FUNDAMENTALS OF

ENGLISH GRAMMAR

Third Edition

LONGMAN ON THE WEB

Visit us at **longman.com** for online resources for teachers and students.
For the Azar Companion Website, visit **longman.com/grammarexchange**.
Longman English Success **(englishsuccess.com)** offers online courses covering
General English, Business English, and Exam Preparation.

FUNDAMENTALS OF

ENGLISH GRAMMAR

Third Edition

Longman

Betty Schrampfer Azar

Fundamentals of English Grammar
Third Edition

Azar Associates
Shelley Hartle, Editor
Susan Van Etten, Manager

Pearson Education, 10 Bank Street, White Plains, NY 10606

Vice president, director of publishing: Allen Ascher
Editorial manager: Pam Fishman
Project manager: Margo Grant
Development editor: Janet Johnston
Vice president, director of design and production: Rhea Banker
Director of electronic production: Aliza Greenblatt
Executive managing editor: Linda Moser
Production manager: Ray Keating
Production editor: Robert Ruvo
Director of manufacturing: Patrice Fraccio
Senior manufacturing buyer: Edie Pullman
Cover design: Monika Popowitz
Illustrations: Don Martinetti
Text composition: Carlisle Communications, Ltd.
Text font: 10.5/12 Plantin

Library of Congress Cataloging-in-Publication Data

Azar, Betty Schrampfer, 1941-
    Fundamentals of English grammar / Betty Schrampfer Azar.—3rd ed.
        p.   cm.
Includes index.
    ISBN 0-13-013631-X
    1.   English language—Textbooks for foreign speakers. 2.   English
language—Grammar—Problems, exercises, etc.   I. Title.
    PE1128 .A965 2002
    428.2'4—dc21

2002069436

ISBN: 0-13-013631-X   (Regular Edition)   8 9 10–CRK–07 06 05

ISBN: 0-13-193019-2   (International Edition)   4 5 6 7 8 9 10–CRK–07 06

To my sister
~ ~ ~ ~
Jo

CONTENTS

APPENDIX 1 PHRASAL VERBS

APPENDIX 2 PREPOSITION COMBINATIONS

Preface to the Third Edition

Fundamentals of English Grammar is a developmental skills text for lower-intermediate and intermediate students of English as a second or foreign language. It combines clear and understandable grammar information with a variety of exercises and activities.

Fundamentals of English Grammar is the second in a series of three texts: *Basic English Grammar* (red cover), *Fundamentals of English Grammar* (black cover), and *Understanding and Using English Grammar* (blue cover).

The principal aims of all three texts in this series are to present clear, cogent information about English grammar and usage, to provide extensive and varied practice that encourages growth in all areas of language use, and to be interesting, useful, and fun for student and teacher alike. The approach is eclectic, with the texts seeking to balance form-focused language-learning activities with abundant opportunities for engaged and purposeful communicative interaction.

The new editions of the texts in the Azar Grammar Series include these changes:

- The communicative aspects are more fully developed and explicit in the third editions. This edition of *Fundamentals of English Grammar* includes a greatly increased number of "real communication" opportunites for the teacher to exploit. The text often uses the students' own life experiences as context and regularly introduces topics of interest to stimulate the free expression of ideas in structured as well as open discussions.

    The Azar Grammar Series texts support the view of many experienced teachers that grammar-based and communicative approaches are not mutually exclusive, but rather mutually supportive, and can advantageously co-exist in the same language program, even in the same class, even in the same lesson.

- Similarly, the interactive aspects of the texts receive greater emphasis in the third editions. Many of the exercises formerly designated ORAL or ORAL (BOOKS CLOSED) are now reformatted to be more clearly available for pair work or group work, in addition to still being viable as class work led by a teacher. This edition of *Fundamentals of English Grammar* encourages interactivity but leaves it open for the users to decide what degree of interactivity best suits their needs.

- There is now an even wider variety of exercise types. This edition has a much larger number of free-response exercises and open-ended communicative tasks, while still providing ample controlled-response exercises to aid initial understanding of the form, meaning, and usage of the target structures. It also includes more writing topics, more speaking activities, new error-analysis exercises in every chapter, and additional extended-context exercises. Classroom teaching materials formerly found in the *Workbook* are now included in this student text, with the *Workbook* devoted solely to self-study exercises. The *Workbook* has a variety of practice approaches for independent study.

- A specific change in this edition of *Fundamentals of English Grammar* is the two Appendices, one with phrasal verbs and one with preposition combinations. Rather than asking students to study a whole chapter of these phrases at one time, the text uses appendices to present them in smaller groupings for teachers to intersperse throughout the teaching term. Another specific change is the omission of conditional sentences, which are presented in *Understanding and Using English Grammar.*

- The accompanying *Teacher's Guide* is written for both experienced and inexperienced teachers. It contains amplified grammar notes the teacher might want to present to the class or will find useful as background information. It outlines various ways of approaching the materials in the classroom and frequently suggests fresh teaching ideas for individual exercises beyond the directions in the text. It seeks to share with the teacher an understanding of the rationale behind the text's content and approaches. Its principal purpose is to make the busy teacher's job easier.

Fundamentals of English Grammar consists of
- a *Student Book* without an answer key
- a *Student Book* with an answer key
- a *Workbook,* consisting of self-study exercises for independent work
- a *Chartbook,* a reference book consisting of only the grammar charts
- a *Teacher's Guide,* with teaching suggestions and additional notes on grammar, as well as the answers to the exercises
- a *Test Bank*

Acknowledgments

The third edition of *FEG* was reviewed by nine ESL/EFL professionals. I wish to express my thanks to these colleagues for their exceedingly helpful insights and suggestions. They are Stephanie La Qua, International Center for American English; Diane Mahin, University of Miami; Amy Parker, Embassy CES Intensive English Program; Gary Pietsch, Green River Community College; Thomas Pinkerton, North Miami Senior High School; Haydée Alvarado Santos, University of Puerto Rico; Hye-Young Um, Myongji University, Seoul, Korea; Lyn Waldie, Helenic-American Union, Athens, Greece; Aida Zic, Montgomery College.

My wholehearted thanks go to Shelley Hartle, who makes my job easy, and Editor Janet Johnston, who guides and assists us in so very many ways. Editor Margo Grant is simply super to work with, as are the many other skilled professionals at Pearson Education for their contributions to the publication of this work; in particular, Joanne Dresner, Anne Boynton-Trigg, Allen Ascher, Pam Fishman, Rhea Banker, Linda Moser, Aliza Greenblatt, Ray Keating, Barry Katzen, Kate McLoughlin, Sylvia Herrera-Alaniz, Bruno Paul, Hugo Loyola, Mike Bennett, Stacy Whittis, Monika Popowicz, Julie Hammond, and Amy Durfy.

A special thank you is reserved for Production Editor Robert Ruvo, who stayed on top of everything and remained unflappable.

I'd like to thank Carlisle Communications, Ltd., whose staff so excellently turned our disks into print pages. Without a doubt, they are the most skilled and reliable compositors I've worked with in twenty years.

I also once again thank Don Martinetti, the illustrator, whose touches of whimsy are so delightful. My appreciation also goes to graphic designer Christine Shrader, creator of the swallow that heralds this third edition.

My great appreciation goes to Stacy Hagen, an experienced ESL author,* who created new materials for the revised *Fundamentals of English Grammar Workbook,* bringing fresh approaches and ideas. Working with her was a very good experience.

I wish to express special acknowledgment of the contributing writers for the previous edition of the *Workbook:* Rachel Spack Koch, Susan Jamieson, Barbara Andrews, and Jeanie Francis. Some of the exercise material originally created for that workbook has been woven into this third edition of the student book, and I thank them for the ways in which this material has enriched the text. I am additionally very grateful to Rachel Spack Koch for her devotion and expertise in answering grammar and usage questions from teachers on the current Azar Companion Web Site.

Sound Advice: A Basis for Listening, 2000, Pearson Education; *Better Writing through Editing,* 1999, McGraw-Hill (co-author Jan Peterson); and *Sound Advantage: A Pronunciation Book,* 1992, Pearson Education (co-author Pat Grogan).

I am indebted especially and always to my many students through the years; I learned so much from them. I also am indebted to my fellow ESL/EFL materials writers, past and present; we learn much from each other. I would like to make special mention of Thomas Crowell and Irene Schoenberg.

In addition, my thanks go to Donna Cowan, University of Washington, Patti Gulledge-White, Sue Van Etten, Joy Edwards, my great girls Chelsea and Rachel, and my wonderfully supportive husband, Larry Harris.

CHAPTER 1
Present Time

CONTENTS

□ EXERCISE 1. Introductions.

Directions: You and your classmates are going to interview each other and then introduce each other to the rest of the class.

PART I.   Read and discuss the dialogue.

    A: Hi. My name is Kunio.

    B: Hi. My name is Maria. I'm glad to meet you.

KUNIO: I'm glad to meet you, too. Where are you from?

MARIA: I'm from Mexico. Where are you from?

KUNIO: I'm from Japan.

MARIA: Where are you living now?

KUNIO: On Fifth Avenue in an apartment. And you?

MARIA: I'm living in a dorm.

KUNIO: How long have you been in (this city)?

MARIA: Three days.

KUNIO: Why did you come here?

MARIA: To study English at this school before I go to another school to study computer programming. How about you?

KUNIO: I came here two months ago. Right now I'm studying English. Later, I'm going to study engineering at this school.

MARIA: What do you do in your free time?

KUNIO: I read a lot. How about you?

MARIA: I like to get on the Internet.

KUNIO: Really? What do you do when you're online?

MARIA: I visit many different Web sites. It's a good way to practice my English.

KUNIO: That's interesting. I like to get on the Internet, too.

MARIA: I have to write your full name on the board when I introduce you to the class. How do you spell your name?

KUNIO: My first name is Kunio. K-U-N-I-O. My family name is Akiwa.

MARIA: Kunio Akiwa. Is that right?

KUNIO: Yes, it is. And what is your name again?

MARIA: My first name is Maria. M-A-R-I-A. My last name is Lopez.

KUNIO: Thanks. It's been nice talking with you.

MARIA: I enjoyed it, too.

PART II. Use the information in the dialogue to complete Kunio's introduction of Maria to the class.

KUNIO: I would like to introduce Maria Lopez. Maria, would you please stand up?

Thank you. Maria is from _____Mexico_____ . Right now, she's living

_____ . She has been here _____ .

She came here to _____ before she _____

_____ . In her free time, she _____

_____ .

PART III. Now it is Maria's turn to introduce Kunio to the class. What is she going to say? Create an introduction. Begin with *"I would like to introduce Kunio . . . ."*

PART IV. Pair up with another student in the class. Interview each other. Then introduce each other to the rest of the class. In your conversation, find out your classmate's:

name   **length of time in this city**
native country or hometown   **reason for being here**
residence   **free-time activities or hobbies**

Take notes during the interview.

PART V. Write the names of your classmates on a sheet of paper as they are introduced in class.

☐ EXERCISE 2. Introducing yourself in writing.
Directions: Write answers to the questions. Use your own paper. With your teacher, decide what to do with your writing.

Suggestions:
  a. Give it to a classmate to read. Your classmate can then summarize the information in a spoken report to a small group.
  b. Pair up with a classmate and correct errors in each other's writing.
  c. Read your composition aloud in a small group and answer any questions about it.
  d. Hand it in to the teacher, who will correct the errors and return it to you.
  e. Hand it in to the teacher, who will keep it and return it at the end of the term, when your English has progressed, for you to correct your own errors.

QUESTIONS:
1. What is your name?
2. Where are you from?
3. Where are you living?
4. Why are you here (in this city)?
   a. Are you a student? If so, what are you studying?
   b. Do you work? If so, what is your job?
   c. Do you have another reason for being here?
5. What do you like to do in your free time?
6. What is your favorite season of the year? Why?
7. What are your three favorite books? Why do you like them?
8. Describe your first day in this class.

☐ EXERCISE 3. Pretest (error analysis): present verbs. (Charts 1-1 → 1-6)
Directions: All the sentences contain mistakes. Find and correct the mistakes.

Example: I no like cold weather.
   → *I don't like cold weather.*

1. Student at this school.

2. I no living at home right now.

3. I be living in this city.

4. I am study English.

5. I am not knowing my teacher's name.

6. *(supply name)* teach our English class.

7. She/He* expect us to be in class on time.

8. We always are coming to class on time.

9. Omar does he going to school?

10. Tom no go to school.

11. My sister don't have a job.

12. Does Anna has a job?

_____

*Choose the appropriate pronoun for your teacher, *he* or *she*.

1-1 THE SIMPLE PRESENT AND THE PRESENT PROGRESSIVE

THE SIMPLE PRESENT past — now — future XXXXXXXXXX	(a) Ann **takes** a shower *every day*. (b) I *usually* **read** the newspaper in the morning. (c) Babies **cry**. Birds **fly**. (d) NEGATIVE: It **doesn't snow** in Bangkok. (e) QUESTION: **Does** the teacher **speak** slowly?	The SIMPLE PRESENT expresses *daily habits* or *usual activities*, as in (a) and (b). The simple present expresses *general statements of fact*, as in (c). In sum, the simple present is used for events or situations that exist always, usually, or habitually in the past, present, and future.
THE PRESENT PROGRESSIVE start — now — finish? in progress	(f) Ann can't come to the phone *right now* because she **is taking** a shower. (g) I **am reading** my grammar book *right now*. (h) Jimmy and Susie are babies. They **are crying**. I can hear them *right now*. Maybe they are hungry. (i) NEGATIVE: It **isn't snowing** *right now*. (j) QUESTION: **Is** the teacher **speaking** *right now?*	The PRESENT PROGRESSIVE expresses *an activity that is in progress (is occurring, is happening) right now*. The event is in progress at the time the speaker is saying the sentence. The event began in the past, is in progress now, and will probably continue into the future. FORM: **am, is, are** + **-ing**.

1-2 FORMS OF THE SIMPLE PRESENT AND THE PRESENT PROGRESSIVE

	SIMPLE PRESENT	PRESENT PROGRESSIVE
STATEMENT	I-You-We-They **work**. He-She-It **works**.	I **am working**. You-We-They **are working**. He-She-It **is working**.
NEGATIVE	I-You-We-They **do not work**. He-She-It **does not work**.	I **am not working**. You-We-They **are not working**. He-She-It **is not working**.
QUESTION	**Do** I-you-we-they **work?** **Does** he-she-it **work?**	**Am** I **working?** **Are** you-we-they **working?** **Is** he-she-it **working?**
CONTRACTIONS pronoun + *be*	*I* + *am* = **I'm** working. *you, we, they* + *are* = **You're, We're, They're** working. *he, she, it* + *is* = **He's, She's, It's** working.	
do + not	*does* + *not* = **doesn't** *do* + *not* = **don't**	She **doesn't** work. I **don't** work.
be + not	*is* + *not* = **isn't** *are* + *not* = **aren't** (*am* + *not* = am not*	He **isn't** working. They **aren't** working. I am not working.)

*Note: *am* and *not* are not contracted.

Directions: Discuss the verbs in *italics*. Is the activity of the verb
    (a) a daily or usual habit? OR
    (b) happening right now (i.e., in progress in the picture)?

It's 7:30 A.M., and the Wilsons are in their kitchen. Mrs. Wilson *is sitting* at the
                                                                         1

breakfast table. She *is reading* a newspaper. She *reads* the newspaper every morning. Mr.
                    2   3

Wilson *is pouring* a cup of coffee. He *drinks* two cups of coffee every morning before he
        4   5

goes to work. There is a cartoon on TV, but the children *aren't watching* it. They
 6   7

are playing with their toys instead. They usually *watch* cartoons in the morning, but this
   8   9

morning they *aren't paying* any attention to the TV. Mr. and Mrs. Wilson *aren't watching*
        10   11

the TV either. They often *watch* the news in the evening, but they *don't watch* cartoons.
             12   13

□ EXERCISE 5. Simple present vs. present progressive. (Charts 1-1 and 1-2)
Directions: Complete the sentences by using the words in parentheses. Use the simple
present or the present progressive.

1. Shhh. The baby *(sleep)* _____is sleeping_____ . The baby *(sleep)*

_____sleeps_____ for ten hours every night.

2. Right now I'm in class. I *(sit)* _____ at my desk. I usually

   (sit) _____ at the same desk in class every day.

3. Ali *(speak)* _____ Arabic. Arabic is his native language, but

   right now he *(speak)* _____ English.

4. A: *(it, rain)* _____ a lot in southern California?

   B: No. The weather *(be)* _____ usually warm and sunny.

5. A: Look out the window. *(it, rain)* _____ ? Should I take

   my umbrella?

   B: It *(start)* _____ to sprinkle.

6. A: Look. It's Youssef.

   B: Where?

   A: Over there. He *(walk)* _____ out of the bakery.

7. A: Oscar usually *(walk)* _____ to work. *(walk, you)*

   _____ to work every day, too?

   B: Yes.

   A: *(Oscar, walk)* _____ with you?

   B: Sometimes.

8. A: Flowers! Flowers for sale!

   Yes sir! Can I help you?

   B: I'll take those—the yellow ones.

   A: Here you are, mister. Are they

   for a special occasion?

   B: I *(buy)* _____

   them for my wife. I *(buy)*

   _____

her flowers on the first day of every month.

☐ EXERCISE 6. Activity: using the present progressive. (Charts 1-1 and 1-2)

Directions: Student A performs an action. Student B describes the action, using Student A's name and the present progressive.

Example: stand next to your desk
TEACHER: (Maria), would you please stand next to your desk? Thank you.
STUDENT A: *(Student A stands up.)*
TEACHER: Who is standing next to her desk? OR What is (Maria) doing?
STUDENT B: (Maria) is standing next to her desk.

1. stand up

2. smile

3. whistle

4. open or close the door

5. hum

6. bite your fingernails

7. read your grammar book

8. erase the board

9. look at the ceiling

10. hold your pen in your left hand

11. rub your palms together

12. kick your desk (softly)

13. knock on the door

14. sit on the floor

15. shake hands with someone

16. look at your watch

17. count aloud the number of people in the room

18. shake your head "no"

19. scratch your head

20. Perform any action you choose. Use objects in the classroom if you wish.

☐ EXERCISE 7. Activity: using the present progressive. (Charts 1-1 and 1-2)

Directions: Use the present progressive to discuss your classmates' immediate activities. Divide into two groups, I and II.

GROUP I. Do anything you each feel like doing (stand up, talk, look out the window, etc.). You may wish to do some interesting or slightly unusual things. Perform these activities at the same time.

GROUP II. Describe the immediate activities of the students in Group I (e.g., *Ali is talking to Ricardo. Yoko is scratching her chin. Spyros is leaning against the wall.*). Be sure to use your classmates' names.

Later, Group I and Group II should reverse roles, with Group II acting and Group I describing.

☐ **EXERCISE 8. Activity: using the present progressive. (Charts 1-1 and 1-2)**

Directions: Use the present progressive to describe activities in progress. Work in groups or as a class.

> **FIRST:** One member of the group pretends to do something, and the rest of the group tries to guess what the action is and describe it, using the present progressive.

> *Example:* painting a wall
> STUDENT A: *(pretends to be painting a wall)*
> OTHERS: You're conducting an orchestra. (No.)
> Are you washing a window? (No.)
> You're painting a wall. (Yes!)

> **SECOND:** Student A repeats the performance and describes his/her actions aloud.

> *Example:*
> STUDENT A: I am standing in front of an unpainted wall. I'm opening a can of paint. Now I'm picking up a paintbrush. I'm dipping the brush in the can of paint. I'm lifting the brush. Now I'm painting the wall.

Suggestions for actions:

painting a wall	playing the piano
drinking a cup of tea/coffee	diving into a pool and swimming
petting a dog	driving a car
dialing a telephone	watching a tennis match
climbing a tree	pitching a baseball

1-3 FREQUENCY ADVERBS

100%
 	
positive {
always
almost always
usually†
often†
frequently†
generally†
sometimes†
occasionally†
 	
negative {
seldom
rarely
hardly ever
almost never
not ever, never
0%
	Frequency adverbs usually occur in the middle of a sentence and have special positions, as shown in examples (a) through (e) below.
	The adverbs with the symbol "†" may also occur at the beginning or end of a sentence.
	    I **sometimes** get up at 6:30.
	    Sometimes I get up at 6:30.
	    I get up at 6:30 **sometimes**.
	
	The other adverbs in the list (the ones not marked by "†") rarely occur at the beginning or end of a sentence. Their usual position is in the middle of a sentence.

(a) SUBJECT + FREQ ADV + VERB Karen **always** **tells** the truth.	Frequency adverbs usually come between the subject and the simple present verb (except main verb *be*).
(b) SUBJECT + BE + FREQ ADV Karen **is** **always** on time.	Frequency adverbs follow *be* in the simple present (*am, is, are*) and simple past (*was, were*).
(c) Do **you always** eat breakfast?	In a question, frequency adverbs come directly after the subject.
(d) Ann **usually doesn't eat** breakfast. (e) Sue **doesn't always** eat breakfast.	In a negative sentence, most frequency adverbs come in front of a negative verb (except *always* and *ever*). **Always** follows a negative helping verb or negative *be*.
(f) CORRECT: Anna **never eats** meat. (g) INCORRECT: *Anna doesn't never eat meat.*	Negative adverbs (*seldom, rarely, hardly ever, never*) are NOT used with a negative verb.
(h) — *Do* you **ever** *take* the bus to work? — Yes, I do. I often take the bus. (i) I **don't ever** walk to work. (j) INCORRECT: *I ever walk to work.*	**Ever** is used in questions about frequency, as in (h). It means "at any time." **Ever** is also used with **not**, as in (i). **Ever** is NOT used in statements.

☐ **EXERCISE 9. The meaning of frequency adverbs. (Chart 1-3)**

Directions: Answer the questions. Discuss the meaning of the frequency adverbs.

What is something that . . .
1. you seldom do?
2. you often do before you go to bed?
3. a polite person often does?
4. a polite person never does?
5. I frequently do in class?
6. I usually don't do in class?
7. you rarely eat?
8. you occasionally do after class?
9. drivers generally do?
10. people in your country always or usually do to celebrate the New Year?

☐ **EXERCISE 10. Position of frequency adverbs. (Chart 1-3)**

Directions: Add the word in *italics* to the sentence. Put the word in its usual midsentence position.

                  always

1. *always*   Tom ∧ studies at home in the evening.

2. *always*   Tom is at home in the evening.

3. *usually*   The mail comes at noon.

4. *usually*   The mail is here by noon.

5. *generally*   I eat lunch around one o'clock.

6. *generally*   Tom is in the lunch room around one o'clock.

7. *generally*   What time do you eat lunch?

8. *usually*   Are you in bed by midnight?

☐ **EXERCISE 11. Frequency adverbs in negative sentences. (Chart 1-3)**

Directions: Add the given words to the sentence. Put the adverbs in their usual midsentence position. Make any necessary changes in the sentence.

1. *Sentence:* Jack doesn't shave in the morning.
   - a. usually   →   *Jack usually doesn't shave in the morning.*
   - b. often   →   *Jack often doesn't shave in the morning.*
   - c. frequently   f. always   i. hardly ever
   - d. occasionally   g. ever   j. rarely
   - e. sometimes   h. never   k. seldom

2. I don't eat breakfast.
   - a. usually   b. always   c. seldom   d. ever

3. My roommate isn't home in the evening.
   - a. generally   b. sometimes   c. always   d. hardly ever

☐ **EXERCISE 12. Using the simple present with frequency adverbs. (Charts 1-1 → 1-3)**

Directions: Work in pairs. Use frequency adverbs to talk about yourself.
Speaker A: Your book is open. Tell your classmate about yourself, using the given ideas and frequency adverbs.
Speaker B: Your book is closed. Repeat the information Speaker A just gave you.
Speaker A: If Speaker B did not understand correctly, repeat the information.
              If Speaker B understood the information say, "Right. How about you?"
Speaker B: Answer the question, using a frequency adverb.

Example: walk to school
SPEAKER A *(book open):*   I usually walk to school.
SPEAKER B *(book closed):* You usually walk to school.
SPEAKER A *(book open):*   Right. How about you? Do you ever walk to school?
SPEAKER B *(book closed):* I seldom walk to school. I usually take the bus. OR I usually walk to school too.

1. wear a suit to class
2. go to sleep before eleven-thirty
3. get at least one e-mail a day
4. read in bed before I go to sleep
5. listen to the radio in the morning
6. speak to people who sit next to me on an airplane

Switch roles.
7. wear jeans to class
8. read poetry in my spare time
9. believe the things I read in newspapers
10. get up before nine o'clock in the morning
11. call my family or a friend if I feel homesick or lonely
12. have chocolate ice cream for dessert

☐ EXERCISE 13. Activity: topics for discussion or writing. (Charts 1-1 → 1-3)
Directions: Discuss the topics in pairs, in groups, or as a class. Topics can also be used for writing practice. Use several frequency adverbs with each topic. See Chart 1-3 for a list of frequency adverbs.

Example: What are some of the things you do when you get up in the morning?
→ *I generally turn on the news.*
I always brush my teeth.
I seldom make my bed.
I usually take a shower.
I never take a bath.

PART I. What are some things you do . . .
1. when you get ready to go to bed at night?
2. when you travel abroad?
3. in this classroom?
4. when you're on vacation?
5. when your airplane flight is delayed?
6. when you use a computer?

PART II. What are some things people in your country do . . .
7. at the dinner table?
8. to celebrate their birthdays?
9. when a child misbehaves?
10. when they meet someone for the first time?
11. when they want to have fun?
12. at a wedding?

1-4 FINAL -S

(a) SINGULAR: *one bird* (b) PLURAL: *two birds, three birds, many birds, all birds, etc.*	SINGULAR = one, not two or more PLURAL = two, three, or more
(c) **Bird**s sing. (d) A bird **sings**.	**A plural noun** ends in **-s**, as in (c). **A singular verb** ends in **-s**, as in (d).
(e) A **bird** *sings* outside my window. 　　**It** *sings* loudly. 　**Ann** *sings* beautifully. 　**She** *sings* songs to her children. 　**Tom** *sings* very well. 　　**He** *sings* in a chorus.	A singular verb follows a singular subject. Add **-s** to the simple present verb if the subject is 　(1) a singular noun (e.g., *a bird, Ann, Tom*) or 　(2) *he, she,* or *it.*★

★*He, she,* and *it* are third person singular personal pronouns. See Chart 6-10, p. 171, for more information about personal pronouns.

□ **EXERCISE 14. Using final -S. (Chart 1-4)**

Directions: Look at each word that ends in **-s**. Is it a noun or a verb? Is it singular or plural?

1. Ali lives in an apartment. → *"lives" = a singular verb*

2. Plants grow. → *"plants" = a plural noun*

3. Ann listens to the radio in the morning.

4. The students at this school work hard.

5. A doctor helps sick people.

6. Planets revolve around the sun.

7. A dictionary lists words in alphabetical order.

8. Mr. Lee likes to go to Forest Park in the spring. He takes the bus. He sits on a bench near a pond and feeds the birds. Ducks swim toward him for food, and pigeons land all around him.

□ **EXERCISE 15. Preview: spelling of final -S/-ES. (Chart 1-5)**

Directions: Add final **-s/-es**.

1. talk **s**_____

2. wish **es**_____

3. hope _____

4. reach _____

5. move _____

6. kiss _____

7. push _____

8. wait _____

9. mix _____

10. blow _____

11. study _____

12. buy _____

13. enjoy _____

14. fly _____

15. carry _____

1-5 SPELLING OF FINAL -S/-ES

(a) visit → **visits** speak → **speaks** (b) ride → **rides** write → **writes**	Final **-s**, not **-es**, is added to most verbs. *INCORRECT: visites, speakes* Many verbs end in **-e**. Final **-s** is simply added.
(c) catch → **catches** wash → **washes** miss → **misses** fix → **fixes** buzz → **buzzes**	Final **-es** is added to words that end in **-ch**, **-sh**, **-s**, **-x**, and **-z**. PRONUNCIATION NOTE: Final **-es** is pronounced /əz/ and adds a syllable.★
(d) **fly** → **flies**	If a word ends in a consonant + **-y**, change the **-y** to **-i** and add **-es**. *(INCORRECT: flys)*
(e) **pay** → **pays**	If a word ends in a vowel + **-y**, simply add **-s**.★★ *(INCORRECT: paies or payes)*
(f) go → **goes** /gowz/ do → **does** /dəz/ have → **has** /hæz/	The singular forms of the verbs *go*, *do*, and *have* are irregular.

★See Chart 6-1 for more information about the pronunciation of final **-s/-es**.
★★Vowels = a, e, i, o, u. Consonants = all other letters in the alphabet.

☐ **EXERCISE 16. Simple present verbs: using final -S/-ES. (Charts 1-4 and 1-5)**

Directions: <u>Underline</u> the verb in each sentence. Add final **-s/-es** to the verb if necessary. Do not change any other words.

1. A dog <u>bark</u>. → **barks**

2. Dogs <u>bark</u>. → **OK** *(no change)*

3. Wood float on water.

4. Rivers flow toward the sea.

5. My mother worry about me.

6. A student buy a lot of books at the beginning of each term.

7. Airplanes fly all around the world.

8. Mr. Wong teach Chinese at the university.

9. The teacher ask us a lot of questions in class every day.

10. Mr. Cook watch game shows on TV every evening.

11. Music consist of pleasant sounds.

12. Cats usually sleep eighteen hours a day.

13. The front page of a newspaper contain the most important news of the day.

14. Water freeze at 32°F (0°C) and boil at 212°F (100°C).

15. Mrs. Taylor never cross the street in the middle of a block. She always walk to the

    corner and use the pedestrian walkway.

16. Many parts of the world enjoy four seasons: spring, summer, autumn, and winter.

    Each season last three months and bring changes in the weather.

□ EXERCISE 17. Simple present verbs: using final -S/-ES. (Charts 1-4 and 1-5)
Directions: Count aloud around the class to the number 24. Find your number(s) in the exercise list, and write the words that appear beside it on a slip of paper. Then close your book.

    Walk around the classroom and read your words aloud to classmates. You are looking for the other half of your sentence.

    When you find the person with the other half, combine the information on your two slips of paper into a sentence. Write the sentence on the chalkboard or on a piece of paper. Make changes in the verb if necessary.

Example (using items 1 and 8): A star shine**s** in the sky at night.

1. a star
2. causes air pollution
3. stretch when you pull on it
4. a hotel
5. newspaper ink
6. supports a huge variety of marine life
7. a bee
8. shine in the sky at night
9. cause great destruction when it reaches land
10. a river
11. improves your circulation and general health
12. an elephant
13. a hurricane
14. produce one-fourth of the world's coffee
15. oceans
16. use its long trunk like a hand to pick things up
17. Brazil
18. supply its guests with clean towels
19. a rubber band
20. gather nectar from flowers
21. flow downhill
22. stain my hands when I read the paper
23. automobiles
24. does physical exercise

Directions: Create three sentences about the activity shown in each picture. Work in pairs, in groups, or as a class.

Sentence 1: **Activity in progress:** Describe what the person in the picture is doing.
Sentence 2: **Usual frequency:** Describe how often this person probably does this activity.
Sentence 3: **Generalization:** Make a general statement or two about this activity.

Example:

Sentence 1: The man in the picture *is swimming.*
Sentence 2: It looks like he's near a tropical island. If he's on vacation there, he probably *swims* every day. If he lives there all the time, he probably *swims* once or twice a week.
Sentence 3: People *swim* for enjoyment and exercise. Swimming in the ocean *is* fun.

1-6 NON-ACTION VERBS

(a) I **know** Ms. Chen.
    INCORRECT: I am knowing Ms. Chen.
(b) I'm hungry. I **want** a sandwich.
    INCORRECT: I am wanting a sandwich.
(c) This book **belongs** to Mikhail.
    INCORRECT: This book is belonging to Mikhail.
	Some verbs are not used in progressive tenses. These verbs are called "non-action verbs." They express a situation that exists, not an action in progress.

NON-ACTION VERBS★

hear	*believe*	*be*	*own*	*need*	*like*	*forget*
see	*think*†	*exist*	*have*†	*want*	*love*	*remember*
sound	*understand*		*possess*	*prefer*	*hate*	
	know		*belong*			

†COMPARE (d) I **think** that grammar is easy. (e) I **am thinking** about grammar right now. (f) Tom **has** a car. (g) I**'m having** a good time.	*Think* and *have* can be used in the progressive. In (d): When ***think*** means "believe," it is nonprogressive. In (e): When ***think*** expresses thoughts that are going through a person's mind, it can be progressive. In (f): When ***have*** means "own" or expresses possession, it is not used in the progressive. In (g): In expressions where ***have*** does not mean "own" (e.g., *have a good time, have a bad time, have trouble, have a problem, have company, have an operation*), ***have*** can be used in the progressive.

★Non-action verbs are also called "stative verbs" or "nonprogressive verbs."

☐ **EXERCISE 19. Progressive verbs vs. non-action verbs. (Chart 1-6)**

Directions: Complete the sentences with the words in parentheses. Use the simple present or the present progressive.

1. Right now I *(look)* _____ **am looking** _____ at the board. I *(see)*
   _____ some words on the board.

2. A: *(you, need)* _____ some help, Mrs. Brown?

   (you, want) _____ me to carry that box for you?

   B: Yes, thank you. That's very kind of you.

3. A: Who is that man? I *(think)* _____ that I *(know)*
   _____ him, but I *(forget)* _____ his name.

   B: That's Mr. Martinez.

   A: That's right! I *(remember)* _____ him now.

4. A: *(you, believe)* _____ in flying saucers?

   B: What *(you, talk)* _____ about?

   A: You know, spaceships from outer space with alien creatures aboard.

   B: In my opinion, flying saucers *(exist)* _____ only in people's
      imaginations.

5. Right now the children *(be)* _____ at the beach. They *(have)*
_____ a good time. They *(have)* _____ a beach
ball, and they *(play)* _____ catch with it. They *(like)*
_____ to play catch. Their parents *(sunbathe)* _____
_____ . They *(try)* _____ to get a tan.
They *(listen)* _____ to music on a radio. They also *(hear)*
_____ the sound of seagulls and the sound of the waves.

6. A: What *(you, think)* _____ about right now?

   B: I *(think)* _____ about seagulls and waves.

   A: *(you, like)* _____ seagulls?

   B: Yes. I *(think)* _____ seagulls are interesting birds.

7. A: Which color *(you, prefer)* _____ , red or blue?

   B: I *(like)* _____ blue better than red. Why?

   A: I *(read)* _____ a magazine article right now. According
   to the article, people who *(prefer)* _____ blue to red
   (be) _____ calm and *(value)* _____ honesty and
   loyalty in their friends. A preference for red *(mean)* _____ that a
   person *(be)* _____ aggressive and *(love)* _____
   excitement.

   B: Oh? That *(sound)* _____ like a bunch of nonsense to me.

8. A: Does the earth turn around and around?

B: Yes, Jimmy. The earth *(spin)* _____ around and around on its axis as it circles the sun. The earth *(spin)* _____ rapidly at this very moment.

B: Really? I can't feel it moving. *(you, try)* _____ to fool me?

A: Of course not! *(you, think, really)* _____ that the earth isn't moving?

B: I guess so. Yes. I can't see it move. Yes. It isn't moving.

A: *(you, believe)* _____ only those things that you can see? Look at the trees out the window. All of them *(grow)* _____ at this very moment, but you can't see the growth. They *(get)* _____ bigger and bigger with every second that passes. You can't see the trees grow, and you can't feel the earth spin, but both events *(take)* _____ place at this moment while you and I *(speak)* _____ .

B: Really? How do you know?

1-7 PRESENT VERBS: SHORT ANSWERS TO YES/NO QUESTIONS

	QUESTION	SHORT ANSWER	LONG ANSWER
QUESTIONS WITH *DO/DOES*	*Does* Bob *like* tea?	Yes, he **does**. No, he **doesn't**.	Yes, he likes tea. No, he doesn't like tea.
	Do you *like* tea?	Yes, I **do**. No, I **don't**.	Yes, I like tea. No, I don't like tea.
QUESTIONS WITH *BE*	*Are* you *studying*?	Yes, I **am**.★ No, I**'m not**.	Yes, I am (I'm) studying. No, I'm not studying.
	Is Yoko a student?	Yes, she **is**.★ No, she**'s not**. OR No, she **isn't**.	Yes, she is (she's) a student. No, she's not a student. OR No, she isn't a student.
	Are they *studying*?	Yes, they **are**.★ No, they**'re not**. OR No, they **aren't**.	Yes, they are (they're) studying. No, they're not studying. OR No, they aren't studying.

★*Am, is,* and *are* are not contracted with pronouns in short answers.
   INCORRECT SHORT ANSWERS: Yes, I'm. Yes, she's. Yes, they're.

> *Directions:* Complete the following dialogues by using the words in parentheses. Also give short answers to the questions as necessary. Use the simple present or the present progressive.

1. A: *(Mary, have)* ___Does Mary have___ a bicycle?

   B: Yes, ___she does___ . She *(have)* ___has___ a ten-speed bike.

2. A: *(it, rain)* _____ right now?

   B: No, _____ . At least, I *(think, not)* _____ so.

3. A: *(your friends, write)* _____ a lot of e-mails?

   B: Yes, _____ . I *(get)* _____ lots of e-mails all the time.

4. A: *(the students, take)* _____ a test in class right now?

   B: No, _____ . They *(do)* _____ an exercise.

5. A: *(the weather, affect*)* _____ your mood?

   B: Yes, _____ . I *(get)* _____ grumpy when it's rainy.

6. A: *(Jean, study)* _____ at the library this evening?

   B: No, _____ . She *(be)* _____ at the recreation center.

   She *(play)* _____ pool with her friend.

   A: *(Jean, play)* _____ pool every evening?

   B: No, _____ . She usually *(study)*

   _____ at the library.

   A: *(she, be)* _____ a
   good player?

   B: Yes, _____ . She
   (play) _____ pool a lot.

   A: *(you, play)* _____ pool?

   B: Yes, _____ .
   But I *(be, not)* _____
   very good.

---

*The word *affect* is a verb: *The weather **affects** my mood.*

The word *effect* is a noun: *Warm, sunny weather has a good **effect** on my mood.*

□ EXERCISE 21. Short answers to yes/no questions. (Chart 1-7)

Directions: Answer the questions with books closed. Give both a short and a long answer. Work in pairs or as a class.

Example: Is Texas south of the equator?
→ *No, it isn't. Texas isn't south of the equator.* OR *I don't know.*

1. Do you wear a wristwatch every day?
2. Is (. . .) sitting next to (. . .) today?*
3. Does (. . .) usually sit in the same place every day?
4. Are (. . .) and (. . .) standing up?
5. Are you interested in politics?
6. Is Toronto in western Canada?

(Switch roles if working in pairs.)

7. Do whales lay eggs?
8. Does your country have bears in the wild?
9. Are dogs intelligent?
10. Is (. . .) from Cambodia?
11. Is the earth turning on its axis and rotating around the sun at the same time?
12. Do all mosquitoes carry malaria?

□ EXERCISE 22. Review: present verbs. (Chapter 1)

Directions: Complete the sentences by using the words in parentheses. Use the simple present or the present progressive. Supply the short answer to a question if necessary.

1. A: My sister *(have)* ____has____ a new car. She bought it last month.

   B: *(you, have)* ___Do you have___ a car?

   A: No, I ___don't___ . Do you?

   B: No, but I have a ten-speed bike.

2. A: Where are the children?

   B: In the living room.

   A: What are they doing? *(they, watch)* _____ TV?

   B: No, they _____ . They *(play)* _____ a game.

3. A: Shhh. I *(hear)* _____ a noise. *(you, hear)* _____ it, too?

   B: Yes, I _____ . I wonder what it is.

4. A: Johnny, *(you, listen)* _____ to me?

   B: Of course I am, Mom. You *(want)* _____ me to take out the garbage. Right?

   A: Right! And right now!

---

*The symbol (. . .) means "supply the name of a person."

5. A: Knock, knock! Anybody home? Hey, Bill! Hi! It's me. I'm here with Tom. Where are you?

   B: I *(be)* _____ in the bedroom.

   A: What *(you, do)* _____ ?

   B: I *(try)* _____ to sleep!

   A: Oh. Sorry. I won't bother you. Tom, shhh. Bill *(rest)* _____ .

6. A: What *(you, think)* _____ about at night before you fall asleep?

   B: I *(think)* _____ about all of the pleasant things that happened during the day. I *(think, not)* _____ about my problems.

7. A: A penny for your thoughts.

   B: Huh?

   A: What *(you, think)* _____ about right now?

   B: I *(think)* _____ about English grammar. I *(think, not)* _____ about anything else right now.

   A: I *(believe, not)* _____ you!

8. A: *(you, see)* _____ that man over there?

   B: Which man? The man in the brown jacket?

   A: No, I *(talk)* _____ about the man who *(wear)* _____ the blue shirt.

   B: Oh, that man.

   A: *(you, know)* _____ him?

   B: No, I *(think, not)* _____ so.

9. A: *(you, know)* _____ any tongue-twisters?

   B: Yes, I _____ . Here's one: She sells seashells down by the seashore.

   A: That *(be)* _____ hard to say! Can you say this: Sharon wears Sue's shoes to zoos to look at cheap sheep?

   B: That *(make, not)* _____ any sense.

   A: I *(know)* _____ .

Directions: Correct the errors in verb tense usage.

(1) My friend Omar ~~is owning~~ his own car now. It's brand new.* Today he driving
owns.

to a small town north of the city to visit his aunt. He love to listen to music, so the CD

player is play one of his favorite CDs—loudly. Omar is very happy: he is drive his own

car and listen to loud music. He's look forward to his visit with his aunt.

(2) Omar is visiting his aunt once a week. She's elderly and live alone. She is

thinking Omar a wonderful nephew. She love his visits. He try to be helpful and

considerate in every way. His aunt don't hearing well, so Omar is speaks loudly and

clearly when he's with her.

(3) When he's there, he fix things for her around her apartment and help her with

her shopping. He isn't staying with her overnight. He usually is staying for a few hours

and then is heading back to the city. He kiss his aunt good-bye and give her a hug

before he is leaving. Omar is a very good nephew.

---

*Brand new means "completely new."

CHAPTER 2
Past Time

CONTENTS

☐ **EXERCISE 1. Review of present verbs and preview of past verbs. (Chapters 1 and 2)**
   Directions: Discuss the *italicized* verbs. Do they express present time or past time? Do the verbs describe an activity or situation that . . .
      a. is in progress right now?
      b. is usual or is a general statement of fact?
      c. began and ended in the past?
      d. was in progress at a time in the past?

1. Jennifer *works* for an insurance company.

2. When people *need* help with their automobile insurance, they *call* her.

3. Right now it is 9:05 A.M., and Jennifer *is sitting* at her desk.

4. She *came* to work on time this morning.

5. Yesterday Jennifer *was* late to work because she *had* a minor auto accident.

6. While she *was driving* to work, her cell phone *rang.*

7. She *answered* it. It *was* her friend Rob.

8. She *was* happy to hear from him because she *likes* Rob a lot and always *enjoys* her conversations with him.

9. While they *were talking*, Jennifer, who *is* allergic to bee stings, *noticed* two bees in her car.

10. She quickly *opened* the car windows and *swatted* at the bees while she *was talking* to Rob on the phone.

11. Her hands *left* the steering wheel, and she *lost* control of the car. Her car *ran* into a row of mailboxes beside the road and *stopped*.

12. Fortunately, no one *was* hurt in the accident.

13. Jennifer *is* okay, but her car *isn't*. It *needs* repairs.

14. When Jennifer *got* to work this morning, she *talked* to her own automobile insurance agent.

15. That *was* easy to do because he *works* at the desk right next to hers.

2-1 EXPRESSING PAST TIME: THE SIMPLE PAST

(a) Mary **walked** downtown *yesterday*. (b) I **slept** for eight hours *last night*.	The simple past is used to talk about activities or situations that began and ended in the past (e.g., *yesterday, last night, two days ago, in 1999*).
(c) Bob **stayed** home yesterday morning. (d) Our plane **arrived** on time last night.	Most simple past verbs are formed by adding **-ed** to a verb, as in (a), (c), and (d).
(e) I **ate** breakfast this morning. (f) Sue **took** a taxi to the airport yesterday.	Some verbs have irregular past forms, as in (b), (e), and (f). See Chart 2-7, p. 33.
(g) I **was** busy yesterday. (h) They **were** at home last night.	The simple past forms of **be** are **was** and **were**.

2-2 FORMS OF THE SIMPLE PAST: REGULAR VERBS

STATEMENT	I-You-She-He-It-We-They **worked** yesterday.
NEGATIVE	I-You-She-He-It-We-They **did not (didn't) work** yesterday.
QUESTION	**Did** I-you-she-he-it-we-they **work** yesterday?
SHORT ANSWER	Yes, I-you-she-he-it-we-they **did**. No, I-you-she-he-it-we-they **didn't**.

2-3 FORMS OF THE SIMPLE PAST: *BE*

STATEMENT	I-She-He-It **was** in class yesterday. We-You-They **were** in class yesterday.
NEGATIVE	I-She-He-It **was not (wasn't)** in class yesterday. We-You-They **were not (weren't)** in class yesterday.
QUESTION	**Was** I-she-he-it in class yesterday? **Were** we-you-they in class yesterday?
SHORT ANSWER	Yes, I-she-he-it **was**. Yes, we-you-they **were**. No, I-she-he-it **wasn't**. No, we-you-they **weren't**.

☐ **EXERCISE 2. Present and past time: statements and negatives.**
       (Chapter 1 and Charts 2-1 → 2-3)

Directions: All of the following sentences have inaccurate information. Correct them by
   (a) making a negative statement, and
   (b) making an affirmative statement with accurate information.

1. Thomas Edison invented the telephone.
   → (a) *Thomas Edison didn't invent the telephone.*
      (b) *Alexander Graham Bell invented the telephone.*

2. You live in a tree.

3. You took a taxi to school today.

4. You're sitting on a soft, comfortable sofa.

5. Our teacher wrote *Romeo and Juliet.*

6. Our teacher's name is William Shakespeare.

7. You were on a cruise ship in the Mediterranean
   Sea yesterday.

8. Rocks float and wood sinks.

9. The teacher flew into the classroom today.

10. Spiders have six legs.

EXERCISE 3. Present and past time: statements and negatives.
(Chapter 1 and Charts 2-1 → 2-3)

Directions: Correct the inaccurate statements by using negative then affirmative sentences. Some verbs are past, and some are present. Work as a class (with the teacher as Speaker A) or in pairs. Only Speaker A's book is open.

Example: (. . .)* left the classroom ten minutes ago.
SPEAKER A *(book open):*   Rosa left the classroom ten minutes ago.
SPEAKER B *(book closed):*   No, that's not true. Rosa didn't leave the classroom. Rosa is still here. She's sitting next to Kim.

1. You got up at 4:30 this morning.
2. (. . .) is standing in the corner of the classroom.
3. (. . .) stands in a corner of the classroom during class each day.
4. (. . .) stood in a corner during class yesterday.
5. This book has a green cover.
6. Shakespeare wrote novels.
7. A river flows from the bottom of a valley to the top of a mountain.
8. We cook food in a refrigerator.

(Switch roles if working in pairs.)
9. (. . .) taught this class yesterday.
10. Butterflies have ten legs.
11. This morning, you drove to school in a *(name of a kind of car)*.
12. (. . .) takes a helicopter to get to school every day.
13. You speak (French and Arabic).
14. This room has *(supply an incorrect number)* windows.
15. (. . .) and you studied together at the library last night.
16. (. . .) went to *(an impossible place)* yesterday.

□ EXERCISE 4. Present and past time: statements and negatives.
(Chapter 1, Charts 2-1 → 2-3)

Directions: Work in pairs.
Speaker A: Your book is open. Complete each sentence to make an INACCURATE statement.
Speaker B: Your book is closed. Correct Speaker A's statement, first by using a negative sentence and then by giving correct information.

Example: . . . has/have tails.
SPEAKER A *(book open):*   People have tails.
SPEAKER B *(book closed):*   No, people don't have tails. Dogs have tails. Cats have tails. Birds have tails. But people don't have tails.

1. . . . is/are blue.
2. You ate . . . for breakfast this morning.

———————
*The symbol (. . .) means "supply the name of a person."

3. Automobiles have . . . .

4. You . . . last night.

5. . . . sat next to you in class yesterday.

6. . . . is from Russia. He/She speaks Russian.

7. . . . is talking to . . . right now.

8. . . . was late for class today.

Switch roles.

9. . . . left class early yesterday.

10. . . . has/have six legs.

11. . . . was singing a song when the teacher walked into the room today.

12. . . . wore a black suit to class yesterday.

13. . . . is/are watching a video right now.

14. You . . . last weekend.

15. People . . . in ancient times.

16. . . . is/are delicious, inexpensive, and good for you.

2-4 REGULAR VERBS: PRONUNCIATION OF -*ED* ENDINGS

(a) talked = talk/t/ stopped = stop/t/ hissed = hiss/t/ watched = watch/t/ washed = wash/t/	Final -*ed* is pronounced /t/ after voiceless sounds. You make a voiceless sound by pushing air through your mouth. No sound comes from your throat. Examples of voiceless sounds: /k/, /p/, /s/, /ch/, /sh/.
(b) called = call/d/ rained = rain/d/ lived = live/d/ robbed = rob/d/ stayed = stay/d/	Final -*ed* is pronounced /d/ after voiced sounds. You make a voiced sound from your throat. Your voice box vibrates. Examples of voiced sounds: /l/, /n/, /v/, /b/, and all vowel sounds.
(c) waited = wait/əd/ needed = need/əd/	Final -*ed* is pronounced /əd/ after "t" and "d" sounds. /əd/ adds a syllable to a word.

□ **EXERCISE 5. Pronunciation of -ED endings. (Chart 2-4)**

Directions: Write the correct pronunciations and practice saying the words aloud.

1. cooked = cook/ t /
2. served = serve/ ∂ /
3. wanted = want/ ∂∂ /
4. asked = ask/   /
5. started = start/   /

6. dropped = drop/   /
7. pulled = pull/   /
8. pushed = push/   /
9. added = add/   /
10. passed = pass/   /

11. returned = return/   /
12. touched = touch/   /
13. waved = wave/   /
14. pointed = point/   /
15. agreed = agree/   /

□ **EXERCISE 6. Pronunciation of -ED endings.** (Chart 2-4)

□ **EXERCISE 6. Pronunciation of -ED endings.** (Chart 2-4)
Directions: Practice saying these words. Use them in sentences.

1. answered	6. finished	11. worked
2. arrived	7. fixed	12. invited
3. continued	8. helped	13. suggested
4. ended	9. looked	14. smelled
5. explained	10. planned	15. crossed

2-5 SPELLING OF *-ING* AND *-ED* FORMS

END OF VERB	DOUBLE THE CONSONANT?	SIMPLE FORM	*-ING*	*-ED*	
-e	NO	(a) smile hope	smiling hoping	smiled hoped	*-ing* form: Drop the *-e*, add *-ing*. *-ed* form: Just add *-d*.
Two Consonants	NO	(b) he**lp** lea**rn**	helping learning	helped learned	If the verb ends in two consonants, just add *-ing* or *-ed*.
Two Vowels + One Consonant	NO	(c) **rain** **heat**	raining heating	rained heated	If the verb ends in two vowels + a consonant, just add *-ing* or *-ed*.
One Vowel + One Consonant	YES	ONE-SYLLABLE VERBS (d) sto**p** pla**n**	sto**pp**ing pla**nn**ing	sto**pp**ed pla**nn**ed	If the verb has one syllable and ends in one vowel + one consonant, double the consonant to make the *-ing* or *-ed* form.★
	NO	TWO-SYLLABLE VERBS (e) **vís**it **óff**er	visiting offering	visited offered	If the first syllable of a two-syllable verb is stressed, do not double the consonant.
	YES	(f) pre**fér** ad**mít**	preferring admitting	preferred admitted	If the second syllable of a two-syllable verb is stressed, double the consonant.
-y	NO	(g) play enjoy	playing enjoying	played enjoyed	If the verb ends in a vowel + *-y*, keep the *-y*. Do not change the *-y* to *-i*.
		(h) wor**ry** stu**dy**	wor**ry**ing stu**dy**ing	wor**ri**ed stu**di**ed	If the verb ends in a consonant + *-y*, keep the *-y* for the *-ing* form, but change the *-y* to *-i* to make the *-ed* form.
-ie		(i) **die** **tie**	dying tying	died tied	*-ing* form: Change the *-ie* to *-y* and add *-ing*. *-ed* form: Just add *-d*.

★Exceptions: Do not double "w" or "x": *snow, snowing, snowed, fix, fixing, fixed.*

EXERCISE 7. -ING and -ED forms. (Chart 2-5)

Directions: Write the **-ing** and **-ed** forms of the following verbs. (The simple past/past participle of irregular verbs is given in parentheses.)

		-ING	**-ED**
1.	start	*starting*	*started*
2.	wait		
3.	hit		(hit)
4.	write		(wrote/written)
5.	shout		
6.	cut		(cut)
7.	meet		(met)
8.	hope		
9.	hop		
10.	help		
11.	sleep		(slept)
12.	step		
13.	tape		
14.	tap		
15.	rain		
16.	run		(ran/run)
17.	whine		
18.	win		(won)
19.	explain		
20.	burn		

EXERCISE 8. -ING and -ED forms. (Chart 2-5)

Directions: Write the **-ing** and **-ed** forms of the following verbs.

		-ING	**-ED**
1.	open		
2.	begin		(began/begun)
3.	occur		
4.	happen		

5. refer   _____   _____

6. offer   _____   _____

7. listen   _____   _____

8. admit   _____   _____

9. visit   _____   _____

10. omit   _____   _____

11. hurry   _____   _____

12. study   _____   _____

13. enjoy   _____   _____

14. reply   _____   _____

15. stay   _____   _____

16. buy   _____   *(bought)* _____

17. try   _____   _____

18. tie   _____   _____

19. die   _____   _____

20. lie★   _____   _____

☐ EXERCISE 9. -ING and -ED forms. (Chart 2-5)

Directions: Write the **-ing** and **-ed** forms of the following verbs.

	-ING	**-ED**
1. lift	lifting	lifted
2. promise		
3. slap		
4. wipe		
5. carry		
6. cry		
7. pray		
8. smile		

★**Lie** is a regular verb when it means "not tell the truth." **Lie** is an irregular verb when it means "put one's body flat on a bed or another surface": *lie, lay, lain.*

9. fail   _____   _____

10. file   _____   _____

11. drag   _____   _____

12. use   _____   _____

13. prefer   _____   _____

14. sign   _____   _____

15. point   _____   _____

16. appear   _____   _____

17. relax   _____   _____

18. borrow   _____   _____

19. aim   _____   _____

20. cram   _____   _____

2-6 THE PRINCIPAL PARTS OF A VERB

	SIMPLE FORM	SIMPLE PAST	PAST PARTICIPLE	PRESENT PARTICIPLE
REGULAR VERBS	finish stop hope wait play try	finished stopped hoped waited played tried	finished stopped hoped waited played tried	finishing stopping hoping waiting playing trying
IRREGULAR VERBS	see make sing eat put go	saw made sang ate put went	seen made sung eaten put gone	seeing making singing eating putting going
PRINCIPAL PARTS OF A VERB (1) the simple form	English verbs have four principal forms or "parts." **The simple form** is the form that is found in a dictionary. It is the base form with no endings on it (no final *-s, -ed,* or *-ing*).			
(2) the simple past	**The simple past** form ends in *-ed* for regular verbs. Most verbs are regular, but many common verbs have irregular past forms. See the reference list of irregular verbs that follows in Chart 2-7.			
(3) the past participle	**The past participle** also ends in *-ed* for regular verbs. Some verbs are irregular. It is used in perfect tenses (see Chapter 4) and the passive (Chapter 10).			
(4) the present participle	**The present participle** ends in *-ing* (for both regular and irregular verbs). It is used in progressive tenses (e.g., the present progressive and the past progressive).			

2-7 IRREGULAR VERBS: A REFERENCE LIST

SIMPLE FORM	SIMPLE PAST	PAST PARTICIPLE	SIMPLE FORM	SIMPLE PAST	PAST PARTICIPLE
awake	awoke	awoken	lie	lay	lain
be	was, were	been	light	lit/lighted	lit/lighted
beat	beat	beaten	lose	lost	lost
become	became	become	make	made	made
begin	began	begun	mean	meant	meant
bend	bent	bent	meet	met	met
bite	bit	bitten	pay	paid	paid
blow	blew	blown	prove	proved	proved/proven
break	broke	broken	put	put	put
bring	brought	brought	quit	quit	quit
broadcast	broadcast	broadcast	read	read	read
build	built	built	ride	rode	ridden
burn	burned/burnt	burned/burnt	ring	rang	rung
buy	bought	bought	rise	rose	risen
catch	caught	caught	run	ran	run
choose	chose	chosen	say	said	said
come	came	come	see	saw	seen
cost	cost	cost	seek	sought	sought
cut	cut	cut	sell	sold	sold
dig	dug	dug	send	sent	sent
dive	dived/dove	dived	set	set	set
do	did	done	shake	shook	shaken
draw	drew	drawn	shave	shaved	shaved/shaven
dream	dreamed/dreamt	dreamed/dreamt	shoot	shot	shot
drink	drank	drunk	shut	shut	shut
drive	drove	driven	sing	sang	sung
eat	ate	eaten	sink	sank	sunk
fall	fell	fallen	sit	sat	sat
feed	fed	fed	sleep	slept	slept
feel	felt	felt	slide	slid	slid
fight	fought	fought	speak	spoke	spoken
find	found	found	spend	spent	spent
fit	fit	fit	spread	spread	spread
fly	flew	flown	stand	stood	stood
forget	forgot	forgotten	steal	stole	stolen
forgive	forgave	forgiven	stick	stuck	stuck
freeze	froze	frozen	strike	struck	struck
get	got	got/gotten	swear	swore	sworn
give	gave	given	sweep	swept	swept
go	went	gone	swim	swam	swum
grow	grew	grown	take	took	taken
hang	hung	hung	teach	taught	taught
have	had	had	tear	tore	torn
hear	heard	heard	tell	told	told
hide	hid	hidden	think	thought	thought
hit	hit	hit	throw	threw	thrown
hold	held	held	understand	understood	understood
hurt	hurt	hurt	upset	upset	upset
keep	kept	kept	wake	woke/waked	woken/waked
know	knew	known	wear	wore	worn
lay	laid	laid	weave	wove	woven
lead	led	led	weep	wept	wept
leave	left	left	win	won	won
lend	lent	lent	withdraw	withdrew	withdrawn
let	let	let	write	wrote	written

Directions: Complete each sentence with the simple past of any irregular verb that makes sense. There may be more than one possible completion.

1. Maria walked to school today. Rebecca _____*drove*_____ her car. Olga _____ her bicycle. Yoko _____ the bus.

2. Last night I had a good night's sleep. I _____ nine hours.

3. Ann _____ a beautiful dress to the wedding reception.

4. It got so cold last night that the water in the pond _____ .

5. Frank was really thirsty. He _____ four glasses of water.

6. Karen had to choose between a blue raincoat and a tan one. She finally _____ the blue one.

7. My husband gave me a painting for my birthday. I _____ it on a wall in my office.

8. Last night around midnight, when I was sound asleep, the telephone _____ . It _____ me up.

9. The sun _____ at 6:04 this morning and will set at 6:59.

10. I _____ an e-mail to my cousin after I finished studying yesterday evening.

11. Ms. Manning _____ chemistry at the local high school last year.

12. The police _____ the bank robbers. They are in jail now.

13. Oh my gosh! Call the police! Someone _____ my car!

14. Today Victor has on slacks and a sports jacket, but yesterday he _____ jeans and a sweatshirt to work.

15. My friend told me that he had a singing dog. When the dog _____ , I _____ my hands over my ears.

16. When I introduced Pedro to Ming, they _____ hands and greeted each other.

17. I _____ the kitchen floor with a broom.

18. A bird _____ into our apartment through an open window.

19. I caught the bird and _____ it gently in my hands until I could put it back outside.

20. The children had a good time at the park yesterday. They _____ the ducks small pieces of bread.

21. My dog _____ a hole in the yard and buried his bone.

22. Ahmed _____ his apartment in a hurry this morning because he was late for school. That's why he _____ to bring his books to class.

☐ **EXERCISE 11. Simple past: irregular verbs. (Chart 2-7)**
Directions: Complete each sentence with the simple past of any irregular verb that makes sense. There may be more than one possible completion.

1. Alex hurt his finger when he was fixing his dinner last night. He accidentally _____ it with a sharp knife.

2. I don't have any money in my pocket. I _____ it all yesterday. I'm flat broke.

3. Ann didn't throw her old shoes away. She _____ them because they were comfortable.

4. I _____ an interesting article in the newspaper yesterday.

5. Jack _____ his pocketknife at the park yesterday. This morning he _____ back to the park to look for it. Finally, he _____ it in the grass. He was glad to have it back.

6. Mr. Litovchenko was very happy but a little nervous when he _____ his baby in his arms for the first time.

7. I _____ Jennifer's parents when they visited her. She introduced me to them.

8. A: Is Natasha still angry with you?

B: No, she _____ me for what I did, and she's speaking to me again.

9. I dropped my favorite vase. It fell on the floor and _____ into a hundred pieces.

10. When I went shopping yesterday, I _____ some light bulbs and a cooking pot.

11. The soldiers _____ the battle through the night and into the morning.

12. I used to have a camera, but I _____ it because I needed the money.

13. Jane didn't want anyone to find her diary, so she _____ it in a shoe box in her closet.

14. I didn't want anyone else to see the note, so I _____ it into tiny pieces and _____ them in the wastebasket.

15. The children _____ pictures of themselves in art class yesterday.

16. I have a cold. Yesterday I _____ terrible, but I'm feeling better today.

17. Last night I _____ a strange noise in the house around 2:00 A.M., so I _____ up to investigate.

18. Sam ran the fastest, so he _____ the race.

19. My dog isn't very friendly. Yesterday she _____ my neighbor's leg. Luckily, my dog is very old and doesn't have sharp teeth, so she didn't hurt my neighbor.

20. Steve _____ on the campfire to make it burn.

21. When I went fishing yesterday, I _____ a fish right away. But the fish was too small to keep. I carefully returned it to the water. It quickly _____ away.

22. Amanda _____ a lie. I didn't believe her because I _____ the truth.

☐ EXERCISE 12. Simple past. (Charts 2-1 → 2-7)

Directions: Perform the action and then describe the action, using the simple past. Most of the verbs are irregular; some are regular.

Work in groups or as a class. Only Speaker A's book is open.

Example: Give (. . .) your pen.
SPEAKER A *(book open):* Give Pablo your pen.
SPEAKER B *(book closed):* *(Speaker B performs the action.)*
SPEAKER A *(book open):* What did you do?
SPEAKER B *(book closed):* I gave Pablo my pen.

1. Give (. . .) your dictionary.
2. Open your book.
3. Shut your book.
4. Stand up.
5. Hold your book above your head.
6. Put your book in your lap.
7. Bend your elbow.
8. Touch the tip of your nose.
9. Spell the word "happened."
10. Shake hands with (. . .).
11. Bite your finger.
12. Hide your pen.
13. Leave the room.
14. Speak to (. . .).
15. Tear a piece of paper.
16. Tell (. . .) to stand up.
17. Throw your pen to (. . .).
18. Draw a triangle on the board.
19. Turn to page ten in your book.
20. Choose a pen, this one or that one.
21. Invite (. . .) to have lunch with you.
22. Thank (. . .) for the invitation.
23. Steal (. . .)'s pen.
24. Sell your pen to (. . .) for a (penny).
25. Hit your desk with your hand.
26. Stick your pen in your pocket/purse.
27. Read a sentence from your book.
28. Repeat my sentence: This book is black.
29. Hang your (jacket) on your chair.
30. Take (. . .)'s grammar book.
31. Write your name on the board.

☐ EXERCISE 13. Simple past: questions and short answers. (Charts 2-1 → 2-7)

Directions: Use the words in parentheses. Give short answers to questions where necessary.

1. A: *(you, sleep)* _____Did you sleep_____ well last night?

   B: Yes, _____I did_____ . I *(sleep)* _____slept_____ very well.

2. A: *(Tom's plane, arrive)* _____ on time yesterday?

   B: Yes, _____ . It *(get)* _____ in at 6:05 on the dot.

3. A: *(you, go)* _____ to class yesterday?

   B: No, _____ . I *(stay)* _____ home because I

   (feel, not) _____ good.

4. A: *(Mark Twain, write)* _____

   Tom Sawyer?

   B: Yes, _____ . He also *(write)*

   _____ Huckleberry Finn.

5. A: *(you, eat)* _____ breakfast this morning?

   B: No, _____ . I *(have, not)* _____ enough

      time. I was late for class because my alarm clock *(ring, not)* _____ .

☐ **EXERCISE 14. Simple past: questions, short answers, and irregular verbs.**
   (Charts 2-1 → 2-7)

Directions: Pair up with a classmate.

Speaker A: Ask questions beginning with *"Did you . . . ?"* Listen carefully to Speaker B's
            answers to make sure he or she is using the irregular verbs correctly. Look at
            Chart 2-7 if necessary to check the correct form of an irregular verb. Your
            book is open.

Speaker B: In order to practice using irregular verbs, answer "yes" to all of Speaker A's
            questions. Give both a short answer and a long answer. Your book is closed.

Example: eat breakfast this morning

SPEAKER A *(book open):* Did you eat breakfast this morning?

SPEAKER B *(book closed):* Yes, I did. I ate breakfast this morning.

1. sleep well last night
2. wake up early this morning
3. come to class early today
4. bring your books to class
5. put your books on your desk

6. lose your grammar book yesterday
7. find your grammar book
8. take a bus somewhere yesterday
9. ride in a car yesterday
10. drive a car

Switch roles.

11. hear about the earthquake
12. read the newspaper this morning
13. catch a cold last week
14. feel terrible
15. see a doctor
16. go to a party last night

17. have a good time
18. think about me
19. meet (. . .) the first day of class
20. shake hands with (. . .) when you first met
    him/her

Switch roles.

21. buy some books yesterday
22. begin to read a new novel
23. fly to this city
24. run to class today
25. write your parents a letter

26. send your parents a letter
27. lend (. . .) some money
28. wear a coat yesterday
29. go to the zoo last week
30. feed the birds at the park

Switch roles.

31. make your own dinner last night
32. leave home at eight this morning
33. drink a cup of tea before class
34. fall down yesterday
35. hurt yourself when you fell down

36. break your arm
37. understand the question
38. speak to (. . .) yesterday
39. tell him/her your opinion of this class
40. mean what you said

☐ EXERCISE 15. Past time. (Charts 2-1 → 2-7)

Directions: Pair up with a classmate.

Speaker A: Tell Speaker B about your activities yesterday. Think of at least five things you did yesterday to tell Speaker B about. Also think of two or three things you didn't do yesterday.

Speaker B: Listen carefully to Speaker A. Make sure that Speaker A is using past tenses correctly. Ask Speaker A questions about his/her activities if you wish. Take notes while Student A is talking.

When Speaker A finishes talking, switch roles: Speaker B tells Speaker A about his/her activities yesterday.

Use the notes from the conversation to write a composition about the other student's activities yesterday.

2-8 THE SIMPLE PAST AND THE PAST PROGRESSIVE

THE SIMPLE PAST	(a) Mary **walked** downtown yesterday. (b) I **slept** for eight hours last night.	The SIMPLE PAST is used to talk about *an activity or situation that began and ended at a particular time in the past (e.g., yesterday, last night, two days ago, in 1999)*, as in (a) and (b).
THE PAST PROGRESSIVE	(c) I sat down at the dinner table at 6:00 P.M. yesterday. Tom came to my house at 6:10 P.M. **I was eating** dinner *when Tom came.* (d) I went to bed at 10:00. The phone rang at 11:00. **I was sleeping** *when the phone rang.*	The PAST PROGRESSIVE expresses *an activity that was in progress (was occurring, was happening) at a point of time in the past* (e.g., *at 6:10*) or at the time of another action (e.g., *when Tom came*). In (c): eating was in progress at 6:10; eating was in progress *when Tom came.* FORM: **was**/**were** + **-ing**.
(e) **When** *the phone rang*, I was sleeping. (f) The phone rang **while** *I was sleeping*.		**when** = at that time **while** = during that time (e) and (f) have the same meaning.

2-9 FORMS OF THE PAST PROGRESSIVE

STATEMENT	I-She-He-It **was working**. You-We-They **were working**.	
NEGATIVE	I-She-He-It **was not (wasn't) working**. You-We-They **were not (weren't) working**.	
QUESTION	**Was** I-she-he-it **working?** **Were** you-we-they **working?**	
SHORT ANSWER	Yes, I-she-he-it **was**. No, I-she-he-it **wasn't**.	Yes, you-we-they **were**. No, you-we-they **weren't**.

☐ EXERCISE 16. Simple past and past progressive. (Charts 2-8 and 2-9)

Directions: Complete the sentences with the words in parentheses. Use the simple past or the past progressive.

1. At 6:00 P.M., Bob sat down at the table and began to eat. At 6:05, Bob *(eat)* ____was eating____ dinner.

2. While Bob *(eat)* _____ _____ dinner, Ann *(come)* _____ through the door.

3. In other words, when Ann *(come)* _____ through the door, Bob *(eat)* _____ dinner.

4. Bob went to bed at 10:30. At 11:00 Bob *(sleep)* _____ .

5. While Bob *(sleep)* _____ , the phone *(ring)* _____ .

6. In other words, when the phone *(ring)* _____ , Bob *(sleep)* _____ .

7. Bob left his house at 8:00 A.M. and *(begin)* _____ to walk to class.

8. While he *(walk)* _____ to class, he *(see)* _____ Mrs. Smith.

9. When Bob *(see)* _____ Mrs. Smith, she *(stand)* _____ on her front porch. She *(hold)* _____ a broom.

10. Mrs. Smith *(wave)* _____ at Bob when she *(see)* _____ him.

Directions: Perform the actions and answer the questions. Only the teacher's book is open.

> *Example:* A: write on the board   B: open the door
>
> To STUDENT A: Please write on the board. Write anything you wish. *(Student A writes on the board.)* What are you doing?
>
> *Response:* I'm writing on the board.
>
> To STUDENT A: Good. Please continue.
>
> To STUDENT B: Open the door. *(Student B opens the door.)* What did you just do?
>
> *Response:* I opened that door.
>
> To STUDENT A: *(Student A),* thank you. You may stop now.
>
> To STUDENT C: Describe the two actions that just occurred, using *when.*
>
> *Response:* When *(Student B)* opened the door, *(Student A)* was writing on the board.
>
> To STUDENT D: Again, using *while.*
>
> *Response:* While *(Student A)* was writing on the board, *(Student B)* opened the door.

1. A: write a note to (. . .)   B: knock on the door

2. A: walk around the room   B: clap your hands once

3. A: talk to (. . .)   B: come into the room

4. A: read your book   B: tap (Student A)'s shoulder

5. A: look out the window   B: ask (Student A) a question

6. A: whistle   B: leave the room

7. A: look at your watch   B: ask (Student A) a question

8. A: pantomime eating (pretend to eat)   B: sit down next to (Student A)

9. A: pantomime sleeping   B: take (Student A)'s grammar book

10. A: pantomime drinking a glass of water   B: come into the room

☐ EXERCISE 18. Present progressive and past progressive. (Charts 1-1, 2-8, and 2-9)

Directions: <u>Underline</u> the present progressive and past progressive verbs in the following pairs of sentences. Discuss their use. What are the similarities between the two tenses?

1. A: Where are Ann and Rob? I haven't seen them for a couple of weeks.
   B: They're out of town. They<u>'re traveling.</u>

2. A: I invited Ann and Rob to my birthday party, but they didn't come.
   B: Why not?
   A: They were out of town. They <u>were traveling</u>.

3. A: What was I talking about when the phone interrupted me? I lost my train of thought.
   B: You were describing the website you found on the Internet yesterday.

4. A: I missed the beginning of the news report. What's the announcer talking about?
   B: She's describing conditions in Bangladesh after the flood.

5. A: Good morning, Kim.
   B: Hello, Tom. Good to see you.
   A: Good to see you, too. On your way to work?
   B: Yup. I'm walking to work today to take advantage of the beautiful spring morning.
   A: It certainly is a beautiful spring morning.

6. A: Guess who I saw this morning.
   B: Who?
   A: Jim.
   B: Oh? How is he?
   A: He looks fine.
   B: Where did you see him?
   A: On the sidewalk near the corner of 5th and Pine. He was walking to work.

☐ EXERCISE 19. Present and past verbs. (Chapters 1 and 2)
   Directions: Complete the sentences with the simple present, present progressive, simple past, or past progressive.

   PART I. PRESENT TIME

   SITUATION:

   Right now Toshi *(sit)* _____<u>is sitting</u>_____ at his desk. He

   (study) _____ his grammar book. His roommate, Oscar, *(sit)*

   _____ at his desk, but he *(study, not)* _____ .

   He *(stare)* _____ out the window. Toshi *(want)*

   _____ to know what Oscar *(look)* _____ at.

   TOSHI: Oscar, what *(you, look)* _____ at?

OSCAR: I *(watch)* _____ 9 _____ the bicyclists. They are very skillful. I

(know, not) _____ 10 _____ how to ride a bike, so I *(admire)*

_____ 11 _____ anyone who can. Come over to the window. Look at

that guy in the blue shirt. He *(steer)* _____ 12 _____ his bike with one

hand while he *(drink)* _____ 13 _____ a soda with the other. At the

same time, he *(weave)* _____ 14 _____ in and out of the heavy street

traffic. He *(seem)* _____ 15 _____ fearless.

TOSHI: Riding a bike *(be, not)* _____ 16 _____ as hard as it *(look)* _____ 17 _____ .

I'll teach you to ride a bicycle if you'd like.

OSCAR: Really? Great!

TOSHI: How come you don't know how to ride a bike?*

OSCAR: I *(have, never)* _____ 18 _____ a bike when I *(be)* _____ 19 _____

a kid. My family *(be)* _____ 20 _____ too poor. Once I *(try)*

_____ 21 _____ to learn on the bike of one of my friends, but the other kids

all *(laugh)* _____ 22 _____ at me. I never *(try)* _____ 23 _____ again

because I *(be)* _____ 24 _____ too embarrassed. But I'd really like to learn

now! When can we start?

PART II. PAST TIME

Yesterday, Toshi *(sit)* _____ was sitting 25 _____ at his desk and *(study)*

_____ 26 _____ his grammar book. His roommate, Oscar, *(sit)*

_____ 27 _____ at his desk, but he *(study, not)* _____ 28 _____ .

He *(stare)* _____ 29 _____ out the window. He *(watch)* _____ 30 _____

bicyclists on the street below.

_____

*"How come?" means "Why?" For example, "How come you don't know how to ride a bike?" means "Why don't you know how to ride a bike?"

Toshi *(walk)* _____ over to the window. Oscar *(point)* _____

<u>31</u>   <u>32</u>

out one bicyclist in particular. This bicyclist *(steer)* _____ with one

<u>33</u>

hand while he *(drink)* _____ a soda with the other. At the same

<u>34</u>

time, he *(weave)* _____ in and out of the heavy traffic. To Oscar,

<u>35</u>

the bicyclist *(seem)* _____ fearless.

<u>36</u>

Oscar *(learn, never)* _____ how to ride a bike when he *(be)*

<u>37</u>

_____ a child, so Toshi *(offer)* _____ to teach him. Oscar

<u>38</u>   <u>39</u>

(accept) _____ gladly.

<u>40</u>

☐ **EXERCISE 20. Verb tense and irregular verb review. (Chapters 1 and 2)**

Directions: Complete the sentences with the verbs in parentheses. Use the simple past, simple present, or past progressive.

(1) Once upon a time, a king and his three daughters *(live)* ____lived____ in a

castle in a faraway land. One day while the king *(think)* __was thinking__ about his

daughters, he *(have)* ____had____ an idea. He *(form)* ____formed____ a

plan for finding husbands for them.

(2) When it *(come)* ____came____ time for the three daughters to marry, the

king *(announce)* __announced__ his plan. He said, "I'm going to take three jewels to

the fountain in the center of the village. The young men *(meet)* ____meet*____

together there every day. The three young men who find the jewels will become my

daughters' husbands."

(3) The next day, the king *(choose)* _____ three jewels—an emerald, a

ruby, and a diamond—and *(take)* _____ them into the village. He *(hold)*

_____ them in his hand and *(walk)* _____ among the young

men. First he *(drop)* _____ the emerald, then the ruby, and then the

diamond. A handsome man *(pick)* _____ up the emerald. Then a wealthy

prince *(spot)* _____ the ruby and *(bend)* _____

down to pick it up. The king *(be)* _____ very pleased.

_____

*The simple present is used here because the story is giving the king's exact words in a quotation. Notice that quotation marks ("...") are used. See Chart 14-8, p. 420, for more information about quotations.

(4) But then a frog *(hop)* _____ toward the diamond and *(pick)* _____ it up. The frog *(bring)* _____ the diamond to the king and said, "I *(be)* _____ the Frog Prince. I *(claim)* _____ your third daughter as my wife."

(5) When the king *(tell)* _____ Tina, his third daughter, about the Frog Prince, she *(refuse)* _____ to marry him. When the people of the land *(hear)* _____ the news about the frog and the princess, they *(laugh)* _____ and *(laugh)* _____ . "Have you heard the news?" the people *(say)* _____ to each other. "Princess Tina is going to marry a frog!"

(6) Tina *(feel)* _____ terrible. She said, "I *(be)* _____ the unluckiest person in the world." She *(fall)* _____ to the floor and *(sob)* _____ . No one *(love)* _____ her, she *(believe)* _____ . Her father *(understand, not)* _____ her. She *(hide)* _____ from her friends and *(keep)* _____ her pain in her heart. Every day, she *(grow)* _____ sadder and sadder. Her two sisters *(have)* _____ grand weddings. Their wedding bells *(ring)* _____ with joy across the land.

(7) Eventually, Tina *(leave)* _____ the castle. She *(run)*

_____ away from her family and *(go)* _____ to live in the

woods by herself. She *(eat)* _____ simple food, *(drink)* _____

water from the lake, *(cut)* _____ her own firewood, *(wash)*

_____ her own clothes, *(sweep)* _____ the floor herself,

(make) _____ her own bed, and *(take)* _____ care of all her

own needs. But she *(be)* _____ very lonely and unhappy.

(8) One day Tina *(go)* _____ swimming. The water *(be)* _____

deep and cold. Tina *(swim)* _____ for a long time and *(become)*

_____ very tired. While she *(swim)* _____ back

toward the shore, she *(lose)* _____ the desire to live. She *(quit)*

_____ trying to swim to safety. She *(drown)* _____

when the frog suddenly *(appear)* _____ and with all his strength

(push) _____ Tina to the shore. He *(save)* _____ her life.

(9) "Why *(save, you)* _____ my life, Frog?"

"Because you *(be)* _____ very young and you *(have)* _____

a lot to live for."

"No, I *(do, not)* _____," said the princess. "I *(be)* _____

the most miserable person in the whole universe."

(10) "Let's talk about it," *(say)* _____ the frog. And they *(begin)*

_____ to talk. Tina and the Frog Prince *(sit)* _____

together for hours and hours. Frog *(listen)* _____ and *(understand)*

_____ . He *(tell)* _____ her about himself and his own

unhappiness and loneliness. They *(share)* _____ their minds and hearts.
Day after day, they *(spend)* _____ hours with each other. They
(talk) _____ , *(laugh)* _____ , *(play)* _____ ,
and *(work)* _____ together.

(11) One day while they *(sit)* _____ near the lake, Tina *(bend)*
_____ down and, with great affection, *(kiss)* _____ the frog
on his forehead. Poof! Suddenly the frog *(turn)* _____ into a man!
He *(take)* _____ Tina in his arms, and said, "You *(save)* _____

me with your kiss. Outside, I *(look)* _____ like a frog, but you *(see)*
_____ inside and *(find)* _____ the real me. Now I *(be)*
_____ free. An evil wizard had turned me into a frog until I found the love
of a woman with a truly good heart." When Tina *(see)* _____ through
outside appearances, she *(find)* _____ true love.

(12) Tina and the prince *(return)* _____ to the castle and *(get)*
_____ married. Her two sisters, she discovered, *(be)* _____
very unhappy. The handsome husband *(ignore)* _____ his wife and
(talk, not) _____ to her. The wealthy husband *(make)* _____
fun of his wife and *(give)* _____ her orders all the time. But Tina and her
Frog Prince *(live)* _____ happily ever after.

□ **EXERCISE 21. Past time. (Chapter 2)**

Directions: Write a story that begins "Once upon a time, ..."

Choose one:

1. Invent your own story. For example, write about a lonely bee who finds happiness, a poor orphan who succeeds in life with the help of a fairy godmother, a hermit who rediscovers the joys of human companionship, etc. Discuss possible story ideas in class.

2. Write a fable that you are familiar with, perhaps one that is well known in your culture.

3. Write a story with your classmates. Each student writes one or two sentences at a time. One student begins the story. Then he or she passes the paper on to another student, who then writes a sentence or two and passes the paper on—until everyone in the class has had a chance to write part of the story, or until the story has an ending. This story can then be reproduced for the class to revise and correct together. The class may want to "publish" the final product on the Internet or in a small booklet.

2-10 EXPRESSING PAST TIME: USING TIME CLAUSES

(a) ⎡time clause⎤ ⎡main clause⎤ **After I finished my work,** I went to bed. (b) ⎡main clause⎤ ⎡time clause⎤ I went to bed **after I finished my work.**	*After I finished my work* = a time clause★ *I went to bed* = a main clause★ (a) and (b) have the same meaning. A time clause can (1) come in front of a main clause, as in (a). (2) follow a main clause, as in (b).
(c) I went to bed **after** *I finished my work.* (d) **Before** *I went to bed*, I finished my work. (e) I stayed up **until** *I finished my work.* (f) **As soon as** *I finished my work,* I went to bed. (g) The phone rang **while** *I was watching* TV. (h) **When** *the phone rang*, I was watching TV.	These words introduce time clauses: *after* *before* *until* ⎫ *as soon as* ⎬ + *subject and verb* = a time clause *while* *when* ⎭ In (e): *until* = "to that time and then no longer"★★ In (f): *as soon as* = "immediately after" PUNCTUATION: Put a comma at the end of a time clause when the time clause comes first in a sentence (comes in front of the main clause): **time clause + comma + main clause** **main clause + NO comma + time clause**
(i) When the phone **rang**, I **answered** it.	In a sentence with a time clause introduced by *when*, both the time clause verb and the main verb can be simple past. In this case, the action in the *when*-clause happened first. In (i): *First: The phone rang. Then: I answered it.*
(j) While I **was doing** my homework, my roommate **was watching** TV.	In (j): When two actions are in progress at the same time, the past progressive can be used in both parts of the sentence.

★A *clause* is a structure that has a subject and a verb.

★★*Until* can also be used to say that something does NOT happen before a particular time: *I didn't go to bed until I finished my work.*

☐ EXERCISE 22. Past time clauses. (Chart 2-10)

> *Directions:* Combine the two sentences into one sentence by using time clauses. Discuss correct punctuation.

1. *First:* I got home.
   Then: I ate dinner.

   → After . . . .   OR   . . . after . . . .
   After I got home, I ate dinner.   OR   *I ate dinner after I got home.*

2. *First:* I unplugged the coffee pot.
   Then: I left my apartment this morning.

   → Before . . . .   OR   . . . before . . . .

3. *First:* I lived on a farm.
   Then: I was seven years old.

   → Until . . . .   OR   . . . until . . . .

4. *First:* I heard the doorbell.
   Then: I opened the door.

   → As soon as . . . .   OR   . . . as soon as . . . .

5. *First:* The rabbit was sleeping.
   Then: The fox climbed through the window.

   → While . . . .   OR   . . . while . . . .
   → When . . . .   OR   . . . when . . . .

6. *First:* It began to rain.
   Then: I stood under a tree.

   → When . . . .   OR   . . . when . . . .

7. *At the same time:* I was lying in bed with the flu.
   My friends were swimming at the beach.

   → While . . . .   OR   . . . while . . . .

□ **EXERCISE 23. Past time clauses. (Charts 2-1 → 2-10)**

Directions: Complete the sentences using the words in parentheses. Use the simple past or the past progressive. Identify the time clauses.

1. My mother called me around 5:00. My husband came home a little after that.

   [When he *(come)* _____**came**_____ home,] I *(talk)* _____**was talking**_____ to my mother on the phone.

2. I *(buy)* _____ a small gift before I *(go)* _____ to the hospital yesterday to visit my friend.

3. Yesterday afternoon I *(go)* _____ to visit the Smith family. When I *(get)* _____ there around two o'clock, Mrs. Smith *(be)* _____ in the yard. She *(plant)* _____ flowers in her garden. Mr. Smith *(be)* _____ in the garage. He *(work)* _____ on their car. He *(change)* _____ the oil. The children *(play)* _____ in the front yard. In other words, while Mr. Smith *(change)* _____ the oil in the car, the children *(play)* _____ with a ball in the yard.

4. I *(hit)* _____ my thumb while I *(use)* _____ the hammer. Ouch! That *(hurt)* _____ .

5. As soon as we *(hear)* _____ the news of the approaching hurricane, we *(begin)* _____ our preparations for the storm.

6. It was a long walk home. Mr. Chu *(walk)* _____ until he *(get)* _____ tired. Then he *(stop)* _____ and *(rest)* _____ until he *(be)* _____ strong enough to continue.

7. While I *(lie)* _____ in bed last night, I *(hear)* _____ a strange noise. When I *(hear)* _____ this strange noise, I *(turn)* _____ on the light. I *(hold)* _____ my breath and *(listen)* _____ carefully. A mouse *(chew)* _____ on something under the floor.

8. I work at a computer all day long. Yesterday while I *(look)* _____ at my computer screen, I *(start)* _____ to feel a little dizzy, so I *(take)* _____ a break. While I *(take)* _____ a short break outdoors and *(enjoy)* _____ the warmth of the sun on my face, an elderly gentleman *(come)* _____ up to me and *(ask)* _____ me for directions to the public library. After I *(tell)* _____ him how to get there, he *(thank)* _____ me and *(go)* _____ on his way. I *(stay)* _____ outside until a big cloud *(come)* _____ and *(cover)* _____ the sun, and then I reluctantly *(go)* _____ back inside to work. As soon as I *(return)* _____ to my desk, I *(notice)* _____ that my computer *(make)* _____ a funny noise. It *(hum)* _____ loudly, and my screen was frozen. I *(think)* _____ for a moment, then I *(shut)* _____ my computer off, *(get)* _____ up from my desk, and *(leave)* _____ . I *(spend)* _____ the rest of the day in the sunshine.

2-11 EXPRESSING PAST HABIT: *USED TO*

(a) I **used to live** with my parents. Now I live in my own apartment. (b) Ann **used to be** afraid of dogs, but now she likes dogs. (c) Al **used to smoke,** but he doesn't anymore.	**Used to** expresses a past situation or habit that no longer exists at present. FORM: **used to** + *the simple form of a verb*
(d) **Did** you **used to** *live* in Paris? (OR **Did** you **use to** *live* in Paris?)	QUESTION FORM: **did** + *subject* + **used to** (OR **did** + *subject* + **use to**)★
(e) I **didn't used to** *drink* coffee at breakfast, but now I always have coffee in the morning. (OR I **didn't use to** *drink* coffee.) (f) I *never* **used to** *drink* coffee at breakfast, but now I always have coffee in the morning.	NEGATIVE FORM: **didn't used to** (OR **didn't use to**)★ *Didn't use(d)* to occurs infrequently. More commonly, people use *never* to express a negative idea with *used to,* as in (f).

*Both forms (spelled *used to* or *use to* in questions and negatives) are possible. There is no consensus among English language authorities on which is preferable.

☐ **EXERCISE 24. Past habit with USED TO. (Chart 2-11)**
Directions: Correct the errors.

1. Alex used to ~~living~~ live in Cairo.

2. Jane used to worked at an insurance company.

3. Margo was used to teach English, but now she works at a publishing company.

4. Where you used to live?

5. I didn't was used to get up early, but now I do.

6. Were you used to live in Singapore?

7. My family used to going to the beach every weekend, but now I don't.

☐ **EXERCISE 25. Past habit with USED TO. (Chart 2-11)**
Directions: Make sentences with a similar meaning by using **used to**. Some of the sentences are negatives, and some of them are questions.

1. When I was a child, I was shy. Now I'm not shy.

   → I ___used to be___ shy, but now I'm not.

2. When I was young, I thought that people over forty were old.

   → I _____ that people over forty were old.

3. Now you live in this city. Where did you live before you came here?

→ Where _____?

4. Did you at some time in the past work for the telephone company?

→ _____ for the telephone company?

5. When I was younger I slept through the night. I never woke up in the middle of the night.

→ I _____ in the middle of the night, but now I do.

→ I _____ through the night, but now I don't.

6. When I was a child, I watched cartoons on TV. I don't watch cartoons anymore. Now I watch news programs. How about you?

→ I _____ cartoons on TV, but I don't anymore.

→ I _____ news programs, but now I do.

→ What _____ on TV when you were a little kid?

☐ **EXERCISE 26. Past habit with USED TO. (Chart 2-11)**
Directions: Complete the sentences with a form of ***used to*** and your own words.

1. I ____*used to ride*____ my bicycle to work, but now I take the bus.

2. What time ____*did you use(d) to go*____ to bed when you were a child?

3. I ____*didn't use(d) to stay up*____ past midnight, but now I often go to bed very late because I have to study.

4. Tom _____ tennis after work every day, but now he doesn't.

5. I _____ breakfast, but now I always have something to eat in the morning because I read that students who eat breakfast do better in school.

6. I _____ interested in _____, but now I am.

7. A: When you were a little kid, what _____ after school?

B: I _____. How about you?

A: I _____.

□ **EXERCISE 27. Past habit with USED TO. (Chart 2-11)**

Directions: Work in pairs. Use ***used to***.
Speaker A: Ask the given question.
Speaker B: Answer the question, using ***used to***. Then ask Speaker A the same question.

Example: Where did you used to live?

SPEAKER A: Where did you used to live?

SPEAKER B: I used to live in Tel Aviv. How about you? Where did you used to live?

SPEAKER A: I used to live in Manila.

1. What did you used to watch on TV when you were a child, and what do you watch now?

2. You are living in a foreign country (OR a different city). What did you used to do in your own country (OR your hometown) that you don't do now?

3. You are an adult now. What did you used to do when you were a child that you don't do now?

4. Think of a particular time in your past (for example, when you were in elementary school, when you lived in Paris, when you worked at your uncle's store). Describe a typical day in your life at that time. What did you used to do?

□ **EXERCISE 28. Past habit with USED TO. (Chart 2-11)**

Directions: Write about the following topics. Use ***used to***. Try to think of at least two or three differences for each topic.

Topics:

1. Compare past and present clothing. How are they different?
   (e.g., *Shoes used to have buttons, but now they don't.*)

2. Compare past and present means of transportation.
   (e.g., *It used to take months to cross the Atlantic Ocean by ship, but now people fly from one continent to another in a few hours.*)

3. Compare the daily lives of people fifty years ago to the daily lives of people today.
   (e.g., *Fifty years ago people didn't use to watch rented movies on TV, but today people often watch movies at home for entertainment.*)

4. Compare past and present beliefs.
   (e.g., *Some people used to believe the sun revolved around the earth, but now we know that the earth revolves around the sun.*)

CHAPTER 3
Future Time

CONTENTS

☐ **EXERCISE 1. Preview: future time. (Charts 3-1 → 3-6)**

Directions: Use the given words to make sentences about the future. Work in pairs, in groups, or as a class.

Examples: I . . . around four this afternoon.
 → *I'm going to go home around four this afternoon.*

 you . . . tomorrow?
 → *Will you be in class tomorrow?*

 1. I . . . this evening.
 2. the teacher . . . next week?
 3. I . . . probably . . . later today.
 4. what time . . . you . . . tomorrow morning?
 5. you . . . later this (morning/afternoon/evening)?
 6. computers . . . in the future.*
 7. what . . . you . . . this weekend?
 8. I may . . . in a few days.
 9. we . . . after we finish this exercise.
10. I . . . before I . . . tomorrow.

_____

In the future = American English; *in future* = British English.

3-1 EXPRESSING FUTURE TIME: *BE GOING TO* AND *WILL*

FUTURE 	(a) I **am going to leave** at nine tomorrow morning. (b) I **will leave** at nine tomorrow morning. (c) Marie **is going to be** at the meeting today.★ (d) Marie **will be** at the meeting today.	**Be going to** and **will** are used to express future time. (a) and (b) have the same meaning. (c) and (d) have the same meaning. **Will** and **be going to** often give the same meaning, but sometimes they express different meanings. The differences are discussed in Chart 3-5, p. 63.
(e) **I shall** leave at nine tomorrow morning. (f) **We shall** leave at nine tomorrow morning.		The use of *shall* (with *I* or *we*) to express future time is possible but infrequent.

★**Today**, **tonight**, and **this** + **morning**, **afternoon**, **evening**, **week**, etc., can express present, past, or future time.

PRESENT: *Sam **is** in his office **this morning**.*
PAST: *Ann **was** in her office **this morning** at eight, but now she's at a meeting.*
FUTURE: *Bob **is going to be** in his office **this morning** after his dentist appointment.*

3-2 FORMS WITH *BE GOING TO*

(a) We *are going to* **be** late. (b) She's *going to* **come** tomorrow. *INCORRECT: She's going to comes tomorrow.*	**Be going to** is followed by the simple form of the verb, as in (a) and (b).

(c) **Am**   I
     Is   he, she, it   } *going to be* late?
     Are   they, we, you
	QUESTION: **be** + *subject* + **going to**

(d)   I   **am not**
   He, she, it   **is not**   } *going to be* late.
   They, we, you   **are not**
	NEGATIVE: **be** + *not* + **going to**

(e) "Hurry up! We're **gonna** be late!"	**Be going to** is more common in speaking and in informal writing than in formal writing. In informal speaking, it is sometimes pronounced "gonna" /gənə/. "Gonna" is not usually a written form.

☐ EXERCISE 2. BE GOING TO. (Charts 3-1 and 3-2)
    Directions: Complete the sentences with **be going to** and the words in parentheses.

    1. A: What *(you, do)* ___are you going to do___ this afternoon?

       B: I *(work)* ___am going to work___ on my report.

    2. A: Where *(Alex, be)* _____ later tonight?

       B: He *(be)* _____ at Kim's house.

3. A: (you, finish) _____ this exercise soon?

    B: Yes, I (finish) _____ it in less than a minute.

4. A: When (you, call) _____ your sister?

    B: I (call, not) _____ her. I (send)

        _____ her an e-mail.

5. A: What (Dr. Price, talk) _____ about in her

        speech tonight?

    B: She (discuss) _____ the economy of Southeast

        Asia.

☐ EXERCISE 3. BE GOING TO. (Charts 3-1 and 3-2)
   Directions: Pair up with a classmate. Use ***be going to*** to talk about plans and intentions.
   (NOTE: You may wish to practice saying "gonna," but also practice enunciating the full
   form.)
   Speaker A: Ask a question using ***be going to*** and the given words. Your book is open.
   Speaker B: Answer the question in a complete sentence, using ***be going to***. Your book is
               closed.

   Example: What . . . do next Monday?
   SPEAKER A *(book open):*   What are you going to do next Monday?
   SPEAKER B *(book closed):* I'm going to go to my classes as usual.

   Example: watch TV tonight?
   SPEAKER A *(book open):*   Are you going to watch TV tonight?
   SPEAKER B *(book closed):* Yes, I'm going to watch TV tonight. OR No, I'm not going to
               watch TV tonight.

    1. where . . . go after your last class today?
    2. have pizza for dinner tonight?
    3. what . . . do this evening?
    4. when . . . visit my hometown?
    5. visit . . . sometime in the future?
    6. what . . . do this coming Saturday?

   Switch roles.
    7. what time . . . go to bed tonight?
    8. what . . . wear tomorrow?
    9. wear your . . . tomorrow too?
   10. how long . . . stay in this city?
   11. take a trip sometime this year or next?
   12. where . . . go and what . . . do?

☐ **EXERCISE 4. Review of verb forms: past, present, and future.**
        (Chapters 1 and 2; Charts 3-1 and 3-2)

Directions: Complete the dialogue with your own words. The dialogue reviews the forms (statement, negative, question, short answer) of the simple present, simple past, and *be going to*.

Example:

A: I *hitchhiked to school* yesterday.

B: Oh? That's interesting. *Do* you *hitchhike to school* every day?

A: Yes, I *do*. I *hitchhike to school* every day.

B: *Do* you also *hitchhike home* every day?

A: No, I *don't*. Etc.

1. A: I _____ yesterday.

2. B: Oh? That's interesting. _____ you _____ every day?

3. A: Yes, I _____ . I _____ every day.

4. B: _____ you also _____ every day?

5. A: No, I _____ . I _____ every day.

6. B: _____ you _____ yesterday?

7. A: Yes, I _____ . I _____ yesterday.

8. B: _____ you also _____ yesterday?

9. A: No, I _____ . I _____ yesterday.

10. B: ____Are____ you _____ tomorrow?

11. A: Yes, I _____ . I _____ tomorrow.

12. B: _____ you also _____ tomorrow?

13. A: No, I _____ . I _____ tomorrow.

☐ **EXERCISE 5. Present, past, and future time. (Chapters 1 and 2; Charts 3-1 and 3-2)**

Directions: Pair up with a classmate.

Speaker A: Ask Speaker B a question about his or her activities. Use *what* and the given
                time expressions. Your book is open.

Speaker B: Answer the question in a complete sentence. Your book is closed.

Example: this evening

SPEAKER A *(book open):* What are you going to do this evening?

SPEAKER B *(book closed):* I'm going to get on the Internet for a while and then read.

Switch roles.

1. yesterday	7. tonight
2. tomorrow	8. the day after tomorrow
3. right now	9. last week
4. every day	10. next week
5. later today	11. every week
6. the day before yesterday	12. this weekend

3-3 FORMS WITH *WILL*

STATEMENT	I-You-She-He-It-We-They **will come** tomorrow.	
NEGATIVE	I-You-She-He-It-We-They **will not (won't) come** tomorrow.	
QUESTION	**Will** I-you-she-he-it-we-they **come** tomorrow?	
SHORT ANSWER	Yes,⎫ No,⎬ I-you-she-he-it-we-they ⎰**will.**★ ⎱**won't.**	
CONTRACTIONS	*I'll* *she'll* *we'll* *you'll* *he'll* *they'll* *it'll*	**Will** is usually contracted with pronouns in both speech and informal writing.
	Bob + **will** = "Bob*'ll*" the teacher + **will** = "the teacher*'ll*"	**Will** is often contracted with nouns in speech, but usually not in writing.

*Pronouns are NOT contracted with helping verbs in short answers.
  CORRECT: Yes, I will.
  INCORRECT: Yes, I'll.

☐ **EXERCISE 6. Forms with WILL. (Chart 3-3)**

Directions: Practice using contractions with **will**. Write the correct contraction for the words in parentheses. Practice pronunciation.

1. (I will) _____I'll_____ be home at eight tonight.

2. (We will) _____ do well in the game tomorrow.

3. (You will) _____ probably get a letter today.

4. Karen is collecting shells at the beach. (She will) _____ be home around sundown.

5. Henry hurt his heel climbing a hill. (He will) _____ probably stay home today.

6. (It will) _____ probably be too cold to go swimming tomorrow.

7. I invited some guests for dinner. (They will) _____ probably get here around seven.

☐ **EXERCISE 7. Forms with WILL. (Chart 3-3)**

Directions: Read the following sentences aloud. Practice contracting **will** with nouns in speech.

1. Rob will probably call tonight. (*"Rob'll probably call tonight."*)
2. Dinner will be at seven.
3. Mary will be here at six tomorrow.
4. The weather will probably be a little colder tomorrow.
5. The party will start at eight.
6. Sam will help us move into our new apartment.
7. My friends will be here soon.
8. The sun will rise at 6:08 tomorrow morning.

3-4 SURENESS ABOUT THE FUTURE

100% sure	(a) I **will be** in class tomorrow. OR I **am going to be** in class tomorrow.	In (a): The speaker uses **will** or **be going to** because he feels sure about his future activity. He is stating a fact about the future.
90% sure	(b) Po **will probably be** in class tomorrow. OR Po **is probably going to be** in class tomorrow. (c) Anna **probably won't be** in class tomorrow. OR Anna **probably isn't going to be** in class tomorrow.	In (b): The speaker uses **probably** to say that he expects Po to be in class tomorrow, but he is not 100% sure. He's almost sure, but not completely sure. Word order with **probably:** * (1) in a statement, as in (b): *helping verb* + **probably** (2) with a negative verb, as in (c): **probably** + *helping verb*
50% sure	(d) Ali **may come** to class tomorrow, or Ali **may not come** to class tomorrow. I don't know what he's going to do.	**May** expresses a future possibility: maybe something will happen, and maybe it won't happen.** In (d): The speaker is saying that maybe Ali will come to class, or maybe he won't come to class. The speaker is guessing.
	(e) **Maybe** Ali **will come** to class, and **maybe** he **won't**. OR **Maybe** Ali **is going to come** to class, and **maybe** he **isn't**.	**Maybe** + **will/be going to** gives the same meaning as **may**. (d) and (e) have the same meaning. **Maybe** comes at the beginning of a sentence.

*See Chart 1-3, p. 9, for more information about placement of midsentence adverbs such as **probably**.
See Chart 7-3, p. 193, for more information about **may.

□ **EXERCISE 8. Sureness about the future. (Chart 3-4)**
    Directions: Discuss how sure the speaker is in each sentence.

1. The bank will be open tomorrow.
    → *The speaker is very sure.*

2. I'm going to go to the bank tomorrow.

3. I'll probably go to the post office too.

4. I may stop at the market on my way home.

5. Ms. White will probably be in the office around nine tomorrow morning.

6. Mr. Wu will be in the office at seven tomorrow morning.

7. Mr. Alvarez may be in the office early tomorrow morning.

8. The sun will rise tomorrow.

9. I'm going to go to the art museum this Saturday, and I may go to the natural history museum too.

10. Abdul is probably going to come with me.

Directions: For each situation, predict what will probably happen and what probably won't happen. Include ***probably*** in your prediction. Use either ***will*** or ***be going to***.

1. Antonio is late to class almost every day.
   (be on time tomorrow? be late again?)
   → *Antonio probably won't be on time tomorrow. He'll probably be late again.*

2. Rosa has a terrible cold. She feels miserable.
   (go to work tomorrow? stay home and rest?)

3. Sam didn't sleep at all last night.
   (go to bed early tonight? stay up all night again tonight?)

4. Ms. Bok needs to travel to a nearby city. She hates to fly.
   (take a plane? travel by bus or train?)

5. Mr. Chu is out of town on business. He needs to contact his assistant right away.
   (call her on the phone or e-mail her? wait until she calls him?)

6. Gina loves to run, but right now she has sore knees and a sore ankle.
   (run in the marathon race this week? skip the race?)

☐ EXERCISE 10. Sureness about the future. (Chart 3-4)

Directions: First the teacher will find out some information from Speaker A, and then ask Speaker B a question. Speaker B will answer using ***may*** or ***maybe*** if s/he's simply guessing or ***probably*** if s/he's fairly sure. Only the teacher's book is open.

Example:

TEACHER *(book open):*   Who's going to visit an interesting place in this city soon?
SPEAKER A *(book closed):* *(Speaker A raises his/her hand.)* I am.
TEACHER *(book open):*   Where are you going to go?
SPEAKER A *(book closed):* To the zoo.
TEACHER *(book open):*   *(Speaker B)*, how is *(Speaker A)* going to get to the zoo?
SPEAKER B *(book closed):* I have no idea. He may walk, or he may take a bus. Maybe he'll ride his bike. OR Well, it's pretty far from here, so he'll probably take a bus.

1. Who's going to visit an interesting place soon?
   Where are you going to go?
   Question to Speaker B: How is *(Speaker A)* going to get to *(name of place)*?

2. Who is going to stay home tonight?
   Question to Speaker B: What is *(Speaker A)* going to do at home tonight?

3. Who's going to go out this evening?
   Question to Speaker B: What is *(Speaker A)* going to do this evening?

4. Who's going to take a trip soon?
   Where are you going?
   Question to Speaker B: How is *(Speaker A)* going to get to *(name of place)*?

5. *(Speaker A)*, please tell us three things you would like to do this weekend.
   Question to Speaker B: What is *(Speaker A)* going to do this weekend?

EXERCISE 11. Sureness about the future. (Chart 3-4)

Directions: Answer the questions using ***will***, ***be going to***, or ***may***. Include ***probably*** or ***maybe*** as appropriate. Work in pairs or as a class.

Example: What will you do after class tomorrow?
→ *I'll probably go back to my apartment.* OR
I'm not sure. I may go to the bookstore.

1. Will you be in class tomorrow?

2. Will (. . .) be in class tomorrow?

3. Is (. . .) going to be in class a month from now?

4. What will the weather be like tomorrow?

5. Will the sun rise tomorrow morning?

6. Is (. . .) going to sit in the same seat in class again tomorrow?

(Switch roles if working in pairs.)

7. What are you going to do after class tomorrow?

8. What is (. . .) going to do after class tomorrow?

9. Will we *(do a particular activity)* in class tomorrow?

10. Who will be the next *(head of state in this country)*?

11. How will the Internet change students' lives?

12. How will the Internet change everyone's life?

□ **EXERCISE 12. Activity: using WILL, BE GOING TO, and MAY. (Charts 3-1 → 3-4)**

Directions: In groups or as a class, use the given topics to discuss the future. The topics can also be used for writing practice.

1. *Clothes:* Will clothing styles change much in the next 10 years? The next 100 years? What kind of clothing will people wear in the year 3000?

2. *Education:* Will computers replace teachers?

3. *Communications:* Will computers take the place of telephones? Will we be able to see the people we're talking to?

4. *Space:* Will we discover other forms of life in the universe? Will humans colonize other planets someday?

5. *Environment:* What will the earth's environment—its water, air, and land—be like in 100 years? Will we still have rainforests? Will animals live in the wild? Will the sea still be a plentiful source of food for humans?

6. *Music:* Will any of today's popular music still be popular 50 years from now? Which songs or singers will last?

7. *Transportation:* Will we still use fossil fuels to power automobiles by the end of this century? Will most automobiles use electric motors in the future? Will cars use other sources of power?

8. *Science:* How will genetic engineering affect our food supply in the future?

3-5 *BE GOING TO* vs. *WILL*

(a) She *is going to succeed* because she works hard. (b) She *will succeed* because she works hard.	*Be going to* and *will* mean the same when they are used to make predictions about the future. (a) and (b) have the same meaning.
(c) I bought some wood because I *am going to build* a bookcase for my apartment.	*Be going to* (but not *will*) is used to express a prior plan (i.e., a plan made before the moment of speaking). In (c): The speaker plans to build a bookcase.
(d) This chair is too heavy for you to carry alone. *I'll help* you.	*Will* (but not *be going to*) is used to express a decision the speaker makes at the moment of speaking. In (d): The speaker decides to help at the immediate present moment; he did not have a prior plan or intention to help.

☐ EXERCISE 13. BE GOING TO vs. WILL. (Charts 3-1 → 3-5)

Directions: Discuss the *italicized* verbs in the following dialogues. Are the speakers expressing

(1) plans they made **before** the moment of speaking, or

(2) decisions they are making **at** the moment of speaking?

1. A: Did you return Pam's phone call?

    B: No, I forgot. Thanks for reminding me. *I'll call* her right away.

    → *Speaker B makes the decision at the moment of speaking.*

2. A: *I'm going to call* Martha later this evening. Do you want to talk to her too?

    B: No, I don't think so.

3. A: Jack is in town for a few days.

    B: Really? Great! *I'll give* him a call. Is he staying at his Aunt Rosa's?

4. A: Alex is in town for a few days.

    B: I know. He called me yesterday. We*'re going to get* together for a drink after I get off work tonight.

5. A: Are you leaving?

    B: Yes. *I'm going to go* for a short walk. I need some fresh air.

    A: *I'll join* you.

    B: Great! Where should we go?

6. A: *I'm going to take* Mohammed to the airport tomorrow morning. Do you want to come along?

    B: Sure.

7. A: We*'re going to go* to Uncle Jacob's over the holiday. Do you want to come with us?

    B: Gee, I don't know. *I'll think* about it. When do you need to know?

8. A: Children, I have a very special job to do, and I need some help. *I'm going to feed* Mr. Whiskers, the rabbit. Who would like to help me?

    B: Me!

    C: I *will!*

    D: Me! Me! I *will!*

    E: I *will!* I *will!*

Directions: Complete the sentences with **be going to** or **will**.

1. A: Why did you buy this flour?

   B: I <u>'m going to</u> make some bread.

2. A: Could someone get me a glass of water?

   B: Certainly. I <u>'ll</u> get you one. Would you like some ice in it?

3. A: Are you going to go to the post office soon?

   B: Yes. Why?

   A: I need to send this letter today.

   B: I _____ mail it for you.

   A: Thanks.

4. A: Why are you carrying that box?

   B: I _____ mail it to my sister. I'm on my way to the post office.

5. A: Could someone please open the window?

   B: I _____ do it.

   A: Thanks.

6: A: What are your vacation plans?

   B: We _____ spend two weeks on a Greek island.

7. A: I have a note for Joe from Rachel. I don't know what to do with it.

   B: Let me have it. I _____ give it to him. He's in my algebra class.

   A: Thanks. But you have to promise not to read it.

8. A: Did you know that Sara and I are moving? We found a great apartment on
      45th Street.

   B: That's terrific. I _____ help you on moving day if you like.

   A: Hey, great! We'd really appreciate that.

9. A: Do you have a car?

   B: Yes, but I _____ sell it. I don't need it now that I live in the city.

10. A: Do you want to walk to the meeting together?

    B: Okay. I _____ meet you by the elevator. Okay?

    A: Okay. I _____ wait for you there.

3-6 EXPRESSING THE FUTURE IN TIME CLAUSES AND *IF*-CLAUSES

<table>
<tr>
<td>

                 time clause
(a) *Before I go* to class tomorrow , I'm going to eat breakfast.

(b) I'm going to eat breakfast *before I go* to class tomorrow.

</td>
<td>

In (a) and (b): *before I go to class tomorrow* is a future time clause.

> *before*
> *after*
> *when*
> *as soon as*
> *until*
> *while*

+ subject and verb = a time clause

</td>
</tr>
<tr>
<td>

(c) *Before I go* home tonight, I'm going to stop at the market.

(d) I'm going to eat dinner at 6:00 tonight. *After I eat* dinner, I'm going to study in my room.

(e) I'll give Rita your message *when I see* her.

(f) It's raining right now. *As soon as the rain stops*, I'm going to walk downtown.

(g) I'll stay home *until the rain stops*.

(h) *While you're* at school tomorrow, I'll be at work.

</td>
<td>

The simple present is used in a future time clause. *Will* and *be going to* are NOT used in a future time clause.
INCORRECT: Before I will go to class, I'm going to eat breakfast.
INCORRECT: Before I am going to go to class tomorrow, I'm going to eat breakfast.
All of the example sentences, (c) through (h), contain future time clauses.

</td>
</tr>
<tr>
<td>

(i) Maybe it will rain tomorrow. *If it rains tomorrow*, I'm going to stay home.

</td>
<td>

In (i): *If it rains tomorrow* is an *if*-clause.
        if + subject and verb = an *if*-clause
When the meaning is future, the simple present (not *will* or *be going to*) is used in an *if*-clause.

</td>
</tr>
</table>

☐ EXERCISE 15. Future time clauses and IF-clauses. (Chart 3-6)
    Directions: <u>Underline</u> the time clauses and correct any errors in verb use.

1. <u>Before I ~~'m going to~~ return to my country next year,</u> I'm going to finish my graduate

    degree in computer science.

2. The boss will review your work after she will return from vacation next week.

3. I'll give you a call on my cell phone as soon as my plane will land.

4. I don't especially like my current job, but I'm going to stay with this company until I

    will find something better.

5. I need to know what time the meeting starts. Please be sure to call me as soon as you

    will find out anything about it.

6. When you will be in Australia next month, are you going to go snorkeling at the Great

    Barrier Reef?

7. If it won't be cold tomorrow, we'll go to the beach. If it will be cold tomorrow, we'll

    go to a movie.

☐ **EXERCISE 16. Future time clauses and IF-clauses. (Chart 3-6)**
  Directions: Use the given verbs to complete the sentences. Give a future meaning to the
  sentences.

  1. *take/read*

     I ___'ll read___ the textbook **before** I ___take___ the final exam next month.

  2. *return/call*

     Mr. Lee _____ his wife **as soon as** he _____ to the

     hotel tonight.

  3. *come/be, not*

     I _____ home tomorrow **when** the painters _____ to

     paint my apartment. Someone else will have to let them in.

  4. *prepare/go*

     Before I _____ to my job interview tomorrow, I _____

     a list of questions I want to ask about the company.

5. *visit/take*

   When Sandra _____ us this coming weekend, we _____
   her to our favorite seafood restaurant.

6. *stay/call*

   I _____ by the phone **until** Rosa _____.★

7. *miss/come, not*

   If Adam _____ to work tomorrow morning, he _____ a
   very important meeting.

8. *get/be/eat*

   If Barbara _____ home on time tonight, we _____
   dinner at 6:30. **If** she _____ late, dinner _____ late.

☐ **EXERCISE 17. Future IF-clauses. (Chart 3-6)**
    Directions: Make sentences about the following possible conditions. Use *if* and add your
    own ideas. Pay special attention to the verb in the *if*-clause. Work in pairs.
    Speaker A: Give the cue as written in the text. Your book is open.
    Speaker B: Use the cue to create a sentence with an *if*-clause. Your book is closed.

Example:
SPEAKER A: Maybe you'll go downtown tomorrow.
SPEAKER B: If I **go** downtown tomorrow, I'm going to buy some new clothes/go to the post
            office/etc.

1. Maybe you'll have some free time tomorrow.

2. Maybe it'll rain tomorrow.

3. Maybe it won't rain tomorrow.

4. Maybe the teacher will be absent tomorrow.

Switch roles.

5. Maybe you'll be tired tonight.

6. Maybe you won't be tired tonight.

7. Maybe it'll be nice tomorrow.

8. Maybe we won't have class tomorrow.

★Time clauses beginning with **until** usually **follow** the main clause.
    Usual: I'm going to stay by the phone **until** *Rosa calls.*
    Possible but less usual: **Until** *Rosa calls,* I'm going to stay by the phone.

☐ **EXERCISE 18. Future time clauses with BEFORE and AFTER. (Chart 3-6)**

Directions: Each item consists of two actions. Decide which action you want to do first. Use **before** or **after** to say what you intend to do. Then perform the actions. Work in pairs, groups, or as a class. Pay special attention to the verb in the time clause.

1. touch your ear / close your grammar book
   → *I'm going to close my grammar book before/after I touch my ear.* OR
   Before/After I close my grammar book, I'm going to touch my ear.

2. raise your hand, touch your foot

3. sit down, stand up

4. clap your hands, slap your knee

5. shake hands with (. . .), shake hands with (. . .)

6. scratch your chin, pick up your pen

7. *Think of other actions to perform.*

☐ **EXERCISE 19. Future time clauses with UNTIL and AS SOON AS. (Chart 3-6)**

Directions: Listen to the directions; state what you're going to do; then perform the actions. Work as a class with the teacher as the leader or in groups with one student designated as leader. Only the leader's book is open; everyone else has a closed book.

Example: *(Student A)*, stand up **until** *(Student B)* stands up. Then sit down.
 (Student A), please tell us what you're going to do.
 (Student B), please tell us what *(Student A)* is going to do.
 (Student C), please tell us what *(Student A)* is going to do **until** *(Student B)*
    stands up.

LEADER: Ali, I'd like you to stand up **until** Kim stands up, and then sit down.
 Ali, please tell us what you're going to do.

ALI: I'm going to stand up **until** Kim stands up. Then I'm going to sit down.

LEADER: Kim, please tell us what Ali is going to do.

KIM: He's going to stand up **until** I stand up. Then he's going to sit down.

LEADER: Maria, tell us what Ali is going to do **as soon as** Kim stands up.

MARIA: **As soon as** Kim stands up, Ali is going to sit down.

Students A and B then perform the actions.

1. *(Student A)*, sit at your desk **until** *(Student B)* knocks on the door. Then get up and
    walk to the door.
   (Student A), please tell us what you're going to do.
   (Student B), please tell us what *(Student A)* is going to do.
   (Student C), please tell us what *(Student A)* is going to do **as soon as** *(Student B)*
    knocks on the door.

2. *(Student A)*, hold your breath **until** *(Student B)* snaps his/her fingers. Then breathe
    again.
   (Student A), please tell us what you're going to do.
   (Student B), please tell us what *(Student A)* is going to do.
   (Student C), please tell us what *(Student A)* is going to do **as soon as** *(Student B)*
    snaps his/her fingers.

3. (*Student A*), clap your hands **until** (*Student B*) bows. Then stop clapping your hands.
    (*Student A*), please tell us what you're going to do.
    (*Student B*), please tell us what (*Student A*) is going to do.
    (*Student C*), please tell us what (*Student A*) is going to do **as soon as** (*Student B*)
    bows.

☐ **EXERCISE 20. Review of time clauses and IF-clauses. (Chapters 1 → 3)**
   Directions: Complete the sentences by using a form of the words in parentheses. Read
   carefully for time expressions.

1. a. Before Tom *(go)* _____goes_____ to bed, he always *(brush)* _____
        his teeth.

    b. Before Tom *(go)* _____ to bed later tonight, he *(e-mail)* _____
        his girlfriend.

    c. Before Tom *(go)* _____ to bed last night, he *(take)* _____
        a shower.

    d. While Tom *(take)* _____ a shower last night, the phone *(ring)*
        _____ .

    e. As soon as the phone *(ring)* _____ last night, Tom *(jump)*
        _____ out of the shower to answer it.

    f. As soon as Tom *(get)* _____ up tomorrow morning, he *(brush)*
        _____ his teeth.

    g. Tom always *(brush)* _____ his teeth as soon as he *(get)*
        _____ up.

2. a. After I *(get)* _____ home from work every afternoon, I usually
        (drink) _____ a cup of tea.

    b. After I *(get)* _____ home from work tomorrow afternoon, I *(drink)*
        _____ a cup of tea.

    c. I *(have, not)* _____ any tea until I *(get)* _____
        home from work tomorrow.

    d. After I *(get)* _____ home from work yesterday, I *(drink)*
        _____ a cup of tea.

    e. While I *(drink)* _____ a cup of tea yesterday afternoon,
        my neighbor *(come)* _____ over, so I *(offer)* _____
        her a cup of tea too.

    f. My neighbor *(drop, probably)* _____ over again
        tomorrow. If she *(come)* _____ , I *(make)* _____
        a cup of tea for her.

Directions: Write two paragraphs. Show the time relationships by using words such as
before, after, when, while, as soon as, next, then, later, after that.

Paragraph 1: a detailed description of your day yesterday.

Paragraph 2: a detailed description of your day tomorrow.

3-7 USING THE PRESENT PROGRESSIVE TO EXPRESS FUTURE TIME

(a) Tom *is going to come* to the party tomorrow. (b) Tom *is coming* to the party tomorrow. (c) We*'re going to go* to a movie tonight. (d) We*'re going* to a movie tonight. (e) I*'m going to stay* home this evening. (f) I*'m staying* home this evening.	The present progressive can be used to express future time. Each pair of example sentences has the same meaning. The present progressive describes *definite plans for the future, plans that were made before the moment of speaking.*
(g) Ann *is going to fly* to Chicago next week. (h) Ann *is flying* to Chicago next week.	A future meaning for the present progressive is indicated either by future time words (e.g., *tomorrow*) or by the situation.*
(i) You*'re going to laugh* when you hear this joke. (j) INCORRECT: *You're laughing when you hear this joke.*	The present progressive is NOT used for predictions about the future. In (i): The speaker is predicting a future event. In (j): The present progressive is not possible; laughing is a prediction, not a planned future event.

*COMPARE: Present situation: *Look! Mary's coming. Do you see her?*

Future situation: *Are you planning to come to the party? Mary's coming. So is Alex.*

☐ **EXERCISE 22. Using the present progressive to express future time.** (Chart 3-7)

Directions: Complete the dialogues with any of the following verbs that make sense. Use
the present progressive if possible. Discuss whether the present progressive expresses
present or future time.

cut	go	spend
do	leave	stay
drive	meet	take
fly		

1. A: What _____are_____ you _____doing_____ tomorrow afternoon?

   B: I _____am going_____ to the mall.

   A: Why?

   B: I _____am going_____ shopping for some new clothes. How about you?

   What _____ you _____ tomorrow afternoon?

   A: I _____ to a movie with Tom. After the movie, we

   _____ out to dinner. Would you like to meet us for dinner?

B: No, thanks. I can't. I _____ Heidi at 6:30 at the new seafood restaurant on Fifth Street.

2. A: What courses _____ you _____ this year?

   B: I _____ English, biology, math, and psychology.

   A: What courses _____ you _____ next year?

   B: I _____ English literature, chemistry, calculus, and history.

   A: That should keep you busy!

3. A: I _____ on vacation tomorrow.

   B: Where _____ you _____ ?

   A: To San Francisco.

   B: How are getting there? _____ you _____ or _____ your car?

   A: I _____ . I have to be at the airport by seven tomorrow morning.

   B: Do you need a ride to the airport?

   A: No, thanks. I _____ a taxi. Are you planning to go somewhere over vacation?

   B: No. I _____ here.

4. A: Stop! Annie! What _____ you _____ ?

   B: I _____ my hair, Mom.

   A: Oh dear!

5. A: You haven't seen my passport, have you?

   B: No. Why?

   A: I need it because I _____ for Taipei next Monday.

   B: Oh? How long will you be there?

   A: A week. I _____ the first few days with my brother, who _____ to school there. After that I _____ some old friends I went to school with in Australia several years ago. They've invited me to be their house guest.

   B: Sounds like a great trip. Hope you find your passport.

☐ **EXERCISE 23. Using the present progressive to express future time. (Chart 3-7)**
Directions: Pair up with a classmate. Tell each other your plans. Use the present progressive.

Example: What are your plans for this evening?
SPEAKER A: I'm staying home. How about you?
SPEAKER B: I'm going to a cybercafe to send some e-mails. Then I'm going to the English Conversation Club. I'm meeting Anna there.

What are your plans . . .
   1. for the rest of today?
   2. for tomorrow or the next day?
   3. for this coming weekend?
   4. for the rest of this month?

☐ **EXERCISE 24. Writing: using the present progressive to express future time. (Chart 3-7)**
Directions: Think of a place you would like to visit. Pretend you are going to take a trip there this weekend. You have already made all of your plans. Write a paragraph in which you describe your trip. Use the present progressive where appropriate.

Example: This coming weekend, my friend Gisella and I are taking a trip. We're going to Nashville, Tennessee. Gisella likes country music and wants to go to some shows. I don't know anything about country music, but I'm looking forward to going to Nashville. We're leaving Friday afternoon as soon as Gisella gets off work. (Etc.)

Possible questions to answer in your paragraph:
   1. Where are you going?
   2. When are you leaving?
   3. Are you traveling alone?
   4. How are you getting there?
   5. Where are you staying?
   6. Are you visiting anyone? Who?
   7. How long are you staying there?
   8. When are you getting back?

3-8 USING THE SIMPLE PRESENT TO EXPRESS FUTURE TIME

(a) My plane **arrives** at 7:35 *tomorrow evening*. (b) Tom's new job **starts** *next week*. (c) The semester **ends** *in two more weeks*. (d) There **is** a meeting at ten *tomorrow morning*.	The simple present can express future time when events are on a definite schedule or timetable. Only a few verbs are used in the simple present to express future time. The most common are **arrive, leave, start, begin, end, finish, open, close, be**.
(e) INCORRECT: *I wear my new suit to the wedding next week.* CORRECT: *I am wearing/am going to wear my new suit to the wedding next week.*	Most verbs **cannot** be used in the simple present to express future time. For example, in (e): The verb **wear** does not express an event on a schedule or timetable. It cannot be used in the simple present to express future time.

☐ **EXERCISE 25. Using present verb forms to express future time. (Charts 3-7 and 3-8)**
Directions: Circle the correct possible completions and cross out those that are incorrect.

1. The concert _____ at eight tonight.

   (a.) begins   (b.) is beginning/is going to begin

2. I _____ seafood pasta for dinner tonight.

   a. make   (b.) am making/am going to make

3. I _____ to school tomorrow morning. I need the exercise.

   a. walk   b. am walking/am going to walk

4. The bus _____ at 8:15 tomorrow morning.

   a. leaves   b. is leaving/is going to leave

5. I _____ the championship game on TV at Jim's house tomorrow.

   a. watch   b. am watching/am going to watch

6. The game _____ at one tomorrow afternoon.

   a. starts   b. is starting/is going to start

7. Alex's plane _____ at 10:14 tomorrow morning.

   a. arrives   b. is arriving/is going to arrive

8. I can't pick him up tomorrow, so he _____ the airport bus into the city.

   a. takes   b. is taking/is going to take

3-9 IMMEDIATE FUTURE: USING *BE ABOUT TO*

(a) Ann's bags are packed, and she is wearing her coat. She *is about to leave* for the airport. (b) Shhh. The movie *is about to begin*.	The idiom "be about to do something" expresses an activity that will happen *in the immediate future,* usually within minutes or seconds. In (a): Ann is going to leave sometime in the next few minutes.

☐ EXERCISE 26. Using BE ABOUT TO. (Chart 3-9)

Directions: Describe the actions that are about to happen in the pictures. Use *be about to*.

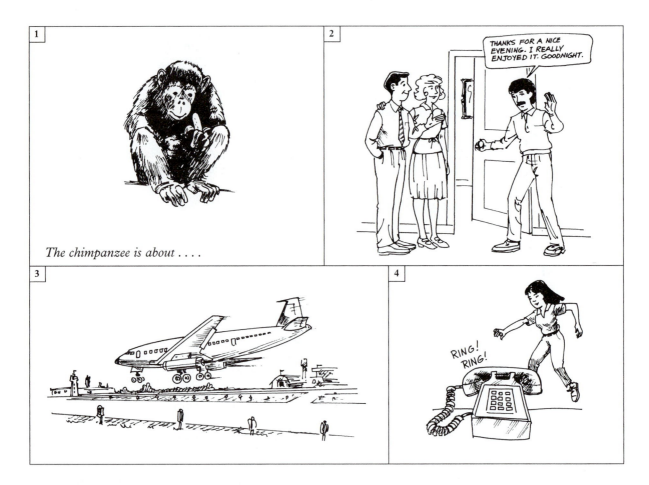

1.

The chimpanzee is about . . . .

2. THANKS FOR A NICE EVENING. I REALLY ENJOYED IT. GOODNIGHT.

3.

4. RING! RING!

☐ EXERCISE 27. Using BE ABOUT TO. (Chart 3-9)

Directions: What are the following people probably about to do? Create pictures of them in your imagination.

1. Jack is holding his camera to his eye. He has his finger on the button.

→ *He's about to take a picture.*

2. The door is closed. Sally has her hand on the doorknob.

3. Eric is on the last question of the examination.

4. Nancy has dirty hands from working in the garden. She is holding a bar of soap. She is standing at the bathroom sink.

5. Ben is putting on his coat and heading for the door.

6. Rita is holding a fly swatter and staring at a fly on the kitchen table.

7. Mr. Tomko has just checked to make sure the doors are locked and turned off the lights in the living room. He's heading toward the bedroom.

□ EXERCISE 28. Using BE ABOUT TO. (Chart 3-9)
Directions: Think of an action to perform. Don't reveal what it is. Get ready to do it, but just before you perform the action, ask the class to describe what you are about to do. Perform with a partner if you wish.

Examples: (. . .) walks to the chalkboard and picks up the eraser. The class guesses correctly that he is about to erase the board.

(. . .) and (. . .) hold out their hands to each other. They are about to shake hands.

Suggestions for actions to prepare to perform:
1. stand up
2. open the door
3. close the window
4. pick up your pen
5. close your book
6. etc.

□ EXERCISE 29. Preview: parallel verbs. (Chart 3-10)
Directions: Correct the errors.

1. Fifteen years from now, my wife and I will retire and travel ~~ing~~ all over the world.

2. I opened the door and invite my friend to come in.

3. If I feel tense, I close my eyes and thinking about nothing at all.

4. Pete is in the other room. He's listening to music and study for his chemistry exam.

5. It's hot in here. I'm going to open the window and turning on the fan.

3-10 PARALLEL VERBS

(a) Jim **makes** his bed *and* **cleans** up his room every morning.	Often a subject has two verbs that are connected by **and**. We say that the two verbs are parallel: v + **and** + v *makes and cleans* = parallel verbs
(b) Ann **is cooking** dinner *and (is)* **talking** on the phone at the same time. (c) I **will stay** home and *(will)* **study** tonight. (d) I **am going to stay** home and *(am going to)* **study** tonight.	It is not necessary to repeat a helping verb (an auxiliary verb) when two verbs are connected by **and**.

□ **EXERCISE 30. Parallel verbs. (Chart 3-10)**

Directions: Complete the sentences with the correct forms of the words in parentheses.

1. When I *(walk)* _____walked_____ into the living room yesterday, Grandpa *(read)* _____ a newspaper and *(smoke)* _____ his pipe.

2. Helen will graduate soon. She *(move)* _____ to New York and *(look)* _____ for a job after she *(graduate)* _____ .

3. Every day my neighbor *(call)* _____ me on the phone and *(complain)* _____ about the weather.

4. Look at Erin! She *(cry)* _____ and *(laugh)* _____ at the same time. I wonder if she is happy or sad?

5. I'm beat! I can't wait to get home. After I *(get)* _____ home, I *(take)* _____ a hot shower and *(go)* _____ to bed.

6. Yesterday my dog *(dig)* _____ a hole in the back yard and *(bury)* _____ a bone.

7. I'm tired of this cold weather. As soon as spring *(come)* _____ , I *(play)* _____ tennis and *(jog)* _____ in the park as often as possible.

8. While Paul *(carry)* _____ brushes and paint and *(climb)* _____ a ladder, a bird *(fly)* _____ down and *(sit)* _____ on his head. Paul *(drop)* _____ the paint and *(spill)* _____ it all over the ground.

9. When I first *(arrive)* _____ in this city and *(start)* _____

going to school here, I knew no one. I was lonely and felt that I didn't have a friend in

the world.

One day while I *(watch)* _____ TV alone in my room

and *(feel)* _____ sorry for myself, a woman I had met in one of

my classes *(knock)* _____ on my door and *(ask)* _____

me if I wanted to accompany her to the student center. That was the beginning of my

friendship with Lisa King.

Now we *(see)* _____ each other every day and usually *(spend)*

_____ time talking on the phone, too. Later this week we *(borrow)*

_____ her brother's car and *(go)* _____ to visit her

aunt in the country. Next week we *(take)* _____ a bus to

Fall City and *(go)* _____ to a football game. I'm really enjoying our

friendship.

☐ **EXERCISE 31. Review: verb forms. (Chapters 1 → 3)**
   Directions: Complete the sentences with the correct forms of the words in parentheses.

1. I usually *(ride)* __ride__ my bicycle to work in the morning, but it *(rain)*

   _____ when I left my house early this morning, so I *(take)*

   _____ the bus. After I *(arrive)* _____ at work, I

   (discover) _____ that I had left my briefcase at home.

2. A: Are you going to take the kids to the amusement park tomorrow morning?

   B: Yes. It *(open)* _____ at 10:00. If we *(leave)* _____

      here at 9:30, we'll get there at 9:55. The kids can be the first ones in the park.

3. A: Ouch!

   B: What happened?

   A: I *(cut)* _____ my finger.

   B: It *(bleed)* _____ !

   A: I know!

   B: Put pressure on it. I *(get)* _____ some antibiotic and a

      bandage.

   A: Thanks.

4. A: I *(go)* _____ to a lecture on Shakespeare tomorrow evening. Want to join me?

   B: Nah. Brian and I *(go)* _____ to a movie — *Godzilla Eats the Earth.*

5. A: Your phone *(ring)* _____ .

   B: I *(know)* _____ .

   A: *(you, answer)* _____ it?

   B: No.

   A: *(you, want)* _____ me to get it?

   B: No thanks.

   A: Why *(you, want, not)* _____ to answer your phone?

   B: I *(expect)* _____ another call from the bill collector. I have a bunch of bills I haven't paid. I *(want, not)* _____ to talk to her.

   A: Oh.

6. A: What *(you, wear)* _____ to Eric's wedding tomorrow?

   B: My blue dress, I guess. How about you?

   A: I *(plan)* _____ to wear my new outfit. I *(buy)* _____ it just a few days ago. It *(be)* _____ a yellow suit with a white blouse. Just a minute. I *(show)* _____ it to you. Wait right here. I *(get)* _____ it from my closet and *(bring)* _____ it out.

7. A: Look! There *(be)* _____ a police car behind us. Its lights *(flash)* _____ .

   B: I *(know)* _____! I *(know)* _____! I *(see)* _____ it.

   A: What *(go)* _____ on? *(you, speed)* _____?

   B: No, I'm not. I *(drive)* _____ the speed limit.

   A: Ah, look. The police car *(pass)* _____ us.

   B: Whew!

8. A: *(the sun, keep)* _____ burning forever, or *(it, burn, eventually)* _____ itself out?

   B: It *(burn, eventually)* _____ itself out, but that *(happen, not)* _____ for billions of years.

9. Sometime in the next twenty-five years, a spaceship with a human crew (land) _____ on Mars. I (think) _____ they (find) _____ evidence of some kind of life forms there, but I (expect, not) _____ _____ them to encounter sentient beings. Someday, however, I (believe) _____ that humans (make) _____ contact with other intelligent beings in the universe.

☐ EXERCISE 32. Review: verb forms. (Chapters 1 → 3)

Directions: Complete the sentences with a form of the verb in parentheses.

(1) Three hundred and fifty years ago, people *(make)* _____**made**_____ their own clothes. They *(have, not)* _____ machines for making clothes. There *(be, not)* _____ any clothing factories. People *(wear)* _____ homemade clothes that were sewn by hand.

(2) Today, very few people *(make)* _____ their own clothes. Clothing *(come)* _____ ready-made from factories. People *(buy)* _____ almost all their clothes from stores.

(3) The modern clothing industry *(be)* _____ international. As a result, people from different countries often *(wear)* _____ similar clothes. For example, people in many different countries throughout the world *(wear)* _____ jeans and T-shirts.

(4) However, some regional differences in clothing still *(exist)* _____ . For instance, people of the Arabian deserts *(wear)* _____ loose, flowing robes to protect themselves from the heat of the sun. In parts of northern Europe, fur hats *(be)* _____ common in the winter.

(5) In the future, there *(be, probably)* _____ fewer and fewer differences in clothing. People throughout the world *(wear)* _____ clothes from the same factories. *(we all, dress)* _____ alike in the future? TV shows and movies about the future often *(show)* _____ everybody in a uniform of some kind. What *(you, think)* _____ ?

□ **EXERCISE 33. Error analysis: summary review of present, past, and future time. (Chapters 1 → 3)**

Directions: Correct the errors.

1. I used to kick ~~ed~~ my sister's legs.

2. We had a test last week, and I past it.

3. I not like the food in the United State.

4. I use to get up at noon, but now I have to be at work by eight.

5. I study hardly every day, but my english is not be improve.

6. Everyone enjoy these English classes.

7. At the picnic, we sang songs and talk to each other.

8. I learn the english in my school in hong Kong before I come here.

9. I like to travel. I gonna go to new and interesting places all my life.

10. Now I study at this school and I living with my cousin. I am always meet my friends in the cafeteria and we talking about our classes.

11. When I wake up in the morning. I am turning on the radio. Before get up.

12. I am live with an American family. They are having four childrens.

13. When I was at the outdoor market, I pointed at the chicken I wanted to buy. The man was taking it from a wooden cage and kill it without mercy.

14. Every day I wake up when the birds begin to sing. If the weather not to be cloudy, I am seeing a beautiful sunrise from my bed.

15. My husband and children they are going to join me after I will finish my English course.

□ EXERCISE 34. Error analysis: summary review of present, past, and future time. (Chapters 1 → 3)

Directions: Rewrite the paragraphs. Correct any errors in grammar, spelling, or punctuation. If you wish, change the wording to improve the expression of the ideas.

1. I want to tell you about Oscar. He my cousin. He comes here four years ago. Before he came here, he study statistics in Chile. When he leaves Chile to come here. He came with four friends. They were studying English in Ohio. Then he went to New york stayed there for three years. He graduated from New York University. Now he study at this school. After he finish his Master's degree, he return to Chile.

2. Long ago in a faraway place, a lonely man move into a new neighborhood. His first project is his new garden. He begun to work on it right away. He wanting to make a perfect garden. One day some friendly neighbors and their children visitted the man in his garden and helpped him with the work. They planting flowers and build a small bridge across a little stream. All of them were very happy during they were building the bridge and work on the garden. The man was especially happy because he's no longer lonely. While the adults working, some of their children plaied with a ball in the garden while they were play, one of them step on a flower. Suddenly the man was getting very angry and tell everyone to leave. All the neighbors leaved and go back to their own homes. After that, the man built a wall around his garden and lock the gate. For the rest of his life, the man sat alone in his garden every evening and crying.

□ EXERCISE 35. Review: verb forms. (Chapters 1 → 3)

Directions: Complete the sentences with the correct forms of the words in parentheses.

A: Okay, let's all open our fortune cookies.

B: What *(yours, say)* _____ ?
1

A: Mine says, "An unexpected gift *(add)* _____ to your pleasure."
2

Great! *(you, plan)* _____ to give me a gift soon?
3

B: Not that I know of. Mine says, "Your trust in a friend *(prove)* _____
4
well-founded." Good. I *(like)* _____ having trustworthy friends.
5

C: This one says, "A smile *(overcome)* _____ a language
6
barrier." Well, that's good! After this, when I *(understand, not)* _____
7
people who *(speak)* _____ English to me, I *(smile, just)*
8
_____ at them!
9

D: My fortune is this: "Your determination *(make)* _____ you
10
succeed in everything."

A: Well, it *(look)* _____ like all of us *(have)* _____
11   12
good luck in the future!

☐ **EXERCISE 36. Future time. (Chapter 3)**

Directions: Do you believe that some people are able to predict the future? Pretend that you have the ability to see into the future. Choose several people you know (classmates, teachers, family members, friends) and tell them in writing about their future lives. Discuss such topics as jobs, contributions to humankind, marriage, children, fame, and exciting adventures. With your words, paint interesting and fun pictures of their future lives.

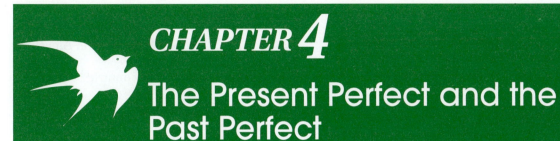

CONTENTS

☐ EXERCISE 1. Review and preview: present and past verbs. (Chapters 1, 2, and 4)
   Directions: Complete the sentences with the words in parentheses. Some of the completions review verb tenses studied in Chapters 1 and 2. Some of them preview verb tenses that will be studied in this chapter: the present perfect and the past perfect. Discuss the form and meaning of the new tenses.
      There may be more than one possible correct completion.

My name *(be)* ___is___ Surasuk Jutukanyaprateep. I *(be)* _____ from
                    1   2
Thailand. Right now I *(study)* _____ English at this school. I *(be)*
                                       3
_____ at this school since the beginning of January. I *(arrive)*
        4
_____ here January 2, and my classes *(begin)* _____
        5   6
January 6.

      Since I *(come)* _____ here, I *(do)* _____
                              7   8
many things, and I *(meet)* _____ many people. Last week, I *(go)*
                                    9
_____ to a party at my friend's house. I *(meet)* _____
        10   11
some of the other students from Thailand at the party. Of course, we *(speak)*

_____ Thai, so I *(practice, not)* _____ my English
        12   13
that night. There *(be)* _____ only people from Thailand at the party.
                                 14

However, since I *(come)* _____ here, I *(meet)* _____
15   16

a lot of other people, too. I *(meet)* _____ people from Latin America,
17

Africa, the Middle East, and Asia. I enjoy meeting people from other countries. Before I

came here, I *(meet, never)* _____ anyone from the Ukraine
18

or Bolivia. Now I *(know)* _____ people from both these places, and they
19

(become) _____ my friends.
20

4-1 PAST PARTICIPLE

	SIMPLE FORM	SIMPLE PAST	**PAST PARTICIPLE**
REGULAR VERBS	finish stop wait	finished stopped waited	**finished** **stopped** **waited**
IRREGULAR VERBS	see make put	saw made put	**seen** **made** **put**

The **past participle** is one of the principal parts of a verb. (See Chart 2-6, p. 32.)

The past participle is used in the PRESENT PERFECT tense and the PAST PERFECT tense.*

The past participle of regular verbs is the same as the simple past form: both end in *-ed*.
See Chart 2-7, p. 33, for a list of irregular verbs.

*The past participle is also used in the passive. See Chapter 10.

☐ EXERCISE 2. Past participle. (Chart 4-1)
Directions: Write the past participle.

	SIMPLE FORM	SIMPLE PAST	PAST PARTICIPLE		SIMPLE FORM	SIMPLE PAST	PAST PARTICIPLE
1.	finish	finished	*finished*	11.	come	came	_____
2.	see	saw	*seen*	12.	study	studied	_____
3.	go	went	_____	13.	stay	stayed	_____
4.	have	had	_____	14.	begin	began	_____
5.	meet	met	_____	15.	start	started	_____
6.	call	called	_____	16.	write	wrote	_____
7.	fall	fell	_____	17.	eat	ate	_____
8.	do	did	_____	18.	cut	cut	_____
9.	know	knew	_____	19.	read	read	_____
10.	fly	flew	_____	20.	be	was/were	_____

4-2 FORMS OF THE PRESENT PERFECT

(a) I **have finished** my work. (b) The students **have finished** Chapter 3. (c) Jim **has eaten** lunch.	STATEMENT: **have/has** + *past participle*
(d) **I've/You've/We've/They've** *eaten* lunch. (e) **She's/He's** *eaten* lunch. (f) **It's** *been* cold for the last three days.	CONTRACTION *pronoun* + **have** = **'ve** *pronoun* + **has** = **'s**★
(g) I **have not (haven't) finished** my work. (h) Ann **has not (hasn't) eaten** lunch.	NEGATIVE: **have/has** + **not** + *past participle* NEGATIVE CONTRACTION **have** + **not** = **haven't** **has** + **not** = **hasn't**
(i) **Have you finished** your work? (j) **Has Jim eaten** lunch? (k) How long **have you lived** here?	QUESTION: **have/has** + *subject* + *past participle*

(l) A: Have you seen that movie?
     B: *Yes, I* **have**. OR *No, I* **haven't**.
 (m) A: Has Jim eaten lunch?
     B: *Yes, he* **has**. OR *No, he* **hasn't**.
	SHORT ANSWER: **have/haven't** or **has/hasn't**
	 Note: The helping verb in the short answer is not contracted with the pronoun.
	 INCORRECT: Yes, I've. OR *Yes, he's.*

★COMPARE: **It's** cold today. [*It's* = *It is*: **It is** *cold today.*]
        It's been cold since December. [*It's* = *It has*: **It has** *been cold since December.*]

☐ EXERCISE 3. Forms of the present perfect. (Chart 4-2)

Directions: Complete the dialogues with the words in parentheses. Use the present perfect.

1. A: *(you, eat, ever)* ____Have you ever eaten____ seaweed?

   B: No, I ____haven't____ . I *(eat, never)* ____'ve never eaten____ seaweed.

2. A: *(you, stay, ever)* _____ at a big hotel?

   B: Yes, I _____ . I *(stay)* _____ at a big hotel
   lots of times.

3. A: *(you, meet, ever)* _____ a movie star?

   B: No, I _____ . I *(meet, never)* _____
   a movie star.

4. A: *(Tom, visit, ever)* _____ you at your house?

   B: Yes, he _____ . He *(visit)* _____ me lots
   of times.

5. A: *(Ann, be, ever)* _____ in Mexico?

   B: No, she _____ . She *(be, never)* _____ in
   Mexico. She *(be, not)* _____ in any Spanish-speaking
   countries.

Jim has eaten lunch.

Ann hasn't eaten lunch.

PRESENT PERFECT, MEANING #1: SOMETHING HAPPENED BEFORE NOW AT AN UNSPECIFIED TIME.

	(a) Jim **has** already **eaten** lunch. (b) Ann **hasn't eaten** lunch yet. (c) **Have** you ever **eaten** at that restaurant?	The PRESENT PERFECT expresses an activity or situation that occurred (or did not occur) *before now, at some unspecified time in the past.* In (a): Jim's lunch occurred before the present time. The exact time is not mentioned; it is unimportant or unknown. For the speaker, the only important information is that Jim's lunch occurred in the past, sometime before now.
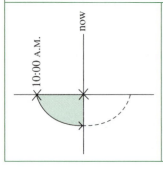	(d) Pete **has eaten** at that restaurant *many times.* (e) I **have eaten** there *twice.*	An activity may be repeated two, several, or more times *before now,* at *unspecified times in the past,* as in (d) and (e).

PRESENT PERFECT, MEANING #2: A SITUATION BEGAN IN THE PAST AND CONTINUES TO THE PRESENT.

10:00 A.M. ... *now*	(f) We'**ve been** in class **since** *ten o'clock this morning.* (g) I **have known** Ben **for** *ten years.* I met him ten years ago. I still know him today. We are friends.	When the present perfect is used with **since** or **for**, it expresses situations that began in the past and continue to the present. In (f): Class started at ten. We are still in class now, at the moment of speaking. *INCORRECT: We are in class since ten o'clock this morning.*

□ **EXERCISE 4. Present perfect. (Chart 4-3)**

Directions: When speakers use the present perfect, they often contract **have** and **has** with nouns in everyday speech. Listen to your teacher say these sentences in normal contracted speech and practice saying them yourself. Discuss the meaning of the present perfect.

1. Bob has been in Montreal since last Tuesday. *("Bob's been in . . . .")*
2. Jane has been out of town for two days.
3. The weather has been warm since the beginning of April.
4. My parents have been active in politics for forty years.
5. Mike has already eaten breakfast.
6. My friends have moved into a new apartment.
7. My roommate has traveled a lot. She's visited many different countries.
8. My aunt and uncle have lived in the same house for twenty-five years.

4-4 SIMPLE PAST vs. PRESENT PERFECT

SIMPLE PAST (a) I **finished** my work *two hours ago*. PRESENT PERFECT (b) I **have** already* **finished** my work.	In (a): I finished my work at a specific time in the past *(two hours ago)*. In (b): I finished my work at an unspecified time in the past *(sometime before now)*.
SIMPLE PAST (c) I **was** in Europe *last year/three years ago/in 1999/in 1995 and 1999/when I was ten years old*. PRESENT PERFECT (d) I **have been** in Europe *many times/several times/a couple of times/once/(no mention of time)*.	The SIMPLE PAST expresses an activity that occurred at a specific time (or times) in the past, as in (a) and (c). The PRESENT PERFECT expresses an activity that occurred at an unspecified time (or times) in the past, as in (b) and (d).
SIMPLE PAST (e) Ann **was** in Miami *for two weeks*. PRESENT PERFECT (f) Bob **has been** in Miami *for two weeks/since May first*.	In (e): In sentences where **for** is used in a time expression, the simple past expresses an activity that began and ended in the past. In (f): In sentences with **for** or **since**, the present perfect expresses an activity that began in the past and continues to the present.

*For more information about **already**, see Chart 4-8, p. 102.

□ **EXERCISE 5. Simple past vs. present perfect. (Chart 4-4)**

Directions: Discuss the meanings of the verb tenses.

1. All of the verbs in the following talk about past time, but the verb in (a) is different from the other three verbs. What is the difference?

(a) I *have had* several bicycles in my lifetime.

(b) I *had* a red bicycle when I was in elementary school.

(c) I *had* a blue bicycle when I was a teenager.

(d) I *had* a green bicycle when I lived and worked in Hong Kong.

2. What are the differences in the ideas the verb tenses express?

    (e) I *had* a wonderful bicycle last year.

    (f) I*'ve had* many wonderful bicycles.

3. What are the differences in the ideas the verb tenses express?

    (g) Ann *had* a red bike for two years.

    (h) Sue *has had* a red bike for two years.

4. Who is still alive, and who is dead?

    (i) In his lifetime, Uncle Alex *had* several red bicycles.

    (j) In his lifetime, Grandpa *has had* several red bicycles.

☐ **EXERCISE 6. Simple past vs. present perfect. (Chart 4-4)**

    Directions: Look at the verb in *italics*. Is it simple past, or is it present perfect? Check the box that describes whether the verb expresses something that happened at a specified time in the past or at an unspecified time in the past.

SPECIFIED TIME IN THE PAST	UNSPECIFIED TIME IN THE PAST	
☐	☒	1. Ms. Parker *has been* in Tokyo many times. (→ *present perfect*)
☒	☐	2. Ms. Parker *was* in Tokyo last week. (→ *simple past*)
☐	☐	3. I*'ve met* Ann's husband. He's a nice guy.
☐	☐	4. I *met* Ann's husband at a party last week.
☐	☐	5. Mr. White *was* in Rome three times last month.
☐	☐	6. Mr. White *has been* in Rome many times.
☐	☐	7. I like to travel. I*'ve been* in more than thirty foreign countries.
☐	☐	8. I *was* in Morocco in 2001.
☐	☐	9. Mary *has never been* in Morocco.
☐	☐	10. Mary *wasn't* in Morocco when I was there in 2001.

☐ **EXERCISE 7. Simple past vs. present perfect. (Chart 4-4)**

    Directions: Complete the sentences with the words in parentheses. Use the present perfect or the simple past.

1. A: Have you ever been in Europe?

    B: Yes, I   <u> have </u> . I *(be)*   <u> have been </u>   in Europe several times.

    In fact, I *(be)*   <u> was </u>   in Europe last year.

2. A: Are you going to finish your work before you go to bed?

    B: I *(finish, already*)*   <u> have already finished </u>   it. I *(finish)*   <u> finished </u>

    my work two hours ago.

---

*In informal spoken English, the simple past is sometimes used with ***already***. Practice using the present perfect with ***already*** in this exercise.

3. A: Have you ever eaten at Al's Steak House?

   B: Yes, I _____ . I (eat) _____ there many times.
   In fact, my wife and I (eat) _____ there last night.

4. A: Do you and Erica want to go to the movie at the Palace Theater with us tonight?

   B: No thanks. We (see, already) _____ it. We
   (see) _____ it last week.

5. A: When are you going to write your report for Mr. Goldberg?

   B: I (write, already) _____ it. I (write)
   _____ it two days ago and gave it to him.

6. A: (Antonio, have, ever) _____ a job?

   B: Yes, he _____ . He (have) _____ lots of
   part-time jobs. Last summer he (have) _____ a job at his
   uncle's waterbed store.

7. A: This is a good book. Would you like to read it when I'm finished?

   B: Thanks, but I (read, already) _____ it. I (read)
   _____ it a couple of months ago.

8. A: What European countries (you, visit) _____ ?

   B: I (visit) _____ Hungary, Germany, and Switzerland. I
   (visit) _____ Hungary in 1998. I (be) _____ in
   Germany and Switzerland in 2001.

□ **EXERCISE 8. Simple past vs. present perfect. (Chart 4-4)**
   Directions: Ask and answer questions, using the present perfect and the simple past.
   Speaker A: You are the questioner. Ask a question using the present perfect, and then
   immediately follow up with a related question that prompts the use of the
   simple past. Ask two or three people the same question.

   Work as a class with the teacher as Speaker A or in groups with one person selected to be
   the leader.

   Example:
   SPEAKER A: (. . .), what countries have you been in?
   SPEAKER B: Well, I've been in Norway, and I've been in Peru.
   SPEAKER A: Oh? When were you in Norway?
   SPEAKER B: I was in Norway three years ago.
   SPEAKER A: How about you, (. . .)? What countries have you been in?
   SPEAKER C: I've never been in Norway or Peru, but I've been in . . . .
   ETC.

1. What countries have you been in?
   When were you in . . . ?

2. What cities *(in Canada, in the United States, etc.)* have you been in?
   When were you in . . . ?

3. What are some of the things you have done since you came to *(this city)*?
   When did you . . . ?

4. What are some of the things we've done in class since the beginning of the term?
   When did we . . . ?

5. What are some of the most interesting or unusual things you have done in your lifetime?
   When did you . . . ?

☐ **EXERCISE 9. Present perfect.** (Charts 4-2 → 4-4)
   Directions: Ask and answer questions using the present perfect. Work in pairs.
   Speaker A: Use *ever* in the question. *Ever* comes between the subject *(you)* and the main verb.★
   Speaker B: Give a short answer first and then a complete sentence answer.

   Use
   $\begin{cases} \textbf{\textit{many times}} \\ \textbf{\textit{lots of times}} \\ \textbf{\textit{several times}} \\ \textbf{\textit{a couple of times}} \\ \textbf{\textit{once in my lifetime}} \\ \textbf{\textit{never}} \end{cases}$
   in the complete sentence.

   Example: be in Florida★★
   SPEAKER A: Have you ever been in Florida?
   SPEAKER B: Yes, I have. I've been in Florida many times. OR
             No, I haven't. I've never been in Florida.

   Switch roles.

   1. be in Europe
   2. be in Africa
   3. be in Asia
   4. eat Chinese food
   5. eat Italian food
   6. eat *(a certain kind of)* food
   7. ride a horse
   8. ride a motorcycle
   9. ride an elephant
   10. be in *(name of a city)*
   11. be in *(name of a state/province)*
   12. be in love
   13. play soccer
   14. play chess
   15. play a video game
   16. walk to *(a place in this city)*
   17. stay up all night
   18. buy something on the Internet

   ────────────
   ★In these questions, *ever* means *in your lifetime, at any time(s) in your life before now.*
   ★★When using the present perfect, a speaker might also use the idiom *be to* *(a place): Have you ever been **to** Florida?*

☐ EXERCISE 10. Irregular verbs. (Chart 2-5)

Directions: Write the simple past and the past participles. You will use these irregular verbs in the next exercise (Exercise 11).

1. see   <u>saw</u>   <u>seen</u>

2. eat   _____   _____

3. give   _____   _____

4. fall   _____   _____

5. take   _____   _____

6. shake   _____   _____

7. drive   _____   _____

8. ride   _____   _____

9. write   _____   _____

10. bite   _____   _____

11. hide   _____   _____

☐ EXERCISE 11. Practicing irregular verbs. (Charts 2-5 and 4-2 → 4-4)

Directions: In order to practice using the past participles of irregular verbs, ask and answer questions that use the present perfect. Work in pairs, in groups, or as a class.

Speaker A: Ask a question beginning with "Have you ever . . . ?"

Speaker B: Answer the question, using the present perfect. Add another sentence about the topic if you wish.

Example: eat at the student cafeteria

SPEAKER A: Have you ever eaten at the student cafeteria?

SPEAKER B: Yes, I have. I've eaten there many times. In fact, I ate breakfast there this morning. OR No, I haven't. I usually eat all my meals at home.

1. take a course in chemistry
2. ride in a hot-air balloon
3. write a poem
4. give the teacher an apple
5. shake hands with (. . .)
6. bite into an apple that had a worm inside

(Switch roles if working in pairs.)

7. drive a semi (a very large truck)
8. eat raw fish
9. hide money under your mattress
10. fall down stairs
11. see the skeleton of a dinosaur

□ EXERCISE 12. Irregular verbs. (Chart 2-5)

Directions: Write the simple past and the past participles.

1. break _____ _____
2. speak _____ _____
3. steal _____ _____
4. get _____ _____
5. wear _____ _____
6. draw _____ _____
7. grow _____ _____

8. throw _____ _____
9. blow _____ _____
10. fly _____ _____
11. drink _____ _____
12. sing _____ _____
13. swim _____ _____
14. go _____ _____

□ EXERCISE 13. Practicing irregular verbs. (Charts 2-5 and 4-2 → 4-4)

Directions: Ask questions beginning with "Have you ever . . . ?" and give answers.

1. fly a private plane
2. break your arm
3. draw a picture of a mountain
4. swim in the ocean
5. speak to (. . .) on the phone
6. wear a costume to a party
7. go to a costume party

(Switch roles if working in pairs.)
8. get a package in the mail
9. steal anything
10. grow tomatoes
11. sing (name of a song)
12. drink carrot juice
13. throw a football
14. blow a whistle

□ EXERCISE 14. Irregular verbs. (Chart 2-5)

Directions: Write the simple past and the past participles.

1. have _____ _____
2. make _____ _____
3. build _____ _____
4. lend _____ _____
5. send _____ _____
6. spend _____ _____
7. leave _____ _____

8. lose _____ _____
9. sleep _____ _____
10. feel _____ _____
11. meet _____ _____
12. sit _____ _____
13. win _____ _____
14. hang★ _____ _____

★*Hang* is a regular verb *(hang, hanged, hanged)* when it means to kill a person by putting a rope around his/her neck.
Hang is an irregular verb when it refers to suspending a thing on a wall, in a closet, on a hook, etc.

□ **EXERCISE 15. Practicing irregular verbs. (Charts 2-5 and 4-2 → 4-5)**

Directions: Ask questions beginning with "Have you ever . . . ?" and give answers.

1. lose the key to your house
2. meet (. . .)
3. have the flu
4. feel terrible about something
5. send a telegram
6. leave your sunglasses at a restaurant
7. sit on a cactus

(Switch roles if working in pairs.)
8. spend one whole day doing nothing
9. lend (. . .) any money
10. sleep in a tent

11. make a birthday cake
12. build sand castles

13. win money at a racetrack
14. hang a picture on the wall

□ **EXERCISE 16. Irregular verbs. (Chart 2-5)**

Directions: Write the simple past and the past participles.

1. sell _____ _____
2. tell _____ _____
3. hear _____ _____
4. hold _____ _____
5. feed _____ _____
6. read _____ _____
7. find _____ _____
8. buy _____ _____

9. think _____ _____
10. teach _____ _____
11. catch _____ _____
12. cut _____ _____
13. hit _____ _____
14. quit* _____ _____
15. put _____ _____

_____

*****Quit** can be used as a regular verb in British English: *quit, quitted, quitted.*

□ EXERCISE 17. Practicing irregular verbs. (Charts 2-5 and 4-2 → 4-4)

Directions: Ask questions beginning with "Have you ever . . . ?" and give answers.

(Switch roles if working in pairs.)

1. teach a child to count to ten
2. hold a newborn baby
3. find any money on the sidewalk
4. cut your own hair
5. think about the meaning of life
6. hear strange noises at night
7. read *Tom Sawyer* by Mark Twain
8. feed pigeons in the park
9. tell a little white lie
10. quit smoking
11. buy a refrigerator
12. sell a car
13. hit another person with your fist
14. put off doing your homework
15. catch a fish

□ EXERCISE 18. Preview: SINCE vs. FOR. (Chart 4-5)

Directions: Complete the sentence "I have been here . . . ." Use **since** or **for** with the given expressions.

I have been here . . .

1. _____for_____ two months.
2. _____since_____ September.
3. _____ 1998.
4. _____ last year.
5. _____ two years.
6. _____ last Friday.
7. _____ 9:30.
8. _____ three days.
9. _____ the first of January.
10. _____ almost four months.
11. _____ the beginning of the term.
12. _____ the semester started.
13. _____ a couple of hours.
14. _____ fifteen minutes.
15. _____ yesterday.
16. _____ about five weeks.

4-5 USING *SINCE* AND *FOR*

SINCE			
	(a) I *have been* here	since eight o'clock. since Tuesday. since May. since 1999. since January 3, 2001. since yesterday. since last month.	*Since* is followed by the mention of *a specific point in time*: an hour, a day, a month, a year, etc. *Since* expresses the idea that something began at a specific time in the past and continues to the present.

	(b) CORRECT: I *have lived* here since May.★ CORRECT: I *have been* here since May. (c) INCORRECT: I am living here since May. (d) INCORRECT: I live here since May. (e) INCORRECT: I lived here since May. INCORRECT: I was here since May.	The *present perfect* is used in sentences with **since**. In (c): The present progressive is NOT used. In (d): The simple present is NOT used. In (e): The simple past is NOT used.

	MAIN CLAUSE (present perfect) SINCE-CLAUSE (simple past) (f) I *have lived* here since I *was* a child. (g) Al *has met* many people since he *came* here.	*Since* may also introduce a time clause (i.e., a subject and verb may follow *since*). Notice in the examples: The present perfect is used in the main clause; the simple past is used in the *since*-clause.

FOR			
	(h) I *have been* here	for ten minutes. for two hours. for five days. for about three weeks. for almost six months. for many years. for a long time.	*For* is followed by the mention of a *length of time*: two minutes, three hours, four days, five weeks, etc. Note: If the noun ends in *-s* (hours, days, weeks, etc.), use *for* in the time expression, not *since*.

	(i) I *have lived* here *for two years*. I moved here two years ago, and I still live here. (j) I *lived* in Athens *for two years*. I don't live in Athens now.	In (i): The use of the present perfect in a sentence with *for + a length of time* means that the action began in the past and continues to the present. In (j): The use of the simple past means that the action began and ended in the past.

★ALSO CORRECT: *I have been living* here since May. See Chart 4-7, p. 100, for a discussion of the present perfect progressive.

☐ EXERCISE 19. SINCE vs. FOR. (Chart 4-5)

Directions: Complete the sentences.

1. I've been in this building . . . .   since   nine o'clock this morning.
                                               for   27 minutes.

2. We've been in class . . . .   since _____
                                               for _____

3. I've been in this city . . . .   since _____
                                               for _____

4. I've had a driver's license . . . . {
since _____
for _____
}

5. I've had this book . . . . {
since _____
for _____
}

☐ **EXERCISE 20. SINCE vs. FOR. (Chart 4-5)**
Directions: Answer the leader's questions. Only the leader's book is open. Work as a class or in groups.
Speaker A: Use **since** in your answer.
Speaker B: Use **for**.

Example:
LEADER *(book open):*   How long have you had this book?
SPEAKER A *(book closed):*   I've had this book **since** (the beginning of the term).
LEADER TO B *(book open):*   How long has *(Speaker A)* had this book?
SPEAKER B *(book closed):*   S/He has had this book **for** (five weeks).

1. How long have you been in *(this country/city)?*
2. How long have you been at *(this school)?*
3. How long have you been up today?
4. How long have you known (. . .)?
5. Where do you live? How long have you lived there?
6. How long have you had your wristwatch?
7. Who has a car/bicycle? How long have you had it?
8. How long have you been in this room today?
9. Who is wearing new clothes? What is new? How long have you had it/them?
10. Who is married? How long have you been married?

☐ **EXERCISE 21. Sentences with SINCE-clauses. (Chart 4-5)**
Directions: Complete the sentences with the words in parentheses. Put brackets around the **since**-clauses.

1. I *(know)* __*have known*__ Mark Miller [ever since* we *(be)* ____*were*____ in college.]

2. Pedro *(change)* _____ his major three times since he *(start)* _____ school.

3. Ever since I *(be)* _____ a child, I *(be)* _____ afraid of snakes.

4. I can't wait to get home to my own bed. I *(sleep, not)* _____ well since I *(leave)* _____ home three days ago.

_____
***Ever since** has the same meaning as **since**.

5. Ever since Danny (meet) _____ Nicole, he (be, not) _____ able to think about anything or anyone else. He's in love.

6. Otto (have) _____ a lot of problems with his car ever since he (buy) _____ it. It's a lemon.

7. A: What (you, eat) _____ since you (get) _____ up this morning?

   B: I (eat) _____ a banana and some yogurt. That's all.

8. I'm eighteen. I have a job and am in school. My life is going okay now, but I (have) _____ a miserable home life when I (be) _____ a young child. Ever since I (leave) _____ home at the age of fifteen, I (take) _____ care of myself. I (have) _____ some hard times, but I (learn) _____ how to stand on my own two feet.★

□ EXERCISE 22. SINCE vs. FOR. (Chart 4-5)
   Directions: Describe yourself, orally or in writing, using ***since***, ***for***, or ***never*** with the present perfect.

   Example: have *(a particular kind of watch)*
   → *I've had my Seiko quartz watch for two years.* OR
   → *I've had my Seiko quartz watch since my eighteenth birthday.*

   Example: smoke cigars/cigarettes/a pipe
   → *I've never smoked cigarettes.* OR
   → *I've smoked cigarettes since I was seventeen.*

   1. know *(a particular person)*

   2. live in *(this city)*

   3. study English

   4. be in this class/at this school/with this company

   5. have long hair/short hair/a mustache

   6. wear glasses/contact lenses

   7. have *(a particular article of clothing)*

   8. be interested in *(a particular subject)*

   9. be married

   10. have a driver's license

───────────

★To "stand on one's own two feet" is an idiom meaning to be able to take care of oneself and be independent.

4-6 PRESENT PERFECT PROGRESSIVE

Al and Ann are in their car right now. They are driving home. It is now four o'clock. (a) They **have been driving** since two o'clock. (b) They **have been driving** for two hours. They will be home soon.	The PRESENT PERFECT PROGRESSIVE talks about *how long* an activity has been in progress before now. Note: Time expressions with **since**, as in (a), and **for**, as in (b), are frequently used with this tense. STATEMENT: **have/has + been + -ing**
(c) How long **have** they **been driving**?	QUESTION FORM: **have/has** + *subject* + **been + -ing**

COMPARE the present progressive and the present perfect progressive.

PRESENT PROGRESSIVE 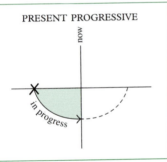	(d) Po **is sitting** in class right now.	The PRESENT PROGRESSIVE describes an activity that is in progress right now, as in (d). It does not discuss duration (length of time). *INCORRECT: Po has been sitting in class right now.*
PRESENT PERFECT PROGRESSIVE 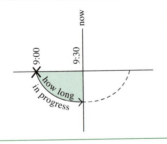	Po is sitting at his desk in class. He sat down at nine o'clock. It is now nine-thirty. (e) Po **has been sitting** in class **since** nine o'clock. (f) Po **has been sitting** in class **for** thirty minutes.	The PRESENT PERFECT PROGRESSIVE expresses the **duration** (length of time) of an activity that began in the past and is in progress right now. *INCORRECT: Po is sitting in class since nine o'clock.*

(g) CORRECT: I **know** Yoko. (h) *INCORRECT: I am knowing Yoko.* (i) CORRECT: I **have known** Yoko **for** two years. (j) *INCORRECT: I have been knowing Yoko for two years.*	Reminder: Non-action verbs (e.g., *know, like, own, belong*) are not used in any progressive tenses.* In (i): With non-action verbs, the present perfect is used with **since** or **for** to express the duration of a situation that began in the past and continues to the present.

*See Chart 1-6 (Non-Action Verbs), p. 17.

□ EXERCISE 23. Present progressive vs. present perfect progressive. (Chart 4-6)
Directions: Complete the sentences. Use the present progressive or the present perfect progressive.

1. I *(sit)* __am sitting__ in class right now. I *(sit)* __have been sitting__ here since one o'clock.

2. Kate is standing at the corner. She *(wait)* _____ for the bus.
   She *(wait)* _____ for the bus for twenty minutes.

3. Scott and Rebecca *(talk)* _____ on the phone right now.
   They *(talk)* _____ on the phone for over an hour.

4. Right now we're in class. We *(do)* _____ an exercise. We
   (do) _____ this exercise for a couple of minutes.

5. A: You look busy right now. What *(you, do)* _____ ?
   B: I *(work)* _____ on my physics experiment. It's a long
      and difficult experiment.
   A: How long *(you, work)* _____ on it?
   B: I started planning it last January. I *(work)* _____
      on it since then.

□ EXERCISE 24. Present perfect progressive. (Chart 4-6)
Directions: Answer the questions. Only the teacher's book is open.

Example:
TEACHER: Where are you living?
RESPONSE: I'm living in an apartment on Fourth Avenue.
TEACHER: How long have you been living there?
RESPONSE: I've been living there since last September.

1. Right now you are sitting in class. How long have you been sitting here?

2. When did you first begin to study English? How long have you been studying English?

3. I began to teach English in *(year)*. How long have I been teaching English?

4. I began to work at this school in *(month or year)*. How long have I been working here?

5. What are we doing right now? How long have we been doing it?

6. (. . .), I see that you wear glasses. How long have you been wearing glasses?

7. Who drives? When did you first drive a car? How long have you been driving?

8. Who drinks coffee? How old were you when you started to drink coffee? How long have you been drinking coffee?

PRESENT PERFECT PROGRESSIVE vs. PRESENT PERFECT

PRESENT PERFECT PROGRESSIVE (a) Rita and Josh are talking on the phone. They *have been talking* on the phone for twenty minutes.	The PRESENT PERFECT PROGRESSIVE expresses the **duration of present *activities*** that are in progress, using action verbs, as in (a).
PRESENT PERFECT (b) Rita *has talked* to Josh on the phone many times (before now). (c) *INCORRECT: Rita has been talking to Josh on the phone many times.* (d) Rita *has known* Josh for two years. (e) *INCORRECT: Rita has been knowing Josh for two years.*	The PRESENT PERFECT expresses (1) repeated activities that occur at **unspecified times in the past**, as in (b), or (2) the **duration of present *situations***, as in (d), using non-action verbs.
(f) I *have been living* here for six months. OR (g) I *have lived* here for six months. (h) Al *has been wearing* glasses since he was ten. OR Al *has worn* glasses since he was ten. (i) I*'ve been going* to school ever since I was five years old. OR I*'ve gone* to school ever since I was five years old.	For some (not all) verbs, duration can be expressed by either the present perfect or the present perfect progressive. (f) and (g) have essentially the same meaning, and both are correct. Often either tense can be used with verbs that express the **duration of usual or habitual activities/situations** (things that happen daily or regularly), e.g., *live, work, teach, smoke, wear glasses, play chess, go to school, read the same newspaper every morning, etc.*

☐ **EXERCISE 25. Present perfect vs. the present perfect progressive. (Chart 4-7)**

Directions: Complete the sentences. Use the present perfect or the present perfect progressive. In some sentences, either form is possible.

1. A: I'm tired. We *(walk)* ___have been walking___ for more than an hour.
   Let's stop and rest for a while.

   B: Okay.

2. A: Is the post office far from here?

   B: Not at all. I *(walk)* ___have walked___ there many times.

3. A: Do you like it here?

   B: I *(live)* __have been living/have lived__ here for only a short while. I don't know yet.

4. A: I *(read)* _____ this chapter in my chemistry text three times, and I still don't understand it!

   B: Maybe I can help.

5. A: My eyes are getting tired. I *(read)* _____ for two hours. I think I'll take a break.

   B: Why don't we go for a walk?

6. A: Do you like the Edgewater Inn?

   B: Very much. I *(stay)* _____ there at least a dozen times. It's my favorite hotel.

7. A: The baby's crying. Shouldn't we do something?
   B: He's all right.

   A: Are you sure? He *(cry)* _____ for almost ten minutes.

   B: Okay. I'll go into his room and see if anything's wrong.

8. A: Who's your daughter's new teacher?
   B: Mrs. Jackson.

   A: She's one of the best teachers at the elementary school. She *(teach)* _____ _____ kindergarten for twenty years.

9. A: Ed *(play)* _____ tennis for ten years, but he still doesn't have a good backhand.

   B: Neither do I, and I *(play)* _____ tennis for twenty years.

10. A: Where does Mr. Alvarez work?

    B: At the power company. He *(work)* _____ there for fifteen years. He likes his job.
    A: What about his neighbor, Mr. Perez?
    B: He's currently unemployed, but he'll find a new job soon.
    A: What kind of job experience does he have?

    B: He *(work)* _____ for a small manufacturing firm, for the telephone company, and at two of the world's leading software companies. With all that work experience, he won't have any trouble finding another job.

4-8 USING *ALREADY, YET, STILL,* AND *ANYMORE*

ALREADY	(a) The mail came an hour ago. **The mail is *already* here.**	Idea of *already:* Something happened before now, before this time. *Position: midsentence.**
YET	(b) I expected the mail an hour ago, but **it hasn't come *yet*.**	Idea of *yet:* Something did not happen before now (up to this time), but it may happen in the future. *Position: end of sentence.*
STILL	(c) It was cold yesterday. **It is *still* cold** today. **We *still* need to wear coats.** (d) I could play the piano when I was a child. **I can *still* play the piano.** (e) The mail didn't come an hour ago. **The mail *still* hasn't come.**	Idea of *still:* A situation continues to exist from past to present without change. *Position: midsentence.**
ANYMORE	(f) I lived in Chicago two years ago, but then I moved to another city. **I don't live in Chicago *anymore*.**	Idea of *anymore:* A past situation does not continue to exist at present; a past situation has changed. *Anymore* has the same meaning as *any longer*. *Position: end of sentence.*

Note:	*Already* is used in *affirmative* sentences.
	Yet and *anymore* are used in *negative* sentences.
	Still is used in either *affirmative* or *negative* sentences.

*See Chart 1-3, p. 9. A midsentence adverb
    (1) precedes a simple present verb: *We **still need** to wear coats.*
    (2) follows *am, is, are, was, were: It is **still** cold.*
    (3) comes between a helping verb and a main verb: *Bob **has already arrived**.*
    (4) precedes a negative helping verb: *Ann **still hasn't** come.*
    (5) follows the subject in a question: *Have **you already** seen that movie?*

☐ **EXERCISE 26. ALREADY, YET, STILL, ANYMORE. (Chart 4-8)**
    Directions: Complete the sentences with *already, yet, still,* or *anymore.*

    1. It's 1:00 P.M. I'm hungry. I haven't eaten lunch _____**yet**_____.

    2. It's 1:00 P.M. I'm not hungry. I've _____ eaten lunch.

    3. Eric was hungry, so he ate a candy bar a few minutes ago. But he's

        _____ hungry, so he's going to have another candy bar.

    4. I used to eat lunch at the cafeteria every day, but now I bring my lunch to school in a

        paper bag instead. I don't eat at the cafeteria _____.

    5. I don't have to study tonight. I've _____ finished all my

        homework.

    6. I started a letter to my parents yesterday, but I haven't finished it _____.

        I'll finish it later today and put it in the mail.

7. I started a letter to my parents yesterday. I thought about finishing it last night before I went to bed, but I didn't. I _____ haven't finished it.*

8. A: Is Mary home _____ ?

   B: No, but I'm expecting her soon.

9. A: Is Mary _____ in class?

   B: Yes, she is. Her class doesn't end until 11:30.

10. A: Has Rob found a new job _____ ?

    B: No. He _____ works at the bookstore.

11. A: When is your sister going to come to visit you?

    B: She's _____ here. She got here yesterday.

12. A: Do you _____ live on Pine Avenue?

    B: No, I don't live there _____ . I moved to another apartment closer to school.

☐ **EXERCISE 27. ALREADY, YET, STILL, ANYMORE. (Chart 4-8)**
Directions: Complete the sentences with your own words.

Example: I . . . not . . . because I've already . . . .
   → **I'm not** hungry **because I've already** eaten.   OR
   → **I'm not** going to go to the movie **because I've already** seen it.   OR
   → **I don't** have to take the English test **because I've already** taken it.

1. I used to . . . , but . . . anymore.
2. I can't . . . because I haven't . . . yet.
3. Are . . . still . . . ?
4. . . . because I've already . . . .
5. I don't . . . anymore, but . . . still . . . .

☐ **EXERCISE 28. Verb tense review. (Chapters 1, 2, and 4)**
Directions: Compare the different meanings of the verb tenses. Identify which sentences express duration.

1. a. Rachel *is taking* English classes.
   b. Nadia *has been taking* English classes for two months.
2. a. Ann *has been* in Jerusalem for two years. She likes it there.
   b. Sue *has been* in Jerusalem. She's also been in Paris. She's been in New York and Tokyo. She's been in lots of cities. She travels a lot.

---

*In negative sentences, **still** and **yet** express similar meanings. The meanings of *I haven't finished it yet* and *I still haven't finished it* are similar.

3. a. Jack **has visited** his aunt and uncle many times.
   b. Matt **has been visiting** his aunt and uncle for the last three days.

4. a. Jack **is talking** on the phone.
   b. Jack **talks** on the phone a lot.
   c. Jack **has been talking** to his boss on the phone for half an hour.
   d. Jack **has talked** to his boss on the phone lots of times.

5. a. Mr. Woods **walks** his dog in Forest Park every day.
   b. Mr. Woods **has walked** his dog in Forest Park many times.
   c. Mr. Woods **walked** his dog in Forest Park five times last week.
   d. Mr. Woods **is walking** his dog in Forest Park right now.
   e. Mr. Woods **has been walking** his dog in Forest Park since two o'clock.

☐ **EXERCISE 29. Verb tenses. (Charts 4-2 → 4-8)**

Directions: Make sentences about your life using the given time expressions. Use the simple past, present perfect, or present perfect progressive.

Example: for the last two weeks
→ *I've had a cold for the last two weeks.*

1. since I was a child
2. for a long time
3. two years ago
4. so far today
5. many times in my lifetime
6. never

7. since last Tuesday
8. for a number of years*
9. a week ago today
10. for the last ten minutes
11. already . . . , but . . . yet
12. still . . . , but . . . anymore

———————

*a number of years = many years.

Directions: Complete the sentences with the words in parentheses.

1. A: *(you, have)* _____Do you have_____ any plans for vacation?

   B: Yes, I do. I *(plan)* _____am planning_____ to go to Toronto.

   A: *(you, be, ever)* _____ there before?

   B: Yes, I have. I *(be)* _____ in Toronto two months ago. My brother

      (live) _____ there, so I *(go)* _____ there often.

2. A: Where's Jessica?

   B: She *(study)* _____ at the library.

   A: When *(she, get)* _____ back home?

   B: In an hour or so. Probably around five o'clock.

   A: How long *(she, study)* _____ at the
      library?

   B: Since two o'clock this afternoon.

   A: *(she, study)* _____ at the library every day?

   B: Not every day, but often.

3. A: Shhh. Irene *(talk)* _____ on the phone long-distance.

   B: Who *(she, talk)* _____ to?

   A: Her brother. They *(talk)* _____ for almost an hour.
      I think her brother is in some kind of trouble.

   B: That's too bad. I hope it's nothing serious.

4. A: *(you, know)* _____ Abdullah's new address?

   B: Not off the top of my head. But I *(have)* _____ it at home in my

      computer. When I *(get)* _____ home this evening, I *(call)*

      _____ and *(give)* _____ you his address.

   A: Thanks. Or you could e-mail it to me.

   B: Okay. I *(do)* _____ that.

5. A: Where's Juan? He *(be)* _____ absent from class for the last three

      days. *(anyone, see)* _____ him lately?

   B: I have. I *(see)* _____ him yesterday. He has a bad cold, so he *(be)*

      _____ home in bed since the weekend. He *(be, probably)*

      _____ back in class tomorrow.

6. A: How long *(you, wear)* _____ glasses?

   B: Since I *(be)* _____ ten years old.

   A: *(you, be)* _____ nearsighted or farsighted?

   B: Nearsighted.

7. A: Let's go to a restaurant tonight.

   B: Okay. Where should we go?

   A: *(you, like)* _____ Thai food?

   B: I don't know. I *(eat, never)* _____ any. What's it like?

   A: It's delicious, but it can be pretty hot!

   B: That's okay. I *(love)* _____ really hot food.

   A: There *(be)* _____ a Thai restaurant downtown. I *(go)* _____
      _____ there a couple of times. The food is excellent.

   B: Sounds good. I *(be, never)* _____ to a Thai
      restaurant, so it *(be)* _____ a new experience for me. After we
      (get) _____ there, can you explain the menu to me?

   A: Sure. And if I can't, our waiter or waitress can.

8. A: *(you, smoke)* _____ ?

   B: Yes, I do.

   A: How long *(you, smoke)* _____ ?

   B: Well, let me see. I *(smoke)* _____ since I *(be)*
      _____ seventeen. So I *(smoke)* _____
      for almost four years.

   A: Why *(you, start)* _____ ?

   B: Because I *(be)* _____ a dumb, stupid kid.

   A: *(you, want)* _____ to quit?

   B: Yes. I *(plan)* _____ to quit very soon. In fact, I *(decide)*
      _____ to quit on my next birthday. My twenty-first
      birthday is two weeks from now. On that day, I *(intend)* _____ to
      smoke my last cigarette.

   A: That's terrific! You *(feel)* _____ much better after you *(stop)*
      _____ smoking.

   B: *(you, smoke, ever)* _____ ?

   A: No, I haven't. I *(smoke, never)* _____ a
      cigarette in my life. When I *(be)* _____ ten years old, I *(smoke)*
      _____ one of my uncle's cigars. My sister and I *(steal)*
      _____ a couple of his cigars and *(go)* _____ behind
      the garage to smoke them. Both of us *(get)* _____ sick. I
      (have, not) _____ anything to smoke since then.

   B: That's smart.

Directions: Correct the errors. Most of the errors are in verb usage, but some are miscellaneous (e.g., capitalization, word order, spelling, agreement, etc.).

1. I have been ~~studied~~ studying ⱻnglish E for eight year^s , but I still have a lot to learn.

2. I want to learn English since I am a child.

3. Our class has have three tests since the beggining of the term.

4. I have started the English classes since three weeks ago and I am learning some English since that time.

5. I have been thinking about how to improve my English ability since I came here, but I still don't find a good way.

6. All of us has learn many thing since we were children.

7. When I was at my sister's house, we had an argument. Since then I didn't talk to her for three days.

8. Since I was very young, I like animals.

9. I have been study english since three and a half month.

10. I like very much the English. Since I was young my father found an American girl to teach my brothers and me English, but when I move to another city my father hasn't find one for five years. Now I'm living here and studying in this English program.

11. I almost die in an automobile accident five year ago. Since that day my life changed completely.

12. In my country, women are soldiers in the army since the 1970s.

13. I meet Abdul in my first English class last June. He was friendly and kind. We are

     friends since that day.

14. My favorite place in the world is my hometown. I live there for twenty years.

15. My wife and I have been in Italy two weeks ago. We went there to ski.

16. My wife broke her leg while she was skiing in Italy. Now she's home, but she can't

     walk without help. A lot of our friends are visiting her since she has broken her leg.

17. I was busy every day since I arrived at this city.

18. I haven't to eaten any kind of chinese food for a week. I miss it a lot!

☐ **EXERCISE 32. Verb tense review. (Chapters 1 → 4)**
   Directions: Complete the sentences with the words in parentheses.

Dear Adam,

     Hi! Remember me? (Just a joke!) I *(write, not)* _____*haven't written*_____
                                                                    1

to you for at least six months, but that's not long enough for you to forget me! I think

about writing to you often, but I *(be, not)* _____ a good correspondent
                                                           2

for the last few months. You *(hear, not)* _____ from me for such a
                                                        3

long time because I *(be)* _____ really busy. For the last few months, I
                                       4

(work) _____ full-time at a shoe store and *(go)* _____
                    5   6

to school at the local community college to study business and computers. When I *(write)*

_____ to you six months ago—last April, I think—I *(go)* _____
            7   8

to the university full-time and *(study)* _____ anthropology. A lot
                                                       9

of things *(happen)* _____ since then.
                                  10

At the end of the spring semester last June, my grades *(be)* _____

11

terrible. As a result, I *(lose)* _____ my scholarship and my parents'

12

support. I really *(mess)* _____ up when I *(get)* _____ those

13   14

bad grades. When I *(show)* _____ my grade report to my parents, they

15

(refuse) _____ to help me with my living expenses at school anymore.

16

They *(feel)* _____ that I was wasting my time and their money, so they *(tell)*

17

_____ me to get a job. So last June I *(start)* _____ working

18   19

at a shoe store: Imperial Shoes at Southcenter Mall. I *(work)* _____

20

there ever since.

It *(be, not)* _____ a bad job, but it *(be, not)* _____

21   22

wonderful either. Every day, I *(fetch)* _____ shoes from the back room for

23

people to try on, boxes and boxes of shoes, all day long. I *(meet)* _____

24

some pretty weird people since I *(start)* _____ this job. A couple of

25

weeks ago, a middle-aged man *(come)* _____ into the store. He

26

(want) _____ to try on some black leather loafers. I *(bring)*

27

_____ the loafers, and he *(put)* _____ them on. While

28   29

he *(walk)* _____ around to see if they fit okay, he *(pull)*

30

_____ from his pocket a little white mouse with pink eyes and

31

(start) _____ talking to it. He *(look)* _____ right at the

32   33

mouse and *(say)* _____ , "George, *(you, like)* _____

34   35

this pair of shoes?" When the mouse *(twitch)* _____ its nose, the man

36

(say) _____ , "Yes, so do I." Then he *(turn)* _____ to me

37   38

and *(say)* _____ , "We'll take them." Can you believe that!?

39

Most of the people I meet are nice—and normal. My favorite customers *(be)*

_____ people who *(know)* _____ what they want when they
40   41

(enter) _____ the store. They *(come)* _____ in, *(point)*
42   43

_____ at one pair of shoes, politely *(tell)* _____ me their
44   45

size, *(try)* _____ the shoes on, and then *(buy)* _____ them,
46   47

just like that. They *(agonize, not)* _____ for a long time over
48

which pair to buy.

I *(learn)* _____ one important thing from working at the
49

shoe store: I *(want, not)* _____ to sell shoes as a career. I *(need)*
50

_____ a good education that *(prepare)* _____ me for a
51   52

job that I can enjoy for the rest of my life. And even though I love studying anthropology,

I *(decide)* _____ that a degree in business and computers will
53

provide the best career opportunities.

Now I (work) _____ part-time at the shoe store and (go)
54
_____ to school at the same time. I (want, always) _____
55   56
to be completely independent and self-reliant, and now I (be) _____ .
57
I (have) _____ to pay every penny of my tuition and living expenses now.
58
Ever since I (lose) _____ my scholarship and (make) _____
59   60
my parents mad, I (be) _____ completely on my own. I'm glad to
61
report that my grades at present (be) _____ excellent, and right now I
62
(enjoy, really) _____ my work with computers. In the
63
future, I (continue) _____ to take courses in anthropology
64
whenever I can fit them into my schedule, and I (study) _____
65
anthropology on my own for the rest of my life, but I (pursue) _____
66
a career in business. Maybe there is some way I can combine anthropology, business, and

computers. Who knows?

There. I (tell) _____ you everything I can think of that is at all
67
important in my life at the moment. I think I (grow) _____ up a
68
lot during the last six months. I (understand) _____ that my education
69
is important. Losing my scholarship (make) _____ my life more difficult,
70
but I (believe) _____ that I (take, finally) _____
71   72
charge of my life. It's a good feeling.

Please write. I'd love to hear from you.

Jessica

☐ **EXERCISE 33. Writing: verb tense review. (Chapters 1 → 4)**
Directions: Think of a friend you haven't spoken or written to since the beginning of this term. Write this friend a letter about your activities from the start of this school term to the present time. Begin your letter as follows:

Dear (. . .),
    I'm sorry I haven't written for such a long time. Lots of things have happened since I last wrote to you.

☐ **EXERCISE 34. Writing: verb tense review. (Chapters 1 → 4)**
Directions: Write about one (or both) of the following topics.

1. Think of two or three important events that have occurred in your life in the past year or two. In a paragraph for each, briefly tell your reader about these events and give your opinions and/or predictions.

2. Think of two or three important events that have occurred in the world in the past year or two. In a paragraph for each, briefly tell your reader about these events and give your opinions and/or predictions.

4-9 PAST PERFECT

Situation: Jack left his apartment at 2:00. Ann arrived at his apartment at 2:15 and knocked on the door. (a) When Ann arrived, Jack wasn't there. He **had left**.	The PAST PERFECT is used when the speaker is talking about two different events at two different times in the past; one event ends before the second event happens. In (a): There are two events, and both happened in the past: *Jack left his apartment. Ann arrived at his apartment.* To show the time relationship between the two events, we use the past perfect *(had left)* to say that the first event (Jack leaving his apartment) was completed before the second event (Ann arriving at his apartment) occurred.

4-9 PAST PERFECT—(continued)

(b) Jack **had left** his apartment when Ann arrived.	FORM: **had** + *past participle*
(c) *He'd* left. *I'd* left. *They'd* left. Etc.	CONTRACTION: *I/you/she/he/it/we/they* + **'d**

COMPARE THE PRESENT PERFECT AND THE PAST PERFECT.

PRESENT PERFECT	(d) I am not hungry now. I **have** already **eaten**.	The PRESENT PERFECT expresses an activity that *occurred before now, at an unspecified time in the past*, as in (d).
PAST PERFECT	(e) I was not hungry at 1:00 P.M. I **had** already **eaten**.	The PAST PERFECT expresses an activity that *occurred before another time in the past*. In (e): I ate at noon. I was not hungry at 1:00 P.M. because I had already eaten before 1:00 P.M.

COMPARE THE PAST PROGRESSIVE AND THE PAST PERFECT.

PAST PROGRESSIVE	(f) I **was eating** when Bob came.	The PAST PROGRESSIVE expresses an activity that was *in progress at a particular time in the past*. In (f): I began to eat at noon. Bob came at 12:10. My meal was in progress when Bob came.
PAST PERFECT	(g) I **had eaten** when Bob came.	The PAST PERFECT expresses an activity that was *completed before a particular time in the past*. In (g): I finished eating at noon. Bob came at 1:00 P.M. My meal was completed before Bob came.

□ EXERCISE 35. Past perfect. (Chart 4-9)

Directions: Identify which action took place first (1st) in the past and which action took place second (2nd).

1. The tennis player **jumped** in the air for joy. She **had won** the match.

   a. _____1st_____ The tennis player won the match.

   b. _____2nd_____ The tennis player jumped in the air.

2. Before I went to bed, I **checked** the front door. My roommate **had** already **locked** it.

   a. _____2nd_____ I checked the door.

   b. _____1st_____ My roommate locked the door.

3. I **looked** for Bob, but he **had left** the building.

   a. _____ Bob left the building.

   b. _____ I looked for Bob.

4. I **laughed** when I saw my son. He **had poured** a bowl of noodles on top of his head.

   a. _____ I laughed.

   b. _____ My son poured a bowl of noodles on his head.

5. Oliver **arrived** at the theater on time, but he couldn't get in. He **had left** his ticket at home.

   a. _____ Oliver left his ticket at home.

   b. _____ Oliver arrived at the theater.

6. I **handed** Betsy the newspaper, but she didn't want it. She **had read** it during her lunch hour.

   a. _____ I handed Betsy the newspaper.

   b. _____ Betsy read the newspaper.

7. After Carl arrived in New York, he **called** his mother. He **had promised** to call her as soon as he got in.

    a. _____ Carl made a promise to his mother.

    b. _____ Carl called his mother.

8. Stella was alone in a strange city. She walked down the avenue slowly, looking in shop windows. Suddenly, she **turned** her head and **looked** behind her. Someone **had called** her name.

    a. _____ Stella turned her head and looked behind her.

    b. _____ Someone called her name.

□ **EXERCISE 36. Present perfect vs. past perfect. (Chart 4-9)**

Directions: Complete the sentences with the present perfect or the past perfect form of the verb in parentheses.

1. A: Oh no! We're too late. The train *(leave, already)* ____**has already left**____ .
   B: That's okay. We'll catch the next train to Athens.

2. Last Thursday, we went to the station to catch a train to Athens, but we were too late. The train *(leave, already)* ____**had already left**____ .

3. A: Go back to sleep. It's only six o'clock in the morning.
   B: I'm not sleepy. I *(sleep, already)* _____ for eight hours. I'm going to get up.

4. I woke up at six this morning, but I couldn't get back to sleep. I wasn't sleepy. I *(sleep, already)* _____ for eight hours.

5. A: I'll introduce you to Professor Newton at the meeting tonight.
   B: You don't need to. I *(meet, already)* _____ him.

6. Jack offered to introduce me to Professor Newton, but it wasn't necessary. I *(meet, already)* _____ him.

7. A: Do you want to go to the movie tonight?
   B: What are you going to see?
   A: *Distant Drums.*
   B: I *(see, already)* _____ it. Thanks anyway.

8. I didn't go to the movie with Francisco last Tuesday night. I *(see, already)* _____ it.

9. A: Jane? Jane! Is that you? How are you? I haven't seen you for ages!

    B: Excuse me? Are you talking to me?

    A: Oh. You're not Jane. I'm sorry. It is clear that I *(make)* _____
    a mistake. Please excuse me.

10. Yesterday I approached a stranger who looked like Jane Moore and started talking to

    her. But she wasn't Jane. It was clear that I *(make)* _____ a
    mistake. I was really embarrassed.

☐ EXERCISE 37. Past progressive vs. past perfect. (Chart 4-9)
Directions: Circle the correct completion.

1. Amanda didn't need to study the multiplication tables in fifth grade. She _____
    them.
    A. was learning   B. had already learned

2. I enjoyed visiting Tommy's class. It was an arithmetic class. The students _____
    their multiplication tables.
    A. were learning   B. had already learned

3. While I _____ up the mountain, I got tired. But I didn't stop until I reached the
    top.
    A. was walking   B. had walked

4. I was very tired when I got to the top of the mountain. I _____ a long distance.
    A. was walking   B. had walked

5. I knocked. No one answered. I turned the handle and pulled sharply on the door, but
    it did not open. Someone _____ it.
    A. was locking   B. had locked

6. "Where were you when the earthquake occurred?"
    "In my office. I _____ to my assistant. We were working on a report."
    A. was talking   B. had already talked

7. "Ahmed's house was destroyed in the earthquake."
    "I know! It's lucky that he and his family _____ for his parents' home before the
    earthquake struck."
    A. were leaving   B. had already left

8. We drove two hundred miles to see the circus in Kansas City. When we got there, we
    couldn't find the circus. It _____ town. We _____ all the way to Kansas City for
    nothing.
    A. was leaving . . . were driving   C. was leaving . . . had driven
    B. had left . . . had driven   D. had left . . . were driving

☐ **EXERCISE 38. Present perfect, past progressive, and past perfect. (Chart 4-9)**
Directions: Complete the sentences with the correct forms of the words in parentheses.
Use the present perfect, past progressive, or past perfect.

1. When I went to bed, I turned on the radio. While I *(sleep)* _____**was sleeping**_____ ,
   somebody turned it off.

2. You're from Jakarta? I *(be, never)* _____ there. I'd like to go
   there someday.

3. I started to tell Rodney the news, but he stopped me. He *(hear, already)* _____
   _____ it.

4. When Gina went to bed, it was snowing. It *(snow, still)* _____
   _____ when she woke up in the morning.

5. Rita called me on the phone to tell me the good news. She *(pass)* _____
   her final exam in English.

6. I couldn't think. The people around me *(make)* _____ too
   much noise. Finally, I gave up and left to try to find a quiet place to work.

7. Are you still waiting for David? *(he, come, not)* _____
   yet? He's really late, isn't he?

8. Otto's back to work today, but was in the hospital last week. He *(be, never)*
   _____ a patient in a hospital before. It was a new
   experience for him.

9. A couple of weeks ago Mr. Fox, our office manager, surprised all of us. When he
   walked into the office, he *(wear)* _____ a T-shirt and jeans.
   Everyone stopped and stared. Mr. Fox is a conservative dresser. Before that time, he
   (wear, never) _____ anything but a blue or gray suit.
   And he *(wear, not)* _____ his jeans to the office since
   that time. He wore them only that one time.

☐ **EXERCISE 39. Verb tense review. (Chapters 1 → 4)**
Directions: Circle the correct completion.

Example:
   I can't come with you. I need to stay here. I _____ for a phone call.
   A. wait   B. will wait   C. am waiting   D. have waited

1. I _____ my glasses three times so far this year. One time I dropped them on a
   cement floor. Another time I sat on them. And this time I stepped on them.
   A. broke   B. was breaking   C. have broken   D. have been breaking

2. Kate reached to the floor and picked up her glasses. They were broken. She _____ on them.
    A. stepped   B. had stepped   C. was stepping   D. has stepped

3. Sarah gets angry easily. She _____ a bad temper ever since she was a child.
    A. has   B. will have   C. had   D. has had

4. Now, whenever Sarah starts to lose her temper, she _____ a deep breath and _____ to ten.
    A. takes . . . counts   C. took . . . counted
    B. has taken . . . counted   D. is taking . . . counting

5. Nicky, please don't interrupt me. I _____ to Grandma on the phone. Go play with your trucks so we can finish our conversation.
    A. talk   B. have talked   C. am talking   D. have been talking

6. We _____ at a hotel in Miami when the hurricane hit southern Florida last month. As soon as the hurricane moved out of the area, we left and went back home.
    A. had stayed   B. stay   C. were staying   D. stayed

7. Now listen carefully. When Aunt Martha _____ tomorrow, give her a big hug.
    A. arrives   B. will arrive   C. arrived   D. is going to arrive

8. My cousin _____ with me in my apartment for the last two weeks. I'm ready for him to leave, but he seems to want to stay forever. Maybe I should ask him to leave.
    A. is staying   B. stayed   C. was staying   D. has been staying

9. Mrs. Larsen discovered a bird in her apartment. It was in her living room. It _____ into her apartment through an open window.
    A. was flying   B. had flown   C. has flown   D. was flown

10. The phone rang, so I _____ it up and _____ hello.
    A. picked . . . had said   C. was picking . . . said
    B. picked . . . said   D. was picking . . . had said

☐ EXERCISE 40. Verb tense review. (Chapters 1 → 4)
Directions: Circle the correct completion.

Example:
I can't come with you. I need to stay here. I _____ for a phone call.
    A. wait   B. will wait   C. am waiting   D. have waited

1. My mother began to drive cars when she was fourteen. Now she is eighty-nine, and she still drives. She _____ cars for seventy-five years.
    A. was driving   B. drives   C. drove   D. has been driving

2. In every culture, people _____ jewelry since prehistoric times.
    A. wear   B. wore   C. have worn   D. had worn

3. It _____ when I left the house this morning, so I opened my umbrella.
   A. rained   B. had rained   C. is raining   D. was raining

4. Australian koala bears are interesting animals. They _____ practically their entire lives in trees without ever coming down to the ground.
   A. are spending   C. have spent
   B. have been spending   D. spend

5. The teacher is late today, so class hasn't begun yet. After she _____ here, class will begin.
   A. will get   B. is going to get   C. gets   D. is getting

6. It's raining hard. It _____ an hour ago and _____ yet.
   A. had started . . . doesn't stop   C. started . . . hasn't stopped
   B. has started . . . didn't stop   D. was starting . . . isn't stopping

7. Alex's bags are almost ready for his trip. He _____ for Syria later this afternoon. We'll say good-bye to him before he _____.
   A. left . . . went   C. is leaving . . . goes
   B. leaves . . . will go   D. has left . . . will go

8. I heard a slight noise, so I walked to the front door to investigate. I looked down at the floor and saw a piece of paper. Someone _____ a note under the door to my apartment.
   A. had pushed   B. is pushing   C. has pushed   D. pushed

9. I walked slowly through the market. People _____ all kinds of fruits and vegetables. I studied the prices carefully before I decided what to buy.
   A. have sold   B. sell   C. had sold   D. were selling

10. I really like my car. I _____ it for six years. It runs beautifully.
   A. have   B. have had   C. had   D. have been having

CHAPTER 5
Asking Questions

CONTENTS

☐ **EXERCISE 1. Preview: asking questions. (Chapter 5)**

Directions: This exercise previews some of the grammar in this chapter. Create questions that fit the given answers. Discuss question forms.

Example: No, I _____ . I'm allergic to them.

→   QUESTION: *Do you like cats?*
    ANSWER: *No, I don't. I'm allergic to them.*

1. Downtown.

2. No, I _____ .

3. Seven-thirty.

4. Two hours.

5. Because I overslept.

6. This one, not that one.

7. Yes, she _____ .

8. Mine.

9. My cousin.

10. Five blocks.

11. Once a week.

12. Answering your question.

5-1 YES/NO QUESTIONS AND SHORT ANSWERS

YES/NO QUESTION	SHORT ANSWER (+ LONG ANSWER)
(a) *Do you like* tea?	*Yes, I do.* (I like tea.) *No, I don't.* (I don't like tea.)
(b) *Did Sue call?*	*Yes, she did.* (Sue called.) *No, she didn't.* (Sue didn't call.)
(c) *Have you met* Al?	*Yes, I have.* (I have met Al.) *No, I haven't.* (I haven't met Al.)
(d) *Is it raining?*	*Yes, it is.* (It's raining.) *No, it isn't.* (It isn't raining.)
(e) *Will Rob be* here?	*Yes, he will.* (Rob will be here.) *No, he won't.* (Rob won't be here.)

A **yes/no question** is a question that can be answered by *yes* or *no*.

In an affirmative short answer (yes), a helping verb is NOT contracted with the subject.

In (c): *INCORRECT: Yes, I've.*
In (d): *INCORRECT: Yes, it's.*
In (e): *INCORRECT: Yes, he'll.*

The spoken emphasis in a short answer is on the verb.

☐ **EXERCISE 2. Short answers to yes/no questions. (Chart 5-1)**

Directions: In these dialogues, the long answer is given in parentheses. Look at the long answer, and then write the appropriate yes/no question and short answer to complete each dialogue. Do not use a negative verb in the question.

1. A: ___Do you know my brother?___

   B: No, ___I don't.___ (I don't know your brother.)

2. A: _____

   B: Yes, _____ (Aspirin relieves pain.)

3. A: _____

   B: No, _____ (Snakes don't have legs.)

4. A: _____

   B: No, _____ (Snakes can't move backward.)

5. A: _____

   B: Yes, _____ (The United States is in North America.)

6. A: _____

   B: Uh-huh, _____ (I enjoyed the movie.)

7. A: _____

   B: Huh-uh, _____ (I won't be at home tonight.)

8. A: _____

    B: Yes, _____ (I have a bicycle.)*

9. A: _____

    B: Yes, _____ (Paul has left.)

10. A: _____

    B: Yes, _____ (He left with Kate.)

☐ **EXERCISE 3. Short answers to yes/no questions. (Chart 5-1)**

Directions: Work in groups of three.
Speaker A: Whisper the cue to Speaker B. Your book is open.
Speaker B: Ask a yes/no question using the information Speaker A gave you. Your book is closed.
Speaker C: Give a short answer to the question. Your book is closed.

Example: (. . .) is wearing jeans today.
SPEAKER A *(book open):* Rosa is wearing jeans today. *(whispered)*
SPEAKER B *(book closed):* Is Rosa wearing jeans today?
SPEAKER C *(book closed):* Yes, she is.

Switch roles.

1. (. . .) has curly hair.
2. (. . .) doesn't have a mustache.
3. (. . .) is sitting down.
4. Isn't talking to (. . .)

Switch roles.

5. (. . .) and (. . .) were in class yesterday.
6. This exercise is easy.
7. That book belongs to (. . .)
8. An ostrich can't fly.

9. (. . .) is wearing earrings.
10. This book has an index.
11. (. . .)'s grammar book isn't open.
12. Giraffes don't eat meat.

---

*In American English, a form of ***do*** is usually used when ***have*** is the main verb:
    Do you have a car?
In British English, a form of ***do*** with main verb ***have*** is not necessary:
    Have you a car?

5-2 YES/NO QUESTIONS AND INFORMATION QUESTIONS

A yes/no question = a question that can be answered by "yes" or "no."
> A: *Does Ann live in Montreal?*
> B: *Yes, she does.* OR *No, she doesn't.*

An information question = a question that asks for information by using a question word: ***where, when, why, who, whom, what, which, whose, how***.
> A: *Where does Ann live?*
> B: *In Montreal.*

	(QUESTION WORD)	HELPING VERB	SUBJECT	MAIN VERB	(REST OF SENTENCE)	The same subject-verb word order is used in both yes/no and information questions.
(a)		***Does***	*Ann*	***live***	in Montreal?	HELPING VERB + SUBJECT + MAIN VERB
(b)	Where	*does*	*Ann*	*live?*		
(c)		***Is***	*Sara*	***studying***	at the library?	(a) is a yes/no question.
(d)	Where	*is*	*Sara*	*studying?*		(b) is an information question.
(e)		***Will***	*you*	***graduate***	next year?	In (i) and (j): Main verb ***be*** in simple present and simple past (***am, is, are, was, were***) precedes the subject. It has the same position as a helping verb.
(f)	When	*will*	*you*	*graduate?*		
(g)		***Did***	*they*	***see***	Jack?	
(h)	Who(m)*	*did*	*they*	*see?*		
(i)		***Is***	*Heidi*		at home?	
(j)	Where	*is*	*Heidi?*			
(k)			*Who*	***came***	to dinner?	When the question word (e.g., ***who*** or ***what***) is the subject of the question, usual question word order is not used. No form of ***do*** is used. Notice (k) and (l).
(l)			*What*	***happened***	yesterday?	

*See Chart 5-4, p. 125, for a discussion of ***who(m)***.

☐ **EXERCISE 4. Yes/no and information questions.** (Chart 5-2)

Directions: Review the patterns of yes/no and information questions.
Speaker A: Create a yes/no question.
Speaker B: Create an information question using ***where***.

Example: I live there.
SPEAKER A: Do you live there?
SPEAKER B: Where do you live?

1. She lives there.

2. The students live there.

3. Bob lived there.

4. Mary is living there.

5. I was living there.

6. They are going to live there.

7. John will live there.

8. The students can live there.

9. Jim has lived there.

10. Tom has been living there.

5-3　WHERE, WHY, WHEN, AND WHAT TIME

QUESTION	ANSWER	
(a) **Where** did you go?	Paris.	**Where** asks about *place*.
(b) **Why** did you stay home?	Because I didn't feel well.*	**Why** asks about *reason*.
(c) **What time** did he come?	Seven-thirty. Around five o'clock. A quarter past ten.	A question with **what time** asks about *time on a clock*.
(d) **When** did he come?	Seven-thirty. Last night. Two days ago. Monday morning. In 1998.	A question with **when** can be answered by any time expression, as in the sample answers in (d).

*See Chart 8-6, p. 239, for the use of *because*. "Because I didn't feel well" is an adverb clause. It is not a complete sentence. In this example, it is the short answer to a question.

☐ EXERCISE 5. Information questions. (Charts 5-2 and 5-3)
　　　Directions: Create information questions. Use **where, why, when,** or **what time.**

　　1. A: ____When are you going to go downtown?____
　　　　B: Tomorrow. (I'm going to go downtown tomorrow.)

　　2. A: _____
　　　　B: At Lincoln Elementary School. (My children go to school at Lincoln Elementary School.)

　　3. A: _____
　　　　B: At 1:10. (Class begins at 1:10.)

　　4. A: _____
　　　　B: Four years ago. (I met the Smiths four years ago.)

　　5. A: _____
　　　　B: It's waiting for a mouse. (The cat is staring at the hole in the wall because it's waiting for a mouse.)

EXERCISE 6. Yes/no and information questions. (Charts 5-2 and 5-3)

Directions: Work in pairs to create dialogues. Switch roles after item 6.
Speaker A: Ask a question that will produce the given answer.
Speaker B: Give the short answer, and then give a long answer.

Example: After midnight.

SPEAKER A: What time did you go to bed last night?
SPEAKER B: After midnight. I went to bed after midnight last night.

1. The day before yesterday.
2. Yes, I do.
3. Because I wanted to.
4. At 8:30.
5. Yes, he is.
6. At a grocery store.

7. Tomorrow afternoon.
8. Viet Nam.
9. No, I can't.
10. Because the weather is . . . today.
11. Yeah, sure. Why not?
12. I don't know. Maybe.

□ **EXERCISE 7. Questions with WHY. (Chart 5-3)**

Directions: Work in pairs to create dialogues. Switch roles after item 4.

Speaker A: Say the sentence in the book.
Speaker B: Ask "Why?" or "Why not?" and then ask the full *why*-question.
Speaker A: Make up an answer to the question.

Example: I can't go with you tomorrow.

SPEAKER A: I can't go with you tomorrow.
SPEAKER B: Why not? Why can't you go with me tomorrow?
SPEAKER A: Because I have to study for a test.

1. I ate two breakfasts this morning.
2. I don't like to ride on airplanes.
3. I'm going to sell my guitar.
4. I didn't go to bed last night.

5. I'm happy today.
6. I had to call the police last night.
7. I can't explain it to you.
8. I'm not speaking to my cousin.

5-4 QUESTIONS WITH *WHO, WHO(M),* AND *WHAT*

QUESTION	ANSWER	
(a) **Who** came? s	**Someone** came. s	In (a): **Who** is used as the subject (**s**) of a question. In (b): **Who(m)** is used as the object (**o**) in a question. **Whom** is used in formal English. In everyday spoken English, **who** is usually used instead of **whom**: FORMAL: Whom did you see? INFORMAL: Who did you see?
(b) **Who(m)** did *you* see? o	*I* saw **someone**. s o	
(c) **What** happened? s	**Something** happened. s	**What** can be used as either the subject or the object in a question. Notice in (a) and (c): When **who** or **what** is used as the subject of a question, usual question word order is not used; no form of **do** is used: CORRECT: Who came? *INCORRECT: Who did come?*
(d) **What** did *you* see? o	*I* saw **something**. s o	

□ EXERCISE 8. Questions with WHO, WHO(M), and WHAT. (Chart 5-4)
   Directions: Create questions with *who, who(m)*, and *what*. Write "s" if the question word is the subject. Write "o" if the question word is the object.

	QUESTION	ANSWER
1.	^s Who knows?	^s **Someone** knows.
2.	^o Who(m) did you ask?	I asked **someone**. ^o
3.	_____	**Someone** knocked on the door.
4.	_____	Sara met **someone**.
5.	_____	Mike learned **something**.
6.	_____	**Something** changed Ann's mind.
7.	_____	Ann is talking about **someone**.★

□ EXERCISE 9. Questions with WHO, WHO(M), and WHAT. (Chart 5-4)
   Directions: Create questions. Use *who, whom,* or *what.*

   1. A: ___What did you see?_____
      B: An accident. (I saw an accident.)

   2. A: _____
      B: An accident. (Mary saw an accident.)

WHO   **WHAT**

   3. A: _____
      B: Mary. (Mary saw an accident.)

   4. A: _____
      B: John. (Mary saw John.)

WHO   **WHO(M)**

★A preposition may come at the beginning of a question in very formal English:
   About whom (NOT *who*) *is Ann talking?*
   In everyday English, a preposition usually does not come at the beginning of a question.

5. A: _____
   B: Mary. (Mary saw John.)

6. A: _____
   B: An accident. (An accident happened.)

7. A: _____
   B. A new coat. (Alice bought a new coat.)

8. A: _____
   B: Alice. (Alice bought a new coat.)

9. A: _____
   B: A map of the world. (I'm looking at a map of the world.)

10. A: _____
    B: Jane. (I'm looking at Jane.)

11. A: _____
    B: The secretary. (I talked to the secretary.)

12. A: _____
    B: His problems. (Tom talked about his problems.)

13. A: _____
    B: The board. (The teacher looked at the board.)

14. A: _____
    B: The teacher. (The teacher looked at the board.)

15. A: _____
    B: The students. (The teacher looked at the students.)

16. A: _____
    B: An amphibian. (A frog is an amphibian.)

17. A: _____
    B: An animal that can live on land or in water. (An amphibian is an animal that can live on land or in water.)

18. A: _____
    B: Mostly insects. (Frogs eat mostly insects.)

□ **EXERCISE 10. Questions with WHO, WHO(M), and WHAT. (Chart 5-4)**

Directions: Work in pairs.
Speaker A: Complete each question with *who, whom,* or *what*.
Speaker B: Answer the question.

Example: . . . are you currently reading?
SPEAKER A: What are you currently reading?
SPEAKER B: A novel about a cowboy.

1. . . . do you like to read?
2. . . . do you like to spend a lot of time with?
3. . . . is your idea of the perfect vacation?
4. . . . do you like to spend your vacations with?
5. . . . are the most important people in your life?

Switch roles.
6. . . . was the most memorable event of your childhood?
7. . . . stresses you out?
8. . . . do you need that you don't have?
9. . . . would you most like to invite to dinner? The person can be living or dead.
10. . . . has had the most influence on you in your life?

5-5 SPOKEN AND WRITTEN CONTRACTIONS WITH QUESTION WORDS

		SPOKEN ONLY	
is	(a)	"*When's* he coming?" "*Why's* she late?"	*Is, are, did,* and *will* are usually contracted with question words in speaking. These contractions are usually NOT written.
are	(b)	"*What're* these?" "*Who're* they?"	
did	(c)	"*Who'd* you see?" "*What'd* you do?"	
will	(d)	"*Where'll* you be?" "*When'll* they be here?"	

		SPOKEN	WRITTEN	
is	(e)	"*Where's* Ed?" "*What's* that?" "*Who's* he?"	(f) Where's Ed? What's that? Who's he?	Only contractions with *is* and *where, what,* or *who* are commonly used in writing.*

*Contractions are used in informal writing, such as letters to friends or e-mails, but are generally not appropriate in more formal writing, such as in magazine articles or reference books.

□ **EXERCISE 11. Spoken contractions with question words. (Chart 5-5)**

Directions: Listen to your teacher say the following questions in contracted speech, and practice saying them yourself.

1. Where is my book?
2. What is in that drawer?
3. Why is Anita absent?
4. Who is that man?

5. Who are those men?
6. Where are you going?
7. What are you doing?
8. Where did Bob go last night?
9. What did you say?

10. Why did you say that?
11. Who did you see at the party?
12. Where will you be?
13. When will you arrive?
14. Who will meet you at the airport?

☐ EXERCISE 12. Information questions. (Charts 5-2 → 5-5)
Directions: Create any appropriate question for the given answer.

Example: Larry.
→ *Who is the fax from?*
Who(m) did you go to the movie with?
Etc.

1. Yesterday.
2. A new pair of shoes.
3. Mr. Soto.
4. Six-thirty.
5. To the zoo.

6. Because I was tired.
7. A sandwich.
8. I don't know.
9. Tomorrow.
10. My brother.

☐ EXERCISE 13. Asking for the meaning of a word. (Chart 5-4)
Directions: Ask your classmates for the meaning of each *italicized* word in the sentences below. Refer to a dictionary as necessary. Work in groups or as a class.

Example: It's raining. *Perhaps* we should take a taxi.
STUDENT A: **What does** "perhaps" **mean?**
STUDENT B: "Perhaps" means "maybe."

1. Water is *essential* to all forms of life on earth.

2. Why do soap bubbles *float?*

3. I think Carol's *mad.*

4. Some fish *bury* themselves in sand on the ocean bottom and live their entire lives there.

5. Mr. Chan gently put his hand *beneath* the baby's head.

6. I *grabbed* my briefcase and started running for the bus.

7. We walked hand in hand through the *orchard.*★

8. Mark and Olivia went to Hawaii on their *honeymoon.*

9. I'm not very good at *small talk,* so I avoid social situations like cocktail parties.

10. Mr. Weatherbee liked to have *hedges* between his house and his neighbors' houses. He planted the bushes close together so that people couldn't see through them.

★To ask for the meaning of a noun, two question forms are common. For example, using the noun "pocket": **What does** *"pocket"* **mean?** OR **What is** *a pocket?*/**What are** *pockets?*

5-6 USING *WHAT* + A FORM OF *DO*

QUESTION	ANSWER	
(a) *What **does** Bob **do** every morning?*	He *goes to class.*	***What*** + a form of ***do*** is used to ask questions about activities. Examples of forms of ***do***: *am doing, will do, are going to do, did, etc.*
(b) *What **did** you **do** yesterday?*	I *went downtown.*	
(c) *What **is** Anna **doing** (right now)?*	She*'s studying.*	
(d) *What **are** you **going to do** tomorrow?*	I*'m going to go to the beach.*	
(e) *What **do** you **want to do** tonight?*	I *want to go to a movie.*	
(f) *What **would** you **like to do** tomorrow?*	I *would like to visit Jim.*	
(g) *What **will** you **do** tomorrow?*	I*'ll go downtown.*	
(h) *What **should** I **do** about my headache?*	You *should take an aspirin.*	

□ **EXERCISE 14. Using WHAT + a form of DO. (Chart 5-6)**
Directions: Create questions. Use ***what*** + a form of ***do***.

1. A: _____What are you doing_____ right now?

   B: I'm studying.

2. A: _____ last night?

   B: I studied.

3. A: _____ tomorrow?

   B: I'm going to visit my relatives.

4. A: _____ tomorrow?

   B: I want to go to the beach.

5. A: _____ this evening?

   B: I would like to go to a movie.

6. A: _____ tomorrow?

   B: I'm planning to stay home and relax most of the day.

7. A: _____ in class every day?

   B: I study English.

8. A: _____ (for a living)?*

   B: I'm a teacher.

---

*What do you do? has a special meaning. It means: *What is your occupation, your job?* Another way of asking the same question: *What do you do for a living?*

9. A: _____ when he stopped you for speeding?

   B: He (the police officer) gave me a ticket.

10. A: _____ in the winter?

    B: It (a bear) hibernates.

11. A: I have the hiccups. _____ ?

    B: You should drink a glass of water.

12. A: _____ ?

    B: He (Mr. Rice) is a businessman. He works for General Electric.

    A: _____ ?

    B: She (Mrs. Rice) designs websites. She works for an Internet company.

□ **EXERCISE 15. Using WHAT + a form of DO and verb tense review. (Chart 5-6)**
  Directions: Work in pairs. Ask a classmate a question. Use **what + do**.

  Example: tomorrow
  SPEAKER A: What are you going to do tomorrow? / What do you want to do tomorrow? /
              What would you like to do tomorrow? / Etc.
  SPEAKER B: *(Answer the question.)*

	Switch roles.
1. last night	7. this morning
2. right now	8. last weekend
3. next Saturday	9. on weekends
4. this afternoon	10. after class yesterday
5. tonight	11. after class today
6. every morning	12. since you arrived in this city

5-7 USING *WHAT KIND OF*

QUESTION	ANSWER	*What kind of* asks for information about a specific type (a specific kind) in a general category.
(a) *What kind of* shoes did you buy?	Boots. Sandals. Tennis shoes. Loafers. Running shoes. High heels. Etc.	In (a): general category = shoes specific kinds = boots 　　　　　　　sandals 　　　　　　　tennis shoes 　　　　　　　etc.

| (b) *What kind of* fruit do you like best? | Apples.
Bananas.
Oranges.
Grapefruit.
Grapes.
Strawberries.
Etc. | In (b):
general category = fruit
specific kinds = apples
　　　　　　　bananas
　　　　　　　oranges
　　　　　　　etc. |

☐ **EXERCISE 16. Using WHAT KIND OF. (Chart 5-7)**
　　Directions: Complete each question. Give other possible answers to the question.

　　1. A: What kind of _____shoes_____ are you wearing?

　　　　B: Boots. (*Other possible answers:* ___loafers/running shoes/etc.___)

　　2. A: What kind of _____meat_____ do you eat most often?

　　　　B: Beef. (*Other possible answers:* ___chicken/lamb/pork/etc.___)

　　3. A: What kind of _____ do you like best?

　　　　B: Rock 'n roll. (*Other possible answers:* _____)

　　4. A: What kind of _____ would you like to have?

　　　　B: A Mercedes-Benz. (*Other possible answers:* _____)

　　5. A: What kind of _____ do you like to read?

　　　　B: Science fiction. (*Other possible answers:* _____)

6. A: What kind of _____ do you have?

   B: _____ . (*Other possible answers:* _____)

7. A: What kind of _____ do you like best?

   B: _____ . (*Other possible answers:* _____)

8. A: What kind of _____ is (. . .) wearing?

   B: _____ . (*Other possible answers:* _____)

□ **EXERCISE 17. Using WHAT KIND OF. (Chart 5-7)**
   Directions: Find classmates who own the following things. Ask them questions using **what kind of**.

   Example: a camera
   SPEAKER A: Do you have a camera?
   SPEAKER B: Yes.★
   SPEAKER A: What kind of camera do you have?
   SPEAKER B: I have a 35-millimeter Kodak camera.

1. a camera	6. a computer
2. a TV	7. a watch
3. a bicycle	8. a dog
4. a car	9. a cell phone
5. a refrigerator	10. *(use your own words)*

5-8 USING *WHICH*

(a) TOM: May I borrow a pen from you?
ANN: Sure. I have two pens. This pen has black ink. That pen has red ink.
    Which pen do you want? OR
    Which one do you want? OR
    Which do you want?
	In (a): Ann uses ***which*** (not ***what***) because she wants Tom to choose.
	Which is used when the speaker wants someone to make a choice, when the speaker is offering alternatives: *this one or that one; these or those.*

(b) SUE: I like these earrings, and I like those, too. BOB: ***Which (earrings/ones)*** are you going to buy? SUE: I think I'll get these.	***Which*** can be used with either singular or plural nouns.
(c) JIM: Here's a photo of my daughter's class. KIM: Very nice. ***Which one*** is your daughter?	***Which*** can be used to ask about people as well as things.
(d) SUE: My aunt gave me some money for my birthday. I'm going to take it with me to the mall. BOB: ***What*** are you going to buy with it? SUE: I haven't decided yet.	In (d): The question doesn't involve choosing from a particular group of items, so Bob uses ***what***, not ***which***.

___

★If the answer is "no," ask another question from the list.

□ **EXERCISE 18. WHICH vs. WHAT. (Chart 5-8)**
Directions: Complete the questions with *which* or *what*.

1. A: This hat comes in brown and in gray. _____Which_____ color do you think
      your husband would prefer?
   B: Gray, I think.

2. A: I've never been to Mrs. Hall's house. _____What_____ color is it?
   B: Gray.

3. A: I have two dictionaries. _____ one do you want?
   B: The Arabic–English dictionary, not the English–English one.

4. A: May I help you?
   B: Please.
   A: _____ are you looking for?
   B: An Arabic–English dictionary.
   A: Right over there in the reference section.
   B: Thanks.

5. A: _____ did you get on your last test?
   B: I don't want to tell you. It was an awful grade.

6. A: If I need only half an onion, _____ half should I use and

      _____ half should I save?
   B: Save the root half. It lasts longer.

□ **EXERCISE 19. WHICH vs. WHAT. (Chart 5-8)**
Directions: Create questions. Use *which* or *what*.

1. A: I have two books. _____Which book/Which one/Which do you want?_____
   B: That one. (I want that book.)

2. A: _____What did you buy when you went shopping?_____
   B: A book. (I bought a book when I went shopping.)

3. A: Could I borrow your pen for a minute?
   B: Sure. I have two. _____
   A: That one. (I would like that one.)

4. A: _____
   B: A pen. (Chris borrowed a pen from me.)

5. A: _____
   B: Two pieces of hard candy. (I have two pieces of hard candy in my hand.) Would
      you like one?
   A: Yes. Thanks.
   B: _____
   A: The yellow one. (I'd like the yellow one.)

6. A: Do you like this tie?
   B: Yes.
   A: Do you like that tie?
   B: It's okay.

   A: _____

   B: This one. (I'm going to buy this one.)

7. A: Tony and I went shopping. I got some new shoes.

   B: _____
   A: A tie. (Tony got a tie.)

8. A: Did you enjoy your trip to Europe?
   B: Yes, I did. Very much.

   A: _____

   B: Poland, Germany, Czechoslovakia, and Italy. (I visited Poland, Germany,
      Czechoslovakia, and Italy.)*

   A: _____

   B: Poland. (I enjoyed visiting Poland the most.)

5-9 USING *WHOSE*

QUESTION	ANSWER	
(a) **Whose (book)** is this?	It's John's (book).	**Whose** asks about possession.* Notice in (a): The speaker of the question may omit the noun *(book)* if the meaning is clear to the listener.
(b) **Whose (books)** are those?	They're mine (OR my books).	
(c) **Whose car** did you borrow?	I borrowed Karen's (car).	
COMPARE		**Who's** and **whose** have the same pronunciation.
(d) **Who's** that?	Mary Smith.	**Who's** = a contraction of **who is**.
(e) **Whose** is that?	Mary's.	**Whose** = asks about possession.

*See Charts 6-11, p. 173, and 6-12, p. 176, for ways of expressing possession.

_____

*The difference between *what country* and *which country* is often very small.

☐ EXERCISE 20. Using WHOSE. (Chart 5-9)

Directions: Create questions with ***whose*** or ***who***. The things near Susan belong to her. The things near Eric belong to him. Point to the things and people in the pictures when you ask some of the questions.

1. A: Whose basketball is ____________ this?
   B: Susan's. (It's Susan's basketball.)
2. A: Who is ____________ this?
   B: Susan. (This is Susan.)
3. A: ____________ that?
   B: Eric's. (It's Eric's notebook.)
4. A: ____________ these?
   B: Eric's. (They're Eric's tapes.)
5. A: ____________ that?
   B: Eric. (That is Eric.)
6. A: ____________ those?
   B: Susan's. (They're Susan's clothes.)
7. A: ____________ that?
   B: Susan's. (It's Susan's coat.)
8. A: ____________ in a gym?
   B: Susan. (Susan is in a gym.)

9. A: _____ sitting down?

   B: Eric. (Eric is sitting down.)

10. A: _____ longer?

    B: Eric's. (Eric's hair is longer than Susan's.)

□ EXERCISE 21. Using WHOSE. (Chart 5-9)
Directions: Ask and answer questions about possession. Follow the pattern in the examples. Talk about things in the classroom.

Example: pen
SPEAKER A: Is this your pen? / Is this (pen) yours?
SPEAKER B: No, it isn't.
SPEAKER A: Whose is it?
SPEAKER B: It's Ali's.

Example: pens
SPEAKER A: Are these Yoko's (pens)? / Are these (pens) Yoko's?
SPEAKER B: No, they aren't.
SPEAKER A: Whose are they?
SPEAKER B: They're mine.

1. dictionary	5. bookbag	9. purse
2. books	6. briefcase	10. calculator
3. notebook	7. glasses	11. things
4. papers	8. backpack	12. stuff★

□ EXERCISE 22. Review: information questions. (Charts 5-2 → 5-9)
Directions: Work in pairs. Create questions for the given answers. Use any appropriate question word.

Example: I'm reading.
SPEAKER A: What are you doing?
SPEAKER B: I'm reading.

1. They're mine.
2. I'm going to study.
3. A Toyota.
4. Mr. (. . .).
5. It's (. . .)'s.
6. It means "small."

Switch roles.
7. Jazz.
8. Because I didn't feel good.
9. This one, not that one.
10. (. . .)'s.
11. A couple of days ago.
12. India.

★*Stuff* is used in informal spoken English to mean miscellaneous things. For example, when a speaker says, "This is my stuff," the speaker may be referring to pens, pencils, books, papers, notebooks, clothes, etc. (Note: *stuff* is a noncount noun; it never has a final *-s*.)

□ **EXERCISE 23. Asking questions.** (Charts 5-1 → 5-9)

Directions: Work in pairs.

Speaker A: Choose any one of the possible answers below and ask a question that would produce that answer.

Speaker B: Decide which answer Speaker A has in mind and answer his/her question. Pay special attention to the form of Speaker A's question. Correct any errors.

Alternate asking questions. (First Speaker A asks a question and Speaker B answers. Next Speaker B asks a question and Speaker A answers.)

Example:

SPEAKER A: What is Maria's favorite color?

SPEAKER B: (Speaker B reviews the list of possible answers below and chooses the appropriate one.) Pink.

Possible answers:

Sure! Thanks!

Call the insurance company.

Next week.

A rat.

Mr. (. . .).

Answering your questions.

Cheese.

Mine.

Eight-thirty.

Her husband.

Probably.

The teacher's.

Not that one. The other one.

A Panasonic or a Sony.

Pink.

No, a friend of mine gave them to me a few days ago.

Historical fiction.

Study, and then watch a movie.

On the Internet.

5-10 USING *HOW*

QUESTION	ANSWER	
(a) ***How*** did you get here?	I drove./By car. I took a taxi./By taxi. I took a bus./By bus. I flew./By plane. I took a train./By train. I walked./On foot.	***How*** has many uses. One use of ***how*** is to ask about means (ways) of transportation.
(b) ***How old*** are you? (c) ***How tall*** is he? (d) ***How big*** is your apartment? (e) ***How sleepy*** are you? (f) ***How hungry*** are you? (g) ***How soon*** will you be ready? (h) ***How well*** does he speak English? (i) ***How quickly*** can you get here?	Twenty-one. About six feet. It has three rooms. Very sleepy. I'm starving. In five minutes. Very well. I can get there in 30 minutes.	***How*** is often used with adjectives (e.g., *old*, *big*) and adverbs (e.g., *well*, *quickly*).

Directions: Create questions with **how**.

1. A: ____How old is your daughter?_____
   B: Ten. (My daughter is ten years old.)

2. A: _____
   B: Very important. (Education is very important.)

3. A: _____
   B: By bus. (I get to school by bus.)

4. A: _____
   B: Very, very deep. (The ocean is very, very deep.)

5. A: _____
   B: By plane. (I'm going to get to Denver by plane.)

6. A: _____
   B: Not very. (The test wasn't very difficult.)

7. A: _____
   B: It's 29,028 feet high. (Mt. Everest is 29,028 feet high.)★

8. A: _____
   B: I walked. (I walked to school today.)

5-11 USING *HOW OFTEN*

QUESTION	ANSWER	*How often* asks about frequency.
(a) **How often** do you go shopping?	Every day. Once a week. About twice a week. Every other day or so.★ Three times a month.	
(b) **How many times a day** do you eat? **How many times a week** do you go shopping? **How many times a month** do you go to the post office? **How many times a year** do you take a vacation?	Three or four. Two. Once. Once or twice.	Other ways of asking **how often:** how many times $\begin{cases} a\ day \\ a\ week \\ a\ month \\ a\ year \end{cases}$

★*Every other day* means "Monday yes, Tuesday no, Wednesday yes, Thursday no," etc. *Or so* means "approximately."

_____

★29,028 feet = 8,848 meters.

Directions: Work in pairs.

Speaker A: Ask a question with ***how often*** or ***how many times a day/week/month/year***.

Speaker B: Answer the question. (Possible answers are suggested in the list of frequency expressions.)

Example: eat lunch at the cafeteria

SPEAKER A: How often do you eat lunch at the cafeteria?

SPEAKER B: About twice a week.

```
FREQUENCY EXPRESSIONS

   a lot                   every  ⎫
   occasionally*      every other  ⎪
   once in a while       once a   ⎪
   not very often       twice a   ⎬ day/week/month/year
   hardly ever      three times a  ⎪
   almost never       ten times a  ⎪
   never                          ⎭
```

Switch roles.

1. play cards
2. get on the Internet
3. go out to eat
4. cook your own dinner
5. read a newspaper
6. get your hair cut

7. buy a toothbrush
8. go to a laundromat
9. go swimming
10. be late for class
11. attend a wedding
12. see a falling star

5-12 USING *HOW FAR*

(a) ***It is*** 289 miles ***from*** St. Louis ***to*** Chicago.* (b) ***It is*** 289 miles ⎰ ***from*** St. Louis ***to*** Chicago. ⎱ ***from*** Chicago ***to*** St. Louis. ⎰ ***to*** Chicago ***from*** St. Louis. ⎱ ***to*** St. Louis ***from*** Chicago.	The most common way of expressing distance: ***It is*** + *distance* + ***from/to*** + ***to/from*** In (b): All four expressions with ***from*** and ***to*** have the same meaning.
(c) A: ***How far is it*** from St. Louis to Chicago? B: 289 miles. (d) A: ***How far do you*** live from school? B: Four blocks.	***How far*** is used to ask questions about distance.
(e) ***How many miles*** is it from St. Louis to Chicago? (f) ***How many kilometers*** is it to Montreal from here? (g) ***How many blocks*** is it to the post office?	Other ways to ask ***how far:*** *how many miles* *how many kilometers* *how many blocks*

*1 mile = 1.60 kilometers.
  1 kilometer = 00.614 mile.

———————

*Notice: *Occasionally* is spelled with *two* "c"s but only *one* "s."

□ **EXERCISE 26. Using HOW FAR.** (Chart 5-12)

Directions: Create questions.

1. A: _____How far is it to Chicago from New Orleans?_____

   B: 919 miles. (It's 919 miles to Chicago from New Orleans.)

2. A: _____

   B: 257 kilometers. (It's 257 kilometers from Montreal to Quebec.)

3. A: _____

   B: Six blocks. (It's six blocks to the post office.)

4. A: I had a terrible day yesterday.

   B: What happened?

   A: I ran out of gas while I was driving to work.

   B: _____ before you ran out of gas?

   A: To the junction of I-90 and 480. (I got to the junction of I-90 and 480.) Luckily, there was a gas station about half a mile down the road.

□ **EXERCISE 27. Using HOW FAR.** (Chart 5-12)

Directions: Bring road maps of your geographical area to class. In small groups, look at a map of your area and ask each other questions with **how far**.

5-13 LENGTH OF TIME: *IT + TAKE* AND *HOW LONG*

IT + TAKE + (SOMEONE) + LENGTH + INFINITIVE OF TIME		**It + take** is often used with time words and an infinitive to express **length of time**, as in (a) and (b). An infinitive = **to** + *the simple form of a verb.** In (a): **to cook** is an infinitive.
(a) **It** takes	20 minutes **to cook** rice.	
(b) **It** took Al	two hours **to drive** to work.	
(c) **How long** does it take to cook rice? —20 minutes. (d) **How long** did it take Al to drive to work today? —Two hours. (e) **How long** did you study last night? —Four hours. (f) **How long** will you be in Hong Kong? —Ten days.		**How long** asks about **length of time**.
(g) **How many days** will you be in Hong Kong?		Other ways of asking **how long**: **how many** + { minutes / hours / days / weeks / months / years

*See Chart 13-3, p. 373.

☐ **EXERCISE 28. Length of time. (Chart 5-13)**

Directions: Create sentences using *it* + *take* to express length of time.

1. I drove to Madrid. *(Length of time: three days)*
   → *It took me three days to drive to Madrid.*
2. I walk to class. *(Length of time: twenty minutes)*
3. Gino finished the test. *(Length of time: an hour and a half)*
4. We will drive to the airport. *(Length of time: forty-five minutes)*
5. Alan hitchhiked to Alaska. *(Length of time: two weeks)*
6. I wash my clothes at the laundromat. *(Length of time: two hours)*

☐ **EXERCISE 29. Length of time. (Chart 5-13)**

Directions: Use *it* + *take*.

1. How long does it take you to . . .
   a. eat breakfast? → *It takes me ten minutes to eat breakfast.*
   b. get to class?
   c. write a short paragraph in English?
   d. read a 400-page novel?
2. Generally speaking, how long does it take to . . .
   a. fly from *(name of a city)* to *(name of a city)*?
   b. get from here to your hometown?
   c. get used to living in a foreign country?
   d. commute from *(name of a local place)* to *(name of a local place)* during rush hour?

☐ **EXERCISE 30. Length of time. (Chart 5-13)**

Directions: Create questions using *how long*.

1. A: *How long did it take you to drive to New York?*
   B: Five days. (It took me five days to drive to New York.)

2. A: _____
   B: A week. (Mr. McNally will be in the hospital for a week.)

3. A: _____
   B: A long time. (It takes a long time to learn a second language.)

4. A: _____
   B: Six months. (I've been living here for six months.)

5. A: _____
   B: Six years. (I lived in Istanbul for six years.)

6. A: _____
   B: A couple of years. (I've known Nho Pham for a couple of years.)

7. A: _____
   B: Since 1999. (He's been living in Canada since 1999.)

8. A: _____
   For 21 to 30 days, according to psychologists. (A person has to do something consistently for 21 to 30 days before it becomes a habit.)

□ **EXERCISE 31. Length of time.** (Chart 5-13)

Directions: Work in groups of three. Only Speaker A's book is open.
Speaker A: Complete the sentence with your own words.
Speaker B: Ask a question about Speaker A's sentence, using ***how long***.
Speaker C: Answer the question. Give both a short answer and a long answer.

Example: It takes me . . . to . . . .
SPEAKER A: It takes me twenty minutes to walk to class from my apartment.
SPEAKER B: How long does it take (Ana) to walk to class from her apartment?
SPEAKER C: Twenty minutes. It takes her twenty minutes to walk to class from her apartment.

1. It took me . . . to get to school today.
2. It usually . . . me . . . to get dressed in the morning.
3. It . . . to fly from . . . to . . . .
4. It . . . 45 minutes to an hour to . . . .

Switch roles.   *Switch roles.*

5. It . . . to change the sheets on a bed.   9. It . . . to walk from . . . to . . .
6. It usually takes me . . . to eat . . . .   10. It takes . . . drive . . . .
7. It took me . . . this morning.   11. It used to take . . . to . . . .
8. It takes only a few minutes to . . . .   12. In class, it takes us approximately . . . to . . . .

5-14 MORE QUESTIONS WITH *HOW*

QUESTION	ANSWER	
(a) ***How do you spell*** "coming"? (b) ***How do you say*** "yes" in Japanese? (c) ***How do you say/pronounce*** this word?	C-O-M-I-N-G. Hai. _____	To answer (a): Spell the word. To answer (b): Say the word. To answer (c): Pronounce the word.
(d) ***How are you getting along?*** (e) ***How are you doing?*** (f) ***How's it going?***	Great. Fine. Okay. So-so.	In (d), (e), and (f): How is your life? Is your life okay? Do you have any problems? Note: (f) is also used in greetings: *Hi, Bob. How's it going?*
(g) ***How do you feel?*** ***How are you feeling?***	Terrific! Wonderful! Great! Fine. Okay. So-so. A bit under the weather. Not so good. Terrible!/Lousy./Awful!	The questions in (g) ask about health or about general emotional state.
(h) ***How do you do?***	How do you do?	***How do you do?*** is used by both speakers when they are introduced to each other in a somewhat formal situation.★

★A: *Dr. Erickson, I'd like to introduce you to a friend of mine, Rick Brown. Rick, this is my biology professor, Dr. Erickson.*
B: ***How do you do,*** *Mr. Brown?*
C: ***How do you do,*** *Dr. Erickson? I'm pleased to meet you.*

☐ **EXERCISE 32. More questions with HOW. (Chart 5-14)**

Directions: Close your books. Divide into two teams. Ask a student on the other team how to spell the word your teacher says. (Alternatively, work in pairs, switching roles after item 9.)

Example: country
SPEAKER A: How do you spell "country"?
SPEAKER B: C-O-N-T-R-Y
SPEAKER A: No, that isn't right. The correct spelling is C-O-U-N-T-R-Y. OR
               Yes, that's right.

1. together	7. different	13. beginning
2. purple	8. foreign	14. intelligent
3. daughter	9. studying	15. writing
4. planned	10. bought	16. occasionally
5. rained	11. people	17. family
6. neighbor	12. beautiful	18. Mississippi

☐ **EXERCISE 33. More questions with HOW. (Chart 5-14)**

Directions: Ask your classmates how to say these words in their native languages.

Example: yes
SPEAKER A: How do you say "yes" in Japanese?
SPEAKER B: Hai.

1. Yes.
2. No.
3. Thank you.
4. I love you.

☐ **EXERCISE 34. More questions with HOW. (Chart 5-14)**

Directions: Ask your classmates how to pronounce these words. Work in groups or as a class.

Example:
SPEAKER A: How do you pronounce the number 9?
SPEAKER B: *(Speaker B pronounces the word.)*
SPEAKER A: Good. OR No, I don't think that's right.

LIST A.	(1)	(2)	(3)	(4)	(5)	(6)	(7)	(8)	(9)	(10)
	beat	bit	bet	bite	bait	bat	but	boot	boat	bought

LIST B.	(1)	(2)	(3)	(4)	(5)	(6)	(7)	(8)	(9)	(10)
	zoos	Sue's	shoes	chews	choose	chose	those	toes	doze	dose

☐ **EXERCISE 35. Review of HOW. (Charts 5-10 → 5-14)**

Directions: Complete the questions.

1. A: _____How often_____ do you get a haircut?
   B: About every six weeks, I think/guess.

2. A: _____ does it take to get a haircut at Bertha's Beauty Boutique?
   B: Half an hour.

3. A: _____ is it from the earth to the moon?
   B: Approximately 239,000 miles or 385,000 kilometers.

4. A: _____ times a day do you brush your teeth?
   B: At least three.

5. A: _____ does a snake shed its skin?
   B: From once a year to more than six times a year, depending on the kind of snake.

6. A: _____ is it from your desk to the door?
   B: I'd say about four regular steps or two giant steps.

7. A: _____ times does the numeral 9 appear in the numerals from 1 to 100?
   B: 20 times.

8. A: _____ does a bird's heart beat?
   B: It depends on size. A big bird's heart beats more than 300 times a minute. A small bird like a hummingbird has a normal heart beat of more than 600 beats a minute.

9. A: _____ volcanoes erupt every year?
   B: About 50. But that's just on Earth.

10. A: _____ 's it going?
    B: Okay, I guess. What about you? What's new with you?
    A: Nothin' much.

11. A: Could you carry this box of books for me?
    B: I'd like to, but I have a bad back. _____ is it?
    A: Pretty heavy. That's okay. I'll ask Jack to carry it.

12. A: You blow on your hands to warm them. You blow on your soup to cool it. Imagine that! Hot and cold from the same mouth. _____ do you explain that?
    B: I don't know. _____ do you explain it?

□ **EXERCISE 36. Review of HOW. (Charts 5-10 → 5-14)**

Directions: Create questions for the given answers. Use ***how*** in each question.

Example: It's very important.
   → *How important is good health?*

1. Very expensive.
2. I took a taxi.
3. Four hours.
4. He's nineteen.
5. In five minutes.
6. With a knife.
7. Every day.
8. Three blocks.
9. Fine.
10. With two "t"s.
11. It gets below zero.
12. Excellent.

□ **EXERCISE 37. Review of questions. (Charts 5-1 → 5-14)**

Directions: Complete the dialogue with questions. Use any appropriate question words. Work in pairs or as a class.

A: _____**What are you going to do**_____ this weekend?
                           1

B: I'm going to go to a baseball game.

A: There are two games this weekend. _____?
                                                    2

B: The one on Sunday.

A: _____ yesterday?
                    3

B: No, I didn't. I didn't know there was a game yesterday. _____?
                                                                          4

A: Yes, I did, and I really enjoyed it.

B: _____ to the game alone?
                    5

A: No.

B: _____ with you?
                    6

A: Linda Rivera. _____ to Sunday's game with?
                                7

B: A guy I work with named Bob Woo. He's a real fan.

A: _____ to the stadium from your apartment?
                    8

B: No, I can't. It's too far.

A: _____ ?
                    9

B: Six miles.

A: _____ get there?
                    10

B: By bus.

A: _____ get there?
                    11

B: Just twenty minutes.

A: _____ start Sunday?
                    12

B: One o'clock.

A: I wish I could join you. _____ to a baseball game?
                                        13

B: About once a month. How about you?

A: I go to a baseball game as often as I can.

B: _____ to baseball games?
                    14

A: Because it's a wonderful game, and it's so much fun to be there and watch it in person.

B: _____ when you go to a game?
                    15

A: I yell, enjoy the sunshine, eat peanuts, and drink soda.

B: That's exactly what I do, too!

☐ **EXERCISE 38. Review of questions. (Charts 5-1 → 5-14)**
   Directions: Create questions for the given answers.

   Example: I'm reading.
   SPEAKER A: What are you doing?
   SPEAKER B: I'm reading.

   1. It means "big."
   2. Three days ago.
   3. Once a week.
   4. Okay.
   5. By bus.
   6. Mine.
   7. Nonfiction.
   8. B-E-A-U-T-I-F-U-L.
   9. The park.
   10. Because I . . . .
   11. 100 (miles/kilometers).
   12. I'm going to study.
   13. A bit under the weather.
   14. How do you do?
   15. Two hours.
   16. Six o'clock.
   17. Mary.
   18. Blue.
   19. Cold and wet.
   20. The one on the red chair.
   21. Chris's.
   22. With two "r"s.
   23. Andy and Ed.
   24. Five blocks.
   25. 1989.
   26. Biochemistry.
   27. Making questions.
   28. Saudi Arabia.
       In the Middle East.
       Oil.
       Riyadh.

☐ **EXERCISE 39. Review of questions. (Charts 5-1 → 5-14)**
   Directions: Work in pairs. Create dialogues from the given words.

   Example: . . . usually get up?
   SPEAKER A: What time do you usually get up?
   SPEAKER B: 6:30.

   1. . . . fruit . . . like best?
   2. . . . is south of . . . ?
   3. . . . times a week do you . . . ?
   4. . . . do tomorrow?
   5. . . . is it from . . . to . . . ?
   6. . . . in this city?

   Switch roles.
   7. . . . is sitting . . . ?
   8. . . . should I . . . ?
   9. . . . do for a living?
   10. . . . spell "happened"?
   11. . . . take to get to . . . from the airport?
   12. . . . getting along in your English classes?

Directions: In small groups (or by yourself), make up questions about some or all of the following topics. What would you like to know about these topics? Share your questions with your classmates. Maybe some of them can answer some of your questions.

Example: tigers

Questions: How long do tigers usually live? Where do they live? What do they eat? Do they kill and eat people? How big is a tiger? Is it bigger than a lion? Can a tiger climb a tree? Do tigers live alone or in groups? How many tigers are there in the world today? How many tigers were there one hundred years ago?

Topics:

1. world geography
2. the universe
3. the weather

4. dinosaurs
5. birds
6. (a topic of your own choosing)

5-15   USING *HOW ABOUT* AND *WHAT ABOUT*

(a) A: We need one more player.
    B: ***How about (what about) Jack?*** Let's ask him if he wants to play.
(b) A: What time should we meet?
    B: ***How about (what about) three o'clock?***
	How about and ***what about*** have the same meaning and usage. They are used to make suggestions or offers.
	How about and ***what about*** are followed by a noun (or pronoun) or the *-ing* form of a verb.

(c) A: What should we do this afternoon?
    B: ***How about going*** to the zoo?
(d) A: ***What about asking*** Sally over for dinner next Sunday?
    B: Okay. Good idea.
	Note: ***How about*** and ***what about*** are frequently used in informal spoken English, but are usually not used in writing.

(e) A: I'm tired. ***How about you?***
    B: Yes, I'm tired too.
(f) A: Are you hungry?
    B: No. ***What about you?***
    A: I'm a little hungry.
	How about you? and ***What about you?*** are used to ask a question that refers to the information or question that immediately preceded it. In (e): *How about you?* = *Are you tired?* In (f): *What about you?* = *Are you hungry?*

☐ EXERCISE 41. HOW ABOUT and WHAT ABOUT. (Chart 5-15)

Directions: Complete the dialogues with your own words.

1. A: ____What time do you want to meet for dinner____?

   B: How about ____nine or nine-thirty____?

   A: That's too late for me. How about ____eight____?

   B: Okay.

2. A: _____?

   B: No, Tuesday's not good for me.

   A: Then what about _____?

   B: Okay. That's fine.

3. A: There's room in the car for one more person. Do you think _____

   would like to go to _____ with us?

   B: _____ can't go with us because _____ .

   A: Then how about _____ ?

   B: _____ .

4. A: Do you like fish?

   B: Yes, very much. How about _____ ?

   A: Yes, I like fish a lot. In fact, I think I'll order fish for dinner tonight. That sounds

   good. What about _____ ?

   B: _____ .

☐ **EXERCISE 42. HOW ABOUT and WHAT ABOUT. (Chart 5-15)**
   Directions: Complete the dialogues by using ***How about you?*** or ***What about you?*** and
   an appropriate response.

   Example:
   SPEAKER A: What are you going to do over vacation?
   SPEAKER B: I'm staying here. *What about (How about) you?*
   SPEAKER A: *I'm going to Texas to visit my sister.*

   1. A: Did you like the movie?
      B: It was okay, I guess . . . . .
      A: . . . .

   2. A: Are you going to the company picnic?
      B: I haven't decided yet . . . . .
      A: . . . .

   3. A: Do you like living in this city?
      B: Sort of . . . . .
      A: . . . .

   4. A: What are you going to have?
      B: Well, I'm not really hungry. I think I might have just a salad . . . . .
      A: . . . .

   5. A: Where are you planning to go to school next year?
      B: A small college in California . . . . .
      A: . . . .

   6. A: Are you married?
      B: . . . .
      A: . . . .

Directions: Work in pairs.

Speaker A: Read the cue. Your book is open.

Speaker B: Respond by asking a question with **how about** or **what about**. Your book is closed.

Speaker A: Respond to Speaker B's suggestion.

Example:

SPEAKER A: I'm looking for a good book to read. Do you have any suggestions?

SPEAKER B: How about (What about) *Tom Sawyer* by Mark Twain? That's a good book.

SPEAKER A: I've already read it. / Okay. Do you have a copy I could borrow? / Etc.

1. I'm glad we're having dinner together this evening, (. . .). What time should we get together?

2. I can't figure out what to give my sister for her birthday.

3. I'm hungry, but I'm not sure what I want to eat.

4. We have a whole week of vacation. Where should we go?

Switch roles.

5. I need to talk to you on the phone this evening. What time should I call you?

6. Where should we go for dinner tonight?

7. I've already asked (. . .) and (. . .) to my party. Who else should I ask?

8. Some friends are coming to visit me this weekend. They said they wanted to see some of the interesting places in the city. I'm wondering where I should take them.

Directions: Work in pairs.

Speaker A: The given questions are conversation openers. Glance at a question quickly, then look up—directly into the eyes of Speaker B—and initiate the conversation. Your book is open.

Speaker B: Answer Speaker A's question. Then ask "How about you?" or "What about you?" to continue the conversation. Your book is closed.

Speaker A: Answer the question. Then continue the conversation by asking related questions.

Example: What kind of books do you like to read?

SPEAKER A: What kind of books do you like to read?

SPEAKER B: Mostly nonfiction. I like books about nature or history. How about you?

SPEAKER A: I like fiction. I read a lot of novels. Mysteries are my favorite. What about you? Do you ever read mysteries?

SPEAKER B: No, not really. But I like to read poetry. How about you? Do you ever read poetry?

SPEAKER A: Etc.

1. How long have you been living in *(this city or country)*?

2. What are you going to do after class today?

3. What kind of movies do you like to watch?

Switch roles.

4. Do you come from a large family?
5. What kind of sports do you enjoy?
6. Do you speak a lot of English outside of class?

5-16 TAG QUESTIONS

AFFIRMATIVE (+)	NEGATIVE (−)	A tag question is a question that is added onto the end of a sentence. An auxiliary verb is used in a tag question.
(a) *You **know** Bob Wilson,*	***don't** you?*	
(b) *Marie **is** from Paris,*	***isn't** she?*	When the main verb is affirmative, the tag question is negative.
(c) *Jerry **can play** the piano,*	***can't** he?*	
NEGATIVE (−)	**AFFIRMATIVE (+)**	When the main verb is negative, the tag question is affirmative.
(d) *You **don't know** Jack Smith,*	***do** you?*	
(e) *Marie **isn't** from Athens,*	***is** she?*	
(f) *Jerry **can't speak** Arabic,*	***can** he?*	

In using a tag question, a speaker gives his idea while asking a question at the same time. In (g) and (h) below: I (the speaker) use a tag question because I expect you (the listener) to tell me that my information or my idea is correct.

As with other kinds of questions, a speaker usually uses a rising intonation at the end of a tag question.*

THE SPEAKER'S IDEA	THE SPEAKER'S QUESTION	EXPECTED ANSWER
(g) I think that you know Bob Wilson.	You **know** Bob Wilson, **don't** you?	**Yes**, I **do**.
(h) I think that you don't know Jack Smith.	You **don't know** Jack Smith, **do** you?	**No**, I **don't**.

COMPARE	
(i) A: Do you know Tom Lee? *(a yes/no question)* B: Yes, I do. OR No, I don't.	In (i): The speaker has no idea. The speaker is simply looking for information.
(j) A: You know Tom Lee, don't you? *(a tag question)* B: Yes, I do.	In (j): The speaker believes that the listener knows Tom Lee. The speaker wants to make sure that his idea is correct.

*Sometimes a falling intonation is used with tag questions. For example:
   A: It's a beautiful day today, *isn't it? (voice falling rather than rising)*
   B: Yes, indeed. The weather's perfect.
A speaker uses falling intonation for a tag question when he is making an observation, commenting on something rather than making sure his information is correct. In the example, the speaker is making a comment about the weather to invite conversation.
   Other examples: *That was a good movie, wasn't it? Mr. Smith is a good teacher, isn't he? It's really hot today, isn't it?*

☐ EXERCISE 45. Tag questions. (Chart 5-16)
   Directions: Add tag questions and give the expected answers.

   1. A: You are a student, _____*aren't you*_____?

      B: _____*Yes, I am*_____.

   2. A: Ahmed came to class yesterday, _____?

      B: _____.

3. A: Pedro was in class too, _____ ?

   B: _____ .

4. A: Anna will be at the meeting tomorrow, _____ ?

   B: _____ .

5. A: You can speak Spanish, _____ ?

   B: _____ .

6. A: Our teacher didn't give us a homework assignment, _____ ?

   B: _____ .

7. A: You haven't eaten dinner yet, _____ ?

   B: _____ .

8. A: All birds lay eggs, _____ ?

   B: _____ .

☐ **EXERCISE 46. Use of auxiliary verbs in tag questions. (Chart 5-16)**
   Directions: Add tag questions.

   1. Mr. Adams was born in England, _____*wasn't he*_____ ?
   2. Flies can fly upside down, _____ ?
   3. Po lives with his brother, _____ ?
   4. Mike isn't married, _____ ?
   5. You would rather have a roommate than live alone, _____ ?
   6. Janet has a car, _____ ?
   7. She's had her car for several years, _____ ?
   8. She has to get a new license plate for her car, _____ ?
   9. If you want to get to work on time, you should leave pretty soon, _____ ?
   10. Ms. Boxlight will be here tomorrow, _____ ?
   11. You didn't forget to finish your homework, _____ ?
   12. This is your pen,* _____ ?

   _____

   *When ***this*** or ***that*** is used in the first part of the sentence, ***it*** is used in the tag question: *This is your book, isn't it?*
   When ***these*** or ***those*** is used in the first part of the sentence, ***they*** is used in the tag question: *These are your shoes, aren't they?*

13. That is Ivana's dictionary, _____?

14. Those are your gloves, _____?

15. The average lifespan of a horse is more than 40 years, _____?

And sea turtles can live to be more than 200, _____?

ONLY 40? YOU'RE JUST A YOUNGSTER.

☐ **EXERCISE 47. Tag questions. (Chart 5-16)**

Directions: Ask and answer tag questions.

Speaker A: Ask a tag question about someone in the room. Ask the person directly or direct the question to another classmate, as you prefer.

Speaker B: Answer.

Example: You think that someone in this room lives in an apartment.

SPEAKER A: (Maria), you live in an apartment, don't you?

SPEAKER B: Yes, I do. OR No, I don't.

Example: You think that someone in this room doesn't own a car.

SPEAKER A: (Maria), (Ali) doesn't own a car, does he?

SPEAKER B: No, he doesn't. OR Yes, he does. OR I don't know.

You think that someone in this room . . .

1. was in class yesterday.
2. didn't come to class a few days ago.
3. isn't married.
4. is from *(country)*.
5. can't speak *(language)*.
6. likes to play *(name of a sport)*.
7. will be in class tomorrow.
8. can whistle.
9. knows *(name of a person)*.
10. has met *(name of a person)*.
11. wore jeans to class yesterday.
12. has brown eyes.

□ **EXERCISE 48. Summary: creating and roleplaying dialogues. (Chapter 5)**
Directions: Work in pairs. Together create a long dialogue for one of the following situations. Present your dialogue to the class. The beginning of the dialogue is given.

1. SITUATION: The dialogue takes place on the telephone.
               Speaker A: You are a travel agent.
               Speaker B: You want to take a trip.

   DIALOGUE: *A: Hello. Worldwide Travel Agency. May I help you?*
               B: Yes. I need to make arrangements to go to . . . .
               A: Etc.

2. SITUATION: The dialogue takes place at a police station.
               Speaker A: You are a police officer.
               Speaker B: You are the suspect of a crime.

   DIALOGUE: *A: Where were you at eleven o'clock on Tuesday night, the 16th of last month?*
               B: I'm not sure I remember. Why do you want to know, Officer?
               A: Etc.

3. SITUATION: The dialogue takes place in an office.
               Speaker A: You are the owner of a small company.
               Speaker B: You are interviewing for a job in Speaker A's company.

   DIALOGUE: *A: Come in, come in. I'm (. . .). Glad to meet you.*
               B: How do you? I'm (. . .). I'm pleased to meet you.
               A: Have a seat, (. . .).
               B: Thank you.
               A: So you're interested in working at (make up the name of a company)?
               B: Yes, I am.
               A: Etc.

CHAPTER 6
Nouns and Pronouns

CONTENTS

☐ **EXERCISE 1. Preview: grammar terms. (Chapter 6)**

Directions: This exercise previews grammar terms used in this chapter. Identify the *italicized* word in each sentence as a NOUN, ADJECTIVE, PREPOSITION, or PRONOUN.

1.	Eric is wearing a new *shirt* today.	*shirt*	noun
2.	Algeria is *in* North Africa.	*in*	preposition
3.	Steve is in Asia. *He* is traveling.	*he*	pronoun
4.	I'm *thirsty*.	*thirsty*	adjective
5.	We have class in this *room* every day.	*room*	
6.	I know my *way* to Joanna's house.	*way*	
7.	The *happy* children squealed with joy.	*happy*	
8.	I walked to class *with* Maria.	*with*	
9.	Hawaii has eight principal *islands*.	*islands*	
10.	The *hungry* man stuffed his mouth with rice.	*hungry*	
11.	Tokyo is the capital of *Japan*.	*Japan*	
12.	Athens is a *beautiful* city.	*beautiful*	
13.	My history book is *under* my desk.	*under*	
14.	Do you like classical *music*?	*music*	
15.	I can't find my keys. Have you seen *them*?	*them*	

6-1 PRONUNCIATION OF FINAL -S/-ES

Final **-s/-es** has three different pronunciations: /s/, /z/, and /əz/.

(a)	seats = seat/s/ maps = map/s/ lakes = lake/s/	/s/ is the sound of "s" in "bus." Final **-s** is pronounced /s/ after voiceless sounds. Examples of voiceless* sounds: /t/, /p/, /k/.
(b)	seeds = seed/z/ stars = star/z/ holes = hole/z/ laws = law/z/	/z/ is the sound of "z" in "buzz." Final **-s** is pronounced /z/ after voiced sounds. Examples of voiced* sounds: /d/, /r/, /l/, /m/, /b/, and all vowel sounds.
(c)	dishes = dish/əz/ matches = match/əz/ classes = class/əz/ sizes = size/əz/ pages = page/əz/ judges = judge/əz/	/əz/ adds a whole syllable to a word. Final **-s/-es** is pronounced /əz/ after -sh, -ch, -s, -z, -ge/-dge sounds.

*See Chart 2-4, p. 28, for more information about voiceless and voiced sounds.

☐ **EXERCISE 2. Pronunciation of final -S/-ES. (Chart 6-1)**

Directions: Write the correct pronunciations and practice saying the words.

1. names = name/ z /
2. clocks = clock/ s /
3. eyes = eye/   /
4. heads = head/   /
5. boats = boat/   /
6. ribs = rib/   /
7. lips = lip/   /
8. hills = hill/   /
9. cars = car/   /
10. ways = way/   /
11. months = month/   /
12. eyelashes = eyelash/   /
13. itches = itch/   /
14. glasses = glass/   /
15. prices = price/   /
16. prizes = prize/   /
17. faxes = fax/   /
18. bridges = bridge/   /
19. cages = cage/   /

☐ **EXERCISE 3. Preview: plural nouns. (Chart 6-2)**

Directions: These sentences have many mistakes in the use of nouns. Underline each noun. Write the correct plural form if necessary. Do not change any of the other words in the sentences.

1. Chicago has busy street and highway. *(streets   highways)*
2. Box have six side.
3. Big city have many problem.
4. Banana grow in hot, humid area.
5. Insect don't have nose.
6. Lamb are the offspring of sheep.
7. Library keep book on shelf.
8. Parent support their child.

9. Indonesia has several active volcano.

10. Baboon are big monkey. They have large head and

sharp tooth. They eat leaf, root, insect, and egg.

6-2 PLURAL FORMS OF NOUNS

SINGULAR	PLURAL	
(a) one bird one street one rose	two *birds* two *streets* two *roses*	To make most nouns plural, add *-s*.
(b) one dish one match one class one box	two *dishes* two *matches* two *classes* two *boxes*	Add *-es* to nouns ending in *-sh*, *-ch*, *-ss*, and *-x*.
(c) one baby one city (d) one toy one key	two *babies* two *cities* two *toys* two *keys*	If a noun ends in a consonant + *-y*, change the *y* to *i* and add *-es*, as in (c). If *-y* is preceded by a vowel, add only *-s*, as in (d).
(e) one knife one shelf	two *knives* two *shelves*	If a noun ends in *-fe* or *-f*, change the ending to *-ves*. (Exceptions: *beliefs, chiefs, roofs, cuffs, cliffs.*)

(f) one tomato
one zoo
one zero
	two *tomatoes*
	two *zoos*
	two *zeroes/zeros*
		The plural form of nouns that end in *-o* is sometimes *-oes* and sometimes *-os*.
		  -oes: *tomatoes, potatoes, heroes, echoes*
		  -os: *zoos, radios, studios, pianos, solos, sopranos, photos, autos, videos*
		  -oes or *-os*: *zeroes/zeros; volcanoes/volcanos, tornadoes/tornados, mosquitoes/mosquitos*

(g) one child one foot one goose one man one mouse one tooth one woman ——————	two *children* two *feet* two *geese* two *men* two *mice* two *teeth* two *women* two *people*	Some nouns have irregular plural forms. (Note: The singular form of *people* can be *person, woman, man, child*. For example, one man and one child = two people.)
(h) one deer one fish one sheep one offspring one species	two *deer* two *fish* two *sheep* two *offspring* two *species*	The plural form of some nouns is the same as the singular form.
(i) one bacterium one cactus one crisis one phenomenon	two *bacteria* two *cacti* two *crises* two *phenomena*	Some nouns that English has borrowed from other languages have foreign plurals.

☐ **EXERCISE 4. Plural nouns. (Chart 6-2)**

Directions: Write the plural forms of the nouns.

1. one potato, two _____**potatoes**_____
2. a library, many _____
3. one child, two _____
4. a leaf, a lot of _____
5. a wish, many _____
6. one fish, two _____
7. an opinion, many _____
8. a mouse, several _____
9. a sandwich, some _____
10. a man, many _____
11. one woman, two _____
12. a flash, three _____
13. one tomato, a few _____
14. one tooth, two _____
15. one half, two _____

16. a tax, a lot of _____
17. a possibility, several _____
18. a thief, many _____
19. a hero, many _____
20. a goose, a lot of _____
21. an attorney, a few _____
22. a butterfly, several _____
23. one category, two _____
24. a mosquito, a lot of _____
25. one sheep, two _____
26. a wolf, some _____
27. one stitch, two _____
28. one foot, three _____
29. one piano, two _____
30. a belief, many _____

6-3 SUBJECTS, VERBS, AND OBJECTS

(a) The **sun** **shines.**
      (noun) (verb)
 	
 (b) **Plants** **grow.**
    (noun) (verb)
	An English sentence has a SUBJECT (**s**) and a VERB (**v**).
	
	 The SUBJECT is a **noun.** In (a): *sun* is a noun; it is the subject of the verb *shines*.

(c) **Plants** **need** **water.** (noun) (verb) (noun) (d) **Bob** **is reading** a **book.** (noun) (verb) (noun)	Sometimes a VERB is followed by an OBJECT (**o**). The OBJECT of a verb is a **noun.** In (c): *water* is the object of the verb *need*.

☐ EXERCISE 5. Subjects, verbs, and objects. (Chart 6-3)

Directions: Identify the subject (**s**) and verb (**v**) of each sentence. Also find the object (**o**) of the verb if the sentence has an object.

                s   v   o

1. The carpenter built a table.

          s   v

2. Birds fly.

3. Cows eat grass.

4. My dog barked.

5. The dog chased the cat.

6. Steam rises.

7. Accidents happen.

8. Most birds build nests.

9. Our guests arrived.

10. Teachers assign homework.

11. My roommate opened the window.

12. Jack raised his hand.

13. Irene is watching her sister's children.

☐ EXERCISE 6. Nouns and verbs. (Charts 6-2 and 6-3)

Directions: Some words can be used both as a noun and as a verb. If the word in *italics* is used as a noun, circle **n.** If the word in *italics* is used as a verb, circle **v.** (**n.** = **noun** and **v.** = **verb**)

1. **n.** (**v.**)   People *smile* when they're happy.

2. (**n.**) **v.**   Mary has a nice *smile* when she's happy.

3. **n.** **v.**   Emily does good *work*.

4. **n.** **v.**   Emily and Mike *work* at the cafeteria.

5. **n.** **v.**   People usually *store* milk in the refrigerator.

6. **n.** **v.**   We went to the *store* to buy some milk.

7. **n.** **v.**   The child wrote her *name* on the wall with a crayon.

8. **n.** **v.**   People often *name* their children after relatives.

9. **n.** **v.**   Airplanes *land* on runways at the airport.

10. **n.** **v.**   The ship reached *land* after seventeen days at sea.

11. **n.** **v.**   I took a *train* from New York to Boston last week.

12. **n.** **v.**   I *train* my dogs to sit on command.

13. **n.** **v.**   Alex *visits* his aunt every week.

14. **n.** **v.**   Alex's aunt enjoys his *visits* every week.

Directions: Use each word in **two** different sentences. Use the word as a noun (**n.**) in the first sentence and as a verb (**v.**) in the second sentence. Consult your dictionary if necessary to find out the different uses and meanings of a word.

Example: watch

→   n. *I am wearing a **watch**.*
     v. *I **watched** TV after dinner last night.*

1. rain	4. phone	7. water
2. paint	5. shop	8. circle
3. tie	6. face	9. fly

Other common words that are used as both nouns and verbs are listed below. Choose several from the list to make additional sentences. Use your dictionary if necessary.

center/centre★	garden	question	snow
date	mail	rock	star
experience	mind	season	tip
e-mail	place	sense	trip
fear	plant	shape	value
fish	promise	smoke	

6-4 OBJECTS OF PREPOSITIONS

S   **V**   **O**   **PREP**   **O OF PREP**
(a) Ann put her books **on** *the* **desk**.
                             (noun)
 	
    S   **V** **PREP**   **O OF PREP**
(b) A leaf fell **to** *the* **ground**.
                    (noun)
	Many English sentences have prepositional phrases. In (a): *on the desk* is a prepositional phrase. A prepositional phrase consists of a PREPOSITION (**PREP**) and an OBJECT OF A PREPOSITION (**O OF PREP**). The object of a preposition is a NOUN.

REFERENCE LIST OF PREPOSITIONS

about	*before*	*despite*	*of*	*to*
above	*behind*	*down*	*off*	*toward(s)*
across	*below*	*during*	*on*	*under*
after	*beneath*	*for*	*out*	*until*
against	*beside*	*from*	*over*	*up*
along	*besides*	*in*	*since*	*upon*
among	*between*	*into*	*through*	*with*
around	*beyond*	*like*	*throughout*	*within*
at	*by*	*near*	*till*	*without*

★American English: *center;* British English: *centre.*

☐ EXERCISE 8. Subjects, verbs, and objects. (Charts 6-3 and 6-4)

Directions: Identify the subjects, verbs, and objects. Also identify the preposition (**PREP**) and the noun that is used as the object of the preposition (**O OF PREP**).

```
        S    V      O      PREP  O of PREP
1.   Sara saw a picture   on    the wall.
```

2. Sara looked at the pictures.

3. Emily waited for her friend at a restaurant.

4. The sun rises in the east.

5. Sue lost her ring in the sand at the beach.

6. The moon usually disappears from view during the day.

7. Eric talked to his friend on the phone for thirty minutes.

8. Children throughout the world play with dolls.

9. Astronauts walked on the moon in 1969.

10. A woman in a blue suit sat beside me until the end of the meeting.

☐ EXERCISE 9. Prepositions of place. (Chart 6-4)

Directions: Review prepositions of place* by using the following phrases in sentences. Demonstrate the meaning of the preposition by some action. Work in pairs, in small groups, or as a class.

Example: above my head
→ *I'm holding my hand above my head.* (The speaker demonstrates this action.)

1. across the room
2. against the wall
3. among my books and papers
4. between two pages of my book
5. around my wrist
6. at my desk
7. on my desk
8. in the room
9. into the room
10. behind me

11. below the window
12. beside my book
13. near the door
14. far from the door
15. off my desk
16. out the window
17. under my desk
18. through the door
19. throughout the room
20. toward(s) the door

---

*Prepositions of place are also called "prepositions of location."

6-5 PREPOSITIONS OF TIME

IN	(a) Please be on time *in the future.* (b) I usually watch TV *in the evening.*	*in* + the past, the present, the future* *in* + the morning, the afternoon, the evening
	(c) I was born *in October.* (d) I was born *in 1985.* (e) I was born *in the twentieth century.* (f) The weather is hot *in (the) summer.*	*in* + { a month a year a century a season }
ON	(g) I was born *on October 31, 1985.* (h) I went to a movie *on Thursday.* (i) I have class *on Thursday morning(s).*	*on* + a date *on* + a weekday *on* + a weekday morning(s), afternoon(s), evening(s)
AT	(j) We sleep at night. I was asleep *at midnight.* (k) I fell asleep *at 9:30 (nine-thirty).* (l) He's busy *at present.* Please call again.	*at* + noon, night, midnight *at* + "clock time" *at* + present, the moment, the present time

*Possible in British English: *in future (Please be on time in future.).*

☐ EXERCISE 10. Prepositions of time. (Chart 6-5)
   Directions: Complete the sentences with *in, at,* or *on*. All the sentences contain time expressions.

   1. We don't know what will happen ____in____ the future.

   2. History is the study of events that occurred _____ the past.

   3. Newspapers report events that happen _____ the present.

   4. Last year I was a junior in high school. _____ present, I am a senior in high school.

   5. I am a student _____ the present time, but I will graduate next month.

   6. Ms. Walker can't come to the phone right now. She's in a meeting _____ the moment.

   7. I usually take a walk _____ the morning before I go to work.

   8. Frank likes to take a nap _____ the afternoon.

   9. Our family enjoys spending time together _____ the evening.

   10. Our children always stay home _____ night.

   11. I ate lunch _____ noon.

   12. I got home _____ midnight.

   13. I moved to this city _____ September.

   14. I moved here _____ 2001.

   15. I moved here _____ September 2001.

   16. I moved here _____ September 3.

   17. I moved here _____ September 3, 2001.

18. I moved here _____ the fall.

19. I work _____ the morning. _____ the afternoon, I have an English class.

20. _____ Wednesday, I work all day. _____ Thursday, I have an English class.

21. _____ Thursday afternoon, I have an English class.

22. My plane was supposed to leave _____ 7:07 P.M., but it didn't take off until 8:30.

□ EXERCISE 11. Prepositions of time. (Chart 6-5)
    Directions: Supply the appropriate preposition and create a sentence.

    Example: _____ the moment
        → **at** *the moment*
        *We're doing an exercise on prepositions **at the moment**.*

1. _____ the future	7. _____ January 1, 1999		
2. _____ present	8. _____ the twenty-first century		
3. _____ the winter	9. _____ the evening		
4. _____ January	10. _____ night		
5. _____ January 1	11. _____ Saturday morning(s)		
6. _____ 1999	12. _____ six o'clock _____ the morning		

6-6 WORD ORDER: PLACE AND TIME

S **V** **PLACE** **TIME** (a) Ann moved *to Paris* *in 1998.* We went *to a movie* *yesterday.*	In a typical English sentence, "place" comes before "time," as in (a). *INCORRECT: Ann moved in 1998 to Paris.*
S **V** **O** **P** **T** (b) We bought a house in Miami in 1995.	S-V-O-P-T = Subject-Verb-Object-Place-Time S-V-O-P-T = a basic English sentence structure.
TIME **S** **V** **PLACE** (c) *In 1998,* Ann moved to Paris. (d) *Yesterday* we went to a movie.	Expressions of time can also come at the beginning of a sentence, as in (c) and (d). A time phrase at the beginning of a sentence is often followed by a comma, as in (c).

□ EXERCISE 12. Word order: place and time. (Chart 6-6)
    Directions: Create sentences from the given words. Add prepositions as necessary.

    Example: Bangkok / we / February / went
        → *We went to Bangkok in February.*   OR   *In February, we went to Bangkok.*

    1. his uncle's bakery / Alex / Saturday mornings / works

    2. the evening / often take / the park / a walk / I

    3. arrived / the morning / the airport / my plane / six-thirty

6-7 SUBJECT–VERB AGREEMENT

SINGULAR SINGULAR (a) The sun shine**s**. PLURAL PLURAL (b) *Bird**s*** *sing*.	A singular subject takes a singular verb, as in (a). A plural subject takes a plural verb, as in (b). Notice: *verb* + **-s** = singular (*shines*) *noun* + **-s** = plural (*birds*)
SINGULAR SINGULAR (c) *My brother* ***lives*** in Jakarta. PLURAL PLURAL (d) *My brother **and** sister* ***live*** in Jakarta.	Two subjects connected by ***and*** take a plural verb, as in (d).
(e) The ***glasses*** over there under the window by the sink ***are*** clean. (f) The ***information*** in those magazines about Vietnamese culture and customs ***is*** very interesting.	Sometimes phrases come between a subject and a verb. These phrases do not affect the agreement of the subject and verb.
v s (g) *There **is** a **book*** on the desk. v s (h) *There **are** some **books*** on the desk.	***There*** + ***be*** + *subject* expresses that something exists in a particular place. The verb agrees with the noun that follows ***be***.
(i) ***Every student is*** sitting down. (j) ***Everybody/Everyone hopes*** for peace.	***Every*** is a singular word. It is used with a singular, not plural, noun. *INCORRECT: Every students . . . .* Subjects with ***every*** take singular verbs, as in (i) and (j).
(k) ***People*** in my country ***are*** friendly.	***People*** is a plural noun and takes a plural verb.

☐ EXERCISE 13. Subject–verb agreement. (Chart 6-7)
Directions: <u>Underline</u> and identify the subject (**s**) and the verb (**v**). Correct errors in agreement.

          s   v
1. <u>Earthquakes</u> <u>occurs</u> every day of the year.

2. <u>Candles</u> <u>burn</u> slowly. OK (*no error*)

3. My mother speak Spanish.

4. My aunt and uncle speak Spanish.

5. Oscar speaks Spanish and English.

6. The students in this class speaks English very well.

7. Every students in my class speak English well.

8. There are five student from Korea in Mr. Brown's class.

9. There's a vacant apartment in my building.

10. Does people in the United States like Chinese food?

11. The people in Brazil speaks Portuguese.

12. There is many different kinds of fish in the ocean.

13. The neighbors in the apartment next to mine is very friendly and helpful.

14. Every students in this room have a grammar book.

6-8 USING ADJECTIVES TO DESCRIBE NOUNS

ADJ NOUN (a) Bob is reading a **good** book.	Words that describe nouns are called *adjectives*. In (a): **good** is an adjective; it describes the book.
(b) The **tall** woman wore a **new** dress. (c) The **short** woman wore an **old** dress. (d) The **young** woman wore a **short** dress.	We say that adjectives "modify" nouns. "Modify" means "change a little." An adjective changes the meaning of a noun by giving more information about it.
(e) Roses are **beautiful** flowers. INCORRECT: *Roses are beautifuls flowers.*	Adjectives are neither singular nor plural. They do NOT have a plural form.
(f) He wore a **white** shirt. INCORRECT: *He wore a shirt white.* (g) Roses *are* **beautiful**. (h) His shirt *was* **white**.	Adjectives usually come immediately before nouns, as in (f). Adjectives can also follow main verb *be*, as in (g) and (h).

☐ EXERCISE 14. Adjectives. (Chart 6-8)
    Directions: <u>Underline</u> and identify the adjectives (**ADJ**) in the sentences.

                     ADJ
1. The students wrote <u>long</u> compositions.

2. Deserts are dry.

3. Crocodiles have big teeth.

4. Knives are sharp.

5. Dark places frighten small children.

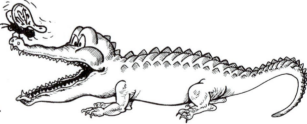

6. The audience laughed at the funny joke.

7. Sensible people wear comfortable shoes.

8. Steve cleaned the shelves of the refrigerator with soapy water.

9. The local police searched the stolen car for illegal drugs.

10. Before the development of agriculture, primitive people gathered wild plants for food.

Directions: Add adjectives to the sentences. Choose **two** of the three adjectives in each item to add to the given sentence.

Example: hard, heavy, strong   A man lifted the box.
   → *A strong man lifted the heavy box.*

1. *beautiful, safe, red*   Roses are flowers.

2. *dark, cold, dry*   Rain fell from the clouds.

3. *empty, wet, hot*   The waiter poured coffee into my cup.

4. *easy, blue, young*   The girl in the dress was looking for a telephone.

5. *quiet, sharp, soft*   Annie sleeps on a bed in a room.

6. *fresh, clear, hungry*   Mrs. Fox gave the children some fruit.

7. *dirty, modern, delicious*   After we finished our dinner, Frank helped me with the dishes.

8. *round, inexperienced, right*   When Tom was getting a haircut, the barber accidentally cut Tom's ear with the scissors.

☐ EXERCISE 16. Adjectives and nouns. (Chart 6-8)

Directions: Don't look at the passage in Part II on the next page. First write the words asked for in Part I. Don't use the same word twice. Then turn the page and use the words to complete Part II.

PART I. Write:

1. an adjective _____old_____

2. a name _____

3. a plural noun _____

4. a plural noun _____

5. a singular noun _____

6. an adjective _____

7. an adjective _____

8. a preposition of place _____

9. an adjective _____

10. a plural noun _____

PART II. Write the words on your list in the blanks. Some of your completions might be a little odd and funny. Read your completed passage aloud in a group or to the rest of the class.

One day a/an _____old_____ girl was walking in the city. Her name was
                     1

_____ . She was carrying a package for her grandmother. It
          2

contained some _____ , some _____ , and
                         3   4

a/an _____ , among other things.
              5

    As she was walking down the street, a/an _____ thief stole
                                                                 6

her package. The _____ girl pulled out her cell phone and called
                          7

the police, who caught the thief _____ a nearby building and
                                           8

returned her package to her. She took it immediately to her _____
                                                                          9

grandmother, who was glad to get the package because she really needed some new

_____ .
          10

6-9 USING NOUNS AS ADJECTIVES

(a) I have a ***flower*** garden. (b) The ***shoe*** store also sells socks. (c) INCORRECT: a flowers garden (d) INCORRECT: the shoes store	Sometimes words that are usually used as nouns are used as adjectives. For example, *flower* is usually a noun, but in (a) it is used as an adjective to modify *garden*. When a noun is used as an adjective, it is singular in form, NOT plural.

☐ **EXERCISE 17. Using nouns as adjectives. (Chart 6-9)**
    Directions: <u>Underline</u> and identify the nouns (N). Use a noun in the first sentence as an adjective in the second sentence.

         N   N
    1. This <u>book</u> is about <u>grammar</u>. It's a ____*grammar book**_____ .

    2. My garden has vegetables. It is a _____ .

    3. The program is on television. It's a _____ .

    4. The soup has beans. It is _____ .

_____

*When one noun modifies another noun, the spoken stress is usually on the first noun: a ***grammar*** book.

5. We made plans for our vacation. We made _____.

6. I read a lot of articles in newspapers. I read a lot of _____.

7. The factory makes automobiles. It's an _____.

8. The lesson concerned history. It was a _____.

9. The villages are in the mountains. They are _____.

10. Flags fly from poles. Many government buildings have _____.

☐ **EXERCISE 18. Using nouns as adjectives. (Chart 6-9)**
Directions: Add *-s* to the *italicized* nouns if necessary.

1. *Computer*ˢ cannot think. They need human operators.

2. *Computer* operators are essential in today's business world. OK *(no change)*

3. *Airplane* allow us to travel to all parts of the world.

4. *Airplane* seats are narrow and uncomfortable.

5. This school has several *language* programs.

6. This school teaches several *language*.

7. *Bicycle* have two tires. *Automobile* have four tires.

8. *Bicycle* tires are considerably smaller and cheaper than *automobile* tires.

☐ **EXERCISE 19. Review: nouns. (Charts 6-1 → 6-9)**
Directions: These sentences contain many mistakes in noun usage. Make the nouns PLURAL whenever possible and appropriate. Do not change any other words.

1. Birdˢ are interesting.

2. There are around 8,600 kind of bird in the world.

3. Bird hatch from egg. Baby bird stay in their nest for several week or month. Their parent feed them until they can fly.

4. People eat chicken egg. Some animal eat bird egg.

5. Fox and snake are natural enemy of bird. They eat bird and their egg.

6. Some bird eat only seed and plant. Other bird eat mainly insect and earthworm.

7. Weed are unwanted plant. They prevent farm crop or garden flower from growing properly. Bird help farmer by eating weed seed and harmful insect.

8. Rat, rabbit, and mouse can cause huge loss on farm by eating stored crop. Certain big bird like hawk help farmer by hunting these animal.

9. The feather of certain kind of bird are used in pillow and mattress. The soft feather from goose are often used for pillow and quilt. Goose feather are also used in winter jacket.

10. The wing feather from goose were used as pen from the sixth century to the nineteenth century, when steel pen were invented.

□ **EXERCISE 20. Review: nouns. (Charts 6-1 → 6-9)**
Directions: Find the nouns. Make them plural if necessary.

(1)   ~~Whale~~ Whales look like fish, but they aren't fish. They are mammal. Mouse, tiger,

(2)   and human being are other example of mammal. Whale are intelligent animal like

(3)   dog and chimpanzee. Even though they live in sea, ocean, and river, whale are

(4)   not fish. Fish lay egg and do not feed their offspring. Mammal give birth to live

(5)   offspring and feed them.

(6)   There are many kind of whale. Most whale are huge creature. The largest

(7)   whale are called blue whale. They can grow to 100 foot (30 meter) in length and

(8)   can weigh 150 ton (135,000 kilogram). Blue whale are much larger than elephant

(9)   and larger than any of the now extinct dinosaur. The heart of an adult blue whale

RELATIVE SIZES OF A BLUE WHALE
AND AN AFRICAN ELEPHANT

(10)   is about the size of a compact car. Its main blood vessel, the aorta, is large

(11)   enough for a person to crawl through.

(12)   Human being have hunted and killed whale since ancient times. Aside from

(13)   people, whale have no natural enemy. Today many people are trying to stop the

(14)   the hunting of whale.

6-10   PERSONAL PRONOUNS: SUBJECTS AND OBJECTS

PERSONAL PRONOUNS

SUBJECT PRONOUNS:	*I*	*we*	*you*	*he, she, it*	*they*
OBJECT PRONOUNS:	*me*	*us*	*you*	*him, her, it*	*them*

(a) **Kate** is married. **She** has two children. *(S)*	A pronoun refers to a noun. In (a): **she** is a pronoun; it refers to **Kate**. In (b): **her** is a pronoun; it refers to **Kate**. **She** is a subject pronoun; **her** is an object pronoun.
(b) **Kate** is my friend. I know **her** well. *(O)*	
(c) Mike has **a new blue bicycle**. He bought **it** yesterday.	A pronoun can refer to a single noun (e.g., *Kate*) or to a noun phrase. In (c): **it** refers to the whole noun phrase *a new blue bicycle*.
(d) *Eric and **I*** are good friends. *(S)*	Guidelines for using pronouns following **and**: If the pronoun is used as part of the subject, use a subject pronoun, as in (d). If it is part of the object, use an object pronoun, as in (e) and (f). *INCORRECT: Eric and me are good friends.* *INCORRECT: Ann met Eric and I at the museum.*
(e) Ann met *Eric and **me*** at the museum. *(O)*	
(f) Ann walked between *Eric and **me***. *(O of PREP)*	

SINGULAR PRONOUNS:	*I*	*me*	*you*	*he, she, it*	*him, her*
PLURAL PRONOUNS:	*we*	*us*	*you*	*they*	*them*

(g) **Mike** is in class. **He** is taking a test. (h) The **students** are in class. **They** are taking a test. (i) **Kate and Tom** are married. **They** have two children.	*Singular* = one. *Plural* = more than one. Singular pronouns refer to singular nouns, plural pronouns to plural nouns, as in the examples.

□ **EXERCISE 21. Personal pronouns: subjects and objects. (Chart 6-10)**
  Directions: Circle the correct words in *italics*.

  1. Nick ate dinner with *I,* (*me.*)

  2. Nick ate dinner with Betsy and *I, me.*

  3. *I, Me* had dinner with Nick last night.

  4. Betsy and *I, me* had dinner with Nick last night.

  5. Please take this food and give *it, them* to the dog.

  6. Please take these food scraps and give *it, them* to the dog.

  7. My brother drove Emily and *I, me* to the store. He didn't come in. He waited for
     we, us in the car. *We, Us* hurried.

  8. A: I want to get tickets for the soccer game.

     B: You'd better get *it, them* right away. *It, They* *is, are* selling fast.

  9. Ms. Lee wrote a note on my test paper. *She, Her* wanted to talk to *I, me* after class.

  10. Between you and *I, me,* I think Ivan made a bad decision to quit his job.
      He, Him and *I, me* see things differently.

□ **EXERCISE 22. Personal pronouns. (Chart 6-10)**
  Directions: Complete the sentences with **she, he, it, her, him, they,** or **them.**

  1. I have a grammar book. _____It_____ is black.

  2. Tom borrowed my books. _____He_____ returned ____them____ yesterday.

  3. Susan is wearing some new earrings. _____ look good on _____ .

  4. Table tennis (also called ping-pong) began in England in the late 1800s. Today

     _____ is an international sport. My brother and I played _____ a

     lot when we were teenagers. I beat

     _____ sometimes, but

     _____ was a better player and

     usually won.

5. Don't look directly at the sun. Don't look at _____ directly even if you are wearing sunglasses. The intensity of its light can injure your eyes.

6. Do bees sleep at night? Or do _____ work in the hive all night long? You never see _____ after dark. What do _____ do after night falls?

7. The apples were rotten, so the children didn't eat _____ even though _____ were really hungry.

8. The scent of perfume rises. According to one expert, you should put _____ on the soles of your feet.

9. Even though clean, safe water is fundamental to human health, an estimated 800 million people in the world are still without _____ . Unsafe water causes illnesses. _____ contributes to high numbers of deaths in children under five years of age.

10. Magazines are popular. I enjoy reading _____ . _____ have news about recent events and discoveries. Recently, I read about "micromachines." _____ are human-made machines that are smaller than a grain of sand. One scientist called _____ "the greatest scientific invention of our time."

6-11 POSSESSIVE NOUNS

SINGULAR: (a) I know the **student's** name. PLURAL: (b) I know the **students'** names. PLURAL: (c) I know the **children's** names.		An apostrophe (') and an **-s** are used with nouns to show possession.

<table>
<tr>
<td rowspan="2">Singular</td>
<td>(d) the student → the **student's** name
my baby → my **baby's** name
a man → a **man's** name</td>
<td>SINGULAR POSSESSIVE NOUN:
   noun + apostrophe (') + -s</td>
</tr>
<tr>
<td>(e) James → **James'/James's** name</td>
<td>A singular noun that ends in -s has two possible possessive forms: *James'* OR *James's*.</td>
</tr>
<tr>
<td rowspan="2">Plural</td>
<td>(f) the students → the **students'** names
my babies → my **babies'** names</td>
<td>PLURAL POSSESSIVE NOUN:
   noun + -s + apostrophe (')</td>
</tr>
<tr>
<td>(g) men → **men's** names
the children → the **children's** names</td>
<td>IRREGULAR PLURAL POSSESSIVE NOUN:
   noun + apostrophe (') + -s
(An irregular plural noun is a plural noun that does not end in **-s**: *children, men, people, women*. See Chart 6-2, p. 158.)</td>
</tr>
<tr>
<td colspan="2">COMPARE
(h) **Tom's** here.
(i) **Tom's** brother is here.</td>
<td>In (h): **Tom's** is not a possessive. It is a contraction of *Tom is*, used in informal writing.
In (i): **Tom's** is a possessive.</td>
</tr>
</table>

Directions: Use the correct possessive form of the nouns in *italics* to complete the sentences.

1. *student*   One student asked several questions. I answered the ___student's___ questions.

2. *students*   Many students had questions after the lecture. I answered the ___students'___ questions.

3. *daughter*   We have one child, a girl. Our _____ bedroom is near ours.

4. *daughters*   We have two children, both girls. They share a bedroom. Our _____ bedroom is next to ours.

5. *man*   Robert is a _____ name.

6. *woman*   Heidi is a _____ name.

7. *men*   Robert and Thomas are _____ names.

8. *women*   Emily and Colette are _____ names.

9. *people*   It's important to be sensitive to other _____ feelings.

10. *person*   I always look straight into a _____ eyes during a conversation.

11. *earth*   The _____ surface is about seventy percent water.

12. *elephant*   An _____ skin is gray and wrinkled.

13. *teachers*   We have class in this building, but all of the _____ offices are in another building.

14. *teacher*   My grammar _____ husband is an engineer.

15. *enemy*   Two soldiers, each faceless and nameless to the other, fought to the death on the muddy river bank. At the end, the victor could not help but admire his _____ courage.

16. *enemies*   Through the years in public office, he made many political enemies. He made a list of his _____ names so that he could get revenge when he achieved political power.

17. *Chris*   Did you add _____ name to the invitation list?

□ EXERCISE 24. Possessive nouns. (Chart 6-11)

Directions: These sentences contain mistakes in the punctuation of possessive nouns. Add apostrophes in the right places.

1. A king's chair is called a throne.

2. Kings' chairs are called thrones.

3. Babies toys are often brightly colored.

4. It's important to make sure your babys toys are safe for babies to play with.

5. Someone called, but because of the static on the cell phone, I couldn't understand the callers words.

6. A receptionists job is to write down callers names and take messages.

7. Newspapers aren't interested in yesterdays news. They want to report todays events.

8. Each flight has at least two pilots. The pilots seats are in a small area called the cockpit.

9. Rainforests cover five percent of the earths surface but have fifty percent of the different species of plants.

10. Mosquitoes wings move incredibly fast.

11. A mosquitos wings move about one thousand times per second. Its wing movement is the sound we hear when a mosquito is humming in our ears.

12. Elephants like to roll in mud. The mud protects the animals skin from insects and the sun.

13. When we were walking in the woods, we saw an animals footprints on the muddy path.

☐ EXERCISE 25. Review of nouns + -S/-ES. (Charts 6-1 → 6-11)
Directions: Add *-s/-es* if necessary. Add apostrophes to possessive nouns as appropriate.

Butterflies
1. ~~Butterfly~~ are beautiful.

David's
2. Nick is ~~David~~ brother.

3. Most leaf are green.

4. My mother apartment is small.

5. Potato are good for us.

6. Do bird have tooth?

7. Tom last name is Miller.

8. Two thief stole Mr. Lee car.

9. Mountain are high, and valley are low.

10. A good toy holds a child interest for a long time.

11. Children toy need to be strong and safe.

12. All of the actor name are listed on page six of your program.

13. Teacher are interested in young people idea.

14. Almost all monkey have opposable thumb on not only their hand but also their foot.

    People have thumb only on their hand.

6-12 POSSESSIVE PRONOUNS AND ADJECTIVES

This pen belongs to me. (a) It's **mine**. (b) It is **my** pen.	(a) and (b) have the same meaning; they both show possession. **Mine** is a *possessive pronoun;* **my** is a *possessive adjective.*
POSSESSIVE PRONOUNS (c) I have **mine**. (d) You have **yours**. (e) She has **hers**. (f) He has **his**. (g) We have **ours**. (h) You have **yours**. (i) They have **theirs**. (j) ———————	POSSESSIVE ADJECTIVES I have **my** pen. You have **your** pen. She has **her** pen. He has **his** pen. We have **our** pens. You have **your** pen. They have **their** pens. I have a book. **Its** *cover* is black.	A **possessive pronoun** is used alone, without a noun following it. A **possessive adjective** is used only with a noun following it. *INCORRECT: I have mine pen.* *INCORRECT: I have my.*
COMPARE *its* vs. *it's:* (k) Sue gave me a book. I don't remember **its** title. (l) Sue gave me a book. **It's** a novel.	In (k): **its** (NO apostrophe) is a possessive adjective modifying the noun *title.* In (l): **It's** (with an apostrophe) is a contraction of *it + is.*
COMPARE *their* vs. *there* vs. *they're:* (m) The students have **their** books. (n) My books are over **there**. (o) Where are the students? **They're** in class.	**Their, there,** and **they're** have the same pronunciation, but not the same meaning. **their** = possessive adjective, as in (m). **there** = an expression of place, as in (n). **they're** = *they are,* as in (o).

☐ **EXERCISE 26. Possessive pronouns and adjectives. (Chart 6-12)**

Directions: Circle the correct words in *italics*.

1. Alice called *(her,) hers* friend.

2. Tom wrote a letter to *his, he's* mother.

3. Children should obey *his, their* parents.

4. A: Excuse me. Is this *my, mine* dictionary or *your, yours?*

    B: This one is *my, mine. Your, Yours* is on *your, yours* desk.

5. The bird cleaned *its, it's* feathers with *its, it's* beak.

6. A: What kind of bird is that?

    B: *Its, It's* a crow.

7. Paula had to drive my car to work.
   Hers, Her had a flat tire.

8. Julie fell off her bicycle and broke *hers, her* arm.

9. Fruit should be a part of *your, yours* daily diet.
   It, They is, are good for *you, your.*

10. a. Adam and Amanda are married. *They, Them* live in an apartment building.

    b. *Their, There, They're* apartment is on the fifth floor.

    c. We live in the same building. *Our, Ours* apartment has one bedroom, but
       their, theirs has two.

    d. *Their, There, They're* sitting
       their, there, they're now because
       their, there, they're waiting for a
       phone call from *their, there, they're*
       son.

11. Alice is a good friend of *me, mine.*★

12. I met a friend of *you, yours* yesterday.

_____

★*A friend of* + possessive pronoun (e.g., *a friend of mine*) is a common expression.

6-13 REFLEXIVE PRONOUNS

myself	(a) *I saw **myself** in the mirror.*	Reflexive pronouns end in *-self/-selves*. They are used when the subject (e.g., *I*) and the object (e.g., *myself*) are the same person. The action of the verb is pointed back to the subject of the sentence.
yourself	(b) *You (one person) saw **yourself**.*	
herself	(c) *She saw **herself**.*	
himself	(d) *He saw **himself**.*	
itself	(e) *It (e.g., the kitten) saw **itself**.*	*INCORRECT: I saw me in the mirror.*
ourselves	(f) *We saw **ourselves**.*	
yourselves	(g) *You (plural) saw **yourselves**.*	
themselves	(h) *They saw **themselves**.*	

(i) *Greg lives **by himself**.*	***By** + a reflexive pronoun* = alone. In (i): Greg lives alone, without family or roommates.
(j) *I sat **by myself** on the park bench.*	

(k) *I **enjoyed myself** at the fair.*	*Enjoy* and a few other verbs are commonly followed by a reflexive pronoun. See the list below.

COMMON EXPRESSIONS WITH REFLEXIVE PRONOUNS

believe in yourself	*help yourself*	*pinch yourself*	*teach yourself*
blame yourself	*hurt yourself*	*be proud of yourself*	*tell yourself*
cut yourself	*give yourself (something)*	*take care of yourself*	*work for yourself*
enjoy yourself	*introduce yourself*	*talk to yourself*	*wish yourself (luck)*
feel sorry for yourself	*kill yourself*		

☐ **EXERCISE 27. Reflexive pronouns. (Chart 6-13)**

Directions: Using a mirror in the classroom, describe who is looking at whom.

Example: (. . .) holds the mirror and looks into it.

TEACHER: What is Spyros doing?

SPEAKER A: He is looking at **himself** in the mirror.

TEACHER: What are you doing, Spyros?

SPYROS: I am looking at **myself** in the mirror.

TEACHER: Tell Spyros what he is doing.

SPEAKER B: Spyros, you are looking at **yourself** in the mirror

Example: (. . .) and (. . .) hold the mirror and look into it.

TEACHER: What are (Min Sok) and (Ivonne) doing? Etc.

☐ EXERCISE 28. Reflexive pronouns. (Chart 6-13)

Directions: Complete the sentences with reflexive pronouns.

1. Are you okay, Heidi? Did you hurt _____yourself_____?

2. David was really embarrassed when he had to go to the job interview with a bandage on his face. He had cut _____ while he was shaving.

3. Do you ever talk to _____? Most people talk to _____ sometimes.

4. It is important for all of us to have confidence in our own abilities. We need to believe in _____ .

5. Sara is self-employed. She doesn't have a boss. She works for _____ .

6. Steve, who is on the wrestling team, wishes _____ good luck before each match.

7. There's plenty of food on the table. Would all of you please simply help _____ to the food?

8. Brian, don't blame _____ for the accident. It wasn't your fault. You did everything you could to avoid it.

9. I couldn't believe my good luck! I had to pinch _____ to make sure I wasn't dreaming.

10. A newborn puppy can't take care of _____ .

11. I know Nicole and Paul have had some bad luck, but it's time for them to stop feeling sorry for _____ and get on with their lives.

12. Jane and I ran into someone she knew. I'd never met this person before. I waited for Jane to introduce me, but she forgot her manners. I finally introduced _____ to Jane's friend.

☐ EXERCISE 29. Reflexive pronouns. (Chart 6-13)

Directions: Complete the sentences with any appropriate expression from the list in Chart 6-13 and reflexive pronouns. Use any appropriate verb tense.

1. The accident was my fault. I caused it. I was responsible. In other words, I _____blamed myself_____ for the accident.

2. Be careful with that sharp knife! You _____ if you're not careful.

3. It was the first day of class. I sat next to another student and started a conversation about the class and the classroom. After we had talked for a few minutes, I said, "Hi. My name is Rita Woo." In other words, I _____ to the other student.

4. When I walked into the room, I heard Joe's voice. I looked around, but the only person I saw and heard was Joe. In other words, Joe _____ _____ when I walked into the room.

5. My wife and I have our own business. We don't have a boss. In other words, we _____ .

6. Mr. and Mrs. Hall own their own business. No one taught them how to be small business managers. In other words, they _____ everything they needed to know about running a small business.

7. Mr. Baker committed suicide. In other words, he _____ .

8. I climbed to the top of the diving tower and walked to the end of the diving board. Before I dived into the pool, I said "Good luck!" to myself. In other words, I _____ luck.

9. Rebecca is home in bed because she has the flu. She's resting and drinking plenty of fluids. She is being careful about her health. In other words, she _____ _____ .

10. Sometimes we have problems in our lives. Sometimes we fail. But we shouldn't get discouraged and sad. We need to have faith that we can solve our problems and succeed. If we _____ , we can accomplish our goals.

11. When I failed to get the new job, I was sad and depressed. I was full of self-pity. In other words, I _____ because I didn't get the job.

12. In a cafeteria, people walk through a section of the restaurant and pick up their food. They are not served by waiters. In other words, in a cafeteria people _____ to the food they want.

Directions: Create sentences with reflexive pronouns. Use imaginary situations.

Example: wish myself

→ *Last week I took my first lesson in skydiving. Before I jumped out of the airplane, I wished myself good luck.*

1. talk to himself
2. hurt myself
3. enjoy themselves
4. take care of herself

5. cut himself
6. wish yourself
7. be proud of yourselves
8. blame ourselves

9. feel sorry for myself
10. introduce herself
11. believe in yourself
12. pinch myself

6-14 SINGULAR FORMS OF *OTHER: ANOTHER* vs. *THE OTHER*

ANOTHER

(a) There is a large bowl of apples on the table. Paul is going to eat one apple. If he is still hungry after that, he can eat **another** apple. There are many apples to choose from.	**Another** means "one more out of a group of similar items, one in addition to the one(s) already mentioned." **Another** is a combination of *an* + *other*, written as one word.

THE OTHER

(b) There are two apples on the table. Paul is going to eat one of them. Sara is going to eat **the other** apple.	**The other** means "the last one in a specific group, the only one that remains from a given number of similar items."
(c) Paul ate one apple. Then he ate { **another** apple. / **another** one. / **another**.	**Another** and **the other** can be used as adjectives in front of a noun (e.g., *apple*) or in front of the word *one*. **Another** and **the other** can also be used alone as pronouns.
(d) Paul ate one apple. Sara ate { **the other** apple. / **the other** one. / **the other**.	

☐ **EXERCISE 31. Singular forms of OTHER. (Chart 6-14)**
   Directions: Complete the sentences with *another* or *the other*.

1. There are two birds in Drawing A. One is an eagle. _____The other_____ is a chicken.

2. There are three birds in Drawing B. One is an eagle.

   a. _____ one is a chicken.

   b. _____ bird is a crow.

3. There are many kinds of birds in the world. One kind is an eagle.

   a. _____ kind is a chicken.

   b. _____ kind is a crow.

   c. _____ kind is a sea gull.

   d. What is the name of _____ kind of bird in the world?

4. I have two brothers. One is named Nick. _____ is named Matt.

5. There are five names on this list. One is Adam. _____ is Greg.

   _____ is Nick.

   _____ one of the names is Eric.

   _____ name on the list (the last of the five) is Jessica.

6. It rained yesterday, and from the look of those dark clouds, we're going to have _____ rainstorm today.

   People I need to call
   ✓ Adam
   Greg
   Eric
   Nick
   Jessica

7. Nicole and Michelle are identical twins. The best way to tell them apart is by looking at their ears. One of them has pierced ears, and _____ doesn't.

8. Of the fifty states in the United States, forty-nine are located on the North American continent. Where is _____ located?

9. France borders on several countries. One is Spain. _____ is Italy.

OTHER(S)

one apple

other apples

other apples

others etc.

There are many apples in Paul's kitchen. Paul is holding one apple.

(a) There are **other** *apples* in a bowl.
      (adjective) + (noun)

(b) There are **other** *ones* on a plate.
      (adjective) + (ones)

(c) There are **others** on a chair.
      (pronoun)

Other(*s*) (without *the*) means "several more out of a group of similar items, several in addition to the one(s) already mentioned." The adjective *other* (without an *-s*) can be used with a plural noun (e.g., *apples*) or with the word *ones*.

Others (with an *-s*) is a plural pronoun; it is not used with a noun.

In (c): *others* = *other apples*.

THE OTHER(S)

one apple

the other apples

There are four apples on the table. Paul is going to take one of them.

(d) Sara is going to take **the other** *apples*.
      (adjective) + (noun)

(e) Sara is going to take **the other** *ones*.
      (adjective) + (ones)

(f) Sara is going to take **the others**.
      (pronoun)

The other(*s*) means "the last ones in a specific group, the remains from a given number of similar items."

The other (without an *-s*) can be used as an adjective in front of a noun or the word *ones*, as in (d) and (e).

The others (with an *-s*) is a plural pronoun; it is not used with a noun.

In (f): *the others* = *the other apples*.

☐ **EXERCISE 32. Forms of OTHER. (Charts 6-14 and 6-15)**

Directions: Perform the following actions.

1. Hold two pens. Use a form of *other* to describe the second pen.
   → *I'm holding two pens. One is mine, and the other belongs to Ahmed.*

2. Hold three pens. Use a form of *other* to describe the second and third pens.

3. Hold up your two hands. One of them is your right hand. Tell us about your left hand, using a form of *other*.

4. Hold up your right hand. One of the five fingers is your thumb. Using forms of *other*, tell us about your index finger (or forefinger), then your middle finger, then your ring finger, and then your little finger, the last of the five fingers on your right hand.

5. Write two names on the board. Use a form of *other* in your description of these names.

6. Write five names on the board and tell us about them, using forms of *other* in your descriptions. Begin with "One of the names on the board is . . . ."

☐ **EXERCISE 33. Plural forms of OTHER. (Chart 6-15)**

Directions: Complete the sentences with **other(s)** or **the other(s)**.

1. There are many kinds of animals in the world. The elephant is one kind. Some

   ___*others*___ are tigers, horses, and whales.

2. There are many kinds of animals in the world. The elephant is one kind. Some

   _____ kinds are tigers, horses, and whales.

3. There are three colors in the U.S. flag. One of the colors is red. _____

   are white and blue.

4. There are three colors in the U.S. flag. One of the colors is red. _____

   colors are white and blue.

5. There are four birds in the picture. One is an eagle, and another one is a crow.

   _____ birds in the picture are chickens.

6. There are four birds in the picture. One is an eagle, and another one is a crow.

   _____ are chickens.

7. There are four seasons. Spring and summer are two. _____ are fall and winter.

8. Spring and summer are two of the four seasons. _____ seasons are fall and winter.

9. There are many kinds of geometric figures. Some are circles. _____ figures are squares. Still _____ are rectangular.

10. There are four geometric figures in the above drawing. One is a square. _____ figures are a rectangle, a circle, and a triangle.

11. Of the four geometric figures in the drawing, only the circle has curved lines. _____ have straight lines.

12. Birds have different eating habits. Some birds eat insects.
    a. _____ birds get their food chiefly from plants.
    b. _____ eat only fish.
    c. _____ hunt small animals like mice and rabbits.
    d. _____ birds prefer dead and rotting flesh.

13. A: There were ten questions on the test. Seven of them were easy. _____ three were really hard.

    B: Any question is easy if you know the answer. Seven of the questions were easy for you because you had studied for them. _____ were hard because you hadn't studied for them.

14. Many people like to get up very early in the morning. _____ like to sleep until noon.

15. A: What do you do when you're feeling lonely?

    B: I go someplace where I can be around _____ people. Even if they are strangers, I feel better when there are _____ around me. How about you?

    A: That doesn't work for me. For example, if I'm feeling lonely and I go to a movie by myself, I look at all _____ people who are there with their friends and family, and I start to feel even lonelier. So I try to find _____ things to do to keep myself busy. If I'm busy, I don't feel lonely.

6-16 SUMMARY OF FORMS OF *OTHER*

	ADJECTIVE	PRONOUN	Notice that the word **others** (*other* + *final* **-s**) is used only as a plural pronoun.
SINGULAR PLURAL	another apple other apples	another others	
SINGULAR PLURAL	the other apple the other apples	the other the others	

☐ **EXERCISE 34. Forms of OTHER. (Charts 6-12 → 6-16)**

Directions: Complete the sentences with correct forms of *other:* **another, other, others, the other, the others**.

1. Jake has only two suits, a blue one and a gray one. His wife wants him to buy

   _____*another*_____ one.

2. Jake has two suits. One is blue, and _____ is gray.

3. Some suits are blue. _____ are gray.

4. Some suits have two buttons. _____ suits have three buttons.

5. Some people keep dogs as pets. _____ have cats. Still

   _____ people have fish or birds as pets. Can you name

   _____ kinds of animals that people keep for pets?

6. When I was a kid, I had two pets. One was a black dog. _____

   was an orange cat.

7. When I walked into the classroom on the first day, the room was empty. I sat down at

   a desk and wondered if I was in the right room. Soon _____

   student came and took a seat. Then a few _____ followed, and

   the room slowly began to fill.

8. My boyfriend gave me a ring. I tried to put it on my ring finger, but it didn't fit. So I

   had to put it on _____ finger.

9. People have two thumbs. One is on the right hand. _____ is on

   the left hand.

10. There are five letters in the word "fresh." One of the letters is a vowel. _____

    _____ are consonants.

11. Smith is a common last name in English. _____ common names

    are Johnson, Jones, Miller, Anderson, Moore, and Brown.

☐ EXERCISE 35. Forms of OTHER. (Charts 6-12 → 6-16)
Directions: Complete the sentences with your own words. Use a form of ***other*** in the blank. If you write the completed sentences, underline the forms of ***other***.

Example: I have . . . books on my desk. One is . . . , and _____ is/are . . . .
   → *I have three books on my desk. One is a grammar book, and <u>the others</u> are my dictionary and a science book.*

1. I have two favorite colors. One is . . . , and _____ is . . . .

2. Some students walk to school. _____ . . . .

3. Ted drank . . . , but he was still thirsty, so . . . _____ one.

4. I speak . . . languages. One is . . . , and _____ is/are . . . .

5. Some people . . . , and _____ . . . .

6. I have . . . sisters, brothers, and/or cousins. One is . . . , and _____ is/are . . . .

7. One of my teachers is . . . . _____ is/are . . . .

8. . . . and . . . are two common names in my country. _____ are . . . .

9. . . . of the students in my class are from . . . . _____ students are from . . . .

10. There are many popular sports in the world. One is . . . . _____ is . . . . _____ are . . . .

☐ EXERCISE 36. Error analysis: summary review of nouns and pronouns. (Chapter 6)
Directions: Correct the errors.

1. The fairy godmother told the boy to make three ~~wish.~~ *wishes*

2. I had some black beans soup for lunch. They were very good.

3. The highways in my country are excellents.

4. My mother and father work in Milan. Their teacher's.

5. Today many womens are miner, pilot, and doctor.

6. My wife likes all kind of flower.

7. We often read story in class and try to understand all the new word. I can't remember all of it.

8. There are two pool at the park. One is for childs. The another is for adults only.

9. My brother has an apple's trees orchard.

10. The windows in our classroom is dirty.

11. In addition to the news about the flood, I heard some others importants news this morning.

12. The population of my hometown in 1975 were about 50,000. Today they are more than 150,000.

13. I don't like my apartment. Its in a bad neighborhood. Is trash on both side of the street. I'm going to move to other neighborhood.

14. Every people needs an education. With a good education, people can improve they're live.

15. Alice when was a child lived in a very little town in the north of Brazil. Today is a very big city with many building and larges highways.

CHAPTER 7
Modal Auxiliaries

CONTENTS

☐ EXERCISE 1. Preview: modal auxiliaries. (Chapter 7)
    Directions: Complete the sentences with *to,* if possible. If not, write **Ø**. Discuss the meanings of the helping verbs in *italics*.

A: I've made a terrible mistake! I put the wrong numbers in my report. My report

    shows that the company made lots of money, but the truth is we lost money. What am

    I going to do!? *Should* I _____**Ø**_____ tell the boss about the accounting error?
                                    1

B: Of course! You *have* _____**to**_____ tell her. That error *could* _____ get the company
                              2   3

    in big trouble.

A: I know that I *ought* _____ be honest about it, but I'm afraid she'll get angry. She
                           4

    might _____ fire me. *Would* you _____ go with me to see her?
             5   6

B: I think you *had better* _____ do this yourself. You *can* _____ do it.
                             7   8

    I'm sure the boss *will* _____ understand. You*'ve got* _____ be brave.
                            9   10

A: No, you *must* _____ go with me. I *can't* _____ face her alone.
                  11   12

189

7-1 THE FORM OF MODAL AUXILIARIES

The verbs listed below are called "modal auxiliaries." They are helping verbs that express a wide range of meanings (ability, permission, possibility, necessity, etc.). Most of the modals have more than one meaning.

AUXILIARY + THE SIMPLE FORM OF A VERB		*Can, could, may, might, should, had better, must, will,* and *would* are immediately followed by the simple form of a verb.
can	(a) Olga *can speak* English.	
could	(b) He *couldn't come* to class.	• They are not followed by *to*.
may	(c) It *may rain* tomorrow.	INCORRECT: Olga can to speak English.
might	(d) It *might rain* tomorrow.	• The main verb does not have a final *-s*.
should	(e) Mary *should study* harder.	INCORRECT: Olga can speaks English.
had better	(f) I *had better study* tonight.	• The main verb is not in a past form.
must	(g) Joe *must see* a doctor today.	INCORRECT: Olga can spoke English.
will	(h) I *will be* in class tomorrow.	• The main verb is not in its *-ing* form.
would	(i) *Would* you please *close* the door?	INCORRECT: Olga can speaking English.
AUXILIARY + *TO* + THE SIMPLE FORM OF A VERB		*To* + the simple form is used with these auxiliaries: *have to, have got to,* and *ought to.*
have to	(j) I *have to study* tonight.	
have got to	(k) I *have got to study* tonight.	
ought to	(l) Kate *ought to study* harder.	

☐ **EXERCISE 2. The form of modal auxiliaries. (Chart 7-1)**
Directions: Add *to* where necessary. If no *to* is necessary, write **Ø**.

1. I have ____to____ go downtown tomorrow.

2. Tom must ____Ø____ see his dentist.

3. Could you please _____ open the window?

4. May I _____ borrow your pen?

5. A good book can _____ be a friend for life.

6. I ought _____ go to the post office this afternoon.

7. Jimmy is yawning and rubbing his eyes. He must _____ be sleepy.

8. I have got _____ go to the post office this afternoon.

9. Shouldn't you _____ save a little money for a rainy day?

10. Poor Edward. He has _____ go to the hospital for an operation.

11. Alex! Stop! You must not _____ run into the street when there's traffic!

EXERCISE 3. Error analysis: the form of modal auxiliaries. (Chart 7-1)
Directions: Correct the errors.

1. Can you ~~to~~ help me, please?

2. I must studying for an exam tomorrow.

3. We couldn't went to the party last night.

4. I am have to improve my English as soon as possible.

5. You shouldn't to spend all your free time at the computer.

6. My mother can't speaking English, but she can speaks several other language.

7-2 EXPRESSING ABILITY: *CAN* AND *COULD*

(a) Bob **can play** the piano. (b) You **can buy** a screwdriver at a hardware store. (c) I **can meet** you at Ted's tomorrow afternoon.	**Can** expresses *ability* in the present or future.
(d) I $\begin{Bmatrix} can't \\ cannot \\ can\ not \end{Bmatrix}$ understand that sentence.	The negative form of **can** may be written **can't**, **cannot**, or **can not**.
(e) Our son **could walk** when he was one year old.	The past form of **can** is **could**.
(f) He **couldn't walk** when he was six months old.	The negative of **could**: **couldn't** or **could not**.

EXERCISE 4. Expressing ability: CAN and CAN'T. (Chart 7-2)
Directions: Complete the sentences with **can** and **can't**.

1. A cat _____can_____ climb trees, but it _____can't_____ fly.

2. A fish _____ walk, but it _____ swim.

3. A dog _____ bark, but it _____ sing.

4. A tiny baby _____ cry, but it _____ talk.

5. You _____ store water in a glass jar, but you _____

    store it in a paper bag.

6. You _____ drive from the Philippines to Australia, but you

    _____ drive from Italy to Austria.

□ **EXERCISE 5. Expressing ability: CAN and CAN'T. (Chart 7-2)**

Directions: Interview a classmate about each item in the list below, then make a report (written or oral) about your classmate's abilities.

Example: read pages that are upside down?

SPEAKER A: (Jose), can you read pages that are upside down?

SPEAKER B: Yes, I can. Here, I'll show you. OR

No, I can't. OR

I don't know. I'll try. Turn your book upside down, and I'll try to read it.

1. speak more than two languages?

2. play chess?

3. drive a stick-shift car?

4. read upside down?

5. play any musical instrument?

6. do card tricks?

7. pat the top of your head up and down with one hand and rub your stomach in a circular motion with the other hand at the same time?

Switch roles.

8. fold a piece of paper in half more than six times?

9. draw well—for example, draw a picture of me?

10. cook?

11. walk on your hands?

12. play tennis?

13. program a computer?

14. write legibly with both your right hand and your left hand?

□ **EXERCISE 6. Expressing past ability: COULD and COULDN'T. (Chart 7-2)**

Directions: Complete the sentences with **could** or **couldn't** and your own words.

Example: A year ago I . . . , but now I can.

→ *A year ago I couldn't speak English well, but now I can.*

1. When I was a baby, I . . . , but now I can.

2. When I was a child, I . . . , but now I can't.

3. When I was thirteen, I . . . , but I couldn't do that when I was three.

4. Five years ago, I . . . , but now I can't.

5. In the past, I . . . , but now I can.

7-3 EXPRESSING POSSIBILITY: *MAY* AND *MIGHT*
EXPRESSING PERMISSION: *MAY* AND *CAN*

(a) It ***may rain*** tomorrow. (b) It ***might rain*** tomorrow. (c) A: Why isn't John in class? B: I don't know. He $\left\{\begin{array}{l}\textbf{\textit{may}}\\\textbf{\textit{might}}\end{array}\right\}$ be sick today.	***May*** and ***might*** express *possibility* in the present or future. They have the same meaning. There is no difference in meaning between (a) and (b).
(d) It ***may not rain*** tomorrow. (e) It ***might not rain*** tomorrow.	Negative: ***may not*** and ***might not***. (Do not contract ***may*** and ***might*** with ***not***.)

(f) ***Maybe*** it will rain tomorrow.
COMPARE
(g) ***Maybe*** John is sick. *(adverb)*
(h) John ***may be*** sick. *(verb)*
	In (f) and (g): ***maybe*** (spelled as one word) is an adverb. It means "possibly." It comes at the beginning of a sentence.
	    INCORRECT: *It will maybe rain tomorrow.*
	In (h): ***may be*** (two words) is a verb form: the auxiliary ***may*** + *the main verb* ***be***.
	    INCORRECT: *John maybe sick.*

(i) Yes, children, you ***may have*** a cookie after dinner. (j) Okay, kids, you ***can have*** a cookie after dinner.	***May*** is also used to give *permission*, as in (i). Often ***can*** is used to give *permission*, too, as in (j). (i) and (j) have the same meaning, but ***may*** is more formal than ***can***.
(k) You ***may not have*** a cookie. You ***can't have*** a cookie.	***May not*** and ***cannot*** (***can't***) are used to deny permission (i.e., to say "no").

☐ **EXERCISE 7. Expressing possibility: MAY, MIGHT, and MAYBE. (Chart 7-3)**

Directions: Answer the questions. Include at least three possibilities in the answer to each question, using ***may***, ***might***, and ***maybe*** as in the example.

Example: What are you going to do tomorrow?

→ I don't know. I ***may*** go downtown. Or I ***might*** go to the laundromat. ***Maybe*** I'll study all day. Who knows?

1. What are you going to do tomorrow night?

2. What's the weather going to be like tomorrow?

3. What is (. . .) going to do tonight?

4. I'm taking something out of my briefcase/ purse/pocket/wallet. It's small, and I'm holding it in my fist. What is it?

5. What does (. . .) have in her purse?

6. What does (. . .) have in his pants pockets?

7. (. . .) isn't in class today. Where is he/she?

8. You have another class after this one. What are you going to do in that class?

9. Look at the picture. What is the man's occupation? What is the woman's occupation?

□ **EXERCISE 8. Ability, possibility, and permission: CAN, MAY, and MIGHT.**
   (Charts 7-2 and 7-3)

Directions: Complete the sentences with ***can, may,*** or ***might***. Use the negative as appropriate. Identify the meaning expressed by the modals: ability, possibility, or permission.

1. I _____*can*_____ play only one musical instrument: the piano. I _____*can't*_____ play a guitar. *(meaning expressed by modals: ability)*

2. Tommy, you _____*may/can*_____ stay up until eight tonight, but you _____*may not/cannot*_____ stay up past that time.
   (meaning expressed by modals: permission)

3. A: What are you going to do this evening?
   B: I don't know. I _____*may/might*_____ stay home, or I _____*may/might*_____ go over to Anita's house. *(meaning expressed by modals: possibility)*

4. A: What are you going to order?
   B: I don't know.* I _____ have the tofu pasta.

5. A: Would you like some more food?
   B: No thanks. I _____ eat another bite. I'm full.

6. A: Is it okay if I have a piece of candy, Mom?
   B: No, but you _____ have an orange.

7. A: Which of these oranges is sweet? I like only sweet oranges.
   B: How should I know? I _____ tell if an orange is sweet just by looking at it. _____ you? Here. Try this one. It _____ be sweet enough for you. If it isn't, put some sugar on it.

8. May I have everyone's attention? The test is about to begin. If you need to leave the room during the examination, please raise your hand. You _____ leave the room without permission. Are there any questions? No? Then you _____ open your test booklets and begin.

9. A: What channel is the news special on tonight?
   B: I'm not sure. It _____ be on Channel Seven. Try that one first.

_____

*In informal spoken English, "I don't know" is often pronounced "I dunno."

7-4 USING *COULD* TO EXPRESS POSSIBILITY

(a) A: Why isn't Greg in class? B: I don't know. He **could be** sick. (b) Look at those dark clouds. It **could start** raining any minute.	***Could*** can mean *past ability*. (See Chart 7-2, p. 191.) But that is not its only meaning. Another meaning of ***could*** is *possibility*. In (a): "He *could* be sick" has the same meaning as "He *may/might* be sick," i.e., "It is possible that he is sick." In (a): ***could*** expresses a **present** possibility. In (b): ***could*** expresses a **future** possibility.

☐ **EXERCISE 9. Meanings of COULD. (Charts 7-2 and 7-4)**

Directions: What is the meaning of ***could*** in the following? Does ***could*** express past, present, or future time?

1. I *could be* home late tonight. Don't wait for me for dinner.
   → *could be = may/might be. It expresses future time.*

2. Thirty years ago, when he was a small child, David *could speak* Arabic fluently. Now he's forgotten a lot.
   → *could speak = was able to speak. It expresses past time.*

3. A: Where's Alicia?
   B: I don't know. She *could be* at the mall.

4. When I was a child, we *could swim* in the Duckfoot River, but now it's too polluted. Today even the fish get sick.

5. A: What's this?
   B: I don't know. It looks like a glass bottle, but it *could be* a flower vase.

6. Let's leave for the airport now. Yuki's plane *could arrive* early, and we want to be there when she arrives.

7. When I was a kid, I *could jump* rope really well.

Directions: Listen to the clues with books closed. Make guesses using **could, may,** and **might.**

Example: is made of metal and you keep it in a pocket

TEACHER: I'm thinking of something that is made of metal. I keep it in my pocket. What could it be?

STUDENTS: It could be a pen. It could be some keys. It might be a paper clip. It may be a small pocket knife. It could be a coin.

TEACHER: (. . .) was right! I was thinking of the keys in my pocket.

1. has wheels and a motor
2. is made of plastic and can be found in my purse/pocket
3. is brown, is made of leather, and is in this room
4. is flat and rectangular
5. is white, hard, and in this room
6. is played with a ball on a large field
7. has *(three)* stories* and is made of *(brick)*
8. has four legs and is found on a farm
9. is green and we can see it out that window
10. is sweet and you can eat it

☐ EXERCISE 11. Expressing possibility: COULD. (Chart 7-4)

Directions: Listen with books closed. Suggest possible courses of actions using **could.** Work in pairs, in groups, or as a class.

Example: (. . .) has to go to work early tomorrow. His car is completely out of gas. His bicycle is broken.

→ *He could take the bus to work.*
  He could take a gas can to a gas station, fill it up, and carry it home to his car.
  He could try to fix his bicycle.
  He could get up very early and walk to work.
  Etc.

1. (. . .) walked to school today. Now she wants to go home. It's raining hard. She doesn't have an umbrella. She doesn't want her hair to get wet.

2. (. . .) and (. . .) want to get some exercise. They have a date to play tennis this morning, but the tennis court is covered with snow.

(Switch roles if working in pairs.)

3. (. . .) just bought a new camera. He has it at home now. He has the instruction manual. It is written in Japanese. He can't read Japanese. He doesn't know how to operate the camera.

4. (. . .) likes to travel around the world. He is twenty-two years old. Today he is alone in *(name of a city)*. He needs to eat, and he needs to find a place to stay overnight. But while he was asleep on the train last night, someone stole his wallet. He has no money.

---

*American English: *story, stories*; British English: *storey, storeys* (floors in a house).
  American and British English: *story, stories* = *tales.*

□ **EXERCISE 12. COULD, MAY, MIGHT, and WILL PROBABLY.** (Charts 3-4 and 7-2 → 7-4)
Directions: Complete the sentences with your own words.

Example: I could _____ today. (. . .) could _____ too, but we'll probably _____ .
→ *I could* skip class and go to a movie *today*. Pedro *could* come along *too, but we'll probably* go to class just like we're supposed to.

1. Tonight I could _____ . Or I might _____ . Of course, I may _____ . But I'll probably _____ .

2. Next year, I might _____ . But I could _____ . I may _____ . But I'll probably _____ .

3. My friend (. . .) may _____ this weekend, but I'm not sure. He/She might _____ . He/She could also _____ . But he/she'll probably _____ .

4. One hundred years from now, _____ may _____ . _____ could _____ . _____ will probably _____ .

7-5 POLITE QUESTIONS: *MAY I, COULD I, CAN I*

POLITE QUESTION	POSSIBLE ANSWERS	
(a) *May I* please borrow your pen? (b) *Could I* please borrow your pen? (c) *Can I* please borrow your pen?	Yes. Yes. Of course. Yes. Certainly. Of course. Certainly. Sure. (informal) Okay. (informal) Uh-huh. (meaning "yes") I'm sorry, but I need to use it myself.	People use *may I, could I,*★ and *can I* to ask polite questions. The questions ask for someone's permission or agreement. (a), (b), and (c) have basically the same meaning. Note: *can I* is less formal than *may I* and *could I*.
		Please can come at the end of the question: *May I borrow your pen, please?* *Please* can be omitted from the question: *May I borrow your pen?*

★In a polite question, *could* is NOT the past form of *can*.

□ **EXERCISE 13. Polite questions: MAY I, COULD I, and CAN I.** (Chart 7-5)
Directions: Following are some phone conversations. Complete the dialogues. Use *may I, could I,* or *can I* + a verb from the list. NOTE: The caller is Speaker B.

> help   leave   speak/talk   take

1. A: Hello?

   B: Hello. Is Ahmed there?

   A: Yes, he is.

   B: _____ to him?

   A: Just a minute. I'll get him.

2. A: Hello. Mr. Black's office.

   B: _____ to Mr. Black?

   A: May I ask who is calling?

   B: Susan Abbott.

   A: Just a moment, Ms. Abbott. I'll connect you.

3. A: Hello?

   B: Hi. This is Bob. _____ to Pedro?

   A: Sure. Hang on.

4. A: Good afternoon. Dr. Wu's office. _____ you?

   B: Yes. I'd like to make an appointment with Dr. Wu.

   A: Fine. Is Friday morning at ten all right?

   B: Yes. Thank you.

   A: Your name?

5. A: Hello?

   B: Hello. _____ to Emily?

   A: She's not at home right now. _____ a message?

   B: No thanks. I'll call later.

6. A: Hello?

   B: Hello. _____ to Maria?

   A: She's not here right now.

   B: Oh. _____ a message?

   A: Certainly. Just a minute. I have to get a pen.

7. A: Hello?

   B: Hello. _____ to Jack?

   A: Who?

   B: Jack. Jack Butler.

   A: There's no one here by that name. I'm afraid you have the wrong number.

   B: Is this 221-3892?

   A: No, it's not.

   B: Oh. I'm sorry.

   A: That's okay.

Directions: Ask and answer polite questions. Use **may I, could I**, or **can I**. Listen to the cues with books closed. Work in groups or as a class. (Alternatively, work in pairs, creating somewhat longer dialogues that you then role-play for the rest of the class.)

Example: (. . .), you want to see (. . .)'s grammar book for a minute.
SPEAKER A: May/Could/Can I (please) see your grammar book for a minute?
SPEAKER B: Of course. / Sure. / Etc.
SPEAKER A: Thank you. / Thanks. I forgot to bring mine to class today.

1. (. . .), you want to see (. . .)'s dictionary for a minute.

2. (. . .), you are at (. . .)'s house. You want to use the phone.

3. (. . .), you are at a restaurant. (. . .) is your waiter/waitress. You have finished your meal. You want the check.

4. (. . .), you run into (. . .) on the street. (. . .) is carrying some heavy packages. What are you going to say to him/her?

5. (. . .), you are speaking to (. . .), who is one of your teachers. You want to leave class early today.

6. (. . .), you want to use (. . .)'s calculator during the algebra test. (. . .) needs to use it himself/herself.

7. (. . .), you are in a store with your good friend (. . .). Your bill is *(a certain amount of money)*. You have only *(a lesser amount of money)*. What are you going to say to your friend?

7-6 POLITE QUESTIONS: *WOULD YOU, COULD YOU, WILL YOU, CAN YOU*

POLITE QUESTION	POSSIBLE ANSWERS	People use **would you, could you, will you**, and **can you** to ask polite questions. The questions ask for someone's help or cooperation. (a), (b), (c), and (d) have basically the same meaning. The use of **can**, as in (d), is less formal than the others.
(a) **Would you** please open the door? (b) **Could you** please open the door? (c) **Will you** please open the door? (d) **Can you** please open the door?	Yes. Yes. Of course. Certainly. I'd be happy to. Of course. I'd be glad to. Sure. (informal) Okay. (informal) Uh-huh. (meaning "yes") I'm sorry. I'd like to help, but my hands are full.	
		Note: **May** is NOT used when **you** is the subject of a polite question. *INCORRECT: May you please open the door?*

Directions: Complete the dialogues. Use a polite question with **would you**/**could you**, **will you**/**can you** in each. Use the expressions in the list or your own words.

answer the phone for me	tell me where the nearest post office is
open the window	turn it down
pick some up	turn the volume up
say that again	

1. TEACHER: It's getting hot in here. ___Would/Could/Will/Can you___
   ___please open the window?___
   STUDENT: ___Of course, I'd be happy to. / Sure. / Etc.___
   TEACHER: ___Thank you. / Thanks.___
   STUDENT: You're welcome.

2. FRIEND A: The phone is ringing, but my hands are full. _____
   _____
   FRIEND B: _____
   FRIEND A: _____
   FRIEND B: No problem.

3. ROOMMATE A: I'm trying to study, but the radio is too loud. _____
   _____
   ROOMMATE B: _____
   ROOMMATE A: _____
   ROOMMATE B: That's okay. No problem.

4. SISTER: I'm trying to listen to the news on television, but I can't hear it.
   _____
   BROTHER: _____
   SISTER: _____
   BROTHER: Don't mention it.

5. HUSBAND: Honey, I'm out of razor blades. When you go to the store, _____
   _____
   WIFE: _____
   HUSBAND: _____
   WIFE: Anything else?

6. PERSON A: Hi.

   PERSON B: Hi. Walabaxitinpundoozit?

   PERSON A: Excuse me? _____

   PERSON B: Walabaxitinpundoozit.

   PERSON A: I'm sorry, but I don't understand.

7. STRANGER A: Pardon me. I'm a stranger here. _____

   _____

   STRANGER B: _____

   STRANGER A: Well, thanks anyway. I'll ask someone else.

☐ EXERCISE 16. Summary: polite questions. (Charts 7-5 and 7-6)

Directions: Work in pairs. Create a dialogue for one or more of the following situations. The beginning of each dialogue is given. Role-play a dialogue for the rest of the class.

Example:

SITUATION: You're in a restaurant. You want the waiter to refill your coffee cup. You catch the waiter's eye and raise your hand slightly. He approaches your table.

DIALOGUE: *Yes? What can I do for you?*

SPEAKER A: Yes? What can I do for you?

SPEAKER B: Could I please have some more coffee?

SPEAKER A: Of course. Right away. Could I get you anything else?

SPEAKER B: No thanks. Oh, on second thought, yes. Would you bring some cream too?

SPEAKER A: Certainly.

SPEAKER B: Thanks.

1. SITUATION: You've been waiting in line at a busy bakery. Finally, the person in front of you is being waited on, and the clerk turns toward you.

   DIALOGUE: *Next!*

2. SITUATION: You are at work. You feel sick. Your head is pounding, and you have a slight fever. You really want to go home. You see your boss, Mr. Jenkins, passing by your desk.

   DIALOGUE: *Mr. Jenkins?*

3. SITUATION: Your cousin, Willy, is in the next room listening to music. You are talking on the telephone. The music is getting louder and louder. Finally, you can no longer hear your conversation over the phone. You put the phone down and turn toward the door to the next room.

   DIALOGUE: *Willy!*

4. SITUATION: The person next to you on the plane has finished reading his newspaper. You would like to read it.

   DIALOGUE: *Excuse me.*

5. SITUATION: You see a car on the side of the road with the hood raised and an older man standing next to it. He looks tired and concerned. You pull over and get out of your car to walk over to him.

   DIALOGUE: *Do you need some help, sir?*

7-7 EXPRESSING ADVICE: *SHOULD* AND *OUGHT TO*

(a) My clothes are dirty I $\left\{ \begin{array}{l} \textbf{\textit{should}} \\ \textbf{\textit{ought to}} \end{array} \right\}$ wash them.
 	
 (b) *INCORRECT: I should to wash them.*
 (c) *INCORRECT: I ought washing them.*
	Should and ***ought to*** have the same meaning. They mean: "This is a good idea. This is good advice."
	
	 FORMS:
	     should + *simple form of a verb* (no ***to***)
	     ought + ***to*** + *simple form of a verb*

(d) You need your sleep. You ***should not (shouldn't)*** stay up late.	NEGATIVE: ***should*** + ***not*** = ***shouldn't*** (*Ought to* is usually not used in the negative.)
(e) A: I'm going to be late. What ***should I do?*** B: Run.	QUESTION: ***should*** + *subject* + *main verb* (*Ought to* is usually not used in questions.)

(f) A: I'm tired today.
    B: You *should/ought to* go home and take a nap.
 	
 (g) A: I'm tired today.
    B: ***Maybe*** you *should/ought to* go home and take a nap.
	The use of ***maybe*** with ***should*** and ***ought to*** "softens" advice. COMPARE:
	
	 In (f): Speaker B is giving definite advice. He is stating clearly that he believes going home for a nap is a good idea and is the solution to Speaker A's problem.
	
	 In (g): Speaker B is making a suggestion: going home for a nap is one possible way to solve Speaker A's problem.

☐ **EXERCISE 17. Expressing advice: SHOULD and OUGHT TO. (Chart 7-7)**

Directions: Work in pairs.
Speaker A: State the problem.
Speaker B: Give advice using ***should*** or ***ought to***. Include ***maybe*** to soften the advice if you wish.

Example: I'm sleepy.
SPEAKER A: I'm sleepy.
SPEAKER B: (Maybe) You should/ought to drink a cup of tea.

1. I'm hungry.

2. I'm cold.

3. I have a toothache.

4. I have the hiccups. What should I do?

5. I left my sunglasses at a restaurant yesterday. What should I do?

Switch roles.

6. I'm hot.

7. I have a headache.

8. Someone stole my bicycle. What should I do?

9. I bought a pair of pants that don't fit. They're too long.

10. I always make a lot of spelling mistakes when I write. I don't know what to do about it. What do you suggest?

7-8 EXPRESSING ADVICE: *HAD BETTER*

(a) My clothes are dirty. I $\left\{\begin{array}{l}\textit{should} \\ \textit{ought to} \\ \textit{had better}\end{array}\right\}$ *wash* them.	***Had better*** has the same basic meaning as *should* and *ought to*: "This is a good idea. This is good advice."
(b) You're driving too fast! You***'d better*** *slow* down.	***Had better*** usually implies a warning about possible bad consequences. In (b): If you don't slow down, there could be a bad result. You could get a speeding ticket or have an accident.
(c) You***'d better not*** *eat* that meat. It looks spoiled.	NEGATIVE: ***had better not***
(d) I***'d*** *better send* my boss an e-mail right away.	In speaking, ***had*** is usually contracted: *'d.*

□ **EXERCISE 18. Expressing advice: HAD BETTER. (Chart 7-8)**
Directions: In the following, the speaker chooses to use ***had better***. What are some possible bad consequences the speaker might be thinking of?

1. The movie starts in ten minutes. We*'d better hurry*.
   → *Possible bad consequences: We'll be late if we don't hurry.*

2. You can't wear shorts and a T-shirt to a job interview! You*'d better change* clothes before you go.

3. I can't find my credit card. I have no idea where it is. I guess I*'d better call* the credit card company.

4. A: My ankle really hurts. I think I sprained it.
   B: You*'d better put* some ice on it right away.

5. You shouldn't leave your car unlocked in the middle of the city. You*'d better lock* it before we go into the restaurant.

□ **EXERCISE 19. Expressing advice: HAD BETTER. (Chart 7-8)**
Directions: Give advice using ***had better***. Explain the possible bad consequence if your advice is not followed. Only the cuer's book is open.

Example: It's raining. I need to go out.
   → *You'd better take your umbrella. If you don't, you'll get wet.*

1. I haven't paid my electric bill.
2. I need to be at the airport for a nine o'clock flight tonight.
3. (. . .) and I want to go out to dinner at *(name of a popular restaurant)* Saturday night, but we don't have reservations yet.
4. (. . .) wants to go to a movie tonight, but she/he has a test tomorrow.
5. I don't feel good today. I think I'm coming down with something.*
6. (. . .) has a job at *(name of a local place)*. She/He has been late to work three times in the last week. Her/His boss is very unhappy about that.

---

*The idiom "come down with something" means "get a sickness" like a cold or the flu.

Directions: Correct the errors.

      had
1. You ~~will~~ better not be late.

2. Anna shouldn't wears shorts into the restaurant.

3. I should to go to the post office today.

4. I ought paying my bills today.

5. You'd had better to call the doctor today.

6. You don't should stay up too late tonight.

7. You'd to better not leaving your key in the door.

8. Mr. Nguyen has a large family and a small apartment. He ought found a new apartment.

□ **EXERCISE 21. Giving advice. (Charts 7-7 and 7-8)**

Directions: Work in pairs. Complete all of the dialogues. Make the dialogues longer if you wish by adding more advice, and present one of your dialogues to the class.
    One of you is Speaker A, and the other is Speaker B.

Example:
SPEAKER A: I don't feel like studying tonight.
SPEAKER B: **Maybe** you **should** . . . . *go to a movie instead / take the night off / etc.*
SPEAKER A: I can't do that. I have a big test tomorrow.
SPEAKER B: Well, then you**'d better** . . . . *study tonight whether you feel like it or not / go to your room and get to work.*

1. A: I don't feel good. I think I'm getting a cold.
   B: That's too bad. You**'d better** . . . .
   A: That's probably a good idea.
   B: You **should** also . . . .
   A: Okay. I will. That's a good idea. And I suppose **I'd better not** . . . .
   B: No, you'd better not do that if you're getting a cold.

2. A: My English isn't progressing as fast as I'd like. What should I do?
   B: You **should** . . . . That's really important when you're learning a second language.
   A: Do you have any other suggestions?
   B: Yes, you **ought to** . . . .
   A: That's a good idea.
   B: And you **shouldn't** . . . .
   A: You're right. Good suggestion.

Switch roles.

3. A: My roommate snores really loudly. I'm losing sleep. I don't know what to do.
   B: **Maybe** you **should** . . . .
   A: I've thought of that, but . . . .
   B: Well then, **maybe** you**'d better** . . . .
   A: Maybe. I guess I really **ought to** . . . .
   B: That's a good idea.

4. A: The refrigerator in my apartment doesn't work. The air conditioner makes so much noise that I can't sleep. And there are cockroaches in the kitchen.
   B: Why do you stay there? You **should** . . . .
   A: I can't. I signed a lease.
   B: Oh. That's too bad. Well, if you have to stay there, you**'d better** . . . .
   A: I suppose I should do that.
   B: And you also **ought to** . . . .
   A: Good idea.

☐ EXERCISE 22. Giving advice. (Charts 7-7 and 7-8)
Directions: Give advice using ***should, ought to,*** and ***had better***. Work in groups of four. Only Speaker A's book is open. Rotate the open book, using a new Speaker A for each item.

Example:
SPEAKER A *(book open):* I study, but I don't understand my physics class. It's the middle of the term, and I'm failing the course. I need a science course in order to graduate. What should I do?★
SPEAKER B *(book closed):* You**'d better** get a tutor right away.
SPEAKER C *(book closed):* You **should** make an appointment with your teacher and see if you can get some extra help.
SPEAKER D *(book closed):* Maybe you **ought to** drop your physics course and enroll in a different science course next term.

1. I forgot my dad's birthday yesterday. I feel terrible about it. What should I do?

2. I just discovered that I made dinner plans for tonight with two different people. I'm supposed to meet my fiancée/fiancé at one restaurant at 7:00, and I'm supposed to meet my boss at a different restaurant across town at 8:00. What should I do?

3. The boss wants me to finish my report before I go on vacation, but I don't have time. I might lose my job if I don't give him that report on time. What should I do?

4. I borrowed Karen's favorite book of poems. It was special to her. A note on the inside cover said "To Karen." The poet's signature was at the bottom of the note. Now I can't find the book. I think I lost it. What am I going to do?

★*Should* (not *ought to* or *had better*) is usually used in a question that asks for advice. The answer, however, can contain *should, ought to,* or *had better.* For example:
> A: My houseplants always die. What ***should*** I do?
> B: You**'d better** get a book on plants. You ***should*** try to find out why they die. Maybe you **ought to** look on the Internet and see if you can find some information.

□ **EXERCISE 23. Giving advice. (Charts 7-7 and 7-8)**

Directions: Discuss problems and give advice. Work in groups.

Speaker A: Think of a problem in your life or a friend's life. Tell your classmates about the problem and then ask them for advice.

Group: Give Speaker A some advice. Use ***should/ought to/had better***.

Example:

SPEAKER A: I can't study at night because the dorm is too noisy. What should I do?

SPEAKER B: You ought to study at the library.

SPEAKER C: You shouldn't stay in your dorm room in the evening.

SPEAKER D: You'd better get some ear plugs.

SPEAKER E: Etc.

7-9 EXPRESSING NECESSITY: *HAVE TO, HAVE GOT TO, MUST*

(a) I have a very important test tomorrow. I $\left\{\begin{array}{l}\textbf{\textit{have to}}\\ \textbf{\textit{have got to}}\\ \textbf{\textit{must}}\end{array}\right\}$ *study* tonight.	***Have to***, ***have got to***, and ***must*** have basically the same meaning. They express the idea that something is *necessary*.
(b) I'd like to go with you to the movie this evening, but I can't. I ***have to go*** to a meeting.	***Have to*** is used much more frequently in everyday speech and writing than ***must***.
(c) Bye now! I***'ve got to go***. My wife's waiting for me. I'll call you later. (d) All passengers ***must present*** their passports at customs upon arrival.	***Have got to*** is typically used in informal conversation, as in (c). ***Must*** is typically found in written instructions, as in (d). It is usually a strong, serious, "no nonsense" word.
(e) ***Do*** we ***have to bring*** pencils to the test? (f) Why ***did*** he ***have to leave*** so early?	QUESTIONS: ***Have to*** is usually used in questions, not ***must*** or ***have got to***. Forms of ***do*** are used with ***have to*** in questions.
(g) I ***had to*** study last night.	The PAST form of ***have to***, ***have got to***, and ***must*** (meaning necessity) is ***had to***.

(h) I ***have to*** ("hafta") *go* downtown today.
(i) Rita ***has to*** ("hasta") *go* to the bank.
(j) I've ***got to*** ("gotta") *study* tonight.
	Usual PRONUNCIATION:
	   have to = /hæftə/ OR /hæftu/
	   has to = /hæstə/ OR /hæstu/
	   (have) ***got to*** = /gadə/ OR /gɔtə/

□ **EXERCISE 24. HAVE TO, HAVE GOT TO, MUST, and SHOULD. (Charts 7-7 and 7-9)**

Directions: Discuss the questions and the meanings of the auxiliaries.

1. What are some things you *have to do* today? tomorrow? every day?
2. What is something you *had to do* yesterday?
3. What is something you*'ve got to do* soon?
4. What is something you*'ve got to do* after class today or later tonight?
5. What is something a driver *must do,* according to the law?
6. What is something a driver *should* always *do* to be a safe driver?
7. What are some things a person *should do* to stay healthy?
8. What are some things a person *must do* to stay alive?

Directions: Read the passage, and then give advice either in a discussion group or in writing.

Mr. and Mrs. Hill don't know what to do about their fourteen-year-old son, Mark. He's very intelligent but has no interest in school or in learning. His grades are getting worse, but he won't do any homework. Sometimes he skips school without permission, and then he writes an excuse for the school and signs his mother's name.

His older sister, Kathy, is a good student and never causes any problems at home. Mark's parents keep asking him why he can't be more like Kathy. Kathy makes fun of Mark's school grades and tells him he's stupid.

All Mark does when he's home is stay in his room and listen to very loud music. Sometimes he doesn't even come downstairs to eat meals with his family. He argues with his parents whenever they ask him to do chores around the house, like taking out the trash.

Mr. and Mrs. Hill can't stay calm when they talk to him. Mrs. Hill is always yelling at her son. She nags him constantly to do his chores, clean up his room, finish his homework, stand up straight, get a haircut, wash his face, and tie his shoes. Mr. Hill is always making new rules. Some of the rules are unreasonable. For instance, one rule Mr. Hill made was that his son could not listen to music after five o'clock. Mark often becomes angry and goes up to his room and slams the door shut.

This family needs a lot of advice. Tell them what changes they should make. What should Mr. and Mrs. Hill do? What shouldn't they do? What about Kathy? What should she do? And what's Mark got to do to change his life for the better?

Use each of the following words at least once in the advice you give:

a. should
b. shouldn't
c. have got to/has got to
d. had better
e. ought to
f. have to/has to
g. must

7-10 EXPRESSING LACK OF NECESSITY: *DO NOT HAVE TO* EXPRESSING PROHIBITION: *MUST NOT*

(a) I finished all of my homework this afternoon. I **don't have to study** tonight.	***Don't/doesn't have to*** expresses the idea that something is *not necessary*.
(b) Tomorrow is a holiday. Mary **doesn't have to go** to class.	
(c) Children, you **must not play** with matches!	***Must not*** expresses *prohibition* (DO NOT DO THIS!).
(d) We **must not use** that door. The sign says PRIVATE: DO NOT ENTER.	
(e) You **mustn't play** with matches.	***Must + not = mustn't.*** (Note: The first "t" is not pronounced.)

☐ **EXERCISE 26. Lack of necessity (DO NOT HAVE TO) and prohibition (MUST NOT).**
(Chart 7-10)

Directions: Complete the sentences with **don't/doesn't have to** or **must not**.

1. You _____**must not**_____ drive when you are tired. It's dangerous.

2. I live only a few blocks from my office. I _____**don't have to**_____ drive to work.

3. Liz finally got a car, so now she usually drives to work. She _____
take the bus.

4. Tommy, you _____ say that word. It's not a nice word.

5. Mr. Moneybags is very rich. He _____ work for a living.

6. A: You _____ tell Jim about the surprise birthday party. Do
you promise?

    B: I promise.

7. According to the rules of the game, one player _____ hit or
trip another player.

8. If you use a toll-free number, you _____ pay for the phone call.

9. A: Did Professor Adams make an assignment?

    B: Yes, she assigned Chapters 4 and 6, but we _____ read
Chapter 5.

10. A: Listen carefully, Annie. If a stranger offers you a ride, you _____
get in the car. Never get in a car with a stranger. Do you understand?

    B: Yes, Mom.

11. A: Do you have a stamp?

    B: Uh-huh. Here.

    A: Thanks. Now I _____ go to the post office to buy
stamps.

12. A: Children, your mother and I are going out this evening. I want you to be good.
You must do everything the baby-sitter tells you to do. You _____
go outside after dark. It's Saturday night, so you _____
go to bed at eight. You can stay up until eight-thirty. And remember: you
_____ pull the cat's tail. Okay?

    B: Okay, Dad.

☐ **EXERCISE 27. Summary: expressing advice, possibility, and necessity.**
    (Charts 7-4 and 7-7 → 7-10)

Directions: Read about each situation and discuss it, orally or in writing. In your discussion, include as many of the following expressions as possible.

should, shouldn't	*have to, not have to*
ought to	*have got to, not have to*
had better, had better not	*must, must not*
could	

Example: Carol is just recovering from the flu. She's at work today. She works for a big company. It's her first day back to work since she got ill. She tires easily and feels a little dizzy.

SPEAKER A: Carol **ought to** talk to her supervisor about leaving work early today.

SPEAKER B: I think Carol **should** go directly home from work, no matter what her boss says. She**'s got to** take care of her health.

SPEAKER C: I agree. She **doesn't have to** stay at work if she doesn't feel well, and she **shouldn't**.

SPEAKER D: She **could** explain to her boss that she doesn't feel well yet and see what her boss says.

SPEAKER E: I think she **should stay** at work until quitting time. If she was well enough to come to work, she's well enough to work a full day. Etc.

1. Steve is a biology major. Chemistry is a required course for biology majors. Steve doesn't want to take chemistry. He would rather take a course in art history or creative writing. His parents want him to become a doctor. He's not interested in medicine or science. He hasn't told his parents because he doesn't want to disappoint them.

2. Matt and Amy are eighteen years old. They are full-time students. Their parents are supporting their education. Matt and Amy met five weeks ago. They fell in love. Matt wants to get married next month. Amy wants to wait four years until they finish their education. Matt says he can't wait that long. Amy loves him desperately. She thinks maybe she should change her mind and marry Matt next month because love conquers all.

3. Georgia has just left the supermarket. She paid for her groceries in cash. When she got her change, the clerk made a mistake and gave her too much money. Georgia put the extra money in her purse. With her ten-year-old son beside her, she walked out of the store. Georgia needs the money and tells herself that the store won't miss it. Nobody needs to know.

4. This is a story about a rabbit named Rabbit and a frog named Frog. Rabbit and Frog are good friends, but Rabbit's family doesn't like Frog, and Frog's family doesn't like Rabbit.

Rabbit's family says, "You shouldn't be friends with Frog. He's too different from us. He's green and has big eyes. He looks strange. You should stay with your own kind."

And Frog's family says, "How can you be friends with Rabbit? He's big and clumsy. He's covered with hair and has funny ears. Don't bring Rabbit to our house. What will the neighbors think?"

7-11 MAKING LOGICAL CONCLUSIONS: *MUST*

(a) A: Nancy is yawning. B: She ***must be*** sleepy.	In (a): Speaker B is making a logical guess. He bases his guess on the information that Nancy is yawning. His logical conclusion, his "best guess," is that Nancy is sleepy. He uses ***must*** to express his logical conclusion.
(b) LOGICAL CONCLUSION: Amy plays tennis every day. She ***must like*** to play tennis. (c) NECESSITY: If you want to get into the movie theater, you ***must buy*** a ticket.	COMPARE: ***Must*** can express • a logical conclusion, as in (b). • necessity, as in (c).
(d) NEGATIVE LOGICAL CONCLUSION: Eric ate everything on his plate except the pickle. He ***must not like*** pickles. (e) PROHIBITION: There are sharks in the ocean near our hotel. We ***must not go*** swimming there.	COMPARE: ***Must not*** can express • a negative logical conclusion, as in (d). • prohibition, as in (e).

☐ **EXERCISE 28. Making logical conclusions: MUST and MUST NOT. (Chart 7-11)**

Directions: Make a logical conclusion about each of the following situations. Use **must**.

Example: Emily is crying.

→ *She must be unhappy.*

1. Mrs. Chu has a big smile on her face.
2. Nadia is coughing and sneezing.
3. Rick is wearing a gold ring on the fourth finger of his left hand.
4. Sam is shivering.
5. Mr. Alvarez just bought three mouse traps.
6. James is sweating.
7. Rita rents ten movies every week.
8. Olga always gets the highest score on every test she takes.
9. Toshi can lift one end of a compact car by himself.

☐ **EXERCISE 29. Making logical conclusions: MUST and MUST NOT. (Chart 7-11)**

Directions: Complete the dialogues with **must** or **must not**.

1. A: Did you offer our guests something to drink?

   B: Yes, but they didn't want anything. They ___must not___ be thirsty.

2. A: You've been out here working in the hot sun for hours. You ___must___ be thirsty.
   B: I am.

3. A: Adam has already eaten one sandwich. Now he's making another.

   B: He _____ be hungry.

4. A: I offered Holly something to eat, but she doesn't want anything.

   B: She _____ be hungry.

5. A: Brian has a red nose and has been coughing and sneezing.

   B: Poor fellow. He _____ have a cold.

6. A: Fido? What's wrong, old boy?
   B: What's the matter with the dog?
   A: He won't eat.

   B: He _____ feel well.

7. A: Erica's really bright. She always gets above ninety-five percent on her math tests.

   B: I'm sure she's bright, but she _____ also study a lot.

8. A: I've called the bank three times, but no one answers the phone. The bank

   _____ be open today. That's strange.
   B: Today's a holiday, remember?
   A: Oh, of course!

9. A: Listen. Someone is jumping on the floor in the apartment above us. Look. Your chandelier is shaking.

   B: Mr. Silverberg _____ be doing his morning exercises. The same thing happens every morning.

☐ **EXERCISE 30. Making logical conclusions: MUST and MUST NOT. (Chart 7-11)**
Directions: Make logical conclusions. Use ***must*** or ***must not***. Use the suggested completions and/or your own words.

1. I am at **Eric**'s apartment door. I've knocked on the door and have rung the doorbell several times. Nobody has answered the door. *be at home? be out somewhere?*
   → *Eric must not be at home. He must be out somewhere.*

2. **Jennifer** reads all the time. She sits in a corner and reads even when people come to visit her. *love books? like books better than people? like to talk to people?*

3. **Kate** has a full academic schedule, plays on the volleyball team, has the lead in the school play, is a cheerleader, takes piano lessons, and has a part-time job at the ice cream store. *be busy all the time? have a lot of spare time?*

4. **David** gets on the Internet every day as soon as he gets home from work. He stays at his computer until he goes to bed. *be a computer addict? have a happy home life?*

5. **Betsy** just talked to Jake on the phone. He asked her to go to a movie. She told him that she had to study. She has just hung up, and now she's going to get ready for bed and go to sleep. *want to go a movie? be tired?*

6. **Debbie** just got home from school. She slammed the front door, threw her books on the floor, and ran to her room. Now her parents can hear music through Debbie's closed door. *be upset? want to talk to her parents right now? want to be alone?*

7-12 GIVING INSTRUCTIONS: IMPERATIVE SENTENCES

COMMAND
(a) *General:* **Open** the door!
    Soldier: Yes, sir!
 	
REQUEST
(b) *Teacher:* **Open** the door, please.
    Student: Okay, I'd be happy to.
 	
DIRECTIONS
(c) *Barbara:* Could you tell me how to get to the post office?
    Stranger: Certainly. **Walk two blocks down this street. Turn left and *walk* three more blocks.** It's on the right-hand side of the street.
	Imperative sentences are used to give commands, make polite requests, and give directions. The difference between a command and a request lies in the speaker's tone of voice and the use of ***please***.
	Please can come at the beginning or end of a request:
	    Open the door, please.
	    Please open the door.

(d) **Close** the window. (e) Please **sit** down. (f) **Be** quiet! (g) **Don't walk** on the grass. (h) Please **don't wait** for me. (i) **Don't be** late.	The simple form of a verb is used in imperative sentences. The understood subject of the sentence is ***you*** (meaning the person the speaker is talking to): *(You) close the window.* NEGATIVE FORM: ***Don't*** + *the simple form of a verb*

☐ EXERCISE 31. Imperative sentences. (Chart 7-12)

Directions: Complete the dialogues with imperative sentences. Try to figure out something the first speaker might say in the given situation.

1.   THE TEACHER: *Read this sentence, please. /Look at page 33. /Etc.*
        THE STUDENT: Okay.

2.   THE DOCTOR: _____
        THE PATIENT: All right.

3.   THE MOTHER: _____
        THE SON: I will. Don't worry.

4.   MRS. JONES: _____
        THE CHILDREN: Yes, ma'am.

5.   THE GENERAL: _____
        THE SOLDIER: Yes, sir! Right away, sir!

6.   THE FATHER: _____
        THE DAUGHTER: Okay, Dad.

7.   A FRIEND: _____
        A FRIEND: Why not?

8.   THE WIFE: _____
        THE HUSBAND: Okay.

9. THE HUSBAND: _____

   THE WIFE: Why?

10. THE BOSS: _____

   THE EMPLOYEE: I'll do it immediately.

11. THE FATHER: _____

   THE SON: Okay. I won't.

☐ **EXERCISE 32. Imperative sentences. (Chart 7-12)**
Directions: Pair up with a classmate.
Student A: Your book is open. Read the directions to Student B.
Student B: Your book is closed. Follow the directions.

STUDENT A to B: Follow these steps to find the answer to a number puzzle.
  • Write down the number of the month you were born. (For example, write "2" if you were born in February. Write "3" if you were born in March.)
  • Double it.
  • Add 5.
  • Multiply by 50.
  • Add your age.
  • Subtract 250.
  • In the final number, the last two digits on the right will be your age, and the one or two digits on the left will be the month you were born.

Switch roles.
STUDENT B to A: Repeat the directions to the number puzzle to Student A.

☐ **EXERCISE 33. Writing activity. (Chart 7-12)**
Directions: Write about one or more of the following.

Give general advice to people who want to
1. improve their health.
2. get good grades.
3. improve their English.
4. make a good first impression.
5. find a job.
6. live life fully every day.
7. get married.
8. help preserve the earth's environment.

Example: handle stress
    Do you want to handle stress in your life? Here are some suggestions for you to consider.
      • Be sure to get daily exercise. You should devote at least half an hour to physical activity every day.
      • Don't overload your daily schedule. Learn to manage your time efficiently.
      • You have to take time for yourself. Don't keep yourself busy doing things for everyone else from morning until night. Do things that are just for you. Read, reflect, listen to music, or just do nothing for a period every day.
      • Don't waste time worrying about things you can't change. Recognize the things you can't change and accept them. Change only the things you can change.

□ **EXERCISE 34. Writing activity. (Charts 7-1 → 7-12)**

Directions: One of your friends wants to come to this city, either to go to school or get a job. Write your friend a letter. Give your friend advice about coming to this city to study or work.

7-13 MAKING SUGGESTIONS: *LET'S* AND *WHY DON'T*

(a) A: It's hot today. ***Let's go*** to the beach. B: Okay. Good idea. (b) A: It's hot today. ***Why don't we go*** to the beach? B: Okay. Good idea.	***Let's*** *(do something)* and ***why don't we*** *(do something)* have the same meaning. They are used to make suggestions about activities for you and me. ***Let's*** = *let us*.
(c) A: I'm tired. B: ***Why don't you take*** a nap? A: That's a good idea. I think I will.	***Why don't you*** *(do something)* is used to make a friendly suggestion, to give friendly advice.

□ **EXERCISE 35. Making suggestions with LET'S and WHY DON'T WE. (Chart 7-13)**

Directions: Make suggestions using ***let's*** and/or ***why don't we***. Work in pairs or as a class.

Example:

SPEAKER A: What would you like to do today?

SPEAKER B: Why don't we go for a walk in the park? / Let's go for a walk in the park.

1. Would you like to do this exercise in pairs or as a class?
2. What would you like to do this afternoon?
3. What do you want to do this weekend?
4. Where should we go for dinner tonight?
5. Who should we ask to join us for dinner tonight?
6. What time should we meet at the restaurant?

□ **EXERCISE 36. Making suggestions with WHY DON'T YOU. (Chart 7-13)**

Directions: Make suggestions using ***why don't you***. Work in pairs or as a class.

Example:

SPEAKER A: I'm hungry.

SPEAKER B: Why don't you have a candy bar?

1. I'm thirsty.
2. I'm sleepy.
3. I have a toothache.
4. It's too hot in this room.
5. I have to take a science course next semester. What should I take?
6. Tomorrow is my sister's birthday. What should I give her?

□ **EXERCISE 37. Making suggestions with LET'S and WHY DON'T.** (Chart 7-13)

Directions: Two students, books open, will read a dialogue aloud. Listen to the dialogue, books closed, and then repeat or write down the suggestion(s) you hear in the dialogue.

Example:
SPEAKER A (Yoko): Are you done with your work?
SPEAKER B (Talal): Yes.
SPEAKER A (Yoko): Good. Let's go to the market. I'm hungry for some fresh fruit.
SPEAKER B (Talal): Okay.
→ (repeated or written): *Yoko said, "Let's go to the market."*

1. A: I'm getting sleepy.
   B: Why don't you have a strong cup of tea?
   A: I suppose I could.

2. A: Are you busy tonight?
   B: No. Why?
   A: Let's rent a video.
   B: Okay.

3. A: Brrr. I'm cold.
   B: Why don't you put on a sweater?
   A: I don't have a sweater.

4. A: Where do you want to go for lunch?
   B: Why don't we go to *(name of a local place)*?
   A: That's too crowded at lunch time. Let's go to *(name of a local place)* instead.
   B: Okay.

5. A: I have a headache.
   B: Why don't you take some aspirin?
   A: I don't like to take aspirin.
   B: Why not?
   A: It upsets my stomach.
   B: Then why don't you lie down and rest? Sometimes that's all it takes to get rid of a headache.

6. A: Why don't we go dancing tonight?
   B: I don't know how to dance.
   A: Oh. Then why don't we go to a movie?
   B: I don't like movies.
   A: You don't like movies?!
   B: No.
   A: Well then, let's go to a restaurant for dinner.
   B: That's a waste of money.
   A: Well, you do what you want to tonight, but I'm going to go to a restaurant for dinner. And after that I'm going to go to a movie. And then I'm going to go dancing!

Directions: Complete the dialogues. Use *let's* or *why don't we*.

1. A: The weather's beautiful today.   *Let's/Why don't we go on a picnic?*
   B: Good idea.

2. A: I'm bored.

   B: Me too. _____

   A: Great idea!

3. A: Are you hungry?
   B: Yes. Are you?

   A: Yes. _____

   B: Okay.

4. A: What are you going to do over the holiday?
   B: I don't know. What are you going to do?
   A: I haven't made any plans.

   B: _____

   A: That sounds like a terrific idea, but I can't afford it.
   B: Actually, I can't either.

5. A: I need to go shopping.
   B: So do I.

   A: _____

   B: I can't go then. _____

   A: Okay. That's fine with me.

6. A: Do you have any plans for this weekend?
   B: Not really.

   A: I don't either. _____

   B: Okay. Good idea.

7. A: What time should we leave for the airport?

   B: _____

   A: Okay.

8. A: What should we do tonight?

   B: _____

   A: Sounds okay to me.

9. A: _____

   B: Let's not. _____ instead.

   A: Okay.

Directions: Work in groups. Make suggestions using *why don't you*. Speaker A states the problem, and then others offer suggestions. Only Speaker A's book is open. Rotate the open book, using a new Speaker A for each item.

Example: I'm at a restaurant with some business clients. I left my wallet at home. I don't have enough money to pay the bill. What am I going to do?

SPEAKER A: Okay, here's the situation. I'm at a restaurant with some business customers. I sell computer parts. I need to impress my clients. I have to pay for dinner, but I left my wallet at home. I'm really embarrassed. What am I going to do?

SPEAKER B: Why don't you call your office and ask someone to bring you some money?

SPEAKER C: Why don't you borrow the money from one of your customers?

SPEAKER D: Why don't you excuse yourself and go home to get your wallet?

SPEAKER E: Why don't you have a private discussion with the manager and arrange to pay the bill later?

1. I feel like doing something interesting and fun tonight. Any suggestions?

2. I need regular physical exercise. What would you suggest?

3. An important assignment is due in Professor Black's history class today. I haven't done it. Class starts in an hour. What am I going to do?

4. I've lost the key to my apartment, so I can't get in. My roommate is at the library. What am I going to do?

5. My friend and I had an argument. We stopped talking to each other. Now I'm sorry about the argument. I want to be friends again. What should I do?

6. I work hard all day, every day. I never take time to relax and enjoy myself. I need some recreation in my life. What do think I should do?

7. I'm trying to learn English, but I'm making slow progress. What can I do to learn English faster?

7-14 STATING PREFERENCES: *PREFER, LIKE . . . BETTER, WOULD RATHER*

(a) I **prefer** apples **to** oranges. (b) I **prefer** watching TV **to** *studying*.	**prefer** + *noun* + **to** + *noun* **prefer** + *-ing verb* + **to** + *-ing verb*
(c) I **like** apples **better than** oranges. (d) I **like** watching TV **better than** studying.	**like** + *noun* + **better than** + *noun* **like** + *-ing verb* + **better than** + *-ing* verb
(e) Ann **would rather have** an apple than an orange. (f) *INCORRECT: Ann would rather has an apple.* (g) I'd rather visit a big city **than live** there. (h) *INCORRECT: I'd rather visit a big city than to live there.* *INCORRECT: I'd rather visit a big city than living there.*	**Would rather** is followed immediately by the simple form of a verb (e.g., *have, visit, live*). Verbs following **than** are also in the simple form.
(i) **I'd/You'd/She'd/He'd/We'd/They'd** rather have an apple.	Contraction of **would** = **'d**.
(j) **Would you rather** have an apple **or** an orange?	In (j): In a polite question, **would rather** can be followed by **or** to offer someone a choice.

EXERCISE 40. Expressing preferences. (Chart 7-14)
Directions: Complete the sentences with **than** or **to**.

1. When I'm hot and thirsty, I **prefer** cold drinks _____to_____ hot drinks.

2. When I'm hot and thirsty, I **like** cold drinks **better** _____than_____ hot drinks.

3. When I'm hot and thirsty, I'**d rather have** a cold drink _____than_____ a hot drink.

4. I **prefer** tea _____ coffee.

5. I **like** tea **better** _____ coffee.

6. I'**d rather** drink tea _____ coffee.

7. When I choose a book, I **prefer** nonfiction _____ fiction.

8. I **like** rock-and-roll **better** _____ classical music.

9. My parents **would rather work** _____ retire. They enjoy their jobs.

10. Do you **like** fresh vegetables **better** _____ frozen or canned vegetables?

11. I **prefer visiting** my friends in the evening _____ watching TV by myself.

12. I **would rather read** a book in the evening _____ visit with friends.

EXERCISE 41. Expressing preferences: WOULD RATHER. (Chart 7-14)
Directions: Answer the questions **in complete sentences**. Work in pairs or as a class.

Example: Which do you prefer, apples or oranges?*
   → *I prefer (oranges) to (apples).*

Example: Which do you like better, bananas or strawberries?
   → *I like (bananas) better than (strawberries).*

Example: Which would you rather have right now, an apple or a banana?
   → *I'd rather have (a banana).*

1. Which do you like better, rice or potatoes?

2. Which do you prefer, peas or corn?

3. Which would you rather have for dinner tonight, beans or potatoes?

4. Name two sports. Which do you like better?

5. Name two movies. Which one would you rather see?

(Switch roles if working in pairs.)

6. What kind of music would you rather listen to, rock or classical?

7. Name two vegetables. Which do you prefer?

8. Which do you like better, Chinese food or Mexican food?

9. Name two sports that you play. Which sport would you rather play this afternoon?

10. Name two TV programs. Which do you like better?

---

*Use a rising intonation on the first choice and a falling intonation on the second choice.
   Which do you prefer, apples or oranges?*

☐ **EXERCISE 42. Expressing preferences: WOULD RATHER. (Chart 7-14)**

Directions: Use **would rather . . . than . . . .** in your answers. Work in pairs, in small groups, or as a class.

Would you rather . . .
1. live in an apartment or (live) in a house?* Why?
2. be a doctor or (be) a dentist? Why?
3. be married or (be) single? Why?
4. be ugly and intelligent or (be) handsome/beautiful and stupid? Why?
5. have a car or (have) an airplane? Why?
6. be rich and unlucky in love or (be) poor and lucky in love? Why?

(Switch roles if working in pairs.)
7. get on the Internet or read a good book? Why?
8. go to Moscow or (go) to London for your vacation? Why?
9. go to a football game or (go) to a soccer game? Why?
10. go to *(name of a place in this city)* or go to *(name of a place in this city)*? Why?
11. have six children or (have) two children? Why?
12. be a bird or (be) a fish? Why?

☐ **EXERCISE 43. Cumulative review. (Chapter 7)**

Directions: Each of the following has a short dialogue. Try to imagine a situation in which the dialogue could take place, and then choose the best completion.

Example: "My horse is sick."
        "Oh? What's the matter? You ___B___ call the vet."
        A. will   B. had better   C. may

1. "Does this pen belong to you?"
   "No. It _____ be Susan's. She was sitting at that desk."
        A. had better   B. will   C. must

2. "Let's go to a movie this evening."
   "That sounds like fun, but I can't. I _____ finish a report before I go to bed tonight."
        A. have got to   B. would rather   C. ought to

3. "Hey, Ted. What's up with Ken? Is he upset about something?"
   "He's angry because you recommended Ann instead of him for the promotion. You _____ sit down with him and explain your reasons. At least that's what I think."
        A. should   B. will   C. can

---

*It is possible but not necessary to repeat a preposition after **than**.

   CORRECT: *I'd rather live in an apartment **than in a house**.*
   CORRECT: *I'd rather live in an apartment **than a house**.*

4. "Does Tom want to go with us to the film festival tonight?"
   "No. He _____ go to a wrestling match than the film festival."
      A. could   B. would rather   C. prefers

5. "I did it! I did it! I got my driver's license!"
   "Congratulations, Michelle. I'm really proud of you."
   "Thanks, Dad. Now _____ I have the car tonight? Please, please!"
   "No. You're not ready for that quite yet."
      A. will   B. should   C. may

6. "I just tripped on your carpet and almost fell! There's a hole in it. You _____ fix
   that before someone gets hurt."
   "Yes, Uncle Ben. I should. I will. I'm sorry. Are you all right?"
      A. can   B. ought to   C. may

7. "Are you going to the conference in Atlanta next month?"
   "I _____ . It's sort of iffy right now. I've applied for travel money, but who knows
   what my supervisor will do."
      A. will   B. have to   C. might

8. "What shall we do after the meeting this evening?"
   "_____ pick Jan up and all go out to dinner together."
      A. Why don't   B. Let's   C. Should

9. "Have you seen my denim jacket? I _____ find it."
   "Look in the hall closet."
      A. may not   B. won't   C. can't

10. "Bye, Mom! I'm going to go play soccer with my friends."
    "Wait a minute, young man! You _____ do your chores first."
      A. had better not   B. have to   C. would rather

11. "Do you think that Scott will quit his job?"
    "I don't know. He _____. He's very angry. We'll just have to wait and see."
      A. must   B. may   C. will

12. "The hotel supplies towels, you know. You _____ pack a towel in your suitcase."
    "This is my bathrobe, not a towel."
      A. don't have to   B. must not   C. couldn't

13. "I heard that Bill was seriously ill."
    "Really? Well, he _____ be sick anymore. I just saw him riding his bike to work."
      A. won't   B. doesn't have to   C. must not

14. "Do you understand how this computer program works?"
    "Sort of, but not really. _____ you explain it to me one more time? Thanks."
      A. Could   B. Should   C. Must

15. "Did you climb to the top of the Statue of Liberty when you were in New York?"
    "No, I didn't. My knee was very sore, and I _____ climb all those stairs."
    A. might not   B. couldn't   C. must not

16. "Rick, _____ work for me this evening? I'll take your shift tomorrow."
    "Sure. I was going to ask you to work for me tomorrow anyway."
    A. should you   B. would you   C. do you have to

17. "How are we going to take care of your little brother and go to the concert at the same time?"
    "I have an idea. _____ we take him with us?"
    A. Why don't   B. Let's   C. Will

18. "Meet me at Tony's at five. Please! I _____ talk to you. It's important."
    "Is something wrong?"
    A. could   B. will   C. must

19. "What are you children doing? Stop! You _____ play with sharp knives."
    "What?"
    A. mustn't   B. couldn't   C. don't have to

20. "Don't wait for me. I _____ late."
    "Okay."
    A. maybe   B. may to be   C. may be

21. "Mr. Wells can't figure out how to assemble his daughter's tricycle."
    "He _____ read the instructions very carefully."
    A. had better   B. can't   C. would rather

Directions: Complete the sentences with any appropriate auxiliary verb in the list. There may be more than one possible completion. Also include any words in parentheses.

am	*do*	*has to*	*might*	*was*
are	*does*	*have to*	*must*	*were*
can	*did*	*is*	*ought to*	*will*
could	*had better*	*may*	*should*	*would*

1. A: Hello?

   B: Hello. This is Gisella Milazzo. ___May (Could/Can)___ I speak with

   Ms. Morgan, please?

2. A: Where's the newspaper?

   B: I *(not)* ____don't____ have it. Ask Kevin.

3. A: _____ you rather go downtown today or tomorrow?

   B: Tomorrow.

4. A: Stop! You *(not)* _____ pick those flowers! It's against the law

   to pick flowers in a national park.

   B: Really? I didn't know that.

5. A: _____ you talk to Amanda yesterday?

   B: Yes. Why?

6. A: _____ I help you, sir?

   B: Yes. _____ you show me the third watch from the left on the

   top shelf?

   A: Of course.

7. A: I'm sorry. _____ you repeat that? I can't hear you because

my dog _____ barking.

B: I said, "Why is your dog making all that noise?"

8. A: I don't know whether to turn left or right at the next intersection.

B: I think you _____ pull over and look at the map.

9. A: Hurry up. Kate and Greg _____ waiting for us.

B: I _____ hurrying!

10. A: Andy can't teach his class tonight.

B: He _____ teach tonight! He'll be fired if he doesn't show up.

11. A: Stop! *(not)* _____ touch that pan! It's hot! You'll burn

yourself.

B: Relax. I had no intention of touching it.

12. A: What _____ you carrying? _____ you

want some help?

B: It's a box of books. _____ you open the door for me, please?

13. A: Hello?

B: Hello. _____ I please speak to Sandra Wilson?

A: I'm sorry. There's no one here by that name. You _____ have

the wrong number.

14. A: _____ Nick going to be at the meeting tomorrow?

B: I hope so.

15. A: Everyone _____ work toward

cleaning up the environment.

B: I agree. Life on earth *(not)* _____

survive if we continue to poison the land, water,

and air.

CHAPTER *8*
Connecting Ideas

CONTENTS

☐ EXERCISE 1. Preview. (Chapter 8)

Directions: Add punctuation (commas and periods) and capital letters if necessary. Do not change or add any words.

1. Butterflies are insects all insects have six legs.
   → *Butterflies are insects. All insects have six legs.*

2. Ants and butterflies are insects. OK *(no change)*

3. Ants butterflies cockroaches bees and flies are insects.

4. Butterflies and bees are insects spiders are different from insects.

5. Spiders have eight legs so they are not called insects.

6. Most insects have wings but spiders do not.

7. Bees are valuable to us they pollinate crops

   and provide us with honey.

8. Some insects bite us and carry diseases.

Free flower pollination with each purchase

Honey for SALE

9. Insects can cause us trouble they bite us carry diseases and eat our food.

10. Insects are essential to life on earth the plants and animals on earth could not live

    without them insects may bother us but we have to share this planet with them.

11. We have to share the earth with insects because they are essential to plant and

    animal life.

12. Because insects are necessary to life on earth it is important to know about them.

8-1 CONNECTING IDEAS WITH *AND*

CONNECTING ITEMS WITHIN A SENTENCE	When *and* connects only **two** words (or phrases) within a sentence, NO COMMA is used, as in (a).
(a) NO COMMA: I saw a cat *and* a mouse. (b) COMMAS: I saw a cat**,** a mouse**,** *and* a dog.	When *and* connects **three or more** items within a sentence, COMMAS are used, as in (b).*
CONNECTING TWO SENTENCES	When *and* connects two complete sentences (also called independent clauses), a comma is usually used, as in (c).
(c) COMMA: I saw a cat**,** *and* you saw a mouse.	
(d) PERIOD: I saw a cat**.** You saw a mouse. (e) *INCORRECT: I saw a cat, you saw a mouse.*	Without ***and***, two complete sentences are separated by a period, as in (d), NOT a comma.** A complete sentence begins with a capital letter; note that *You* is capitalized in (d).

*In a series of three or more items, the comma before *and* is optional.
        ALSO CORRECT: *I saw a cat**,** a mouse and a dog.*
**A "period" (the dot used at the end of a sentence) is called a "full stop" in British English.

☐ EXERCISE 2. Connecting ideas with AND. (Chart 8-1)
    Directions: Underline and label the words (noun, verb, adjective) connected by ***and***. Add commas as necessary.

                    noun + noun
1. My aunt puts <u>milk</u> and <u>sugar</u> in her tea. → *no commas needed*

                    noun + noun + noun
2. My aunt puts <u>milk</u>**,**   <u>sugar</u>**,** and <u>lemon</u> in her tea. → *commas needed*

3. The river is wide and deep.

4. The river is wide deep and dangerous.

5. Goats and horses are farm animals.

6. Giraffes anteaters tigers and kangaroos are wild animals.

7. The children played games sang songs and ate birthday cake.

8. The children played games and sang songs.

9. My mother father and grandfather went to the airport to pick up my brother and

   sister.

10. When he wants to entertain the children, my husband moos like a cow roars like a lion

    and barks like a dog.

□ EXERCISE 3. Connecting ideas with AND. (Chart 8-1)

Directions: Write sentences for some or all of the topics below. Use *and* in your sentences.

Example: three things you are afraid of
→ *I'm afraid of heights, poisonous snakes, and guns.*

1. your three favorite sports
2. three adjectives that describe a person whom you admire
3. four cities that you would like to visit
4. two characteristics that describe *(name of this city)*
5. three or more separate things you did this morning
6. the five most important people in your life
7. two or more things that make you happy
8. three or more adjectives that describe the people in your country

□ EXERCISE 4. Punctuating with commas and periods. (Chart 8-1)

Directions: Add commas and periods where appropriate. Capitalize as necessary.

1. The rain fell the wind blew.
   → *The rain fell.* ***T****he wind blew.*

2. The rain fell and the wind blew.
   → *The rain fell,* *and the wind blew.**

3. I talked he listened.

4. I talked to Ryan about his school grades and he listened to me carefully.

---

*Sometimes the comma is omitted when **and** connects two very short independent clauses.
   ALSO CORRECT: *The rain fell **and** the wind blew.* (NO COMMA)
In longer sentences, the comma is helpful and usual.

5. The man asked a question the woman answered it.

6. The man asked a question and the woman answered it.

7. People and animals must share the earth and its resources.

8. Rome is an Italian city it has a mild climate and many interesting attractions.

9. You should visit Rome its climate is mild and there are many interesting attractions.

10. The United States is bounded by two oceans and two countries the oceans are the Pacific to the west and the Atlantic to the east and the countries are Canada to the north and Mexico to the south.

11. The twenty-five most common words in English are: *the and a to of I in was that it he you for had is with she has on at have but me my* and *not*.

8-2 CONNECTING IDEAS WITH *BUT* AND *OR*

(a) I *went* to bed *but couldn't sleep*. (b) Is a lemon *sweet **or** sour*? (c) Did you order *coffee**,** tea**,** **or** milk*?	***And, but,*** and ***or*** are called "conjunctions."* Like ***and, but*** and ***or*** can connect items within a sentence. Commas are used with a series of three or more items, as in (c).
I dropped the vase. = a sentence *It didn't break.* = a sentence (d) I dropped the vase**,** ***but*** it didn't break. (e) Do we have class on Monday**,** ***or*** is Monday a holiday?	A comma is usually used when ***but*** or ***or*** combines two complete (independent) sentences into one sentence, as in (d) and (e).**

*More specifically, *and, but,* and *or* are called "coordinating conjunctions."

**Except in very formal writing, a conjunction can also come at the beginning of a sentence.
ALSO CORRECT: *I dropped the vase.* ***B****ut it didn't break.*
I saw a cat. ***A****nd you saw a mouse.*

□ EXERCISE 5. Connecting ideas with AND, BUT, and OR. (Charts 8-1 and 8-2)
Directions: Add ***and, but,*** or ***or.*** Add commas if necessary.

1. I washed my shirt ___, but___ it didn't get clean.

2. Would you like some water _____or_____ some fruit juice?

3. I bought some paper, a greeting card ___, and___ some envelopes.

4. The flight attendants served dinner _____ I didn't eat.

5. I was hungry _____ didn't eat on the plane. The food didn't look appetizing.

6. I washed my face, brushed my teeth _____ combed my hair.

7. Golf _____ tennis are popular sports.

8. Sara is a good tennis player _____ she's never played golf.

9. Which would you prefer? Would you like to play tennis _____ golf Saturday morning?

10. Who called whom? Did Bob call you _____ did you call Bob?

☐ EXERCISE 6. Punctuating with commas and periods. (Charts 8-1 and 8-2)
Directions: Add commas, periods, and capital letters as appropriate.

1. Cats are mammals turtles are reptiles.
   → *Cats are mammals.* **T**urtles are reptiles.

2. Cats are mammals but turtles are reptiles.

3. Cows and horses are farm animals but zebras and giraffes are wild animals.

4. Cows and horses are farm animals zebras giraffes and lions are wild animals.

5. Cars use roads trains run on tracks.

6. Cars buses and trucks use roads but trains run on tracks.

7. Most vegetables grow above the ground but some are roots and grow under the ground corn beans and cabbage grow above the ground but carrots and onions grow under the ground.

8. Why do people with different ethnic backgrounds sometimes fear and distrust each other?

9. Nothing in nature stays the same forever today's land sea climate plants and animals are all part of a relentless process of change continuing through millions of years.

10. Mozart was a great composer but he had a short and difficult life at the end of his life, he was penniless sick and unable to find work but he wrote music of lasting beauty and joy.

8-3 CONNECTING IDEAS WITH *SO*

(a) The room was dark, *so* I turned on a light.	*So* can be used as a conjunction. It is preceded by a comma. It connects the ideas in two independent clauses. *So* expresses **results**: cause: *The room was dark.* result: *I turned on a light.*
(b) COMPARE: The room was dark, *but* I didn't turn on a light.	*But* often expresses an unexpected result, as in (b).

☐ **EXERCISE 7. SO vs. BUT. (Charts 8-2 and 8-3)**
   Directions: Add *so* or *but*.

   1. It began to rain, _____so_____ I opened my umbrella.

   2. It began to rain, _____but_____ I didn't open my umbrella.

   3. I didn't have an umbrella, _____ I got wet.

   4. I didn't have an umbrella, _____ I didn't get wet because I was wearing my raincoat.

   5. The water was cold, _____ I didn't go swimming.

   6. The water was cold, _____ I went swimming anyway.

   7. Scott's directions to his apartment weren't clear, _____ George got lost.

   8. The directions weren't clear, _____ I found Scott's apartment anyway.

   9. My friend lied to me, _____ I still like and trust her.

   10. My friend lied to me, _____ I don't trust her anymore.

Directions: Add commas, periods, and capital letters as necessary.

1. African elephants are larger than Asiatic elephants. **E** elephants native to Asia are easier to train and have gentler natures than African elephants.

2. Asiatic elephants are native to the jungles and forests in India Indonesia Malaysia Thailand India China and other countries in southeastern and southern Asia.

3. Elephants spend a lot of time in water and are good swimmers they take baths in rivers and lakes they like to give themselves showers by shooting water from their trunks.

4. After a bath, they often cover themselves with dirt the dirt protects their skin from the sun and insects.

5. A female elephant is pregnant for approximately twenty months and almost always has only one baby a young elephant stays close to its mother for the first ten years of its life.

6. Elephants live peacefully together in herds but some elephants (called *rogues)* leave the herd and become mean these elephants usually are in pain from decayed teeth a disease or a wound.

Directions: Add commas, periods, and capital letters as necessary.

(1)   **A** ⱥ few days ago, a friend and I were driving from Benton Harbor to Chicago.

(2)   **W** ẉe didn't experience any delays for the first hour but near Chicago we ran into

(3)   some highway construction the traffic wasn't moving at all my friend and I sat in the

(4)   car and waited we talked about our jobs our families and the terrible traffic slowly the

(5)   traffic started to move

(6)   we noticed a black sports car at the side of the road the right blinker was blinking

(7)   the driver obviously wanted to get back into the line of traffic car after car passed

(8)   without letting the black sports car get in line I decided to do a good deed so I

(9)   motioned for the black car to get in line ahead of me the driver of the black car waved

(10)   thanks to me and I waved back at him

(11)   all cars had to stop at a toll booth a short way down the road I held out my

(12)   money to pay my toll but the tolltaker just smiled and waved me on she told me that the

(13)   man in the black sports car had already paid my toll wasn't that a nice way of saying

(14)   thank you?

8-4 USING AUXILIARY VERBS AFTER *BUT* AND *AND*

(a) I **don't like** coffee, **but** my husband **does**. (b) I **like** tea, **but** my husband **doesn't**. (c) I **won't be** here tomorrow, **but** Sue **will**. (d) I **'ve seen** that movie, **but** Joe **hasn't**. (e) He **isn't** here, **but** she **is**.*	In (a): **does** = *likes coffee*. After **but** and **and**, often only an auxiliary verb is used. It has the same tense or modal as the main verb.
(f) I **don't like** coffee, **and** Ed **doesn't** either. (g) I **like** tea, **and** Kate **does** too. (h) I **won't be** here, **and** he **won't** either. (i) I **'ve seen** that movie, **and** Pat **has** too. (j) He **isn't** here, **and** Anna **isn't** either.	Notice in the examples: negative + *but* + affirmative affirmative + *but* + negative negative + *and* + negative affirmative + *and* + affirmative

*A verb is not contracted with a pronoun at the end of a sentence after *but* and *and*:
    CORRECT: . . . *but she is*.
    INCORRECT: . . . *but she's*.

☐ **EXERCISE 10. Using auxiliary verbs after BUT. (Chart 8-4)**
    Directions: Complete the sentences with auxiliary verbs.

1. Debra **reads** a lot of books, but her brothers _____don't_____.

2. Sam **isn't** in the school play this year, but Adam _____is_____.

3. I **will be** at home this evening, but my roommate _____.

4. Ducks **like** to swim, but chickens _____.

5. That phone **doesn't work**, but this one _____.

6. Joe **isn't** at home, but his parents _____.

7. Carl **can touch** his nose with his tongue, but most people _____.

8. Jack **has visited** my home, but Linda _____.

9. I**'m not going** to graduate this year, but my best friend _____.

10. My dog **crawls** under the bed when it thunders, but my cat _____.

□ EXERCISE 11. Using auxiliary verbs after BUT. (Chart 8-4)

Directions: Complete the sentences by using the names of your classmates and appropriate auxiliary verbs.

1. _____Maria_____ has long hair, but _____Kutaiba doesn't_____.

2. _____Kunio_____ doesn't live in an apartment, but _____Boris does_____.

3. _____ isn't in class today, but _____.

4. _____ is here today, but _____.

5. _____ can speak (*a language*), but _____.

6. _____ doesn't have brown eyes, but _____.

7. _____ didn't come to class yesterday, but _____.

8. _____ will be at home tonight, but _____.

9. _____ has a mustache, but _____.

10. _____ has lived here for a long time, but _____.

□ EXERCISE 12. Using auxiliary verbs after AND and BUT. (Chart 8-4)

Directions: Complete the sentences by adding appropriate auxiliary verbs. Add *too* and *either* as appropriate.

1. Alex goes to college, and his sisters _____do too_____.

2. Anna goes to college, but her cousin _____doesn't_____.

3. Hugo doesn't go to college, and his brother _____doesn't either_____.

4. Horses are domesticated animals, and camels _____.

5. Lions aren't domesticated animals, and tigers _____.

6. Horses are domesticated animals, but lions _____.

7. Paula didn't go to the picnic, and Jack _____.

8. I work at an airplane factory, and my brother _____.

9. Gray is a dull color, but orange _____.

10. Rita won't be at the party, and Jean _____.

11. Olga was in class yesterday, but Antonio _____.

12. Fatima is in class today, and Pedro _____.

13. I can't sing very well, but my wife _____.

8-5 USING *AND* + *TOO, SO, EITHER, NEITHER*

(a) Sue works, *and* **Tom** $\overset{s}{}$ $\overset{+}{}$ $\overset{aux}{\textbf{does}}$ $\overset{+}{}$ $\overset{\text{TOO}}{\textbf{too}}$.
 (b) Sue works, *and* **so** $\overset{\text{SO}}{}$ $\overset{+}{}$ $\overset{aux}{\textbf{does}}$ $\overset{+}{}$ $\overset{s}{\textbf{Tom}}$.
	(a) and (b) have the same meaning.
	 Word order:
	    subject + *auxiliary* + **too**
	    so + *auxiliary* + *subject*

(c) Ann doesn't work, *and* **Joe** $\overset{s}{}$ $\overset{+}{}$ $\overset{aux}{\textbf{doesn't}}$ $\overset{+}{}$ $\overset{\text{EITHER}}{\textbf{either}}$.
 (d) Ann doesn't work, *and* **neither** $\overset{\text{NEITHER}}{}$ $\overset{+}{}$ $\overset{aux}{\textbf{does}}$ $\overset{+}{}$ $\overset{s}{\textbf{Joe}}$.
	(c) and (d) have the same meaning.
	 Word order:
	    subject + *auxiliary* + **either**
	    neither + *auxiliary* + *subject*
	 Note: An affirmative auxiliary is used with *neither*.

(e) A: I'm hungry.
    B: *I am too.*   (f) A: I'm hungry.
                       B: *So am I.*
 (g) A: I don't eat meat.   (h) A: I don't eat meat.
    B: *I don't either.*   B: *Neither do I.*
	And is usually not used when there are two speakers.
	 (e) and (f) have the same meaning.
	 (g) and (h) have the same meaning.

(i) A: I'm hungry. (j) A: I don't eat meat. B: *Me too.* (informal) B: *Me neither.* (informal)	**Me too** and **me neither** are often used in informal spoken English.

☐ **EXERCISE 13. AND + TOO, SO, EITHER, NEITHER.** (Chart 8-5)
    Directions: Complete the sentences using the given words. Pay special attention to word order.

Omar   James   Marco   Ivan

1. a. *too*   Marco has a mustache, and _____James does too_____.

   b. *so*   Marco has a mustache, and _____.

2. a. *either*   Omar doesn't have a mustache, and _____.

   b. *neither*   Omar doesn't have a mustache, and _____.

3. a. *too*   Marco is wearing a hat, and _____.

   b. *so*   Marco is wearing a hat, and _____.

4. a. *either*   Ivan isn't wearing a hat, and _____.

   b. *neither*   Ivan isn't wearing a hat, and _____.

☐ **EXERCISE 14. AND + TOO, SO, EITHER, NEITHER.** (Chart 8-5)
Directions: Complete the sentences by using **too, so, either,** or **neither.** Use the names of your classmates and appropriate auxiliaries.

1. _____Maria_____ is in class today, and _____so is Po / Po is too_____ .
2. _____ lives in an apartment, and _____ .
3. _____ can't speak Chinese, and _____ .
4. _____ wasn't in class yesterday, and _____ .
5. _____ stayed home and studied last night, and _____ .
6. _____ doesn't have a mustache, and _____ .
7. _____ will be in class tomorrow, and _____ .
8. _____ isn't married, and _____ .
9. _____ has dimples, and _____ .
10. _____ has been in class all week, and _____ .

☐ **EXERCISE 15. AND + TOO, SO, EITHER, NEITHER.** (Chart 8-5)
Directions: Complete by using **too, so, either,** or **neither** and the given words.

1. *clouds*   Snow is white, and _____clouds are too / so are clouds_____ .
2. *salt*   Sugar isn't expensive, and _____ .
3. *cats*   Monkeys have long tails, and _____ .
4. *gorillas*   Human beings don't have tails, and _____ .
5. *the teacher* I forgot to bring my book to class, and _____ .
6. *the teacher* I was late for class today, and _____ .
7. *I*   You've never* been in Nepal, and _____ .
8. *penguins*   Ostriches can't fly, and

_____

_____ .

I WONDER HOW THEY DO THAT?

SO DO I!

---
*__Never__ makes a sentence negative:
The teacher is __never__ late, and __neither__ am I. OR *I'm __not either__.*

□ **EXERCISE 16. AND + TOO, SO, EITHER, NEITHER. (Chart 8-5)**
Directions: Complete the dialogues by agreeing with Speaker A's idea. Use *so* or *neither*.
Use *I*.

1. A: I'm tired.

   B: _____So am I_____ .

2. A: I didn't enjoy the movie last night.

   B: _____Neither did I_____ .

3. A: I always have coffee in the morning.

   B: _____ .

4. A: I don't feel like going to class today.

   B: _____ .

5. A: I didn't eat breakfast this morning.

   B: _____ .

6. A: I've never been in Peru.

   B: _____ .

7. A: I studied last night.

   B: _____ .

8. A: I should study tonight.

   B: _____ .

9. A: I can't speak Hungarian.

   B: _____ .

10. A: But I can speak English.

    B: _____ .

□ **EXERCISE 17. SO and NEITHER. (Chart 8-5)**
Directions: Work in pairs.
Speaker A: Say the given sentence. Complete the sentence with your own words if
  necessary. Your book is open.
Speaker B: Respond to Speaker A's statement by using *so* or *neither*. Your book is closed.

Example: I'm confused.
SPEAKER A *(book open):* I'm confused.
SPEAKER B *(book closed):* So am I.★

Example: Frogs don't have tails.
SPEAKER A *(book open):* Frogs don't have tails.
SPEAKER B *(book closed):* Neither do human beings.

Example: *(Name of a restaurant)* is a good place to eat in *(this city)*.
SPEAKER A *(book open):* Ivar's Seafood Restaurant is a good place to eat in Seattle.
SPEAKER B *(book closed):* So is Hong Kong Gardens.

★This exercise is designed to practice the use of *so* and *neither* in conversational responses. If, however, Speaker B
doesn't want to agree, echo, or support Speaker A's statement, there are alternative responses. For example:
  SPEAKER A: I'm confused.
  SPEAKER B: **You are? What's the matter?**

  SPEAKER A: Frogs don't have tails.
  SPEAKER B: **Really? Is that so? Hmmm. I didn't know that. Are you sure?**

  SPEAKER A: Ivar's Seafood Restaurant is a good place to eat in Seattle.
  SPEAKER B: **Oh? I've never eaten there.**

Switch roles.

1. I studied last night.
2. I study grammar every day.
3. I'm thirsty.
4. I'd like *(a kind of drink)*.
5. I've never been in *(name of a country)*.
6. I don't like *(a kind of food)*.
7. . . . is a *(big/small)* country.
8. Paper burns.
9. Snakes don't have legs.
10. I've never seen an iceberg.

11. San Francisco is a seaport.
12. Chickens lay eggs.
13. I *(like/don't like)* the weather today.
14. Swimming is an Olympic sport.
15. Coffee contains caffeine.
16. Elephants can swim.
17. *(Name of a country)* is in Africa.
18. I've never had caviar* for breakfast.
19. Denmark has no volcanoes.
20. I'd rather go to *(name of a place)* than *(name of a place)*.

☐ EXERCISE 18. TOO, SO, EITHER, NEITHER. (Chart 8-5)
Directions: Create dialogues (either with a partner or in writing).
Speaker A: Use the given verb to make a statement (not a question). Your book is open.
Speaker B: React to Speaker A's idea by using *too, so, either,* or *neither* in a response. Your book is closed.

Example: would like
SPEAKER A *(book open):* I'd like to sail around the world someday.
SPEAKER B *(book closed):* So would I. OR I would too.**

Example: didn't want
SPEAKER A *(book open):* Toshi didn't want to give a speech in front of the class.
SPEAKER B *(book closed):* Neither did Ingrid. OR Ingrid didn't either.**

Switch roles.

1. don't have
2. can't speak
3. enjoy
4. isn't going to be
5. haven't ever seen
6. will be

7. can fly
8. would like
9. didn't go
10. are
11. is sitting
12. wasn't

---

*Caviar = fish eggs (an expensive delicacy in some cultures).

**This exercise asks you to use *too, so, either,* or *neither* in conversational responses. Other responses are, of course, possible. For example:
SPEAKER A: I'd like to sail around the world someday.
SPEAKER B: **Really? Why?**
SPEAKER A: Toshi didn't want to give a speech in front of the class.
SPEAKER B: **Oh? Why not?**

8-6 CONNECTING IDEAS WITH *BECAUSE*

(a) He drank water *because* he was thirsty.	***Because*** expresses a cause; it gives a reason. Why did he drink water? Reason: he was thirsty.
(b) MAIN CLAUSE: *He drank water.*	A main clause is a complete sentence: *He drank water* = a complete sentence.
(c) ADVERB CLAUSE: *because he was thirsty*	An adverb clause is NOT a complete sentence: *because he was thirsty* = NOT a complete sentence. ***Because*** introduces an adverb clause: ***because*** + *subject* + *verb* = *an adverb clause.*
MAIN CLAUSE　　ADVERB CLAUSE (d) ⌐He drank water⌐ ⌐*because he was thirsty.*⌐ 　　　　(no comma) ADVERB CLAUSE　　　MAIN CLAUSE (e) ⌐*Because he was thirsty,*⌐ ⌐he drank water.*⌐ 　　　　(comma)	An adverb clause is connected to a main clause, as in (d) and (e).★ In (d): **main clause** + ***no* comma** + **adverb clause** In (e): **adverb clause** + **comma** + **main clause** (d) and (e) have exactly the same meaning.
(f) *INCORRECT IN WRITING:* *He drank water.* **Because he was thirsty.**	(f) is incorrect in written English: *because he was thirsty* cannot stand alone as a sentence that starts with a capital letter and ends with a period. It has to be connected to a main clause, as in (d) and (e).
(g) CORRECT IN SPEAKING: 　A: Why did he drink some water? 　B: **Because he was thirsty.**	In spoken English, an adverb clause can be used as the short answer to a question, as in (g).

★See Chart 2-10, p. 48, for a discussion of other adverb clauses. "Time clauses" are adverb clauses that are introduced by *when, after, before, while, until,* and *as soon as.*

☐ EXERCISE 19. Adverb clauses with BECAUSE. (Chart 8-6)
　　　　Directions: Combine each pair of sentences in two different orders. Use ***because***. Punctuate carefully.

　　　1. We didn't have class.
　　　　　The teacher was absent.
　　　　　→ *We didn't have class because the teacher was absent.*
　　　　　→ *Because the teacher was absent, we didn't have class.*

　　　2. The children were hungry.
　　　　　There was no food in the house.

　　　3. The bridge is closed.
　　　　　We can't drive to the other side of the river.

　　　4. My car didn't start.
　　　　　The battery was dead.

　　　5. Larry and Patti laughed hard.
　　　　　The joke was very funny.

☐ **EXERCISE 20. Adverb clauses with BECAUSE. (Chart 8-6)**
Directions: Add periods, commas, and capital letters as necessary.

1. Jimmy is very young because he is afraid of the dark he likes to have a light on in his

   bedroom at night.
   → *Jimmy is very young.* ***B****ecause he is afraid of the dark, he likes to have a light on in his*
      bedroom at night.

2. Mr. El-Sayed had a bad cold because he was not feeling well he stayed home from the

   office.

3. Judy went to bed early because she was tired she likes to get at least eight hours of

   sleep a night.

4. Frank put his head in his hands he was angry and upset because he had lost a lot of

   work on his computer.

☐ **EXERCISE 21. BECAUSE and SO. (Charts 8-3 and 8-6)**
Directions: Create sentences with the same meaning. Use commas as appropriate.

PART I. Restate the sentence, using **so**.
1. Jack lost his job because he never showed up for work on time.
   → *Jack never showed up for work on time, so he lost his job.*

2. I opened the window because the room was hot.

3. Because it was raining, I stayed indoors.

PART II. Restate the sentence, using **because**.
4. Jason was hungry, so he ate.
   → *Because Jason was hungry, he ate.* OR *Jason ate because he was hungry.*

5. The water in the river is polluted, so we can't go swimming.

6. My watch is broken, so I was late for my job interview.

☐ **EXERCISE 22. Review: conjunctions and adverb clauses. (Charts 8-1 → 8-6)**
Directions: Add commas, periods, and capital letters as appropriate. Don't change any of
the words or the order of the words.

1. Jim was hot he sat in the shade.
   → *Jim was hot.* ***H****e sat in the shade.*

2. Jim was hot and tired so he sat in the shade.

3. Jim was hot tired and thirsty.

4. Because he was hot Jim sat in the shade.

5. Because they were hot and thirsty Jim and Susan sat in the shade and drank tea.

6. Jim and Susan sat in the shade and drank tea because they were hot and thirsty.

7. Jim sat in the shade drank tea and fanned himself because he was hot tired and thirsty.

8. Because Jim was hot he stayed under the shade of the tree but Susan went back to work.

9. Mules are domestic animals they are the offspring of a horse and a donkey mules are called "beasts of burden" because they can work hard and carry heavy loads.

10. Because mules are strong they can work under harsh conditions but they need proper care.

11. Ann had been looking for an apartment for two weeks yesterday she went to look at an apartment on Fifth Avenue she rented it because it was in good condition and had a nice view of the city she was glad to find a new apartment.

12. The word "matter" is a chemical term matter is anything that has weight this book your finger water a rock air and the moon are all examples of matter radio waves and heat are not matter because they do not have weight happiness daydreams and fear have no weight and are not matter.

8-7 CONNECTING IDEAS WITH *EVEN THOUGH / ALTHOUGH*

(a) ***Even though*** *I was hungry,* I did not eat. I did not eat ***even though*** *I was hungry.* (b) ***Although*** *I was hungry,* I did not eat. I did not eat ***although*** *I was hungry.*	***Even though*** and ***although*** introduce an adverb clause. (a) and (b) have the same meaning. They mean: *I was hungry, but I did not eat.*
COMPARE (c) *Because* I was hungry, *I ate.* (d) *Even though* I was hungry, *I did not eat.*	*Because* expresses an expected result. *Even though/although* expresses an unexpected or opposite result.

☐ **EXERCISE 23. EVEN THOUGH vs. BECAUSE. (Chart 8-7)**

Directions: Complete the sentences by using *even though* or *because*.

1. _____*Even though*_____ the weather is cold, Rick isn't wearing a coat.

2. _____*Because*_____ the weather is cold, Ben is wearing a coat.

3. _____ Jane was sad, she smiled.

4. _____ Jane was sad, she cried.

5. _____ it was cold outside, we went swimming in the lake.

6. _____ I like to swim, I joined my friends in the lake.

7. People ask Tony to sing at weddings _____ he has a good voice.

8. George sings loudly _____ he can't carry a tune.

9. _____ our friends live on an island, it is easy to get there by car

_____ there is a bridge from the mainland.

☐ **EXERCISE 24. EVEN THOUGH/ALTHOUGH and BECAUSE. (Charts 8-6 and 8-7)**

Directions: Choose the best completion.

1. Even though ostriches have wings, ___*C*___ .
   A. their feathers are large
   B. they are big birds
   C. they can't fly

2. My brother came to my graduation ceremony although _____ .
   A. he was sick
   B. he was eager to see everyone
   C. he was happy for me

3. Even though I looked in every pocket and every drawer, _____ .
   A. my keys were under the bed
   B. my roommate helped me look for my keys
   C. I never found my keys

4. Jack hadn't heard or read about the murder even though _____ .
   A. he was the murderer
   B. it was on the front page of every newspaper
   C. he was out of town when it occurred

5. We can see the light from an airplane high in the sky at night before we hear the plane because _____ .
   A. light travels faster than sound
   B. airplanes travel at high speeds
   C. our eyes work better than our ears at night

6. Although _____ , he finished the race in first place.
    A. John was full of energy and strength
    B. John was leading all the way
    C. John was far behind in the beginning

7. My partner and I worked late into the evening. Even though _____ , we stopped at our favorite restaurant before we went home.
    A. we were very hungry
    B. we had finished our report
    C. we were very tired

8. Snakes don't have ears, but they are very sensitive to vibrations that result from noise. Snakes can sense the presence of a moving object even though _____ .
    A. they have ears
    B. they feel vibrations
    C. they can't hear

9. In mountainous areas, melting snow in the spring runs downhill into streams and rivers. The water carries with it sediment, that is, small particles of soil and rock. In the spring, mountain rivers become cloudy rather than clear because _____ .
    A. mountain tops are covered with snow
    B. the water from melting snow brings sediment to the river
    C. ice is frozen water

10. Even though it was a hot summer night, we went inside and shut the windows because _____ .
    A. the rain stopped
    B. we were enjoying the cool breeze
    C. a storm was coming

☐ EXERCISE 25. EVEN THOUGH vs. BECAUSE. (Charts 8-6 and 8-7)
Directions: Answer "yes" or "no," as you wish. Answer in a complete sentence using either *because* or *even though*. Change the wording as you wish. Only the teacher's book is open.

Example: Last night you were tired. Did you go to bed early?
→ *Yes, I went to bed early because I was tired.* OR
Yes, because I was tired, I went to bed before nine. OR
No, I didn't go to bed early even though I was really sleepy. OR
No, even though I was really tired, I didn't go to bed until after midnight.

1. Last night you were tired. Did you stay up late?

2. You are thirsty. Do you want (a glass of water)?

3. You're hungry. Do you want (a candy bar)?

4. Vegetables are good for you. Do you eat a lot of them?

5. Space exploration is exciting. Would you like to be an astronaut?

6. Guns are dangerous. Do you want to own one?

7. *(A local restaurant)* is expensive/inexpensive. Do you eat there?

8. *(A local delicacy)* is/are expensive. Do you buy it/them?

9. The *(name of a local)* river is/isn't polluted. Do you want to swim in it?

10. Who (in this room) can't swim? Do you want to go to (the beach/the swimming pool) with (. . .) and me this afternoon?

11. Who loves to go swimming? Do you want to go to (the beach/the swimming pool) with (. . .) and me this afternoon?

12. What are the winters like here? Do you like living here in winter?

13. *(A recent movie)* has had good reviews. Do you want to see it?

14. Are you a good artist? Do you want to draw a picture of me on the board?

15. Where does your family live? Are you going to go there (over the next holiday)?

□ EXERCISE 26. EVEN THOUGH and BECAUSE. (Chart 8-7)

Directions: Complete the sentences with your own words. Pay attention to proper punctuation.

1. I like our classroom even though . . . .
2. I like my home because . . . .
3. . . . even though I don't . . . . .
4. . . . because I don't . . . .
5. Because we . . . , we . . . .
6. Even though . . . , we . . . .
7. Even though . . . , . . . because . . . .
8. Because . . . , I . . . , but . . . because . . . .

□ EXERCISE 27. Error analysis. (Charts 8-1 → 8-7)

Directions: Correct the errors in these sentences. Pay special attention to punctuation.

1. Even though I was sick, but I went to work.
   → *Even though I was sick, I went to work.*
   → *I was sick, but I went to work.*

2. Gold silver and copper. They are metals.

3. The students crowded around the bulletin board. Because their grades were posted there.

4. I had a cup of coffee, and so does my friend.

5. My roommate didn't go. Neither I went either.

6. Even I am very exhausted, I didn't stop working until after midnight last night.

7. The teacher went too the meeting, and too of the students did to.

8. Although I like chocolate, but I can't eat it because I'm allergic to it.

9. Many tourists visit my country. Warm weather all year. Many interesting landmarks.

10. Because the weather in my country is warm and comfortable all year so many tourists visit it in the winter.

11. I like to eat raw eggs for breakfast and everybody else in my family too.

12. A hardware store sells tools and nails and plumbing supplies and paint and etc.*

13. Because the war broke out in late September we had to cancel our October trip even though we already had our passports visas airplane tickets and hotel reservations.

14. Many of us experience stress on our jobs my job is stressful because my workplace is not pleasant or comfortable it is noisy hot and dirty even though I try to do my best my boss is unhappy with my work and always gives me bad performance reports I need to find another job.

15. I like animals I have a little dog at home her name is Linda she is brown and white.

□ EXERCISE 28. Punctuating with commas and periods. (Chapter 8)
Directions: Add commas, periods, and capital letters as necessary. (There are four adverb clauses in the following passage. Can you find and underline them?)

(1)   What is the most common substance on earth? I it isn't wood, iron, or sand. The most common substance on earth is water it occupies more than seventy percent of the earth's surface it is in lakes rivers and oceans it is in the ground and in the air it is practically everywhere.

---

*__Etc__. is an abbreviation of the Latin *et cetera*. It means "and other things of a similar nature." The word **and** is NOT used in front of **etc**.
    INCORRECT: *The farmer raises cows, sheep, goats, **chickens, and etc**.*
    INCORRECT: *The farmer raises cows, sheep, goats, **and chickens, etc**.*
    CORRECT: *The farmer raises cows, sheep, goats, chickens, **etc**.*
Also, notice the spelling: *etc*., NOT *ect*.

(2)   Water is vital because life on earth could not exist without it people animals and plants all need water in order to exist every living thing is mostly water a person's body is about sixty-seven percent water a bird is about seventy-five percent water most fruit is about ninety percent water.

(3)   Most of the water in the world is saltwater ninety-seven percent of the water on earth is in the oceans because seawater is salty people cannot drink it or use it to grow plants for food only three percent of the earth's water is fresh only one percent of the water in the world is easily available for human use.

(4)   Even though water is essential to life human beings often poison it with chemicals from industry and agriculture when people foul water with pollution the quality of all life—plant life animal life and human life—diminishes life cannot exist without fresh water so it is essential for people to take care of this important natural resource.

CHAPTER 9
Comparisons

CONTENTS

☐ **EXERCISE 1. Preview of comparisons. (Chapter 9)**
   Directions: Use the given words to make comparisons.

1. short/long lines (Compare the lengths of the lines.)

   line A _____
   line B _____
   line C _____
   line D _____
   line E _____

   → *Line C is shorter than lines A and B.*
   → *B is the longest line of all.*
   → *C isn't as long as A.*
   → *(continue to make comparisons)*

2. happy/sad look on his face

   DAVID   MIKE   RICK   JIM

3. large/small country (in total land area)

> Brazil: 3,286,488 sq. mi. (8,511,965 sq km)
> Egypt: 385,229 sq. mi. (997,739 sq km)
> Spain: 194,897 sq. mi. (504,782 sq km)
> Canada: 3,553,303 sq. mi. (9,203,054 sq km)

4. easy/difficult questions

> FIRST QUESTION: What's 2 plus 2?
> SECOND QUESTION: What's the square root of 937 divided by 16?
> THIRD QUESTION: What's 3 times 127?
> FOURTH QUESTION: What's 2 plus 3?

5. good/bad handwriting

> EXAMPLE A: *The meeting shmes al eight!*
> EXAMPLE B: *The meeting starts at eight !*
> EXAMPLE C: *The meeting starts at eight!*

9-1 MAKING COMPARISONS WITH *AS . . . AS*

(a) Tina is 21 years old. Sam is also 21. Tina is *as old as* Sam (is). (b) Mike came *as quickly as* he could.	*As . . . as* is used to say that the two parts of a comparison are equal or the same in some way. In (a): *as* + *adjective* + *as* In (b): *as* + *adverb* + *as*
(c) Ted is 20. Tina is 21. Ted is *not as old as* Tina. (d) Ted is*n't quite as old as* Tina. (e) Amy is 5. She is*n't nearly as* old *as* Tina.	Negative form: *not as . . . as.** *Quite* and *nearly* are often used with the negative. In (d): *not quite as . . . as* = a small difference. In (e): *not nearly as . . . as* = a big difference.
(f) Sam is *just as old as* Tina. (g) Ted is *nearly/almost as old as* Tina.	Common modifiers of *as . . . as* are *just* (meaning "exactly") and *nearly/almost*.

*Also possible: *not so . . . as: Ted is not so old as Tina.*

TINA
age 21

SAM
age 21

TED
age 20

AMY
age 5

EXERCISE 2. Comparisons with AS . . . AS. (Chart 9-1)

Directions: Complete the sentences with one of the following:
- *just as*
- *almost as/not quite as*
- *not nearly as*

PART I. Compare the fullness of the glasses.

1. Glass 4 is ___almost as/not quite as___ full as glass 2.

2. Glass 3 is _____ full as glass 2.

3. Glass 1 is _____ full as glass 2.

PART II. Compare the boxes.

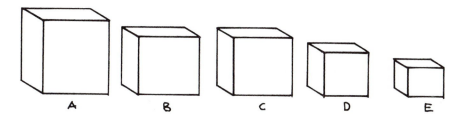

4. Box B is _____ big as Box A.

5. Box E is _____ big as Box A.

6. Box C is _____ big as Box B.

7. Box E is _____ big as Box D.

EXERCISE 3. Comparisons with AS . . . AS. (Chart 9-1)

Directions: Using the given words, complete the sentences with *as . . . as*. Use a negative verb if appropriate.

1. a housefly and an ant

___An ant isn't (quite) as___ big as ___a housefly___ .

2. a lion and a tiger

___A lion is just as___ dangerous and wild as ___a tiger___ .

3. a lake and an ocean

_____ big as _____ .

4. honey and sugar

_____ sweet as _____ .

5. good health and money

_____ important as _____ .

6. adults and children/usually

_____ patient as _____ .

7. a galaxy and a solar system

_____ large as _____ .

8. monkeys and people

_____ agile in climbing trees as _____ .

9. reading a novel and listening to music

In my opinion, _____ relaxing as _____ .

☐ **EXERCISE 4. Comparisons with AS . . . AS. (Chart 9-1)**
   Directions: Complete the sentences by using ***as . . . as*** and your own words.

1. I need you right away! Please come . . . .
   → *Please come as soon as possible.*

2. We can't go any farther. This is . . . .
   → *This is as far as we can go.*

3. I can't work any faster. I'm working . . . .

4. An orange is sweeter than a lemon. In other words, an orange is not . . . .

5. A stream is usually much narrower than a river. In other words, a stream isn't . . . .

6. I had expected the test to be difficult, and it was. In other words, the test was just . . . .

7. It's important to use your English every day. You should practice speaking English . . . .

8. You're only old if you feel old. You are . . . young . . . .

9. You might think it's easy to do, but it's not quite . . . .

10. It takes an hour to drive to the airport. It takes an hour to fly to Chicago. In other words, it takes . . . .

Directions: ***As . . . as*** is used in many traditional phrases. These phrases are generally spoken rather than written. See how many of these phrases you're familiar with by completing the sentences with the given words.

✓*a bear*	*a feather*	*a mule*
a bird	*the hills*	*a rock*
a bull/an ox	*a kite*	*a wet hen*
a cat		

1. When will dinner be ready? I'm as hungry as _____ a bear _____ !

2. Did Bill really lift that heavy box all by himself? He must be as strong as _____ .

3. It was a lovely summer day. School was out, and there was nothing in particular that I had to do. I felt as free as _____ .

4. Marco won't change his mind. He's as stubborn as _____ .

5. How can anyone expect me to sleep in this bed? It's as hard as _____ .

6. Of course I've heard that joke before! It's as old as _____ .

7. Why are you pacing? What's the matter? You're as nervous as _____ .

8. Thanks for offering the help, but I can carry the box alone. It looks heavy, but it isn't. It's as light as _____ .

9. When Erica received the good news, she felt as high as _____ .

10. Was she angry? You'd better believe it! She was as mad as _____ .

□ **EXERCISE 6. Comparisons with AS . . . AS. (Chart 9-1)**

Directions: Complete the sentences with your own words.

Example: . . . not as sharp as . . . .

→ *A pencil point isn't as sharp as a needle.*
   A kitchen knife isn't as sharp as a razor blade.
   My mind isn't as sharp in the afternoon as it is in the morning.

1. . . . just as important as . . . .
2. . . . not as comfortable as . . . .
3. . . . not nearly as interesting as . . . .
4. . . . just as good as . . . .
5. . . . not quite as difficult as . . . .
6. . . . not as quiet as . . . .
7. . . . almost as good as . . . .
8. . . . not as friendly as . . . .
9. . . . not as heavy as . . . .
10. . . . just as nutritious as . . . .
11. . . . as often as I can.
12. . . . as often as I used to.
13. . . . as soon as possible.
14. . . . not as easy as it looks.
15. . . . as much as possible.

9-2   COMPARATIVE AND SUPERLATIVE

(a) "A" is *older than* "B." (b) "A" and "B" are *older than* "C" and "D." (c) Ed is *more generous than* his brother.	The comparative compares *this* to *that* or *these* to *those.* Form: *-er* or *more*. (See Chart 9-3.) Notice: A comparative is followed by *than*.
(d) "A," "B," "C," and "D" are sisters. "A" is *the oldest* of all four sisters. (e) A woman in Turkey claims to be *the oldest person* in the world. (f) Ed is *the most generous person* in his family.	The superlative compares one part of a whole group to all the rest of the group. Form: *-est* or *most*. (See Chart 9-3 for forms.) Notice: A superlative begins with *the*.

□ **EXERCISE 7. Error analysis: comparative and superlative. (Chart 9-2)**

Directions: Correct the errors.

1. Alaska is large than Texas.
   → *Alaska is larger than Texas.*

2. Alaska is largest state in the United States.

3. Texas is the larger from France in land area.

4. Old shoes are usually more comfortable to new shoes.

5. I like Chinese food more better than French food.

6. A pillow is more soft from a rock.

7. My brother is 22. I am 20. My sister is 18. I am the youngest than my brother. My

   sister is the younger person in our family.

□ **EXERCISE 8. Comparative and superlative. (Chart 9-2)**

Directions: Choose five to ten moveable objects (in this room or in the possession of anyone in this room) and put them in a central place. Compare the items using the given words and your own words. Use both the comparative (*-er/more*) and the superlative (*-est/most*).

Example: big/small

SPEAKER A: Omar's pen is bigger than Anya's ring.
SPEAKER B: Sergio's calculator is smaller than Kim's briefcase.
SPEAKER C: The biggest thing on the table is the briefcase.
SPEAKER D: Etc.

1. big/small
2. soft/hard
3. light/heavy
4. cheap/expensive
5. etc.

9-3 COMPARATIVE AND SUPERLATIVE FORMS OF ADJECTIVES AND ADVERBS

		COMPARATIVE	SUPERLATIVE	
ONE-SYLLABLE ADJECTIVES	old wise	older wiser	the oldest the wisest	For most one-syllable adjectives, *-er* and *-est* are added.
TWO-SYLLABLE ADJECTIVES	famous pleasant	more famous more pleasant	the most famous the most pleasant	For most two-syllable adjectives, *more* and *most* are used.
	busy pretty	busier prettier	the busiest the prettiest	*-Er* and *-est* are used with two-syllable adjectives that end in *-y*. The *-y* is changed to *-i*.
	clever gentle friendly	cleverer more clever gentler more gentle friendlier more friendly	the cleverest the most clever the gentlest the most gentle the friendliest the most friendly	Some two-syllable adjectives use either *-er/-est* or *more/most*: *able, angry, clever, common, cruel, friendly, gentle, handsome, narrow, pleasant, polite, quiet, simple, sour.*
ADJECTIVES WITH THREE OR MORE SYLLABLES	important fascinating	more important more fascinating	the most important the most fascinating	*More* and *most* are used with long adjectives.
IRREGULAR ADJECTIVES	good bad	better worse	the best the worst	*Good* and *bad* have irregular comparative and superlative forms.
-LY ADVERBS	carefully slowly	more carefully more slowly	the most carefully the most slowly	*More* and *most* are used with adverbs that end in *-ly*.*
ONE-SYLLABLE ADVERBS	fast hard	faster harder	the fastest the hardest	The *-er* and *-est* forms are used with one-syllable adverbs.
IRREGULAR ADVERBS	well badly far	better worse farther/further**	the best the worst the farthest/furthest	

*Exception: *early* is both an adjective and an adverb. Forms: *earlier, earliest*.

Both *farther* and *further* are used to compare physical distances: *I walked farther/further than my friend did.* **Further (but not *farther*) can also mean "additional": *I need further information.*

☐ **EXERCISE 9. Comparative and superlative forms. (Charts 9-2 and 9-3)**

Directions: Give the comparative and superlative forms of the following adjectives and adverbs.

1. high _higher, the highest_
2. good _____
3. lazy _____
4. hot★ _____
5. neat★ _____
6. late★ _____
7. happy _____

8. dangerous _____
9. slowly _____
10. common _____
11. friendly _____
12. careful _____
13. bad _____
14. far _____

☐ **EXERCISE 10. Comparatives. (Charts 9-2 and 9-3)**

Directions: Complete the sentences with the correct comparative form (***more/-er***) of the given adjectives.

clean	*dangerous*	*funny*	✓*sweet*
confusing	*dark*	*pretty*	*wet*

1. Oranges are _____**sweeter**_____ than lemons.

2. I heard a little polite laughter when I told my jokes, but everyone laughed loudly when Janet told hers. Her jokes are always much _____ than mine.

3. Many more people die in car accidents than in plane accidents. Statistics show that driving your own car is _____ than flying in an airplane.

4. Professor Sato speaks clearly, but I have trouble understanding Professor Larson's lectures. Her lectures are much _____ than Professor Sato's.

5. Bobby! How did you get all covered with mud? Hurry and take a bath. Even the floor is _____ than you are.

_____

*Spelling notes:
   • When a one-syllable adjective ends in **one vowel** + **a consonant**, double the consonant and add ***-er/-est***.
      Example: ***sad, sadder, saddest***.
   • When an adjective ends in **two vowels** + **a consonant**, do NOT double the consonant: ***cool, cooler, coolest***.
   • When an adjective ends in ***-e***, do NOT double the consonant: ***wide, wider, widest***.

6. A: Why does wet sand look _____ than dry sand?

   B: Because wet sand reflects less light.

7. A: The moon is full tonight. There's not a cloud in the sky. Look at the moonlight on the lake. It makes the water sparkle. Have you ever seen a _____ sight than this?

   B: No. It's beautiful.

8. If a cat and a duck are out in the rain, the cat will get much _____ than the duck. The water will simply roll off the duck's feathers but will soak into the cat's hair.

☐ **EXERCISE 11. FARTHER and FURTHER. (Chart 9-3)**
   Directions: Complete the sentences with ***farther*** and/or ***further***. Use both if possible.

1. Ron and his friend went jogging. Ron ran two miles, but his friend got tired after one mile. Ron ran _____farther/further_____ than his friend did.

2. If you have any _____further_____ questions, don't hesitate to ask.

3. Paris is _____ north than Tokyo.

4. I gave my old computer to my younger sister because I had no _____ use for it.

5. I like my new apartment, but it is _____ away from school than my old apartment was.

6. Thank you for your help, but I'll be fine now. I don't want to cause you any _____ trouble.

Directions: Choose any appropriate adjective from the list (or any adjective of your own choosing) to make comparisons between the given items. Use the comparative form (***more/-er***).

bright	*flexible*	*short*
easy	*heavy*	*thick*
enjoyable	*relaxing*	*thin*
fast	*shallow*	*wide and deep*

1. traveling by air \ traveling by bus

   → *Traveling by air is faster than traveling by bus.*
   Traveling by air is easier than traveling by bus.
   Etc.

2. a pool \ a lake

3. an elephant's neck \ a giraffe's neck

4. sunlight \ moonlight

5. iron \ wood

6. walking \ running

7. a river \ a stream

8. rubber \ wood

9. nothing \ sitting in a garden on a quiet summer day

10. a butterfly's wing \ a blade of grass

☐ EXERCISE 13. Comparatives. (Charts 9-2 and 9-3)

Directions: Work in pairs.
Speaker A: Ask the given question. Your book is open.
Speaker B: Answer the question. Begin your response with "**Not really, but at least . . . .**" Your book is closed.

Example:
SPEAKER A *(book open):* Is the mayor of this city famous?
SPEAKER B *(book closed):* Not really, but at least he/she is more famous than I am.

Switch roles.

1. Is a mouse big?

2. Is this room large?

3. Is your desk comfortable?

4. Is an elephant intelligent?

5. Was the last exercise easy?

7. Is the floor clean?

8. Is a pen expensive?

9. Is this book heavy?

10. Is blue a bright color?

11. Is *(name of a city)* close to *(name of this city)*?

9-4 COMPLETING A COMPARATIVE

(a) I'm older *than* **my brother** *(is)*. (b) I'm older *than* **he** *is*. (c) I'm older *than* **him**. *(informal)*	In formal English, a subject pronoun (e.g., *he)* follows ***than***, as in (b). In everyday, informal spoken English, an object pronoun (e.g., *him*) often follows ***than***, as in (c).
(d) He works harder *than* **I do**. (e) I arrived earlier *than* they **did**.	Frequently an auxiliary verb follows the subject after ***than***. In (d): *than I do = than I work*.
(f) *Ann's* hair is longer *than* **Kate's**. (g) *Jack's* apartment is smaller *than* **mine**.	A possessive noun (e.g., *Kate's*) or pronoun (e.g., *mine*) may follow ***than***.

☐ **EXERCISE 14. Completing a comparative. (Chart 9-4)**

Directions: Complete the sentences. Use pronouns in the completions.

1. My sister is only six. She's much younger than _____**I am** OR *(informally)* **me** _____.

2. Peggy is thirteen, and she feels sad. She thinks most of the other girls in school are far more popular than _____.

3. The children can't lift that heavy box, but Mr. Ford can. He's stronger than

   _____.

4. Jim isn't a very good speller. I can spell much better than _____.

5. I was on time. Jack was late. I got there earlier than _____.

6. Ted is out of shape. I can run a lot faster and farther than _____.

7. Isabel's classes are difficult, but my classes are easy. Isabel's classes are more difficult than _____. My classes are easier than _____.

8. Our neighbor's house is very large. Our house is much smaller than

   _____. Their house is larger than _____.

□ **EXERCISE 15. Comparative and superlative forms.** (Charts 9-3 and 9-4)

Directions: As a class or in smaller groups, divide into two teams. Each team will try to score points.

SCORING:
 (1) One point for the correct *meaning* of the given adjective.
 (2) One point for the correct *comparative* and *superlative forms* of that adjective.
 (3) One point for a clear *sentence* with the comparative or superlative form.

The teams should prepare for the contest by discussing the words in the list, looking them up in the dictionary if necessary, and making up possible sentences.

Example: dependable

LEADER: What does "dependable" mean?
TEAM: "Dependable" means "responsible, reliable, trustworthy." For example, it describes people who do their jobs well every day.
LEADER: Yes. That's one point. Now, comparative and superlative forms?
TEAM: *more dependable than, the most dependable of all*
LEADER: Correct. That's another point. And a sentence with one of those forms?
TEAM: Vegetables are more dependable than fruit.
LEADER: What? That doesn't make any sense. No point.
TEAM: Adults are more dependable than children.
LEADER: Good. One point. Your total points as a team: three.

List of adjectives for the leader to choose from:

1. absent-minded	8. confusing	15. fresh	22. pleasant
2. active	9. cute	16. friendly	23. polite
3. attractive	10. dangerous	17. heavy	24. soft
4. bright	11. delightful	18. hectic	25. sour
5. calm	12. dim	19. high	26. straight
6. clever	13. easy	20. humid	27. wild
7. common	14. flexible	21. intelligent	28. wonderful

9-5 MODIFYING COMPARATIVES

(a) Tom is *very old.* (b) Ann drives *very* carefully.	*Very* often modifies adjectives, as in (a), and adverbs, as in (b).
(c) INCORRECT: *Tom is very older than I am.* INCORRECT: *Ann drives very more carefully than she used to.*	*Very* is NOT used to modify comparative adjectives and adverbs.
(d) Tom is *much/a lot/far older* than I am. (e) Ann drives *much/a lot/ far more carefully* than she used to.	Instead, *much, a lot,* or *far* are used to modify comparative adjectives and adverbs, as in (d) and (e).
(f) Ben is *a little (bit) older* than I am / OR (informally) me.	Another common modifier is *a little/a little bit*, as in (f).

□ **EXERCISE 16. Modifying comparatives. (Chart 9-5)**
Directions: Add **very, much, a lot,** or **far** to these sentences.

1. It's hot today. → *It's **very** hot today.*

2. It's hotter today than yesterday. → *It's **much/a lot/far** hotter today than yesterday.*

3. An airplane is fast.

4. Taking an airplane is faster than hitchhiking.

5. Learning a second language is difficult for many people.

6. Learning a second language is more difficult than learning chemistry formulas.

7. You can live more inexpensively in student housing than in a rented apartment.

8. You can live inexpensively in student housing.

9-6 COMPARISONS WITH *LESS . . . THAN* AND *NOT AS . . . AS*

MORE THAN ONE SYLLABLE (a) A pen is **less** expensive **than** a book. (b) A pen is **not as** expensive **as** a book.	The opposite of **-er/more** is expressed by **less** or **not as . . . as.** (a) and (b) have the same meaning.
	Less and **not as . . . as** are used with adjectives and adverbs of **more than one syllable**.
ONE SYLLABLE (c) A pen is **not as** large **as** a book. (d) *INCORRECT: A pen is less large than a book.*	Only **not as . . . as** (NOT **less**) is used with one-syllable adjectives or adverbs, as in (c).

□ **EXERCISE 17. LESS . . . THAN and NOT AS . . . AS. (Chart 9-6)**
Directions: Circle the correct answer or answers.

1. My nephew is _____ ambitious _____ my niece.
   Ⓐ less . . . than   Ⓑ not as . . . as

2. My nephew is _____ old _____ my niece.
   A. less . . . than   Ⓑ not as . . . as

3. A bee is _____ big _____ a bird.
   A. less . . . than   B. not as . . . as

4. My brother is _____ interested in planning for the future _____ I am.
   A. less . . . than   B. not as . . . as

5. I am _____ good at repairing things _____ Diane is.
   A. less . . . than   B. not as . . . as

6. Some students are _____ serious about their schoolwork _____ others.
   A. less . . . than   B. not as . . . as

□ **EXERCISE 18. MORE/-ER, LESS, and NOT AS . . . AS. (Charts 9-1 → 9-6)**
Directions: Use the words in the given order to make comparisons using one of the following:

- *more/-er . . . than*
- *less . . . than*
- *not as . . . as*

1. France \ large \ Brazil
   → *France isn't as large as Brazil.*
2. a river \ big \ a stream
   → *A river is bigger than a stream.*
3. metal \ flexible \ rubber
   → *Metal is less flexible than rubber.* OR *Metal isn't as flexible as rubber.*
4. a sidewalk \ wide \ a road
5. arithmetic \ difficult \ advanced algebra
6. a hill \ high \ a mountain
7. bottled water \ clear and clean \ river water
8. cold, wet weather \ pleasant \ warm weather
9. sitting in an easy chair \ comfortable \ sitting on a park bench
10. hiking along a path \ dangerous \ climbing a mountain peak
11. toes \ long \ fingers
12. toes \ useful \ fingers
13. toes \ long or useful \ fingers
14. fingers \ long and useful \ toes

□ **EXERCISE 19. MORE/-ER, LESS, and AS . . . AS. (Charts 9-1 → 9-6)**
Directions: Compare the following. Use *(not) as . . . as, less,* and *more/-er.* How many points of comparison can you think of? Work in pairs, on teams, or as a class.

Example: trees and flowers *(big, colorful, useful, etc.)*
   → *Trees are bigger than flowers.*
   Trees are rarely as colorful as flowers.
   Flowers are less useful than trees.
   Flowers aren't as sturdy as trees.
   Trees are more important to clean air quality than flowers.

1. the sun and the moon
2. children and adults
3. two restaurants in this city
4. two famous people in the world

9-7 UNCLEAR COMPARISONS	
UNCLEAR (a) Ann likes her dog better than her husband.	Sometimes it is necessary to complete the idea following ***than*** in order to make a comparison clear.
CLEAR (b) Ann likes her dog better than her husband *does.* (c) Ann likes her dog better than she *does* her husband.	In (b): *does* means "likes the dog." In (c): *does* means "likes."

□ **EXERCISE 20. Unclear comparisons. (Chart 9-7)**

Directions: The following are unclear comparisons. Discuss the possible meanings by creating clear comparisons.

1. UNCLEAR: I know John better than Mary.
   → *I know John better than Mary does.* OR *I know John better than I do Mary.*
2. UNCLEAR: Sam likes football better than his wife.
3. UNCLEAR: Frank helps me more than Debra.
4. UNCLEAR: I pay my plumber more than my dentist.

9-8 USING *MORE* WITH NOUNS

(a) Would you like some ***more coffee***? (b) Not everyone is here. I expect ***more people*** to come later.	In (a): *coffee* is a noun. When ***more*** is used with nouns, it often has the meaning of *additional*. It is not necessary to use ***than***.
(c) There are ***more people*** in China ***than*** there are in the United States.	***More*** is also used with nouns to make complete comparisons by adding ***than***.
(d) Do you have enough coffee, or would you like some ***more?***	When the meaning is clear, the noun may be omitted and ***more*** used by itself.

□ **EXERCISE 21. Comparatives with nouns, adjectives, and adverbs.**
       (Charts 9-2, 9-3, and 9-8)

Directions: Use ***-er*** or ***more*** and the words in the list to complete the sentences. Discuss whether the words are nouns, adjectives, or adverbs, and review how comparatives are formed. When do you use ***-er***, and when do you use ***more?***

✓bright	happily	information	responsibilities	salt
✓brightly	happiness	mistakes	responsible	✓traffic
doctors	happy	quick	responsibly	

1. A city has _____ more traffic _____ than a small town.

2. Sunlight is much _____ brighter _____ than moonlight.

3. Did you know that a laser burns billions of times _____ more brightly _____ than the light at the sun's surface?

4. There is _____ about geography in an encyclopedia than (there is) in a dictionary.

5. I used to be sad, but now I'm a lot _____ about my life (than I used to be).

6. Unhappy roommates or spouses can live together _____ if they learn to respect each other's differences.

7. She's had a miserable life. I hope she finds _____ in the future.

8. I made _____ on the last test than (I did) on the first one, so I got a worse grade.

9. My daughter Annie is trustworthy and mature. She behaves much _____ than my nephew Louie.

10. A twelve-year-old has _____ at home and in school than a nine-year-old.

11. My son is _____ about doing his homework than his older sister is.

12. A rabbit is _____ than a turtle.

13. This soup doesn't taste quite right. I think it needs just a little _____.

14. Health care in rural areas is poor. We need _____ to treat people in rural areas.

9-9 REPEATING A COMPARATIVE

(a) Because he was afraid, he walked **faster and faster**. (b) Life in the modern world is becoming **more and more complex**.	Repeating a comparative gives the idea that something becomes progressively greater, i.e., it increases in intensity, quality, or quantity.

☐ **EXERCISE 22. Repeating a comparative. (Chart 9-9)**

Directions: Complete the answers by repeating a comparative. Use the words in the list.

angry	discouraged	hard	weak
big	✓fast	long	wet
cold/warm	good	loud	

1. When I get excited, my heart beats ___ *faster and faster* ___.

2. When you blow up a balloon, it gets _____.

3. My English is improving. It is getting _____ every day.

4. As the ambulance came closer to us, the siren became _____.

5. She sat there quietly, but during all that time she was getting _____
_____. Finally she exploded.

6. The line of people waiting to get into the theater got _____.

7. I've been looking for a job for a month and still haven't been able to find one. I'm
getting _____.

8. The weather is getting _____ with each passing day.

9. As I continued walking in miserable weather, it rained _____.
I got _____. By the time I got home, I was
completely soaked.

10. As I continued to row the boat, my arms got _____
until I had almost no strength left in them at all.

(a) *The harder* you study, *the more* you will learn. (b) *The more* she studied, *the more* she learned. (c) *The warmer* the weather (is), *the better* I like it.	A double comparative has two parts; both parts begin with *the,* as in the examples. The second part of the comparison is the **result** of the first part. In (a): If you study harder, the result will be that you will learn more.

(d) A: Should we ask Jenny and Jim to the party too?
     B: Why not? *The more, the merrier*.
 (e) A: When should we leave?
     B: *The sooner, the better*.
	The more, the merrier and *the sooner, the better* are two common expressions.
	 In (d): It is good to have more people at the party.
	 In (e): It is good if we leave as soon as we can.

Directions: Complete the sentences with double comparatives (*the more/-er ... the more/-er*).

1. If the fruit is *fresh,* it tastes *good.*

   → _____The fresher_____ the fruit (is), _____the better_____ it tastes.

2. We got *close* to the fire. We felt *warm.*

   → _____ we got to the fire, _____ we felt.

3. If a knife is *sharp,* it is *easy* to cut something with.

   → _____ a knife (is), _____ it is to
   cut something.

4. The party got *noisy* next door. I got *angry.*

   → I had a terrible time getting to sleep last night. My neighbors were having a loud
   party. _____ it got, _____ I got.
   Finally, I banged on the wall and told them to be quiet.

5. If a flamingo eats a lot of *shrimp,* it becomes very *pink.*

   → The _____ a flamingo eats,

   the _____ it gets.

   SHRIMP, ALL YOU CAN EAT.

6. She drove *fast.* I became *nervous.*

   → Erica offered to take me to the airport, and I was grateful. But we got a late start,
   so on the way she stepped on the accelerator. I got more than a little
   uncomfortable. The . . . .

7. He *thought* about his family. He became *homesick.*

   → Pierre tried to concentrate on his studying, but his mind would drift to his family
   and his home. The . . . .

8. We ran *fast* to reach the house. The sky grew *dark.*

   → A storm was threatening. The . . . .

9-11 USING SUPERLATIVES

(a) Tokyo is one of *the largest cities in the world*. (b) David is *the most generous person I have ever known*. (c) I have three books. These two are quite good, but this one is the *best* (book) *of all*.	Typical completions when a superlative is used: In (a): superlative + *in* a place *(the world, this class, my family, the corporation, etc.)*. In (b): superlative + adjective clause.* In (c): superlative + *of all*.
(d) I took four final exams. The final in accounting was *the least difficult* of all.	*The least* has the opposite meaning of *the most*.
(e) Ali is *one of* the best *students* in this class. (f) *One of* the best *students* in this class *is* Ali.	Notice the pattern with *one of*: *one of* + PLURAL noun (+ SINGULAR verb)

*See Chapter 12 for more information about adjective clauses.

☐ **EXERCISE 24. Superlatives. (Chart 9-11)**

Directions: Complete the sentences with superlatives and the appropriate preposition, *in* or *of*.

1. Jack is *lazy*. He is _____the laziest_____ student ___in___ the class.

2. Mike and Julie were *nervous*, but Amanda was ___the most nervous of___ all.

3. Costa Rico is *beautiful*. It is one of _____

   countries _____ the world.

4. Scott got a *bad* score on the test. It was one of _____ scores

   _____ the whole school.

5. Pluto is *far* from the sun. In fact, it is _____ planet from the

   sun _____ our solar system.

6. There are a lot of *good* cooks in my family, but my mom is _____ cook

   _____ all.

7. Alaska is *big*. It is _____ state _____ the United States.

8. My grandfather is very *old*. He is _____ person _____ the

   town where he lives.

9. That chair in the corner is *comfortable*. It is _____

   chair _____ the room.

10. Everyone who ran in the race was *exhausted*, but I was _____

    _____ all.

☐ **EXERCISE 25. Superlatives. (Chart 9-11)**
   Directions: Use the given phrases to complete the sentences with superlatives.

> big bird   long river in South America
> clean air   popular forms of entertainment
> ✓deep ocean   three common street names
> high mountains on earth   two great natural dangers

1. The Pacific is ___the deepest ocean___ in the world.

2. There is almost no air pollution at the South Pole. The South Pole has _____
   _____ in the world.

3. _____ are in
   the Himalayan Range in Asia.

4. Most birds are small, but not the flightless North African ostrich. It is _____
   _____ in the world.

5. _____ to
   ships are fog and icebergs.

6. One of _____ throughout
   the world is the motion picture.

7. _____ in the United
   States are Park, Washington, and Maple.

8. _____ is the Amazon.

☐ **EXERCISE 26. Completing superlatives with adjective clauses. (Chart 9-11)**
   Directions: Complete the sentences with an appropriate superlative followed by an adjective clause.

1. I have had many *good experiences.* Of those, my vacation to Honduras was one of . . . .
   → *the best experiences I have ever had.*

2. Sally has had many *nice times,* but her birthday party was one of . . . .

3. I've taken many *difficult courses,* but statistics is one of . . . .

4. I've made some *bad mistakes* in my life, but lending my cousin money was one of . . . .

5. We've seen many *beautiful buildings* in the world, but the Taj Mahal is one of . . . .

6. A: How do you think you did on the exam this morning?
   B: I think I did pretty well. It was an *easy test.* In fact, it was one of . . . .

☐ **EXERCISE 27. Using ONE OF with superlatives. (Chart 9-11)**

Directions: Work in pairs.
Speaker A: Give the cues. (Listen carefully to Speaker B's answer, making sure s/he is using a plural noun following *one of.*) Your book is open.
Speaker B: Answer the questions in complete sentences, using *one of* plus a superlative. Your book is closed.

Example:
SPEAKER A *(book open):*   You have known many interesting people. Who is one of them?
SPEAKER B *(book closed):* **One of the most interesting people** I've ever known *is* (Ms. Lee). OR (Ms. Lee) *is one of* the **most interesting people** I've ever known.

1. There are many beautiful countries in the world. What is one of them?
2. There are many famous people in the world. Who is one of them?
3. What is one of the best movies you've seen recently? And have you seen any bad movies? What is one of them?
4. What is one of the most exciting things you've ever done?
5. You know many wonderful people. Who is one of them?

Switch roles.
6. Think of some happy days in your life. What was one of them?
7. There are a lot of interesting animals in the world. What is one of them?
8. Who is one of the most important people in the history of your country?
9. You have had many good experiences. What is one of them?
10. There are many important people in your life among your family, friends, teachers, co-workers, and others. Who is one of these people?

☐ **EXERCISE 28. Superlatives. (Chart 9-11)**

Directions: Use superlatives of the given words and your own words to complete the sentences.

1. *bad*   . . . is the . . . movie I . . . .
   → *"Sea Monsters" is the worst movie I've ever seen.*

2. *popular*   The . . . sport in . . . is . . . .

3. *large*   The . . . city in . . . is . . . .

4. *good*   . . . is the . . . restaurant in . . . .

5. *interesting* . . . is one of the . . . people I . . . .

6. *valuable*   The . . . thing I . . . is . . . .

7. *important*   The three . . . things in life are . . . .

8. *serious*   The . . . problems in . . . today are . . . .

□ **EXERCISE 29. Review: comparatives and superlatives.** (Charts 9-1 → 9-11)
Directions: Work in pairs.
Speaker A: Ask a question that uses either a comparative or a superlative.
Speaker B: Answer the question. Use complete sentences.

Example: what . . . sweet
SPEAKER A: What is sweeter than sugar?
SPEAKER B: Nothing is sweeter than sugar.

Example: who is . . . wonderful
SPEAKER A: Who is the most wonderful person you've ever known?
SPEAKER B: That's a hard question. Probably my mother is the most wonderful person
I've ever known.

Switch roles.

1. what is . . . important
2. who is . . . famous
3. what is . . . good
4. what is . . . bad
5. whose hair is . . . long
6. what is . . . interesting
7. which car is . . . expensive
8. what country is . . . near
9. what is . . . dangerous
10. who is . . . old
11. what is . . . beautiful
12. who is . . . kind

□ **EXERCISE 30. Review: comparatives and superlatives.** (Charts 9-1 → 9-11)
Directions: Compare the items in each list using the given words. Use **as . . . as,** the
comparative **(-er/more),** and the superlative **(-est/most).** Discuss the topics orally or in
writing.

Example: streets in this city: *wide \ narrow \ busy \ dangerous*
→ *First Avenue is **wider** than Market Street.*
*Second Avenue is **nearly as wide as** First Avenue.*
*First Avenue is **narrower** than Interstate Highway 70.*
***The busiest** street is Main Street.*
*Main Street is **busier** than Market Street.*
***The most dangerous street** in the city is Olive Boulevard.*

1. a lemon, a grapefruit, and an orange:
sweet \ sour \ large \ small

2. three different books in the classroom:
thin \ fat \ interesting \ useful \ good \ bad

3. a kitten, a cheetah, and a lion:
weak \ powerful \ wild \ gentle \ fast

4. air, water, and wood:
heavy \ light \ important to human life

5. boxing, soccer, and golf:
dangerous \ safe \ exciting \ boring

6. the food at *(three places in this city where you have eaten)*:
delicious \ appetizing \ inexpensive \ good \ bad

☐ **EXERCISE 31. Review of comparatives and superlatives. (Charts 9-1 → 9-11)**
Directions: Complete the sentences. Use any appropriate form of the words in parentheses and add any other necessary words. There may be more than one possible completion.

1. Lead is a very heavy metal. It is *(heavy)* ____heavier than____ gold or silver. It is one of *(heavy)* ____the heaviest____ metals __of__ all.

2. Dogs are usually *(friendly)* _____ cats.

3. One of *(famous)* _____ volcanoes _____ the world is Mount Etna in Sicily.

4. A car has two *(wheels)* _____ a bicycle.

5. Mrs. Cook didn't ask the children to clean up the kitchen. It was *(easy)* _____ for her to do it herself _____ to nag them to do it.

6. Duck eggs and chicken eggs are different. Duck eggs are *(large)* _____ chicken eggs. Also, the yolk of a duck egg is *(dark)* _____ yellow _____ the yolk of a chicken egg.

7. The volcanic explosion of Krakatoa near Java in 1883 may have been *(loud)* _____ noise _____ recorded history. It was heard 2,760 miles (4,441 kilometers) away.

8. *(important)* _____ piece of equipment for birdwatching is a pair of binoculars.

9. Although both jobs are important, being a teacher requires *(education)* _____ _____ being a bus driver.

10. The Great Wall of China is *(long)* _____ structure that has ever been built.

11. Howard Anderson is one of (delightful) _____

    people I've ever met.

12. (hard) _____ I tried, (impossible) _____

    _____ it seemed to solve the math problem.

13. Perhaps (common) _____ topic of everyday

    conversation _____ the world is the weather.

14. World Cup Soccer is (big) _____ sporting event _____

    the world. It is viewed on TV by (people) _____ any other

    event in sports.

15. Human beings must compete with other species for the food of the land. (great)

    _____ competitors we have for food are insects.

16. When the temperature stays below freezing for a long period of time, the Eiffel Tower

    becomes six inches (fifteen centimeters) (short) _____ .

17. Have you ever been bothered by a fly buzzing around you? (easy) _____

    _____ way to get a fly out of a room is to darken the room and turn on a

    light somewhere else.

18. Young people have (high) _____ rate of automobile accidents

    _____ all drivers.

19. The wall of a soap bubble is very, very thin. A

    human hair is approximately ten

    thousand times (thick) _____

    _____ the wall of a soap bubble.

20. English has approximately 600,000 words.

    Because of the explosion of scientific discoveries

    and new technologies, there are (words)

    _____ in English

    _____ in any other language.

21. You'd better buy the tickets for the show soon. (long) _____ you

    wait, (difficult) _____ it will be for you to get

    good seats.

22. No animals can travel *(fast)* _____ birds. Birds are *(fast)*

_____ animals _____ all.

23. Most birds have small eyes, but not ostriches. Indeed, the eye of an ostrich is *(large)*

_____ its brain.

24. *(great)* _____ variety of birds _____ a single area can be

found in the rainforests of Southeast Asia and India.

25. It's easy to drown a houseplant. *(houseplants)* _____ die

from too much water _____ not enough water.

9-12 USING *THE SAME, SIMILAR, DIFFERENT, LIKE, ALIKE*

(a) John and Mary have *the same books*. (b) John and Mary have *similar books*. (c) John and Mary have *different books*. (d) Their books are *the same*. (e) Their books are *similar*. (f) Their books are *different*.	*The same, similar,* and *different* are used as adjectives. Notice: *the* always precedes *same*.
(g) This book is *the same as* that one. (h) This book is *similar to* that one. (i) This book is *different from* that one.	Notice: *the same* is followed by *as;* *similar* is followed by *to;* *different* is followed by *from.**
(j) She is *the same age as* my mother. My shoes are *the same size as* yours.	A noun may come between *the same* and *as,* as in (j).
(k) My pen *is like* your pen. (l) My pen and your pen *are alike*.	Notice in (k) and (l): *noun +* ***be like*** *+ noun* *noun and noun +* ***be alike***
(m) She *looks like* her sister. It *looks like* rain. It *sounds like* thunder. This material *feels like* silk. That *smells like* gas. This chemical *tastes like* salt. Stop *acting like* a fool. He *seems like* a nice fellow.	In addition to following *be, like* also follows certain verbs, primarily those dealing with the senses. Notice the examples in (m).
(n) The twins *look alike*. We *think alike*. Most four-year-olds *act alike*. My sister and I *talk alike*. The little boys are *dressed alike*.	*Alike* may follow a few verbs other than *be.* Notice the examples in (n).

*In informal speech, native speakers might use *than* instead of *from* after *different*. *From* is considered correct in formal English, unless the comparison is completed by a clause: *I have a different attitude now than I used to have.*

□ **EXERCISE 32. THE SAME, SIMILAR, DIFFERENT, LIKE, and ALIKE. (Chart 9-12)**

Directions: Complete the sentences with **as, to, from,** or **Ø** if no word is necessary.

1. Geese are similar _____to_____ ducks. They are both large water birds.

2. But geese are not the same _____as_____ ducks. Geese are usually larger and have longer necks.

3. Geese are different _____from_____ ducks.

4. Geese are like _____Ø_____ ducks in some ways, but geese and ducks are not exactly alike _____Ø_____ .

5. An orange is similar _____ a grapefruit. They are both citrus fruits.

6. But an orange is not the same _____ a grapefruit. A grapefruit is usually larger and sourer.

7. An orange is different _____ a grapefruit.

8. An orange is like _____ a grapefruit in some ways, but they are not exactly alike _____ .

9. Gold is similar _____ silver. They are both valuable metals that people use for jewelry. But they aren't the same _____ . Gold is not the same color _____ silver. Gold is also different _____ silver in cost. Gold is more expensive than silver.

10. Look at the two zebras. Their names are Zee and Bee. Zee looks like _____ Bee. Is Zee exactly the same _____ Bee? The pattern of the stripes on each zebra in the world is unique. No two zebras are exactly alike _____ . Even though Zee and Bee are similar _____ each other, they are different _____ each other in the exact pattern of their stripes.

□ EXERCISE 33. THE SAME, SIMILAR, DIFFERENT, LIKE, and ALIKE. (Chart 9-12)
   Directions: Compare the figures. Complete the sentences using ***the same (as)***, ***similar***
   (to), ***different (from)***, ***like***, and ***alike***.

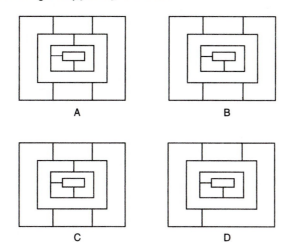

1. All of the figures are _____ *similar to* _____ each other.

2. Figure A is _____ Figure B.

3. Figure A and Figure B are _____ .

4. A and C are _____ .

5. A and C are _____ D.

6. C is _____ A.

7. B isn't _____ D.

□ EXERCISE 34. THE SAME, SIMILAR, DIFFERENT, LIKE, and ALIKE. (Chart 9-12)
   Directions: Compare the figures. Work in pairs or groups.

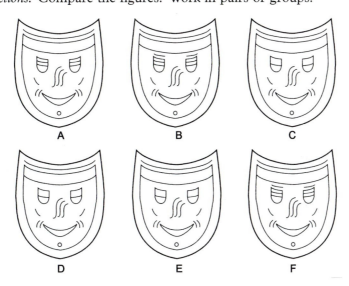

Directions: Use *the same (as)*, *similar (to)*, *different (from)*, *like*, and *alike* in the sentences. There may be more than one possible response in some of them. Use whatever response sounds best to you.

1. Jennifer and Jack both come from Rapid City. In other words, they come from
   _____the same_____ town.

2. This city is ___the same as / similar to / like___ my hometown. Both are quiet and conservative.

3. You and I don't agree. Your ideas are _____ mine.

4. Eric never wears _____ clothes two days in a row.

5. Ants are fascinating. An ant colony is _____ a well-disciplined army.

6. In terms of shape, cabbage looks _____ lettuce. But cabbage and lettuce don't taste _____ .

7. A male mosquito is not _____ size _____ a female mosquito. The female is larger.

8. I'm used to strong coffee. I think the coffee Americans drink tastes _____ dishwater!

9. "Meet" and "meat" are homonyms; i.e., they have _____ pronunciation.

10. The pronunciation of "caught" is _____ the pronunciation of "cot."

11. "Flower" has _____ pronunciation _____ "flour."

12. My dictionary is _____ yours.

13. Trying to get through school without studying is _____ trying to go swimming without getting wet.

14. A crocodile and an alligator are _____ in appearance.

15. If it looks _____ a duck, quacks _____ a duck, and walks _____ a duck, it is a duck.
    (*a humorous saying*)

☐ **EXERCISE 36. Making comparisons. (Chapter 9)**

Directions: Do you have sayings in your language that are similar to or the same as the following English proverbs?

1. Don't count your chickens before they hatch.
2. The early bird gets the worm.
3. Too many cooks spoil the broth.
4. A bird in the hand is worth two in the bush.
5. A stitch in time saves nine.
6. When in Rome, do as the Romans do.
7. Birds of a feather flock together.
8. A rolling stone gathers no moss.

☐ **EXERCISE 37. Making comparisons. (Chapter 9)**

Directions: Write a composition based on one of the following topics.

Compare and contrast:
1. being single and being married.
2. cities you have lived in or have visited.
3. different schools you have attended.
4. your way of life before and after you became a parent.
5. yourself now to yourself ten years ago.
6. your country now to your country 100 years ago.
7. life today to life 100 years from now.
8. two sports.
9. the seasons of the year.
10. food in two countries.

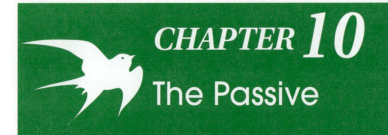

CHAPTER *10*
The Passive

CONTENTS

10-1 ACTIVE SENTENCES AND PASSIVE SENTENCES

(a) **ACTIVE:** The mouse *ate* the cheese. (b) **PASSIVE:** The cheese *was eaten* by the mouse.	(a) and (b) have the same meaning.

ACTIVE   **PASSIVE**

ACTIVE: **S** **O** (c) *Bob* mailed **the package**.	In (c): The object in an active sentence becomes the subject in a passive sentence.
PASSIVE: **S** *by* + **O** (d) **The package** was mailed by *Bob*.	In (d): The subject in an active sentence is the object of **by** in the *by*-phrase in a passive sentence.

10-2 FORM OF THE PASSIVE

	BE + PAST PARTICIPLE	Form of all passive verbs: **be** + *past participle*
(a) Corn	*is* *grown* by farmers.	**Be** can be in any of its forms: *am, is, are, was, were,*
(b) Sara	*was* *surprised* by the news.	*has been, have been, will be, etc.*
(c) The report	*will be* *written* by Mary.	

	ACTIVE	PASSIVE
SIMPLE PRESENT	Farmers *grow* corn. ⟶	Corn *is grown* by farmers.
SIMPLE PAST	The news *surprised* Sara. ⟶	Sara *was surprised* by the news.
PRESENT PERFECT	Jack *has mailed* the letter. ⟶	The letter *has been mailed* by Jack.
FUTURE	Mr. Lee *will plan* the meeting. ⟶ Sue *is going to write* the report. ⟶	The meeting *will be planned* by Mr. Lee. The report *is going to be written* by Sue.

☐ **EXERCISE 1. Active vs. passive. (Charts 10-1 and 10-2)**
Directions: Change the active verbs to passive verbs. Write the subject of the passive sentence.

1. SIMPLE PRESENT

    (a) The teacher *helps* **me**.   (a) ___I___ ___am helped___ by the teacher.

    (b) The teacher *helps* **Jane**.   (b) ___Jane___ ___is helped___ by the teacher.

    (c) The teacher *helps* **us**.   (c) _____ _____ by the teacher.

2. SIMPLE PAST

    (a) The teacher *helped* **me**.   (a) _____ _____ by the teacher.

    (b) The teacher *helped* **them**.   (b) _____ _____ by the teacher.

3. PRESENT PERFECT

    (a) The teacher *has helped* **Joe**.   (a) _____ _____ by the teacher.

    (b) The teacher *has helped* **us**.   (b) _____ _____ by the teacher.

4. FUTURE

    (a) The teacher *will help* **me**.   (a) _____ _____ by the teacher.

    (b) The teacher *is going to help* **Tim**.   (b) _____ _____ by the teacher.

□ EXERCISE 2. Form of the passive. (Charts 10-1 and 10-2)

Directions: Change the verbs to the passive. Do not change the tense.

		BE +	PAST PARTICIPLE	
1. Bob *mailed* the package.	The package	<u>was</u>	<u>mailed</u>	by Bob.
2. That company *employs* many people.	Many people	_____	_____	by that company.
3. That company *has hired* Sue.	Sue	_____	_____	by that company.
4. The secretary *is going to fax* the letters.	The letters	_____	_____	by the secretary.
5. A college student *bought* my old car.	My old car	_____	_____	by a college student.
6. Mrs. Adams *will do* the work.	The work	_____	_____	by Mrs. Adams.
7. Mr. Fox *washed* the windows.	The windows	_____	_____	by Mr. Fox.

□ EXERCISE 3. Active vs. passive. (Charts 10-1 and 10-2)

Directions: Change the sentences from active to passive.

1. Ms. Hopkins invited me to dinner.
   → *I was invited to dinner by Ms. Hopkins.*

2. Thomas Edison invented the phonograph.

3. Water surrounds an island.

4. A plumber is going to fix the leaky faucet.

5. A doctor has examined the sick child.

6. A large number of people speak Spanish.

7. Helicopters fascinate children.

8. Shakespeare wrote *Hamlet*.

9. This news will amaze you.

☐ EXERCISE 4. Active vs. passive: question forms. (Charts 10-1 and 10-2)

Directions: Change the active sentences to passive sentences that have the same meaning and tense.

ACTIVE   PASSIVE

1. (a) The news surprised John.   _John was surprised_   by the news.

    (b) Did the news surprise you?   _Were you surprised_   by the news?

2. (a) The news surprises Erin.   _____   by the news.

    (b) Does the news surprise you?   _____   by the news?

3. (a) The news will shock Steve.   _____   by the news.

    (b) Will the news shock Pat?   _____   by the news?

4. (a) Liz signed the petition.   _____   by Liz.

    (b) Did Ryan sign it?   _____   by Ryan?

PETITION

We, the undersigned, believe that the house at 3205 Tree Street is an historic building. We believe that it should not be destroyed in order to build a fast-food restaurant at that location.

Robert E. Miller   Wm. H. Brock

Elizabeth J. Wilson   Ms. Catherine Ann Jackson

James Walsh   An Binh Nguyen

Alicia Alvarez

---

5. (a) Bob has signed the petition.   _____   by Bob.

    (b) Has Jim signed it yet?   _____   by Jim yet?

6. (a) Sue is going to sign it.   _____   by Sue.

    (b) Is Carol going to sign it?   _____   by Carol?

☐ EXERCISE 5. Active vs. passive. (Charts 10-1 and 10-2)

Directions: Change the sentences from active to passive.

1. A thief stole Ann's purse. → *Ann's purse was stolen by a thief.*

2. Did a cat kill the bird?

3. My cat didn't kill the bird.

4. Do a large number of people speak French?

5. Is the janitor going to fix the window?

6. Will a maid clean our hotel room?

7. Does the hotel provide clean towels?

8. Sometimes my inability to understand spoken English frustrates me.

□ **EXERCISE 6. Active vs. passive. (Charts 10-1 and 10-2)**

Directions: Change the passive sentences to active. Keep the same tense. Some of the sentences are questions.

1. Was the riot stopped by the police?
   → *Did the police stop the riot?*

2. My suitcase was inspected by a customs officer.

3. Love and understanding are needed by all children.

4. Were you taught to read by your parents?

5. I was taught to read by my parents.

6. Are we going to be met at the train station by your cousin?

7. Have the plans for the new hospital already been drawn by the architect?

8. The bear was chased up a tree by a dog.

10-3 TRANSITIVE AND INTRANSITIVE VERBS

(a) **TRANSITIVE**
    S   **V**   **O**
    Bob   *mailed*   *the letter.*
    Mr. Lee *signed* *the check.*
    A cat   *killed*   *the bird.*
	A *transitive* verb is a verb that is followed by an object. An object is a noun or a pronoun.

(b) **INTRANSITIVE**
    S   **V**
    An accident *happened.*
    Kate   *came* to our house.
    I   *slept* well last night.
	An *intransitive* verb is a verb that is not followed by an object.

COMMON INTRANSITIVE VERBS*				
agree	die	happen	rise	stand
appear	exist	laugh	seem	stay
arrive	fall	live	sit	talk
become	flow	occur	sleep	wait
come	go	rain	sneeze	walk

(c) **TRANSITIVE VERBS**
   ACTIVE: Bob *mailed* the letter.
   PASSIVE: The letter *was mailed* by Bob.
	Only transitive verbs can be used in the passive.

(d) **INTRANSITIVE VERBS**
   ACTIVE: An accident *happened.*
   PASSIVE: *(not possible)*
 (e) *INCORRECT: An accident was happened.*
	An intransitive verb is NOT used in the passive.

*To find out if a verb is transitive or intransitive, look in your dictionary. The usual abbreviations are v.t. (transitive) and v.i. (intransitive). Some verbs have both transitive and intransitive uses. For example:
    transitive: *Students study books.*
    intransitive: *Students study.*

Directions: <u>Underline</u> the verbs and identify them as transitive (**v.t.**) or intransitive (**v.i.**). Change the sentences to the passive if possible.

         v.i.
1. Jack <u>walked</u> to school yesterday. *(no change)*

         v.t.
2. Susie <u>broke</u> the window.
   → *The window was broken by Susie.*

3. We stayed in a hotel.

4. The leaves fell to the ground.

5. I slept at my friend's house last night.

6. An accident happened at the corner of Third and Main.

7. Many people saw the accident.

8. Dinosaurs existed millions of years ago.

9. I usually agree with my sister.

10. Many people die during a war.

11. The /*th*/ sound doesn't occur in my native language.

12. Research scientists will discover a cure for AIDS★ someday.

13. A cloud of migrating butterflies appeared out of nowhere.

14. Did the Koreans invent gunpowder?

15. In the fairy tale, a princess kissed a frog.

★AIDS = a disease (**A**uto **I**mmune **D**eficiency **S**yndrome).

10-4 USING THE *BY*-PHRASE

(a) This sweater *was made* **by my aunt**.	The *by*-phrase is used in passive sentences when it is important to know who performs an action. In (a): *by my aunt* is important information.
(b) My sweater *was made* in Korea. (c) Spanish *is spoken* in Colombia. (d) That house *was built* in 1940. (e) Rice *is grown* in many countries.	Usually there is no *by*-phrase in a passive sentence. The passive is used when it is **not known or not important to know exactly who performs an action**. In (b): The exact person (or people) who made the sweater is not known and is not important to know, so there is no *by*-phrase in the passive sentence.
(f) **My aunt** is very skillful. **She** *made* this sweater. (g) — I like your sweaters. — Thanks. **This sweater** *was made by* my aunt. **That sweater** *was made by* my mother.	Usually the active is used when the speaker knows who performed the action, as in (f), where the focus of attention is on *my aunt*. In (g), the speaker uses the passive WITH a *by*-phrase because he wants to focus attention on the subjects of the sentences. The focus of attention is on the two sweaters. The *by*-phrases add important information.

☐ **EXERCISE 8. The BY-phrase. (Chart 10-4)**

Directions: Change the sentences from active to passive. Include the *by*-phrase only if necessary.

1. Bob Smith built that house.
   → *That house was built by Bob Smith.*

2. Someone built this house in 1904.
   → *This house was built in 1904. (Someone = unnecessary)*

3. People grow rice in India.

4. Do people speak Spanish in Peru?

5. Alexander Graham Bell invented the telephone.

6. When did someone invent the first computer?

7. People sell hammers at a hardware store. People use them to pound nails.

8. Someone will list my name in the new telephone directory.

9. Charles Darwin wrote *The Origin of Species*.

10. Someone published *The Origin of Species* in 1859.

11. Has anyone ever hypnotized you?

12. Someone has changed the name of this street from Bay Avenue to Martin Luther King Way.

"DEEP ASLEEP... DEEP ASLEEP..
YOU FEEL VERY SLEEPY... DEEP...."

☐ **EXERCISE 9. The BY-phrase. (Chart 10-4)**

Directions: <u>Underline</u> the passive verbs. Discuss use of the passive. If a *by*-phrase is included, discuss why.

1. The mail <u>is</u> usually <u>delivered</u> to Bob's apartment around eleven o'clock.
   → *The passive is used because it is unknown exactly who delivers the mail.*

2. A: That's a pretty picture.
   B: Yes. It <u>was drawn</u> by my eight-year-old son.
   → *The passive is used with a by-phrase. The focus of attention is on the picture. The by-phrase includes important information. The active could also be used:* "Yes. My eight-year-old son drew it."

3. Our classroom building was built in the 1950s.

4. Coffee is grown in Brazil.

5. A: These tomatoes are delicious!
   B: Yes. They taste so much better than the ones you can get in the grocery store. These tomatoes were grown by my uncle in his greenhouse.

6. Airplane travel is unpredictable. Yesterday Anna's flight was delayed for seven hours. That's a long time to spend in an airport waiting for your plane to leave.

7. We can't go to the school play tonight. All the tickets have already been sold.

8. "Thailand" means "land of the free." The country of Thailand has never been ruled by a foreign power.

9. One of the most significant inventions in the history of civilization was the wheel. It was invented around five thousand years ago. It allowed people to pull things in carts instead of carrying everything on their backs or in their arms.

10. The invention of the printing press changed the world because it allowed many people instead of few to have copies of books. It was invented by Johannes Gutenberg around 1440. Before that, books were copied by hand. Writing books by hand was a slow process.

☐ **EXERCISE 10. Active vs. passive. (Charts 10-1 → 10-4)**

Directions: Complete the sentences with the correct form of the verb (active or passive) in parentheses.

1. Yesterday our teacher *(arrive)* _____**arrived**_____ five minutes late.

2. Our morning paper *(read)* _____ by over 200,000 people every day.

3. Last night my favorite TV program *(interrupt)* _____ by a special news bulletin.

4. That's not my coat. It *(belong)* _____ to Louise.

5. Our mail *(deliver)* _____ before noon every day.

6. The "b" in "comb" *(pronounce, not)* _____ . It is silent.

7. A bad accident *(happen)* _____ on Highway 95 last night.

8. When I *(arrive)* _____ at the airport yesterday, I *(meet)* _____ by my cousin and a couple of her friends.

9. Yesterday I *(hear)* _____ about Margaret's divorce. I *(surprise)* _____ by the news. Janice *(shock)* _____ .

10. A new house *(build)* _____ next to ours next year.

11. Roberto *(write)* _____ this composition last week. That one *(write)* _____ by Abdullah.

12. Radium *(discover)* _____ by Marie and Pierre Curie in 1898.

13. At the soccer game yesterday, the winning goal *(kick)* _____ by Luigi. Over 100,000 people *(attend)* _____ the soccer game.

14. A: Do you understand the explanation in the book?
    B: No, I don't. I *(confuse)* _____ by it.

15. A: Where are you going to go to school next year?
    B: I *(accept)* _____ by Shoreline Community College.

16. A: I think football is too violent.
    B: I *(agree)* _____ with you. I *(prefer)* _____ baseball.

17. A: When *(your bike, steal)* _____ ?

    B: Two days ago.

18. A: *(you, pay)* _____ your electric bill yet?

    B: No, I haven't, but I'd better pay it today. If I don't, my electricity *(shut off)* _____ by the power company.

19. A: Did you hear about the accident?

    B: No. What *(happen)* _____ ?

    A: A bicyclist *(hit)* _____ by a taxi in front of the dorm.

    B: *(the bicyclist, injure)* _____ ?

    A: Yes. Someone *(call)* _____ an ambulance. The bicyclist *(take)* _____ to City Hospital and *(treat)* _____ in the emergency ward for cuts and bruises.

    B: What *(happen)* _____ to the taxi driver?

    A: He *(arrest)* _____ for reckless driving.

    B: He's lucky that the bicyclist *(kill, not)* _____ .

20. The Eiffel Tower *(be)* _____ in Paris, France. It *(visit)* _____ by millions of people every year. It *(design)* _____ by Alexandre Eiffel (1832–1923). It *(erect)* _____ in 1889 for the Paris exposition. Since that time, it *(be)* _____ the most famous landmark in Paris. Today it *(recognize)* _____ by people throughout the world.

☐ **EXERCISE 11. Active vs. passive. (Charts 10-1 → 10-4)**

Directions: Complete the sentences with the correct forms of the verbs in parentheses.

Almost everyone *(enjoy)* _____**enjoys**_____ visiting a zoo. Today zoos are
                                    1

common. The first zoo *(establish)* _____ around 3500 years ago
                                            2

by an Egyptian queen for her personal enjoyment. Five hundred years later, a Chinese

emperor *(establish)* _____ a huge zoo to show his power and wealth.
                              3

Later zoos *(establish)* _____ for the purpose of studying animals.
                                4

Some of the early European zoos were dark holes or dirty cages. At that time, people

(disgust) _____ by the bad conditions and the mistreatment of
                    5

the animals. Later, these early zoos *(replace)* _____ by scientific
                                                        6

institutions where animals *(study)* _____ and *(keep)*
                                            7

_____ in good condition. These research centers *(become)* _____
          8   9

the first modern zoos.

As early as the 1940s, scientists *(understand)* _____ that
                                                        10

many kinds of wild animals faced extinction. Since that time, zoos *(try)* _____
                                                                              11

_____ to save many endangered species, but relying on zoos to save

species such as the rhinoceros is not enough. In the 1980s, the number of rhinos in the

world *(reduce)* _____ from 10,000 to 400. Many rhinos *(kill)*
                          12

_____ by poachers, but many also *(die)* _____ in
          13   14

captivity. Zoo breeding programs for rhinos have not been successful. The best method of

conservation *(be)* _____ to leave them in their natural habitat. By 1999,
                            15

there *(be)* _____ more than 13,000 rhinos again living in the wild. These
16

rhinos *(save)* _____ from extinction by the strong conservation
17

methods of local communities, government agencies, and private landowners. Wildlife

biologists still fear that some subspecies of the rhino in Africa and Indonesia *(become)*

_____ extinct in the near future. Some scientists *(believe)*
18

_____ that half of all animal species in zoos will also be in danger of
19

extinction by the middle of this century.

Because zoos want to treat animals humanely and encourage breeding, today animals

(put) _____ in large, natural settings instead of small cages.
20

They *(watch)* _____ carefully for any signs of disease and *(feed)*
21

_____ a balanced diet. Most zoos *(have)* _____
22   23

specially trained veterinarians and a hospital for animals.

They also have specially trained keepers. Food *(prepare)* _____ in
24

the zoo kitchen. The food program *(design)* _____ to satisfy the
25

animals' particular needs. For example, some snakes *(feed)* _____ only
26

once a week, while some birds *(feed)* _____ several times a day. Today zoo
27

animals *(treat)* _____ well, and zoo breeding programs are important
28

in the attempt to save many species of wildlife.

10-5　THE PASSIVE FORMS OF THE PRESENT AND PAST PROGRESSIVE

ACTIVE	PASSIVE	
The secretary *is copying* some letters. Someone *is building* a new hospital.	(a) Some letters **are being copied** by the secretary. (b) A new hospital **is being built**.	Passive form of the present progressive: $\left.\begin{array}{l}\textbf{\textit{am}}\\\textbf{\textit{is}}\\\textbf{\textit{are}}\end{array}\right\}$ + **being** + *past participle*
The secretary *was copying* some letters. Someone *was building* a new hospital.	(c) Some letters **were being copied** by the secretary. (d) A new hospital **was being built**.	Passive form of the past progressive: $\left.\begin{array}{l}\textbf{\textit{was}}\\\textbf{\textit{were}}\end{array}\right\}$ + **being** + *past participle*

☐ **EXERCISE 12. Passive forms. (Chart 10-5)**

Directions: Complete the sentences with the correct passive forms of the present and past progressive.

1. Mr. Rice is teaching our class today.

   → Our class _____*is being taught*_____ by Mr. Rice today.

2. Someone is building a new house on Elm Street.

   → A new house _____ on Elm Street.

3. The Smith Construction Company is building that house.

   → That house _____ by the Smith Construction Company.

4. We couldn't use our classroom yesterday because someone was painting it.

   → We couldn't use our classroom yesterday because it _____.

5. Someone is organizing a student trip to the art museum.

   → A student trip to the art museum _____.

6. Dogs usually wag their tails while people are petting them.

   → Dogs usually wag their tails while they _____.

7. Many of the older people in the neighborhood were growing vegetables to help with the war effort.

   → Vegetables _____ by many of the older people in the neighborhood to help with the war effort.

8. According to one scientific estimate, we are losing 20,000 species of plants and animals each year due to the destruction of rainforests.

   → According to one scientific estimate, 20,000 species of plants and animals _____ each year due to the destruction of rainforests.

10-6 PASSIVE MODAL AUXILIARIES

ACTIVE MODAL AUXILIARIES	PASSIVE MODAL AUXILIARIES (MODAL + *BE* + PAST PARTICIPLE)		Modal auxiliaries are often used in the passive.
Bob *will mail* it.	It	*will be mailed* by Bob.	FORM: *modal* + *be* + *past participle*
Bob *can mail* it.	It	*can be mailed* by Bob.	(See Chapter 7 for information about
Bob *should mail* it.	It	*should be mailed* by Bob.	the meanings and uses of modal
Bob *ought to mail* it.	It	*ought to be mailed* by Bob.	auxiliaries.)
Bob *must mail* it.	It	*must be mailed* by Bob.	
Bob *has to mail* it.	It	*has to be mailed* by Bob.	
Bob *may mail* it.	It	*may be mailed* by Bob.	
Bob *might mail* it.	It	*might be mailed* by Bob.	
Bob *could mail* it.	It	*could be mailed* by Bob.	

☐ EXERCISE 13. Passive modals. (Chart 10-6)

Directions: Complete the sentences by changing the active modals to passive modals.

1. Someone must send this letter immediately.

   → This letter _____ must be sent _____ immediately.

2. People should plant tomatoes in the spring.

   → Tomatoes _____ in the spring.

3. People cannot control the weather.

   → The weather _____ .

4. Someone had to fix our car before we left for Chicago.

   → Our car _____ before we left for Chicago.

5. People can reach me at 555-3815.

   → I _____ at 555-3815.

6. You can find flowers in almost every part of the world.

   → Flowers _____ in almost every part of the world.

7. Someone ought to wash these dirty dishes soon.

   → These dirty dishes _____ soon.

8. People may cook carrots or eat them raw.

   → Carrots _____ or _____ raw.

9. If the river floods, water could destroy the village.

   → The village _____ if the river floods.

10. You must keep medicine out of the reach of children.

    → Medicine _____ out of the reach of children.

11. You shouldn't pronounce the "b" in "lamb."

    → The "b" in "lamb" _____ .

12. People can wear some watches underwater.

    → Some watches _____

    underwater.

DO YOU HAVE
THE TIME?

□ **EXERCISE 14. Active vs. passive. (Charts 10-1 → 10-6)**

Directions: Complete the sentences with any appropriate tense, active or passive, of the verbs in parentheses.

In prehistoric times, huge herds of horses *(live)* _____lived_____ throughout the

Americas. But then, for some unknown reason, they *(disappear)* _____

completely from North and South America. Even though the early horses *(die)*

_____ out in the Americas, they *(survive)* _____ in Asia.

Long ago, horses *(domesticate)** _____ by central Asian

nomads. At first, horses *(use)* _____ in war and in hunting, and oxen

(use) _____ for farming. Later, horses also *(become)* _____

farm animals.

Horses *(reintroduce)* _____ into the Americas by

Spaniards early in the fifteenth century. Spanish explorers *(come)* _____ in

ships to the New World with their horses on board. When the explorers *(return)*

_____ to Spain, they *(leave)* _____ some of their horses

behind. These *(develop)* _____ into wild herds. Native American

tribes in the western plains *(begin)* _____ to use horses around 1600. Wild

horses *(capture)* _____ and *(tame)* _____ for

use in war and in hunting.

In the 1800s, there were several million wild horses in North America. By the 1970s,

that number had become less than 20,000. The wild horses *(hunt)* _____

and *(kill)* _____ principally for use as pet food. Today in the United

States, wild horses *(protect)* _____ by law. They *(can kill, not)*

_____ for sport or profit. What is your opinion?

(wild horses, should protect) _____ by law?

_____

*People domesticate (tame) animals.

Directions: All of the sentences in the following passage are active. Some of the sentences should be passive because it is unknown or unimportant to know exactly who performs certain actions. Change sentences to the passive as appropriate. Discuss your reasons for making changes and for not making changes.

(1) Cheese has been a principal food throughout much of the world for thousands of years.

(2) ~~Someone probably made the first cheese~~ *The first cheese was probably made* in Asia around four thousand years ago. (3) Today people eat it in almost all the countries of the world. (4) People can eat it alone, or they may eat it with bread. (5) People can melt it and add it to noodles or vegetables. (6) People can use it as part of a main course or as a snack. (7) Throughout most of the world, cheese adds enjoyment and nutrition to many people's daily diets.

(8) Cheese is a milk product. (9) Cheesemakers make most cheese from cow's milk, but they can make it from the milk of goats, camels, yaks, and other animals, including zebras. (10) Some kinds of cheese, such as cheddar, are common in many parts of the world, but you can find other kinds only in small geographical areas.

(11) Cheesemakers produce cheese in factories. (12) They have to treat the milk in special ways. (13) They must heat it several times during the process. (14) At the end, they add salt, and they pack it into molds. (15) They age most cheese for weeks or months before they package and sell it. (16) They usually sell cheese to stores in large round pieces that they seal in wax.

(17) You can see these big rounds of cheese in food stores like delicatessens. (18) I like cheese and buy it often. (19) I don't know all the names of different kinds of cheese. (20) Often I can't pronounce the foreign name of the cheese I want. (21) When I go to the delicatessen near my apartment, I simply point to a kind of cheese that looks good to me. (22) I hold my

thumb and forefinger wide apart if I want a lot of cheese or close together if I want just a little.

(23) Frank and Anita, who work behind the cheese counter at the deli, always seem to give me just the right amount. (24) I'm glad cheese is nutritious because it's one of my favorite kinds of food.

10-7 USING PAST PARTICIPLES AS ADJECTIVES (STATIVE PASSIVE)

<table>
<tr>
<td>

(a) Paul **is** **young**.
(b) Paul **is** **tall**.
(c) Paul **is** **hungry**.

BE + **PAST PARTICIPLE**
(d) Paul **is** **married**.
(e) Paul **is** **tired**.
(f) Paul **is** **frightened**.

</td>
<td>

Be can be followed by an adjective. The adjective describes or gives information about the subject of the sentence.
Be can be followed by a past participle (the passive form). The past participle is often like an adjective. The past participle describes or gives information about the subject of the sentence. Past participles are used as adjectives in many common, everyday expressions.

</td>
</tr>
<tr>
<td>

(g) Paul *is married* **to** Susan.
(h) Paul *was excited* **about** the game.
(i) Paul *will be prepared* **for** the exam.

</td>
<td>

Often the past participles in these expressions are followed by particular prepositions + an object.
For example:
    married is followed by **to** (+ an object)
    excited is followed by **about** (+ an object)
    prepared is followed by **for** (+ an object)

</td>
</tr>
</table>

SOME COMMON EXPRESSIONS WITH BE + PAST PARTICIPLE

1. *be acquainted (with)*
2. *be bored (with, by)*
3. *be broken*
4. *be closed*
5. *be composed of*
6. *be crowded (with)*
7. *be devoted (to)*
8. *be disappointed (in, with)*
9. *be divorced (from)*
10. *be done (with)*
11. *be drunk (on)*
12. *be engaged (to)*

13. *be excited (about)*
14. *be exhausted (from)*
15. *be finished (with)*
16. *be frightened (of, by)*
17. *be gone (from)*
18. *be hurt*
19. *be interested (in)*
20. *be involved (in, with)*
21. *be located in, south of, etc.*
22. *be lost*
23. *be made of*
24. *be married (to)*

25. *be opposed (to)*
26. *be pleased (with)*
27. *be prepared (for)*
28. *be qualified (for)*
29. *be related (to)*
30. *be satisfied (with)*
31. *be scared (of, by)*
32. *be shut*
33. *be spoiled*
34. *be terrified (of, by)*
35. *be tired (of, from)* *
36. *be worried (about)*

*I'm **tired of** the cold weather. = *I've had enough cold weather. I want the weather to get warm.*
 I'm **tired from** working hard all day. = *I'm exhausted because I worked hard all day.*

Directions: Complete the sentences with the appropriate form of the verbs in *italics*. Include prepositions as necessary. Use the simple present.

1. *scare*   Most children ___*are scared of*___ loud noises.

2. *interest*   Jane _____ ecology.

3. *disappoint* My parents _____ me because of my low grades.

4. *please*   My boss _____ my work.

5. *satisfy*   I _____ my progress in English.

6. *marry*   Tony _____ Sonia.

7. *relate*   Alice Jones _____ Anna Jones. They're first cousins.

8. *do*   This is the last item in this exercise. We _____ this exercise now.

□ EXERCISE 17. Stative passive. (Chart 10-7)
Directions: Complete the sentences with the expressions in the list. Use the simple present.

be acquainted	*be exhausted*	*be related*
be broken	*be located*	*be satisfied*
be composed	*be lost*	*be scared*
be crowded	*be made*	*be spoiled*
be disappointed	*be qualified*	✓*be worried*

1. Dennis isn't doing well in school this semester. He ___*is worried*___ about his grades.

2. My shirt _____ of cotton.

3. I live in a three-room apartment with six other people. Our apartment _____ _____ .

4. Vietnam _____ in Southeast Asia.

5. I'm going to go straight to bed tonight. It's been a hard day. I _____ _____ .

6. Excuse me, sir, but I _____ . Could you please tell me how to get to the bus station from here?

7. My tape recorder doesn't work. It _____ .

8. Holly and I are sisters. We _____ to each other.

9. We leave a light on in our son's bedroom at night because he _____

_____ of the dark.

10. Alice thinks her boss should pay her more money. She _____ not

_____ with her present salary.

11. The children _____ . I had promised to take them to

the beach today, but now we can't go because it's raining.

12. _____ you _____ with Mrs. Novinsky? Have you

ever met her?

13. According to the job description, an applicant must have a Master's degree and at least

five years of teaching experience. Unfortunately, I _____ not

_____ for that job.

14. This milk doesn't taste right. I think it _____ . I'm not going to

drink it.

15. Water _____ of hydrogen and oxygen.

□ **EXERCISE 18. Stative passive. (Chart 10-7)**
  Directions: Complete the sentences with appropriate prepositions.

1. The day before a holiday, the food stores are usually crowded _____**with**_____

last-minute shoppers.

2. Are you qualified _____ that job?

3. Mr. Heath loves his family very much. He is devoted _____ them.

4. Our dog runs under the bed during storms. He's terrified _____ thunder.

5. My sister is married _____ a law student.

6. Are you prepared _____ the test?

7. I'll be finished _____ my work in another minute or two.

8. Jason is excited _____ going to Hollywood.

9. Ms. Brown is opposed _____ the new tax plan.

10. Jane isn't satisfied _____ her present apartment. She's looking for a

new one.

11. Janet doesn't take good care of herself. I'm worried _____ her health.

12. I'm tired _____ this rainy weather. I hope the sun shines tomorrow.

13. In terms of evolution, a hippopotamus is related _____ a horse.

14. The students are involved _____ many extracurricular activities.

15. Are you acquainted _____ this author? I think her books are excellent.

16. When will you be done _____ your work?

17. I'm starving! Right now I'm interested _____ only one thing: food.

18. The children want some new toys. They're bored _____ their old ones.

19. Sam is engaged _____ his childhood sweetheart.

20. Our daughter is scared _____ dogs.

21. You've done a good job. You should be very pleased _____ yourself.

☐ **EXERCISE 19. Stative passive. (Chart 10-7)**
Directions: Work in pairs.
Speaker A: Begin the item. Don't lower your intonation. Your book is open.
Speaker B: Finish the item with *a preposition* + **someone** or **something**.
Speaker A: Decide whether B has used the correct preposition. (Refer to Chart 10-7, p. 292, if necessary.) Repeat the entire item, emphasizing the preposition.

Example:
SPEAKER A *(book open):* I'm worried . . . .
SPEAKER B *(book closed):* . . . about something.
SPEAKER A *(book open):* Right. I'm worried **about** something.

Switch roles.

1. I'm interested	10. I'm opposed . . . .
2. I'm married	11. I'm frightened . . . .
3. I'm scared	12. I'm excited . . . .
4. I'm related	13. I'm engaged . . . .
5. I'm disappointed	14. I'm exhausted . . . .
6. I'm qualified	15. I'm tired . . . .
7. I'm satisfied	16. I'm finished . . . .
8. I'm prepared	17. I'm done . . . .
9. I'm acquainted . . .	18. I'm involved . . . .

Repeat the exercise. Use only the past participles as cues, and make your own sentences.

Example: worried
SPEAKER A: worried
SPEAKER B: The students are worried about the next test.

Directions: Complete the sentences with the words in *italics*. Use the passive form, simple present, or simple past. Include prepositions where necessary.

1. *close*   When we got to the post office, it ___was closed___ .

2. *make*   My earrings ___are made of___ gold.

3. *divorce*   Sally and Tom used to be married, but now they _____ .

4. *relate*   Your name is Tom Hood. _____ you _____ Mary Hood?

5. *spoil*   This fruit _____ . I think I'd better throw it out.

6. *exhaust*   Last night I _____ , so I went straight to bed.

7. *involve*   Last week I _____ a three-car accident.

8. *locate*   The University of Washington _____ Seattle.

9. *drink*   Ted _____ . He's making a fool of himself.

10. *interest*   I _____ learning more about that subject.

11. *devote*   Linda loves her job. She _____ her work.

12. *lose*   What's the matter, little boy? _____ you _____ ?

13. *terrify*   Once when we were swimming at the beach, we saw a shark. All of us _____ .

14. *acquaint*   _____ you _____ Sue's roommate?

15. *qualify*   I didn't get the job. The interviewer said that I _____ not _____ it.

16. *disappoint*   My son brought home a report card with all D's and F's. I can't understand it. I _____ him.

17. *do*   At last, I _____ my homework. Now I can go to bed.

18. *crowd*   There are too many students in our class. The classroom _____ .

19. *shut*   It's starting to rain. _____ all of the windows

_____ ?

20. *go*   Where's my wallet? It _____ ! Did you take it?

10-8 PARTICIPIAL ADJECTIVES: *-ED* vs. *-ING*

Indian art interests me. (a) I am ***interested*** in Indian art. INCORRECT: *I am interesting in Indian art.* (b) Indian art is ***interesting***. INCORRECT: *Indian art is interested.*	The past participle *(-ed)** and the present participle *(-ing)* can be used as adjectives. In (a): The past participle *(interested)* describes how a person feels. In (b): The present participle *(interesting)* describes the **cause** of the feeling. The cause of the interest is Indian art.
The news surprised Kate. (c) Kate was ***surprised***. (d) The news was ***surprising***.	In (c): *surprised* describes how Kate felt. The past participle carries a passive meaning: *Kate was surprised **by the news**.* In (d): *the news* was the cause of the surprise.
(e) Did you hear the ***surprising news?*** (f) Roberto fixed the ***broken window.***	Like other adjectives, participial adjectives may follow *be*, as in examples (a) through (d), or come in front of nouns, as in (e) and (f).

*The past participle of regular verbs ends in *-ed*. Some verbs have irregular forms. See Chart 2-6, p. 32.

☐ **EXERCISE 21. Participial adjectives. (Chart 10-8)**
   Directions: Complete the sentences with the *-ed* or *-ing* form of the verbs in *italics*.

1. Greg's classes *interest* him.

   a. Greg's classes are _____ interesting _____ .

   b. Greg is an _____ interested _____ student.

2. Emily is going to Australia. The idea of going on this trip *excites* her.

   a. Emily is _____ about going on this trip.

   b. She thinks it is going to be an _____ trip.

3. I like to study sea life. The subject of marine biology *fascinates* me.

   a. I'm _____ by marine biology.

   b. Marine biology is a _____ subject.

4. Mike heard some bad news. The bad news *depressed* him.

   a. Mike is very sad. In other words, he is _____ .

   b. The news made Mike feel sad. The news was _____ .

5. The exploration of space *interests* me.

    a. I'm _____ in the exploration of space.

    b. The exploration of space is _____ to me.

6. The nation's leader stole money. The scandal *shocked* the nation.

    a. It was a _____ scandal.

    b. The _____ nation soon replaced the leader.

7. I bought a new camera. I read the directions twice, but I didn't understand them. They *confused* me.

    a. I was _____ when I tried to understand the directions.

    b. They were _____ directions.

8. I spilled my drink on the dinner table. This *embarrassed* me.

    a. I was very _____ when I spilled my drink.

    b. That was an _____ experience.

9. Jane's classes *bore* her.

    a. Jane's classes are _____ .

    b. Jane is a _____ student.

10. An article in the newspaper *surprised* Mrs. Perez.

    a. It was a very _____ article to her.

    b. Mrs. Perez was very _____ when she read it.

11. The loud noise *frightened* the children.

    a. It was a _____ sound.

    b. The _____ children ran into their house.

□ **EXERCISE 22. Participial adjectives. (Chart 10-8)**

Directions: Complete the sentences with the appropriate **-ed** or **-ing** form of the words in italics.

Julie was walking along the edge of the fountain outside her office building. She was with her co-worker and friend Paul. Suddenly she lost her balance and accidentally fell in.

1. *embarrass*   Julie was really _____embarrassed_____ .

2. *embarrass*   Falling into the fountain was really _____embarrassing_____ .

3. *shock*   Her friend Paul was _____ .

4. *shock*   It was a _____ sight.

5. *surprise*   The people around the office building were very _____
    when they saw Julie in the fountain.

6. *surprise*   It was a _____ sight.

7. *depress*   The next day Julie was _____ because she thought she
    had made a fool of herself.

8. *depress*   When she fell into the fountain, some people laughed at her. It was a
    _____ experience.

9. *interest*   Her friend Paul told her not to lose her sense of humor. He told her it was
    just another _____ experience in life.

10. *interest*   He said that people would be _____ in hearing about
    how she fell into a fountain.

EXERCISE 23. Participial adjectives. (Charts 10-7 and 10-8)

Directions: Complete the sentences with an *-ed* or *-ing* adjective and the **boldface** noun.

1. If you *spoil* **children**, they become _____ spoiled children. _____

2. If a **door** *revolves*, it is called a _____ revolving door. _____

3. If someone *steals* a **car**, it is a _____

4. If people *crowd* into a **room**, it is a _____

5. If **costs** *rise*, they are _____

6. If a **danger** *exists*, it is an _____

7. If you *dry* **fruit**, it becomes _____

8. If you *plan* an **event**, it is called a _____

9. If a **committee** *plans* something, it is called a _____

10. If **water** *is boiling*, we call it _____

11. If a **person** *is missing*, we call him or her a _____

12. If you *freeze* **vegetables**, they are called _____

13. If the **weather** *freezes* things, it is called _____

14. If you *break* your **pencil**, you have a _____

10-9 *GET* + ADJECTIVE; *GET* + PAST PARTICIPLE

GET + **ADJECTIVE** (a) I **am getting hungry.** Let's eat. (b) Eric **got nervous** before the job interview.	***Get*** can be followed by an adjective. ***Get*** gives the idea of change—the idea of becoming, beginning to be, growing to be. In (a): *I'm getting hungry.* = *I wasn't hungry before, but now I'm beginning to be hungry.*
GET + **PAST PARTICIPLE** (c) **I'm getting tired.** Let's stop working. (d) Steve and Rita **got married** last month.	Sometimes ***get*** is followed by a past participle. The past participle after ***get*** is like an adjective; it describes the subject of the sentence.

GET + ADJECTIVE

get angry	*get dry*	*get quiet*
get bald	*get fat*	*get rich*
get big	*get full*	*get serious*
get busy	*get hot*	*get sick*
get close	*get hungry*	*get sleepy*
get cold	*get interested*	*get thirsty*
get dark	*get late*	*get well*
get dirty	*get nervous*	*get wet*
get dizzy	*get old*	

GET + PAST PARTICIPLE

get acquainted	*get drunk*	*get involved*
get arrested	*get engaged*	*get killed*
get bored	*get excited*	*get lost*
get confused	*get finished*	*get married*
get crowded	*get frightened*	*get scared*
get divorced	*get hurt*	*get sunburned*
get done	*get interested*	*get tired*
get dressed	*get invited*	*get worried*

☐ **EXERCISE 24. GET + adjective/past participle. (Chart 10-9)**

Directions: Complete the sentences. Use each word in the list only one time.

angry	dirty	full	rich
bald	dizzy	hot	sick
busy	dressed	hurt	sleepy
✓ cold	drunk	lost	tired

1. In winter, the weather gets _____ cold _____ .

2. In summer, the weather gets _____ .

3. This food is delicious, but I can't eat any more. I'm getting _____ .

4. I think I'll go to bed. I'm getting _____ .

5. Let's stop working and take a break. I'm getting _____ .

6. Sam is wearing one brown sock and one blue sock today. He got _____ in a hurry this morning and didn't pay attention to the color of his socks.

7. This work has to be done before we leave. We'd better get _____ and stop wasting time.

8. I didn't understand Jane's directions very well, so on the way to her house last night I got _____ . I couldn't find her house.

9. It's hard to work in a garage and stay clean. Paul's clothes always get _____ from all the grease and oil.

10. Don't waste your money gambling. You won't ever get _____ that way.

11. Mr. Anderson is losing some of his hair. He's getting _____ .

12. Was it a bad accident? Did anyone get _____ ?

13. Calm down! Take it easy! You shouldn't get so _____ . It's not good for your blood pressure.

14. When I turned around and around in a circle, I got _____ .

15. I don't feel very good. I think I'm getting _____. Maybe I should see
    a doctor.

16. My friends got _____ at the party Saturday night, so I drove them
    home in my car. They were in no condition to drive.

☐ **EXERCISE 25. GET + adjective/past participle. (Chart 10-9)**
   Directions: Complete the sentences with appropriate forms of ***get*** and the words in the list.

cold	*excite*	*lose*	*thirsty*
crowd	*hungry*	*marry*	*tired*
dark	*involve*	*sleep*	*well*
dry	*kill*	✓*sunburn*	*worry*

1. When I stayed out in the sun too long yesterday, I ___got sunburned___.

2. If you're sick, stay home and take care of yourself. You won't _____
   if you don't take care of yourself.

3. Jane and Greg are engaged. They are going to _____ a year
   from now.

4. Sarah doesn't eat breakfast, so she always _____ by ten or
   ten-thirty.

5. In the winter, the sun sets early. It _____ outside by six or even
   earlier.

6. Put these socks back in the dryer. They didn't _____ the
   first time.

7. Let's stop working for a while. I'm _____. I need to rest.

8. Sue has to vacate her apartment next week, and she hasn't found a new place to live.
   She's _____.

9. Sitara always _____ after she eats salty food.

10. Toshiro was in a terrible car wreck and almost _____. He's lucky
    to be alive.

11. The temperature is dropping. Brrr! I'm _____. Can I
    borrow your sweater?

12. We were in a strange city without a map. It was easy for us to _____.
    We had to ask a shopkeeper how to get back to our hotel.

13. Did you _____ when your team won the game? Did you
    clap and yell when they won?

14. Good restaurants _____ around dinner time. It's hard to find a seat because there are so many people.

15. When little Annie _____ , her father gave her a bottle and put her to bed.

16. I left when Ellen and Joe began to argue. I never _____ in other people's quarrels.

10-10 USING *BE USED/ACCUSTOMED TO* AND *GET USED/ACCUSTOMED TO*

(a) I *am used to* hot weather. (b) I *am accustomed to* hot weather.	(a) and (b) have the same meaning: "Living in a hot climate is usual and normal for me. I'm familiar with what it is like to live in a hot climate. Hot weather isn't strange or different to me."
(c) I *am used* ***to living*** in a hot climate. (d) I *am accustomed* ***to living*** in a hot climate.	Notice in (c) and (d): *to* (a preposition) is followed by the *-ing* form of a verb (a gerund).
(e) I just moved from Florida to Siberia. I have never lived in a cold climate before, but I *am getting used to (accustomed to)* the cold weather here.	In (e): *I'm getting used to/accustomed to* = something is beginning to seem usual and normal to me.

☐ EXERCISE 26. BE USED/ACCUSTOMED TO. (Chart 10-10)

Directions: Complete the sentences with *be used to,* affirmative or negative.

1. Juan is from Mexico. He ___is used to___ hot weather. He ___isn't used to___ cold weather.

2. Alice was born and raised in Chicago. She _____ living in a big city.

3. My hometown is New York City, but this year I'm going to school in a town with a population of 10,000. I _____ living in a small town. I _____ living in a big city.

4. We do a lot of exercises in class. We _____ doing exercises.

Complete the sentences with *be accustomed to,* affirmative or negative.
NOTICE: *accustomed* is spelled with two "c"s and one "m."

5. Spiro recently moved to Canada from Greece. He ___is accustomed to___ eating Greek food. He ___isn't accustomed to___ eating Canadian food.

6. I always get up around 6:00 A.M. I _____ getting up early. I _____ sleeping late.

7. Our teacher always gives us a lot of homework. We _____

    having a lot of homework every day.

8. Young schoolchildren rarely take multiple choice tests. They _____

    _____ taking that kind of test.

☐ **EXERCISE 27. BE USED/ACCUSTOMED TO. (Chart 10-10)**
Directions: Talk about yourself. Use *be used/accustomed to*.

Example: cold weather
    → *I am* (OR *I am not) used / accustomed to cold weather.*

1. hot weather
2. cold weather
3. living in a warm climate
4. living in a cold climate
5. living in a big city
6. living in a small town
7. getting up early
8. sleeping late
9. eating a big breakfast
10. drinking coffee in the morning
11. *(a kind of)* food
12. being on my own★

☐ **EXERCISE 28. BE USED/ACCUSTOMED TO. (Chart 10-10)**
Directions: Work in pairs.
Speaker A: Pose the question. Your book is open.
Speaker B: Answer the question in a complete sentence. Your book is closed.

Example:
SPEAKER A *(book open):* What time are you accustomed to getting up?
SPEAKER B *(book closed):* I'm accustomed to getting up (at 7:30).

1. What time are you used to going to bed?

2. Are you accustomed to living in *(name of this city)*?

3. Are you used to speaking English every day?

4. Do you live with a roommate or do you live alone? Are you accustomed to that?

5. What are you accustomed to eating for breakfast?

Switch roles.
6. What kind of food are you accustomed to eating?

7. What time are you accustomed to getting up?

8. Are you accustomed to living in a big city or a small town?

9. Our weather right now is (hot/cold/humid/cold) and (wet/dry/etc.) Are you used to this kind of weather?

10. Are you used to speaking English every day, or does it seem strange to you?

_____

★*To be on one's own* is an idiom. It means to be away from one's family and responsible for oneself.

☐ **EXERCISE 29. GET USED/ACCUSTOMED TO. (Chart 10-10)**

Directions: Discuss or write about one or more of the following topics.

1. James graduated from high school last month. Three days after graduation, he got married. The next week he started a job at a paint store. Within two weeks, his life changed a lot. What did he have to get used to?

2. Jane is going to leave her parents' house next week. She is going to move in with two of her cousins who work in the city. Jane will be away from her home for the first time in her life. What is she going to have to get accustomed to?

3. Think of a time you traveled in or lived in a foreign country. What weren't you used to? What did you get used to? What didn't you ever get used to?

4. Think of the first day of a job you have had. What weren't you used to? What did you get used to?

10-11 USED TO vs. BE USED TO

(a) I *used to* **live** in Chicago, but now I live in Tokyo. *INCORRECT: I used to living in Chicago.* *INCORRECT: I am used to live in a big city.*	In (a): ***Used to*** expresses the habitual past (see Chart 2-11, p. 52). It is followed by the **simple form of a verb**.
(b) I *am used to* **living** in a big city.	In (b): ***be used to*** is followed by the ***-ing* form of a verb** (a gerund).*

*NOTE: In both **used to** (habitual past) and **be used to**, the "d" is not pronounced in *used*.

☐ **EXERCISE 30. USED TO vs. BE USED TO. (Chart 10-11)**

Directions: Add an appropriate form of **be** if necessary. If no form of **be** is needed, write **Ø** in the blank.

1. I have lived in Malaysia for a long time. I _____*am*_____ used to warm weather.

2. I _____*Ø*_____ used to live in Finland, but now I live in France.

3. I _____ used to sitting at this desk. I sit here every day.

4. I _____ used to sit in the back of the classroom, but now I prefer to sit in the front row.

5. When I was a child, I _____ used to play games with my friends in a big field near my house after school every day.

6. It's hard for my children to stay inside on a cold, rainy day. They _____ used to playing outside in the big field near our house. They play there almost every day.

7. A teacher _____ used to answering questions. Students, especially good students, always have a lot of questions.

8. People _____ used to believe the world was flat.

☐ EXERCISE 31. USED TO vs. BE USED TO. (Chart 10-11)

Directions: Complete the sentences with **used to** or **be used to** and the correct form of the verb in parentheses.

1. Nick stays up later now than he did when he was in high school. He *(go)*
_____*used to go*_____ to bed at ten, but now he rarely gets to bed before
midnight.

2. I got used to going to bed late when I was in college, but now I have a job and I need
my sleep. These days I *(go)* __*am used to going*__ to bed around ten-thirty.

3. I am a vegetarian. I *(eat)* _____ meat, but now I
eat only meatless meals.

4. Ms. Wu has had a vegetable garden all her life. She *(grow)* _____
_____ her own vegetables.

5. Oscar has lived in Brazil for ten years. He *(eat)* _____
Brazilian food. It's his favorite.

6. Georgio moved to Germany to open his own restaurant. He *(have)* _____
_____ a small bakery in Italy.

7. I have taken the bus to work every day for the past five years. I *(take)* _____
_____ the bus.

8. Juanita travels by plane on company business. She *(go)* _____
by train, but now the distances she needs to travel are too great.

☐ EXERCISE 32. USED TO vs. BE USED TO. (Charts 2-9 and 10-11)

Directions: You are living in a new place (country, city, apartment, dorm, etc.) and going to
a new school. What adjustments have you had to make? Write about them by completing
the sentences with your own words.

1. I'm getting used to . . . .

2. I'm also getting accustomed to . . . .

3. I have gotten accustomed to . . . .

4. I haven't gotten used to . . . .

5. I can't get used to . . . .

6. Do you think I will ever get accustomed to . . . ?

7. I used to . . . , but now . . . .

10-12 USING *BE SUPPOSED TO*

(a) Mike *is supposed to call* me tomorrow. (IDEA: I expect Mike to call me tomorrow.) (b) We *are supposed to write* a composition. (IDEA: The teacher expects us to write a composition.)	*Be supposed to* is used to talk about an activity or event that is expected to occur. In (a): The idea of *is supposed to* is that Mike is expected (by me) to call me. I asked him to call me. He promised to call me. I expect him to call me.
(c) Alice *was supposed to be* home at ten, but she didn't get in until midnight. (IDEA: Someone expected Alice to be home at ten.)	In the past form, *be supposed to* often expresses the idea that an expected event did not occur, as in (c).

☐ **EXERCISE 33. BE SUPPOSED TO. (Chart 10-12)**

Directions: Create sentences with a similar meaning by using *be supposed to*.

1. The teacher expects us to be on time for class.
   → *We are supposed to be on time for class.*

2. People expect the weather to be cold tomorrow.

3. People expect the plane to arrive at 6:00.

4. My boss expects me to work late tonight.

5. I expected the mail to arrive an hour ago, but it didn't.

☐ **EXERCISE 34. BE SUPPOSED TO. (Chart 10-12)**

Directions: Correct the mistakes.

1. I'm supposed ᵗᵒ call my parents tonight.

2. We're not suppose to tell anyone about the surprise.

3. You don't supposed to talk to Alan about the surprise.

4. My friend was supposing to call me last night, but he didn't.

5. Children supposed to respect their parents.

6. Didn't you supposed be at the meeting last night?

□ **EXERCISE 35. BE SUPPOSED TO. (Chart 10-12)**

Directions: Identify who is supposed to do something.

1. TOM'S BOSS: Mail this package.
       TOM: Yes, sir.
   → *Tom is supposed to mail a package.*

2. MARY: Call me at nine.
       ANN: Okay.

3. MS. MARTINEZ: Please make your bed before you go to school.
       JOHNNY: Okay, Mom.

4. MR. TAKADA: Put your dirty clothes in the laundry basket.
       SUSIE: Okay, Dad.

5. MRS. WILSON: Bobby, pick up your toys and put them away.
       BOBBY: Okay, Mom.
   MRS. WILSON: Annie, please hang up your coat.
       ANNIE: Okay, Mom.

6. DR. KETTLE: You should take one pill every eight hours.
       PATIENT: All right, Dr. Kettle. Anything else?
   DR. KETTLE: Drink plenty of fluids.

7. PROF. THOMPSON: Read the directions carefully, and raise your hand if you have any
                    questions.
       STUDENTS: *(no response)*

□ **EXERCISE 36. BE SUPPOSED TO. (Chart 10-12)**

Directions: Create sentences with **be supposed to** by combining the subjects in Column A with the ideas in Column B. Use the simple present.

Example: Visitors at a zoo are not supposed to feed the animals.

Column A	Column B
1. Visitors at a zoo	A. listen to their parents
2. Doctors	B. buckle their seatbelts before takeoff
3. Employees	✓C. not . . . feed the animals
4. Air passengers	D. not . . . talk during a performance
5. Theatergoers	E. be on time for work
6. Soldiers on sentry duty	F. obey its trainer
7. Children	G. pay their rent on time
8. Heads of state	H. care for their patients
9. A dog	I. not . . . fall asleep
10. People who live in apartments	J. be diplomatic

☐ EXERCISE 37. BE SUPPOSED TO. (Chart 10-12)

Directions: Think of things the following people are or were supposed to do. Use **be supposed to**.

Example: a good friend of yours
→ *My friend Ji Ming is supposed to help me paint my apartment this weekend. Benito was supposed to go to dinner with me last Wednesday, but he forgot. Nadia is supposed to call me tonight.*

1. a good friend of yours
2. your roommate or spouse*
3. children
4. a student in your English class
5. your English teacher
6. the leader of your country
7. one or both of your parents
8. one of your siblings or cousins
9. yourself
10. (. . .)

☐ EXERCISE 38. Written. (Chapters 1 → 10)

Directions: In writing, describe how a particular holiday is celebrated in your country. What is done in the morning, in the afternoon, in the evening? What are some of the things that people typically do on this holiday?
NOTE: Many of your sentences will be active, but some of them should be passive.

☐ EXERCISE 39. Error analysis. (Chapter 10)

Directions: Correct the errors.

Example: I am agree with him.
→ *I agree with him.*

1. An accident was happened at the corner yesterday.

2. This pen is belong to me.

3. I am very surprise by the news.

4. I'm interesting in that subject.

5. He is marry with my cousin.

6. Thailand is locate in Southeast Asia.

7. Mary's dog was died last week.

8. Were you surprise when you saw him?

---

*If you have neither a roommate nor a spouse, invent one or simply skip to the next item.

9. When I went downtown, I get lost.

10. Last night I very tire.

11. The bus was arrived ten minutes late.

12. I am disagreed with that statement.

13. Our class is compose from immigrants.

14. I am not acustomed to cold weather.

15. We're not suppose to have pets in our apartment.

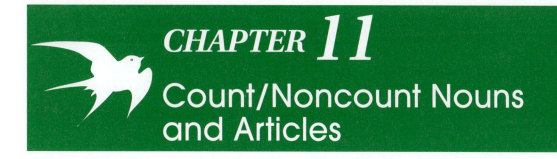

CHAPTER 11
Count/Noncount Nouns and Articles

□ EXERCISE 1. Preview: using A and AN. (Charts 11-1 and 11-2)
Directions: Add *a* or *an* as necessary.

1. I never wear ∧ *a* hat.

2. We had ∧ *an* easy test yesterday.

3. I rarely put salt on my food. OK *(no change)*

4. Jack has wallet in his back pocket.

5. We had good weather for our picnic yesterday.

6. There was earthquake in Turkey last week.

7. Ball is round object.

8. Linda likes to wear jewelry.

9. Anna is wearing ring on her fourth finger.

10. My father enjoys good health.

11. Simon Bolivar is hero to many people.

12. I called Jim by the wrong name. It was honest mistake.

13. I had unusual experience yesterday.

14. Ann had unique experience yesterday.

15. I often ask my parents for advice.

11-1 *A* vs. *AN*

(a) I have *a pencil*. (b) I live in *an apartment*. (c) I have *a small apartment*. (d) I live in *an old building*.	*A* and *an* are used in front of a singular noun (e.g., *pencil*, *apartment*). They mean "one." If a singular noun is modified by an adjective (e.g., *small*, *old*), *a* or *an* comes in front of the adjective, as in (c) and (d). *A* is used in front of words that begin with a consonant (*b, c, d, f, g,* etc.): *a boy, a bad day, a cat, a cute baby.* *An* is used in front of words that begin with the vowels *a, e, i,* and *o*: *an apartment, an angry man, an elephant, an empty room,* etc.

(e) I have *an umbrella*.
(f) I saw *an ugly picture*.
(g) I attend *a university*.
(h) I had *a unique experience*.
	For words that begin with the letter *u*:
	    (1) *An* is used if the *u* is a vowel sound, as in *an umbrella, an uncle, an unusual day.*
	    (2) *A* is used if the *u* is a consonant sound, as in *a university, a unit, a usual event.*

(i) He will arrive in *an hour*.
(j) New Year's Day is *a holiday*.
	For words that begin with the letter *h*:
	    (1) *An* is used if the *h* is silent: *an hour, an honor, an honest person.*
	    (2) *A* is used if the *h* is pronounced: *a holiday, a hotel, a high point.*

☐ **EXERCISE 2. A vs. AN. (Chart 11-1)**
Directions: Write *a* or *an* in the blanks.

1. _*a*_ mistake
2. ____ abbreviation
3. ____ dream
4. ____ interesting dream
5. ____ empty box
6. ____ box

7. ____ uniform
8. ____ union
9. ____ untrue story
10. ____ urgent message
11. ____ universal problem
12. ____ unhappy child

13. ____ hour or two
14. ____ hole in the ground
15. ____ hill
16. ____ handsome man
17. ____ honest man
18. ____ honor

☐ **EXERCISE 3. A vs. AN. (Chart 11-1)**
Directions: Define the given words in complete sentences. Begin each sentence with *a* or *an*. Refer to a dictionary if necessary.

Example: indecisive person
→ *An indecisive person is a person who can't make up his mind.*

1. astronaut
2. microscope
3. enemy
4. ferry
5. absent-minded person

6. camel
7. umbrella
8. unicorn
9. onion
10. honeymoon trip

11. hourly wage
12. horn
13. unlit hallway
14. utensil
15. orchard

11-2 COUNT AND NONCOUNT NOUNS

	SINGULAR	PLURAL	A count noun:
COUNT NOUN	*a* chair *one* chair	Ø★ chairs *two* chairs *some* chairs	(1) can be counted with numbers: *one chair, two chairs, ten chairs, etc.* (2) can be preceded by *a/an* in the singular: *a chair.* (3) has a plural form ending in *-s* or *-es: chairs.*★★

NONCOUNT NOUN	Ø furniture
	some furniture
		Ø
		Ø
			A noncount noun:
			(1) cannot be counted with numbers.
			   INCORRECT: one furniture
			(2) is NOT immediately preceded by *a/an*.
			   INCORRECT: a furniture
			(3) does NOT have a plural form (no final-*s*).
			   INCORRECT: furnitures

★Ø = "nothing."
★★See Chart 1-5, p. 13, and Chart 6-1, p. 157, for the spelling and pronunciation of *-s/-es*.

☐ EXERCISE 4. Count and noncount nouns. (Chart 11-2)

Directions: Correct the mistakes. Some sentences contain no errors. Use *some* with the noncount nouns.

1. I bought one chair for my apartment. OK *(no change)*

2. I bought ~~one~~ ^{some} furniture for my apartment.*

3. I bought four chairs for my apartment.

4. I bought four furnitures for my apartment.

5. I bought a chair for my apartment.

6. I bought a furniture for my apartment.

7. I bought some chair for my apartment.

8. I bought some furnitures for my apartment.

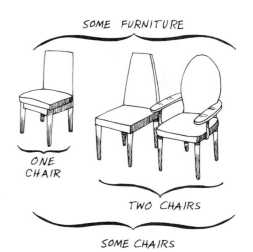

SOME FURNITURE

ONE CHAIR

TWO CHAIRS

SOME CHAIRS

---

*CORRECT: *I bought **some furniture** for my apartment.* OR *I bought **furniture** for my apartment.* See Chart 11–8, p. 326, for more information about the use of Ø and *some*.

Directions: Write *a/an* or *some* in the blanks. Identify count and noncount nouns.

1. I often have _____some_____ **fruit** for dessert.   *fruit*   →   count (noncount)

2. I had _____a_____ **banana** for dessert.   *banana*   →   (count) noncount

3. I got _____ **letter** today.   *letter*   →   count   noncount

4. I got _____ **mail** today.   *mail*   →   count   noncount

5. Anna wears _____ **ring** on her left hand.   *ring*   →   count   noncount

6. Maria is wearing _____ **jewelry** today.   *jewelry*   →   count   noncount

7. I have _____ **homework** to finish.   *homework*   →   count   noncount

8. I have _____ **assignment** to finish.   *assignment*   →   count   noncount

9. I needed _____ **information**.   *information*   →   count   noncount

10. I asked _____ **question**.   *question*   →   count   noncount

11-3   NONCOUNT NOUNS

INDIVIDUAL PARTS = THE WHOLE
(Count Nouns)   (Noncount Nouns)

(a) letters / postcards / bills / etc. ⟩ ***mail***

(b) apples / bananas / oranges / etc. ⟩ ***fruit***

(c) rings / bracelets / necklaces / etc. ⟩ ***jewelry***

Noncount nouns usually refer to a whole group of things that is made up of many individual parts, a whole category made up of different varieties.

For example, *furniture* is a noncount noun; it describes a whole category of things: *chairs, tables, beds, etc.*

INDIVIDUAL PARTS = THE WHOLE

chairs / tables / beds / etc. ⟩ ***furniture***

Mail, fruit, and *jewelry* are other examples of noncount nouns that refer to a whole category made up of individual parts.

SOME COMMON NONCOUNT NOUNS: WHOLE GROUPS MADE UP OF INDIVIDUAL PARTS

A. *clothing*	B. *homework*	E. *grammar*	G. *corn*
equipment	*housework*	*slang*	*dirt*
food	*work*	*vocabulary*	*flour*
fruit			*hair*
furniture	C. *advice*	F. *Arabic*	*pepper*
jewelry	*information*	*Chinese*	*rice*
mail		*English*	*salt*
money	D. *history*	*German*	*sand*
scenery	*literature*	*Indonesian*	*sugar*
stuff	*music*	*Spanish*	
traffic	*poetry*	*Etc.*	

Directions: Add final *-s/-es* if possible. Otherwise, write a slash (*I*) in the blank.

1. I'm learning a lot of **grammar** ___/___ .

2. We're studying count and noncount **noun** __s__ .

3. City streets usually have a lot of **traffic** _____ .

4. The streets are full of **automobile** _____ .

5. We enjoyed the **scenery** _____ in the countryside.

6. Nepal has high **mountain** _____ .

7. I have some important **information** _____ for you.

8. I have some important **fact** _____ for you.

9. Olga knows a lot of English **word** _____ .

10. Olga has learned a lot of new **vocabulary** _____ .

11. The children learned a lot of new **song** _____ in nursery school.

12. I enjoy listening to **music** _____ .

13. Can you give me some **suggestion** _____ ?

14. Can you give me some **advice** _____ ?

15. I like to read good **literature** _____ .

16. I like to read good **novel** _____ .

17. I had **sand** _____ in my shoes from walking on the beach.

18. Florida is famous for its white sand **beach** _____ .

11-4 MORE NONCOUNT NOUNS

(a) LIQUIDS		SOLIDS and SEMI-SOLIDS				GASES
coffee	soup	bread	meat	chalk	paper	air
milk	tea	butter	beef	glass	soap	pollution
oil	water	cheese	chicken	gold	toothpaste	smog
		ice	fish	iron	wood	smoke

(b) THINGS THAT OCCUR IN NATURE		
weather	darkness	thunder
rain	light	lightning
snow	sunshine	

(c) ABSTRACTIONS*					
beauty	fun	health	ignorance	patience	time
courage	generosity	help	knowledge	progress	violence
experience	happiness	honesty	luck		

*An abstraction is an idea. It has no physical form. A person cannot touch it.

☐ EXERCISE 7. Count and noncount nouns. (Charts 11-2 → 11-4)
    Directions: Add final *-s/-es* if possible. Otherwise, write a slash (*/*) in the blank.

1. I made some **mistake** _s_____ on my algebra test.

2. In winter in Alaska, there ((is), *are*) **snow** __/___ on the ground.

3. Alaska has a lot of cold **weather** _____ .

4. We have a lot of **storm** _____ in the winter.

5. There (*is, are*) some **chalk** _____ in this classroom.

6. Be sure to give the new couple my best **wish** _____ .

7. I want to wish them good **luck** _____ .

8. **Thunder** _____ and **lightning** _____ can be scary for children and animals.

9. **Gold** _____ (*is, are*) expensive. **Diamond** _____ (*is, are*) expensive too.

10. I admire Prof. Yoo for her extensive **knowledge** _____ of organic farming methods.

11. Prof. Yoo has a lot of good **idea** _____ and strong **opinion** _____ .

12. Teaching children to read requires **patience** _____ .

13. Doctors take care of **patient** _____ .

14. Mr. Fernandez's English is improving. He's making a lot of **progress** _____ .

15. Automobiles are the biggest source of **pollution** _____ in most cities.

16. Engineers build **bridge** _____ across **river** _____ and other **body** _____ of

    water _____ .

☐ EXERCISE 8. Noncount abstractions. (Chart 11-4)
    Directions: Complete the sentences in Column A with words from Column B. The completed sentences will be common sayings in English.

    Example: Ignorance is bliss.
        ("Ignorance is bliss" is a saying. It means: If you know about problems, you have to worry about them and solve them. If you don't know about problems, you can avoid them and be happy [*bliss = happiness*]. Do you agree with this saying?)

Column A	Column B
1. Ignorance is __D__	A. the best teacher.
2. Honesty is _____	B. the best medicine.
3. Time is _____	C. power.
4. Laughter is _____	✓D. bliss.
5. Beauty is _____	E. in the eye of the beholder.
6. Knowledge is _____	F. money.
7. Experience is _____	G. the best policy.

□ **EXERCISE 9. Noncount abstractions. (Chart 11-4)**

Directions: In groups or by yourself, complete the lists with abstract nouns. (Abstract nouns are usually noncount. To find out if a noun is count or noncount, check your dictionary or discuss it with your teacher.)

a. Name four good qualities you admire in a person.

1. _____ *patience* _____ 3. _____

2. _____ 4. _____

b. Name bad qualities people can have.

1. _____ *greed* _____ 3. _____

2. _____ 4. _____

c. What are some of the most important things in life?

1. _____ *good health* _____ 3. _____

2. _____ 4. _____

d. Certain bad conditions exist in the world. What are they?

1. _____ *hunger* _____ 3. _____

2. _____ 4. _____

□ **EXERCISE 10. Count and noncount nouns. (Charts 11-1 → 11-4)**

Directions: Choose one of the given topics. Make a written list of the things you see.

Example: You're sitting in your office. List the things you see.

Written:
- two windows
- three desk lamps
- a lot of books—around 50 books about English grammar
- office equipment—a Macintosh computer, a printer, a photocopy machine
- typical office supplies—a stapler, paper clips, pens, pencils, a ruler
- some photographs
- etc.

Topics:

1. Sit in any room of your choosing. List the things you see (including things other people are wearing if you wish).
2. Look out a window. List the things and people you see.
3. Go to a place outdoors (a park, a zoo, a city street) and list what you see.
4. Travel in your imagination to a room you lived in when you were a child. List everything you can remember about that room.

11-5 USING *SEVERAL, A LOT OF, MANY/MUCH,* AND *A FEW/A LITTLE*

	COUNT	NONCOUNT	
(a)	*several* chairs	Ø	*Several* is used only with *count* nouns.
(b)	*a lot of* chairs	*a lot of* furniture	*A lot of* is used with both *count* and *noncount* nouns.
(c)	*many* chairs	*much* furniture	*Many* is used with *count* nouns. *Much* is used with *noncount* nouns.
(d)	*a few* chairs	*a little* furniture	*A few* is used with *count* nouns. *A little* is used with *noncount* nouns.

☐ EXERCISE 11. SEVERAL, A LOT OF, and MANY/MUCH. (Charts 11-1 → 11-5)
Directions: Correct the mistakes. Some sentences contain no errors. One sentence contains a spelling error.

1. Jack bought ~~several~~ *some* furniture.

2. He bought several chairs. OK (*no change*)

3. Ted bought a lot of chairs.

4. Sue bought a lot of furniture, too.

5. Alice bought too much furniture.

6. She bought too much chairs.

7. Dr. Lee bought a few furniture for his new office.

8. He bought a few chairs.

9. He has several new furnitures in his office.

10. He has several new chairs in his office.

11. There is alot of desk in this room.

12. There are a lot of furnitures in Dr. Lee's office.

Directions: Create questions with *how many* or *how much*. Use the information in parentheses to form Speaker A's question.

1. A: How ____many children do the Millers have____ ?
   B: Three. (The Millers have three children.)

2. A: How ____much money does Jake make____ ?
   B: A lot. (Jake makes a lot of money.)

3. A: How _____ on a soccer team?
   B: Eleven. (There are eleven players on a soccer team.)

4. A: How _____ to do tonight?
   B: Just a little. (I have just a little homework to do tonight.)

5. A: How _____ in the baskets?
   B: A lot. (There are a lot of apples in the baskets.)

6. A: How _____ in the baskets?
   B: A lot. (There is a lot of fruit in the baskets.)

7. A: How _____ in Canada?
   B: Ten. (There are ten provinces in Canada.)

8. A: How _____ before you moved to Japan?
   B: Just a little. (I knew just a little Japanese before I moved to Japan.)

9. A: How _____ in the world?
   B: Approximately 22,000. (There are approximately 22,000 kinds of fish in the world.)

10. A: How _____ ?
    B: A lot. (You should buy a lot of cheese.) It looks really good.

11. A: How _____ every day?
    B: Two cups. (I drink two cups of coffee every day.)

12. A: How _____ in the chalk tray?
    B: Several pieces. (There are several pieces of chalk in the chalk tray.)

Directions: Work in pairs.
Speaker A: Using the cues, ask a question using *how much* or *how many*. You are looking for the answer to "**x**." Your book is open.
Speaker B: Listen carefully for the correct use of *much* and *many*. Answer the question. If you don't know the answer, guess. Sometimes Speaker A is given the correct answer and can tell you how close you are to the correct answer. Your book is closed.

Example: **water**: You drink **x** every day.
SPEAKER A *(book open):* How much water do you drink every day?
SPEAKER B *(book closed):* I try to drink at least six glasses of water every day.

Example: **page**: There are **x** in this chapter. *(Answer: 32)*
SPEAKER A *(book open):* How many pages are there in this chapter?
SPEAKER B *(book closed):* I don't know. I'd guess there are about thirty.
SPEAKER A *(book open):* Very close! There are 32 pages in this chapter.

1. **tea**:   You usually drink **x** every day.
2. **word**:   There are **x** in the title of this book. *(Answer: 4)*
3. **money**:   A pencil costs **x**.
4. **bone**:   There are **x** in the human body. *(Answer: 206)*
5. **tooth**:   The average person has **x**. *(Answer: 32)*
6. **mail**:   You got **x** yesterday.

Switch roles.
7. **sugar**:   You put **x** in your tea.
8. **language**:   You can speak **x**.
9. **English**:   Had you studied **x** before you started attending this class?
10. **people**:   There were **x** on earth 2,000 years ago. *(Answer: around 250 million)*
11. **human being**: There are **x** in the world today. *(Answer: around six billion)*
12. **butterfly**:   You can see **x** in one hour on a summer day in a flower garden.

□ EXERCISE 14. A FEW vs. A LITTLE. (Charts 11-1 → 11-5)
Directions: Complete the sentences by using *a few* or *a little* and the given noun. Use the plural form of the noun when necessary.

REMINDER: Use *a few* with a count noun: *a few songs*.
             Use *a little* with a noncount noun: *a little music*.

1. *music*   I feel like listening to _____*a little music*_____ tonight.

2. *song*   We sang _____*a few songs*_____ at the party.

3. *help*   Do you need _____ with that?

4. *pepper*   My grandfather doesn't use extra salt, but he always puts _____
                _____ on his hard-boiled egg

5. *thing*   I need to pick up _____ at the market on my
                way home from work tonight.

6. *apple* I bought _____ at the market.*

7. *fruit* I bought _____ at the market.

8. *advice* I need _____ .

9. *money* If I accept that job, I'll make _____ more _____ .

10. *coin* Annie put _____ in her pocket.

11. *friend* _____ came by last night to visit us.

12. *rain* It looks like we might get _____ today. I think I'll take my umbrella with me.

13. *French* I can speak _____ , but I don't know any Italian at all.

14. *hour* Ron's plane will arrive in _____ more _____ .

15. *toothpaste* Tommy, put just _____ on your toothbrush, not half the tube!

16. *chicken* I'm still hungry. I think I'll have _____ more _____ .

17. *chicken* When I was a child, we raised _____ in our backyard.

a little chicken a little chicken a few chickens

a big chicken a lot of chicken a lot of chickens

_____

*I bought *a few apples.* = I bought a small number of apples.
 I bought *a little apple.* = I bought one apple, and it was small, not large.

11-6 NOUNS THAT CAN BE COUNT OR NONCOUNT

Quite a few nouns can be used as either count or noncount nouns. Examples of both count and noncount usages for some common nouns follow.

NOUN	USED AS A **NONCOUNT** NOUN	USED AS A **COUNT** NOUN
glass	(a) Windows are made of **glass**.	(b) I drank **a glass** of water. (c) Janet wears **glasses** when she reads.
hair	(d) Rita has brown **hair**.	(e) There's **a hair** on my jacket.
iron	(f) **Iron** is a metal.	(g) I pressed my shirt with **an iron**.
light	(h) I opened the curtain to let in **some light**.	(i) Please turn off **the lights** (lamps).
paper	(j) I need **some paper** to write a letter.	(k) I wrote **a paper** for Professor Lee. (l) I bought **a paper** (a newspaper).
time	(m) How **much time** do you need to finish your work?	(n) How **many times** have you been in Mexico?
work	(o) I have **some work** to do tonight.	(p) That painting is **a work** of art.
coffee	(q) I had **some coffee** after dinner.	(r) **Two coffees**, please.
chicken/ fish	(s) I ate **some chicken/some fish**.	(t) She drew a picture of **a chicken/a fish**.
experience	(u) I haven't had **much experience** with computers. (I don't have much knowledge or skill in using computers.)	(v) I had **many** interesting **experiences** on my trip. (Many interesting events happened to me on my trip.)

☐ **EXERCISE 15. Nouns that can be count or noncount. (Chart 11-6)**

Directions: Complete the sentences with the given words. Choose words in parentheses as necessary.

1. *chicken*   Joe, would you like *(a, some)* __some chicken__ for dinner tonight?

2. *chicken*   My grandmother raises __chickens__ in her yard.

3. *time*   It took a lot of _____ to write my composition.

4. *time*   I really like that movie. I saw it three _____ .

5. *paper*   Students in Prof. Young's literature class have to write a lot of

     _____ .

6. *paper*   Students who take thorough lecture notes use a lot of _____ .

7. *paper*   *The New York Times* is *(a, some)* famous _____ .

8. *work*   Rodin's statue of "The Thinker" is one of my favorite

_____ of art.

9. *work*   I have a lot of _____ to do tomorrow at my

office.

10. *light*   If _____ accidentally *(get, gets)* in a darkroom, *(it, they)* can

ruin photographic negatives.

11. *light*   There *(is, are)* a lot of fluorescent _____ on the ceilings of

the school building.

12. *hair*   Erin has straight _____ , and Sara has curly _____ .

13. *hair*   Brian has a white cat. When I stood up from Brian's sofa, my black slacks

were covered with short white _____ .

14. *glass*   I wear _____ because I'm nearsighted.

15. *glass*   In some countries, people use _____ for their tea; in other

countries, they use cups.

16. *glass*   Framed paintings are usually covered with _____ to protect

them.

17. *iron*   _____ *(is, are)* necessary to animal and plant life.

18. *iron*   _____ *(is, are)* used to make clothes look neat.

19. *experience*   Grandfather had a lot of interesting _____ in his

long career as a diplomat.

20. *experience*   You should apply for the job at the electronics company only if you have a

lot of _____ in that field.

11-7 USING UNITS OF MEASURE WITH NONCOUNT NOUNS

(a) I had some tea. (b) I had **two cups of** tea. (c) I ate some toast. (d) I ate **one piece of** toast.	To mention a specific quantity of a noncount noun, speakers use units of measure such as *two cups of* or *one piece of.* A unit of measure usually describes **the container** *(a cup of, a bowl of)*, **the amount** *(a pound of, a quart of)*,★ or **the shape** *(a bar of soap, a sheet of paper).*

★Weight measure: *one pound* = 0.45 kilograms/kilos.
   Liquid measure: *one quart* = 0.95 litres/liters; four quarts = one gallon = 3.8 litres/liters.

☐ **EXERCISE 16. Units of measure with noncount nouns. (Chart 11-7)**
   Directions: What units of measure are usually used with the following nouns? More than one unit of measure can be used with some of the nouns.

   PART I. You are going to the store. What are you going to buy? Choose from these units of measure.

bag	bottle	box	can★ (tin)	jar

   1. a ___can/jar___ of olives

   2. a ___box___ of crackers

   3. a _____ of mineral water

   4. a _____ of jam or jelly

   5. a _____ of tuna fish

   6. a _____ of soup

   7. a _____ of sugar

   8. a _____ of wine

   9. a _____ of corn

   10. a _____ of peas

   11. a _____ of flour

   12. a _____ of soda pop

   13. a _____ of paint

   14. a _____ of breakfast cereal

   _____

   ★*a can* in American English = *a tin* in British English.

PART II. You are hungry and thirsty. What are you going to have? Choose from these units of measure.

| bowl | cup | glass | piece | slice |

15. a ___cup/glass___ of green tea

16. a ___bowl___ of cereal

17. a _____ of candy

18. a _____ of bread

19. a _____ of apple pie

20. a _____ of orange juice

21. a _____ of soup

22. a _____ of cantaloupe

23. a _____ of beer

24. a _____ of noodles

25. a _____ of mineral water

26. a _____ of popcorn

27. a _____ of cheese

28. a _____ of rice

29. a _____ of strawberries and ice cream

☐ **EXERCISE 17. Writing activity: count and noncount nouns. (Charts 11-1 → 11-7)**
Directions: In several paragraphs, describe the perfect meal. Use your imagination. If you use the name of a dish that your reader is probably unfamiliar with, describe it in parentheses. For example:

I'm going to imagine for you the perfect meal. I am on a terrace high on a hillside in Nepal. When I look out, I see snow-capped mountains in the distance. The valley below is hazy and beautiful. I'm with my friends Olga and Roberto. The table has a while tablecloth and a vase of blue flowers. I'm going to eat all of my favorite kinds of food.

First the waiter is going to bring escargots. (Escargots are snails cooked in butter and seasoned with garlic and other herbs.) Etc.

11-8 GUIDELINES FOR ARTICLE USAGE

	USING *A* OR Ø (NO ARTICLE)		**USING *A* OR *SOME***
SINGULAR COUNT NOUNS	(a) ***A dog*** makes a good pet. (b) ***A banana*** is yellow. (c) ***A pencil*** contains lead.	A speaker uses ***a*** with a singular count noun when s/he is making a generalization. In (a): The speaker is talking about any dog, all dogs, dogs in general.	(j) I saw ***a dog*** in my yard. (k) Mary ate ***a banana***. (l) I need ***a pencil***.
PLURAL COUNT NOUNS	(d) **Ø *Dogs*** make good pets. (e) **Ø *Bananas*** are yellow. (f) **Ø *Pencils*** contain lead.	A speaker uses no article (**Ø**) with a plural count noun when s/he is making a generalization.* In (d): The speaker is talking about any dog, all dogs, dogs in general. Note: (a) and (d) have the same meaning.	(m) I saw ***some dogs*** in my yard. (n) Mary bought ***some bananas***. (o) Bob has ***some pencils*** in his pocket.
NONCOUNT NOUNS	(g) **Ø *Fruit*** is good for you. (h) **Ø *Coffee*** contains caffeine. (i) I like **Ø *music***.	A speaker uses no article (**Ø**) with a noncount noun when s/he is making a generalization. In (g): The speaker is talking about any fruit, all fruit, fruit in general.	(p) I bought ***some fruit***. (q) Bob drank ***some coffee***. (r) Would you like to listen to ***some music?***

*Sometimes a speaker uses an expression of quantity (e.g., ***almost all***, ***most***, ***some***) when s/he makes a generalization:
Almost all dogs make good pets. Most dogs are friendly. Some dogs have short hair.

	USING *THE*	
A speaker uses *a* with a singular count noun when s/he is talking about one thing (or person) that is not specific. In (j): The speaker is saying, "I saw one dog (not two dogs, some dogs, many dogs). It wasn't a specific dog (e.g., your dog, the neighbor's dog, that dog). It was only one dog out of the whole group of animals called dogs."	(s) Did you feed **the dog**? (t) I had a banana and an apple. I gave **the banana** to Mary. (u) **The pencil** on that desk is Jim's. (v) **The sun** is shining. (w) Please close **the door**. (x) Mary is in **the kitchen**.	**The** is used in front of (1) singular count nouns: *the dog*. (2) plural count nouns: *the dogs*. (3) noncount nouns: *the fruit*. A speaker uses **the** (not *a*, Ø, or *some*) when the speaker and the listener are thinking about the same specific person(s) or thing(s).
A speaker often uses **some*** with a plural count noun when s/he is talking about things (or people) that are not specific. In (m): The speaker is saying, "I saw more than one dog. They weren't specific dogs (e.g., your dogs, the neighbor's dogs, those dogs). The exact number of dogs isn't important (two dogs, five dogs); I'm simply saying that I saw an indefinite number of dogs."	(y) Did you feed **the dogs**? (z) I had some bananas and apples. I gave **the bananas** to Mary. (aa) **The pencils** on that desk are Jim's. (bb) Please turn off **the lights**.	In (s): The speaker and the listener are thinking about the same specific dog. The listener knows which dog the speaker is talking about: the dog that they own, the dog that they feed every day. There is only one dog that the speaker could possibly be talking about. In (t): A speaker uses **the** when s/he mentions a noun the second time. First mention: *I had **a banana** . . . .* Second mention: *I gave **the banana** . . . .* In the second mention, the listener now knows which banana the speaker is talking about: the banana the speaker had (not the banana John had, not the banana in that bowl).
A speaker often uses **some*** with a noncount noun when s/he is talking about something that is not specific. In (p): The speaker is saying, "I bought an indefinite amount of fruit. The exact amount (e.g., two pounds of fruit, four bananas, and two apples) isn't important. And I'm not talking about specific fruit (e.g., that fruit, the fruit in that bowl.)"	(cc) **The fruit** in this bowl is ripe. (dd) I drank some coffee and some milk. **The coffee** was hot. (ee) I can't hear you. **The music** is too loud. (ff) **The air** is cold today.	

*In addition to **some**, a speaker might use **several**, **a few**, **a lot of**, *etc.*, with a plural count noun, or **a little**, **a lot of**, *etc.*, with a noncount noun. (See Chart 11-5, p. 318.)

□ **EXERCISE 18. Count and noncount nouns. (Chart 11-8)**

Directions: Discuss Speaker A's use of articles in the following dialogues. Why does Speaker A use *a*, *some*, *the*, or *Ø*? Discuss what both Speaker A and Speaker B are thinking about.

DIALOGUE 1:

A: ***A dog*** makes a good pet.   B: I agree.

DIALOGUE 2:

A: I saw ***a dog*** in my yard.

DIALOGUE 4:

A: ***Dogs*** make good pets.   B: I agree.

DIALOGUE 5:

A: I saw ***some dogs*** in my yard.

DIALOGUE 7:

A: ***Fruit*** is good for you.   B: I agree.

DIALOGUE 8:

A: I ate ***some fruit***.

DIALOGUE 3:

B: Oh?

A: Did you feed *the dog?*   B: Yes.

DIALOGUE 6:

B: Oh?

A: Did you feed *the dogs?*   B: Yes.

DIALOGUE 9:

B: Oh?

A: *The fruit* in this bowl is ripe.   B: Good.

Directions: Here are some conversations. Try to decide whether the speakers would probably use *the* or *a/an*. Are the speakers thinking about the same objects or persons?

1. A: Did you have a good time at __the__ party last night?

   B: Yes.

   A: So did I. I'm glad that you decided to go with me.

2. A: What did you do last night?

   B: I went to __a__ party.

   A: Oh? Where was it?

3. A: Do you have _____ car?

   B: No. But I have _____ bicycle.

4. A: Do you need _____ car today, honey?

   B: Yes. I have a lot of errands to do. Why don't I drive you to work today?

   A: Okay. But be sure to fill _____ car up with gas sometime today.

5. A: I bought _____ table yesterday.

   B: Oh? I didn't know you went shopping for furniture.

6. A: Have you seen my keys?

   B: Yes. They're on _____ table next to _____ front door.

7. A: Is Mr. Jones _____ graduate student?

   B: No. He's _____ professor.

8. A: Where's _____ professor?

   B: She's absent today.

9. A: Would you like to go to _____ zoo this afternoon?

   B: Sure. Why not?

10. A: Does San Diego have _____ zoo?

    B: Yes. It's world famous.

11. A: Let's listen to _____ radio.

    B: Okay. I'll turn it on.

12. A: Does your car have _____ radio?

    B: Yes, and _____ CD player.

13. A: Did you lock _____ door?

   B: Yes.

   A: Did you check _____ stove?

   B: Yes.

   A: Did you close all _____ windows downstairs?

   B: Yes.

   A: Did you set _____ alarm?

   B: Yes.

   A: Then let's turn out _____ lights.

   B: Goodnight, dear.

   A: Goodnight, dear.

14. A: Where's Dennis?

   B: He's in _____ kitchen.

15. A: Do you like your new apartment?

   B: Yes. It has _____ big kitchen.

□ **EXERCISE 20. Using A or Ø for generalizations. (Chart 11-8)**
   Directions: Write ***a*** or **Ø** in the blank before each singular noun. Then write the plural form of the noun if possible.

Singular Subjects	Plural Subjects
1. __A__ bird has feathers.	Birds have feathers.
2. __Ø__ C ¢orn is nutritious.	Ø *(none possible)*
3. _____ milk is white.	
4. _____ flower is beautiful.	
5. _____ water is a clear liquid.	
6. _____ horse is strong.	
7. _____ jewelry is expensive.	
8. _____ soap produces bubbles.	
9. _____ shirt has sleeves.	
10. _____ honey comes from bees.	

Directions: Complete the sentences with the given nouns. Use **the** for specific statements. Do not use **the** for general statements.

1. *flowers*   a. _____The flowers_____ in that vase are beautiful.

              b. _____Flowers_____ are beautiful.

2. *mountains*   a. _____ are beautiful.

              b. _____ in Colorado are beautiful.

3. *water*   a. _____ consists of hydrogen and oxygen.

              b. I don't want to go swimming today. _____ is too cold.

4. *information*   a. _____ in today's newspaper is alarming.

              b. The Internet is a widely used source of _____ .

5. *health*   a. _____ is more important than money.

              b. Doctors are concerned with _____ of their patients.

6. *men*   a. _____ generally have stronger muscles

   women   than _____ .

              b. At the party last night, _____ sat on one side of the room, and _____ sat on the other.

7. *problems*   a. Everyone has _____ .

              b. Irene told me about _____ she had with her car yesterday.

8. *happiness*   a. I can't express _____ I felt when I heard the good news.

              b. Everyone seeks _____ .

9. *vegetables*   a. _____ are good for you.

              b. _____ we had for dinner last night were overcooked.

10. *gold*   a. _____ is a precious metal.

              b. _____ in Mary's ring is 24 karats.

Directions: Add **the** if necessary. Otherwise, use **Ø** to show that no article is necessary.

1. Please pass me _____the_____ butter.

2. _____Ø_____ B̸utter is a dairy product.

3. _____ air is free.

4. _____ air is humid today.

5. A: _____ windows are closed. Please open them.

   B: Okay.

6. _____ windows are made of _____ glass.

7. As every parent knows, _____ children require a lot of time and attention.

8. A: Frank, where are _____ children?

   B: Next door at the Jacksons'.

9. _____ paper is made from _____ trees or other plants.

10. _____ paper in my notebook is lined.

11. _____ nurses are trained to care for sick and injured people.

12. When I was in Memorial Hospital, _____ nurses were wonderful.

13. I'm studying _____ English. I'm studying _____ grammar.

14. _____ grammar in this chapter isn't easy.

15. All of our food comes from _____ plants. Some food, such as _____ fruit and _____ vegetables, comes directly from _____ plants. Other food, such as _____ meat, comes indirectly from _____ plants.

16. I'm not very good at keeping houseplants alive. _____ plants in my apartment have to be tough. They survive in spite of me.

Directions: Write **a/an, some,** or **the** in the blanks.

1. I had _____a_____ banana and _____an_____ apple. I gave _____the_____ banana to Mary. I ate _____the_____ apple.

2. I had _____some_____ bananas and _____some_____ apples. I gave _____the_____ bananas to Mary. I ate _____the_____ apples.

3. I have _____ desk and _____ bed in my room. _____ desk is hard. _____ bed is hard, too, even though it's supposed to be soft.

4. I forgot to bring my things with me to class yesterday, so I borrowed _____

pen and _____ paper from Joe. I returned _____ pen, but I used

_____ paper for my homework.

5. A: What did you do last weekend?

B: I went on _____ picnic Saturday and saw _____ movie

Sunday.

A: Did you have fun?

B: _____ picnic was fun, but _____ movie was boring.

6. Yesterday I saw _____ dog and _____ cat. _____ dog

was chasing _____ cat. _____ cat was chasing _____

mouse. _____ mouse ran into _____ hole, but _____

hole was very small. _____ cat couldn't get into _____ hole, so it

ran up _____ tree. _____ dog tried to climb _____ tree

too, but it couldn't.

7. I bought _____ bag of flour and _____ sugar to make _____

cookies. _____ sugar was okay, but I had to return _____ flour.

When I opened _____ flour, I found _____ little bugs in it. I took

it back to the people at the store and showed them _____ little bugs. They

gave me _____ new bag of flour. _____ new bag didn't have any

bugs in it.

8. Once upon a time, _____ princess fell in love with _____ prince.

_____ princess wanted to marry _____ prince, who lived in

_____ distant land. She summoned _____ messenger to take

_____ things to _____ prince to show him her love. _____

messenger took _____ jewels and _____ robe made of yellow and red

silk to _____ prince. _____ princess anxiously awaited _____

messenger's return. She hoped that _____ prince would send her _____

tokens of his love. But when _____ messenger returned, he brought back

_____ jewels and _____ beautiful silk robe that _____

princess had sent. Why? Why? she wondered. Then _____ messenger told

her: _____ prince already had _____ wife.

□ **EXERCISE 24. Summary: A/AN vs. Ø vs. THE. (Charts 11-1 → 11-8)**

Directions: Write *a/an, Ø,* or ***the*** in the blanks.

1. I have ___a___ window in my bedroom. I keep it open at night because I like ___Ø___ fresh air. ___The___ window is above my bed.

2. Kathy bought _____ radio. She likes to listen to _____ music when she studies.

3. A: Would you please turn _____ radio down? _____ music is too loud.
   B: No problem.

4. _____ good book is _____ friend for _____ life.

5. Last week I read _____ book about _____ life of Gandhi.

6. A: Let's go swimming in _____ lake today.
   B: That sounds like _____ good idea.

7. _____ lake is a body of _____ water that is smaller than _____ sea but larger than _____ pond. _____ ocean is larger than _____ sea.

8. During our vacation in Brazil, we walked along _____ beach in front of our hotel and looked at _____ ocean.

9. _____ water is essential to human life, but don't drink _____ water in the Flat River. It'll kill you! _____ pollution in that river is terrible.

10. People can drink _____ fresh water. They can't drink _____ seawater because it contains _____ salt.

11. Ted, pass _____ salt, please. And _____ pepper. Thanks.

12. _____ different countries have _____ different geography. Italy is located on _____ peninsula. Japan is _____ island nation.

13. A: How did you get here? Did you walk?
    B: No, I took _____ taxi.

14. There are some wonderful small markets in my neighborhood. You can always get _____ fresh fish at Mr. Rico's fish market.

15. _____ good food keeps us healthy and adds _____ pleasure to our lives.

16. A: Well, are you ready to leave?

    B: Anytime you are.

    A: Let me take just one last sip of coffee. I've really enjoyed this meal.

    B: I agree. _____ food was excellent—especially _____ fish. And _____ service was exceptionally good. Let's leave _____ waitress _____ good tip.

    A: Yes, let's do that. I usually tip around fifteen percent, sometimes eighteen percent. Does that sound about right to you?

17. A: We're ready to go, kids. Get in _____ car.

    B: Just a minute! We forgot something.

    A: Marge, can you get _____ kids in _____ car, please?

    B: Just a minute, Harry. They're coming.

18. In ancient times, people did not use _____ coins for money. Instead they used _____ shells, _____ beads, or _____ salt. The first coins were made around 2600 years ago. Today, most money is made from _____ paper. In the future, maybe we'll use only _____ plastic cards and there will be no paper money.

19. A: Can I have some money, Dad?

    B: What for?

    A: I want to go to the movies with my friends and hang around the mall.

    B: What you need is a job! _____ money doesn't grow on _____ trees, you know.

20. A doctor cures _____ sick people. _____ farmer grows _____ crops. _____ architect designs _____ buildings. _____ artist creates _____ new ways of looking at _____ world and _____ life.

21. _____ earthquakes are _____ rare events in central Africa.

22. My city experienced _____ earthquake recently. I was riding my bicycle when _____ earthquake occurred. _____ ground beneath me trembled so hard that it shook me off my bike.

23. A: I saw _____ good program on TV last night.

    B: Oh? What was it?

    A: It was _____ documentary about wildlife in Indonesia. It was really interesting. Did you see it too?

    B: No, I watched _____ old movie. It wasn't very good. I wish I'd known about _____ documentary. I would have watched it.

24. _____ modern people, just like their ancestors, are curious about _____ universe. Where did _____ moon come from? Does _____ life exist on other planets? What is _____ star? How large is _____ universe? How long will _____ sun continue to burn?

□ **EXERCISE 25. Preview: using THE or Ø with names. (Chart 11-9)**
  Directions: Complete with *the* or *Ø*.

  I would like to know more about . . .

  1. __the__ Amazon River.   6. _____ Australia.

  2. __Ø__ Korea.   7. _____ Mississippi River.

  3. _____ Mexico City.   8. _____ Red Sea.

  4. _____ Indian Ocean.   9. _____ Lake Michigan.

  5. _____ Ural Mountains.   10. _____ Mount Fuji.

11-9 USING *THE* OR Ø WITH NAMES

(a) We met **Ø** *Mr. Wang.* I know **Ø** *Doctor Smith.* **Ø** *President Rice* has been in the news.	**The** is NOT used with titled names. INCORRECT: *We met the Mr. Wang.*
(b) He lives in **Ø** *Europe.* **Ø** *Asia* is the largest continent. Have you ever been in **Ø** *Africa?*	**The** is NOT used with the names of continents. INCORRECT: *He lives in the Europe.*
(c) He lives in **Ø** *France.* **Ø** *Brazil* is a large country. Have you ever been in **Ø** *Thailand?*	**The** is NOT used with the names of most countries. INCORRECT: *He lives in the France.*
(d) He lives in **the** *United States.* **The** *Netherlands* is in Europe. Have you ever been in **the** *Philippines?*	**The** is used in the names of only a few countries, as in the examples. Others: *the Czech Republic, the United Arab Emirates, the Dominican Republic.*
(e) He lives in **Ø** *Paris.* **Ø** *New York* is the largest city in the United States Have you ever been in **Ø** *Istanbul?*	**The** is NOT used with the names of cities. INCORRECT: *He lives in the Paris.*
(f) **The** *Nile River* is long. They crossed **the** *Pacific Ocean.* **The** *Yellow Sea* is in Asia.	**The** is used with the names of rivers, oceans, and seas.
(g) Chicago is on **Ø** *Lake Michigan.* **Ø** *Lake Titicaca* lies on the border between Peru and Bolivia.	**The** is NOT used with the names of lakes.
(h) We hiked in **the** *Alps.* **The** *Andes* are in South America.	**The** is used with the names of mountain ranges.
(i) He climbed **Ø** *Mount Everest.* **Ø** *Mount Fuji* is in Japan.	**The** is NOT used with the names of individual mountains.

□ **EXERCISE 26. Using THE or Ø with names. (Chart 11-9)**
Directions: Complete with **the** or **Ø**.

1. ___Ø___ Rome is in ___Ø___ Italy.

2. ___The___ Rhine River flows through ___Ø___ Germany.

3. _____ Moscow is the capital of _____ Russia.

4. _____ Yangtze is a famous river.

5. _____ Atlantic Ocean is smaller than _____ Pacific.

6. _____ Rocky Mountains are located in _____ Canada and _____ United States.

7. _____ Doctor Anderson is a good physician.

8. _____ Lake Victoria is located in _____ Africa.

11-10 CAPITALIZATION

CAPITALIZE 1. The first word of a sentence	(a) **W**e saw a movie last night. **I**t was very good.	*Capitalize* = use a big letter, not a small letter.
2. The names of people	(b) I met **G**eorge **A**dams yesterday.	
3. Titles used with the names of people	(c) I saw **D**octor (**D**r.) Smith. Do you know **P**rofessor (**P**rof.) Alston?	COMPARE I saw a **d**octor. I saw **D**octor Wilson.
4. Months, days, holidays	(d) I was born in **A**pril. Bob arrived last **M**onday. It snowed on **T**hanksgiving **D**ay.	NOTE: Seasons are not capitalized: *spring, summer, fall/autumn, winter*

5. The names of places:
   city
   state/province
   country
   continent
 	
   ocean
   lake
   river
   desert
   mountain
 	
   school
   business
 	
   street
   building
   park, zoo
	(e) He lives in **C**hicago.
	She was born in **C**alifornia.
	They are from **M**exico.
	Tibet is in **A**sia.
	
	They crossed the **A**tlantic **O**cean.
	Chicago is on **L**ake **M**ichigan.
	The **N**ile **R**iver flows north.
	The **S**ahara **D**esert is in Africa.
	We visited the **R**ocky **M**ountains.
	
	I go to the **U**niversity of **F**lorida.
	I work for the **G**eneral **E**lectric **C**ompany.
	
	He lives on **G**rand **A**venue.
	We have class in **R**itter **H**all.
	I went jogging in **F**orest **P**ark.
		COMPARE
		She lives in a **c**ity.
		She lives in **N**ew **Y**ork **C**ity.
		
		COMPARE
		They crossed a **r**iver.
		They crossed the **Y**ellow **R**iver.
		
		COMPARE
		I go to a **u**niversity.
		I go to the **U**niversity of **T**exas.
		
		COMPARE
		We went to a **p**ark.
		We went to **C**entral **P**ark.

6. The names of courses	(f) I'm taking **C**hemistry 101 this term.	COMPARE I'm reading a book about **p**sychology. I'm taking **P**sychology 101 this term.
7. The titles of books, articles, movies	(g) *Gone with the **W**ind* *The **O**ld **M**an and the Sea*	Capitalize the first word of a title. Capitalize all other words except articles *(the, a/an)*, coordinating conjunctions *(and, but, or)*, and short prepositions *(with, in, at, etc.)*.
8. The names of languages and nationalities	(h) She speaks **S**panish. We discussed **J**apanese customs.	Words that refer to the names of nations, nationalities, and languages are always capitalized.
9. The names of religions	(i) **B**uddism, **C**hristianity, **H**induism, **I**slam, and **J**udaism are major religions in the world. Talal is a **M**oslem.	Words that refer to the names of religions are always capitalized.
10. The pronoun "I"	(j) Yesterday **I** fell off my bicycle.	The pronoun "I" is always capitalized.

□ EXERCISE 27. Capitalization. (Chart 11-10)
Directions: Add capital letters where necessary.

1. We're going to have a test next Tuesday.

2. Do you know richard smith? he is a professor at this university.

3. I know that professor smith teaches at the university of arizona.

4. The nile river flows into the mediterranean sea.

5. John is a catholic. ali is a moslem.

6. Anna speaks french. she studied in france for two years.

7. I'm taking a history course this semester.

8. I'm taking modern european history 101 this semester.

9. We went to vancouver, british columbia, for our vacation last summer.

10. Venezuela is a spanish-speaking country.

11. Canada is in north america.*

12. Canada is north of the united states.

13. The sun rises in the east.

14. The mississippi river flows south.

15. The amazon is a river in south america.

16. We went to a zoo. We went to brookfield zoo in chicago.

17. The title of this book is fundamentals of english grammar.

18. I enjoy studying english grammar.

19. On valentine's day (february 14), sweethearts give each other presents.

20. I read a book entitled *the cat and the mouse in my aunt's house.*

---

*When **north, south, east**, and **west** refer to the direction on a compass, they are not capitalized: *Japan is **east** of China.*
When they are part of a geographical name, they are capitalized: *Japan is in the Far **East**.*

□ **EXERCISE 28. Capitalization. (Chart 11-10)**
Directions: Capitalize as necessary.

                  G

(1) Jane goodall is a famous scientist. She became famous for her studies of chimpanzees in tanzania.

(2) Even though she was born in the heart of london, england, as a child she was always fascinated by animals of all sorts. Her favorite books were *the jungle book,* by rudyard kipling, and books about tarzan, a fictional character who was raised by apes.

(3) Her dream from childhood was to go to africa. After high school, she worked as a secretary and a waitress to earn enough money to go there. During that time, she took evening courses in journalism and english literature. One of her favorite poets was t. s. eliot. She saved every penny. She put her wages under the carpet in her mother's living room until she had enough money for passage to africa.

(4) In the spring of 1957, she sailed through the red sea and southward down the african coast to mombasa in kenya. Her uncle had arranged a job for her in nairobi with a british company. When she was there, she met louis leakey, a famous anthropologist. Under his guidance she began her lifelong study of chimpanzees on the eastern shore of lake tanganyika.

(5) Jane goodall lived alone in a tent near the lake. Through months and years of patience, she won the trust of the chimps and was able to observe them at close hand. Her observations changed forever how we view chimpanzees—and all other animals we share the world with as well.

(6) As a young woman, jane couldn't afford to go to a university. She never received an undergraduate degree, but later in her life she received a Ph.D. from cambridge university and became a professor at stanford university. She has written several books. One of them is *my friends, the wild chimpanzees.* She works tirelessly on behalf of endangered species and in support of the humane treatment of animals in captivity.

☐ **EXERCISE 29. Error analysis. (Chapter 11)**
   Directions: Correct the mistakes.

1. Lions are wild animal ^s.

2. There are a lot of informations in that book.

3. The oil is a natural resource.

4. I was late because there were too many traffics.

5. I drank two waters.

6. Our teacher gives us too many homeworks.

7. Nadia knows a lot of vocabularies.

8. I had a egg for breakfast.

9. There is many kind of trees in the world.

10. I'm studying the english.

11. My cousin living in United State.

12. Only twelve student were in class yesterday.

13. I need some advices.

14. We all have a few problem in the life.

15. There were no job, and people didn't have much moneys.

16. I don't know anything about farm animals except for chicken.

17. When I am a children, my family had a big farm with the Horses.

18. I live with two friend. One is from the chile, and the other is from the Saudi Arabia.

19. I think the english is difficult language.

20. When people use a lot of slangs, I can't understand them.

CHAPTER 12
Adjective Clauses

CONTENTS

12-1 ADJECTIVE CLAUSES: INTRODUCTION

ADJECTIVES	ADJECTIVE CLAUSES
An **adjective** modifies a noun. "Modify" means to change a little. An adjective describes or gives information about the noun. (See Chart 6-8, p. 166.)	An **adjective clause*** modifies a noun. It describes or gives information about a noun.
An adjective usually comes in front of a noun.	An adjective clause follows a noun.
(a) I met a <u>*adjective*</u> **kind** + <u>*noun*</u> man. (b) I met a <u>*adjective*</u> **famous** + <u>*noun*</u> man.	(c) I met a <u>*noun*</u> man + <u>*adjective clause*</u> **who is kind to everybody**. (d) I met a <u>*noun*</u> man + <u>*adjective clause*</u> **who is a famous poet**. (e) I met a <u>*noun*</u> man + <u>*adjective clause*</u> **who lives in Chicago**.

*GRAMMAR TERMINOLOGY	
(1) ***I met a man*** = an independent clause; it is a complete sentence. (2) ***He lives in Chicago*** = an independent clause; it is a complete sentence. (3) ***who lives in Chicago*** = a dependent clause; it is NOT a complete sentence. (4) ***I met a man who lives in Chicago*** = an independent clause + a dependent clause; a complete sentence.	A **clause** is a structure that has a subject and a verb. There are two kinds of clauses: **independent** and **dependent**. • An **independent clause** is a main clause and can stand alone as a sentence. • A **dependent clause** cannot stand alone as a sentence; it must be connected to an independent clause.

12-2 USING *WHO* AND *WHOM* IN ADJECTIVE CLAUSES

(a) The man is friendly.	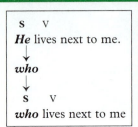 **s v** ***He*** lives next to me. ↓ ***who*** ↓ **s v** ***who*** lives next to me	In (a): ***He*** is a subject pronoun. ***He*** refers to "the man." To make an adjective clause, change ***he*** to ***who***. ***Who*** is a subject pronoun. ***Who*** refers to "the man."
		In (b): An adjective clause immediately follows the noun it modifies. *INCORRECT: The man is friendly who lives next to me.*
(b) The man ***who*** *lives next to me* is friendly.		
(c) The man was friendly.	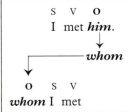 **s v o** I met ***him***. ↓ ───***whom*** **o s v** ***whom*** I met	In (c): ***him*** is an object pronoun. ***Him*** refers to "the man." To make an adjective clause, change ***him*** to ***whom***. ***Whom*** is an object pronoun. ***Whom*** refers to "the man." ***Whom*** comes at the beginning of an adjective clause.
		In (d): An adjective clause immediately follows the noun it modifies. *INCORRECT: The man was friendly whom I met.*
(d) The man ***whom*** *I met* was friendly.		

☐ **EXERCISE 1. Adjective clauses with WHO and WHOM. (Charts 12-1 and 12-2)**
Directions: Combine the two sentences into one sentence. Make "b" an adjective clause. Use ***who*** or ***whom***.

1. a. Do you know the people?   b. They live in the white house.
   → *Do you know the people who live in the white house?*

2. a. The woman gave me some information.   b. I called her.
   → *The woman whom I called gave me some information.*

3. a. The police officer was friendly.   b. She gave me directions.

4. a. The waiter was friendly.   b. He served us dinner.

5. a. The people were very nice.   b. I met them at the party last night.

6. a. The people have three cars.   b. They live next to me.

7. a. The man talked a lot.   b. I met him on the plane.

8. a. The man talked a lot.   b. He sat next to me.

9. a. Three women walked into my office.   b. I didn't know them.

10. a. I talked to the women.   b. They walked into my office.

Directions: Complete the sentences with *who* or *whom*. Put parentheses around the entire adjective clause. Identify the subject and verb of the adjective clause.

1. The children (_____who_____ live down the street in the yellow house) are
   always polite.

2. The children (_____whom_____ we watched in the park) were feeding ducks in a pond.

3. The people _____ we visited gave us tea and a light snack.

4. I know some people _____ live on a boat.

5. I talked to the woman _____ was sitting next to me.

6. I saw the people _____ were playing football at the park.

7. My mother is a person _____ I admire tremendously.

8. Marie and Luis Escobar still keep in touch with many of the students _____
   they met in their English class five years ago.

9. People _____ listen to very loud music may suffer gradual hearing loss.

10. At the supermarket yesterday, one of the store employees caught a man _____
    had put a beefsteak in his coat pocket and attempted to walk out without paying.

11. The couple _____ I invited to dinner at my home were two hours late. I
    thought that was very rude. They didn't call. They didn't have an excuse. They
    didn't apologize. I'll never invite them again.

Directions: Insert **who** where it is necessary.

                      who
1. The man ʌ answered the phone was polite.

2. I liked the people sat next to us at the soccer game.

3. People paint houses for a living are called house painters.

4. I'm uncomfortable around married couples argue all the time.

5. While I was waiting at the bus stop, I stood next to an elderly gentleman started a
   conversation with me about my educational plans.

□ EXERCISE 4. Adjective clauses with WHO. (Charts 12-1 and 12-2)

Directions: Complete the sentences in Column A with the adjective clauses in Column B.
Consult your dictionary if necessary.

Example: A Bostonian is someone . . . .
→ *A Bostonian is someone who lives in Boston.*

Column A

1. A Bostonian is someone . . . .
2. A pilot is a person . . . .
3. A procrastinator is someone . . . .
4. A botanist is a scientist . . . .
5. An insomniac is somebody . . . .
6. A revolutionary is someone . . . .
7. A misanthrope is a person . . . .
8. A meteorologist is a person . . . .
9. A jack-of-all-trades is someone . . . .
10. An expert can be defined as a
    person . . . .

Column B

A. who has trouble sleeping.
B. who seeks to overthrow the government.
C. who flies an airplane.
D. who studies weather phenomena.
✓E. who lives in Boston.
F. who hates people.
G. who always puts off doing things.
H. who knows a lot about a little and
   a little about a lot.
I. who has many skills.
J. who studies plants.

□ EXERCISE 5. Adjective clauses with WHO. (Charts 12-1 and 12-2)

Directions: Complete the sentences with your own words. Consult your dictionary if
necessary.

1. A baker is a person who . . . . *makes bread, cakes, pies, etc.*
2. A mechanic is someone who . . . .
3. A bartender is a person who . . . .
4. A philatelist is someone who . . . .
5. A spendthrift is somebody who . . . .
6. An astronomer is a scientist who . . . .
7. A carpenter is a person who . . . .
8. A miser is someone who . . . .

12-3 USING *WHO, WHO(M),* AND *THAT* IN ADJECTIVE CLAUSES

(a) The man is friendly. **S** v **He** lives next to me. ↓ **who** **that** **s** v (b) The man **who** lives next to me is friendly. (c) The man **that** lives next to me is friendly.	In addition to **who**, **that** can be used as the subject of an adjective clause. (b) and (c) have the same meaning.
	A subject pronoun cannot be omitted: INCORRECT: *The man lives next to me is friendly.* CORRECT: *The man who/that lives next to me is friendly.*

S V
 (d) The man was friendly. I met   **O**
                      him.
                      ↓
                    whom
                    that
 	
            O   **S V**
 (e) The man   **who(m)**   *I met*   was friendly.
 (f) The man   **that**   *I met*   was friendly.
 (g) The man   **Ø**   *I met*   was friendly.
	In addition to **who(m)**,★ **that** can be used as the object in an adjective clause.
	 (e) and (f) have the same meaning.

	An object pronoun can be omitted from an adjective clause. (e), (f), and (g) have the same meaning. In (g): The symbol "**Ø**" means "nothing goes here."

★The parentheses around the "m" in **who(m)** indicate that (especially in everyday conversation) **who** is often used as an object pronoun instead of the more formal **whom**.

☐ EXERCISE 6. Adjective clauses with WHO, WHO(M), and THAT. (Chart 12-3)
    Directions: Complete the sentences using **who, who(m),** and **that**. Write **Ø** if the pronoun can be omitted.

1. The woman _____who(m) / that / Ø_____ I met last night was interesting.

2. The man _____who / that_____ answered the phone was polite.

3. The people _____ Nadia is visiting live on Elm Street.

4. The students _____ came to class late missed the quiz.

5. The man _____ married my mother is now my stepfather.

6. The man _____ my mother married is now my stepfather.

7. Do you know the boy _____ is talking to Anita?

8. I've become good friends with several of the people _____ I met in my English class last year.

9. The woman _____ I saw in the park was feeding the pigeons.

10. The woman _____ was feeding the pigeons had a sackful of bread crumbs.

12-4 USING *WHICH* AND *THAT* IN ADJECTIVE CLAUSES

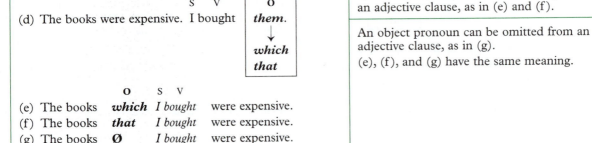

(a) The river is polluted. $\begin{array}{c} \text{s} \quad \text{v} \\ \boxed{\begin{array}{c} \textbf{\textit{It}} \\ \downarrow \\ \textbf{\textit{which}} \\ \textbf{\textit{that}} \end{array}} \end{array}$ flows through the town.	***Who*** and ***whom*** refer to people. ***Which*** refers to things. ***That*** can refer to either people or things.
	In (a): To make an adjective clause, change ***it*** to ***which*** or ***that***. ***It***, ***which***, and ***that*** all refer to a thing (the river). (b) and (c) have the same meaning.
(b) The river ***which*** *flows through the town* is polluted. (c) The river ***that*** *flows through the town* is polluted.	When ***which*** and ***that*** are used as the subject of an adjective clause, they CANNOT be omitted. INCORRECT: *The river flows through town is polluted.*
(d) The books were expensive. I bought $\boxed{\begin{array}{c} \text{o} \\ \textbf{\textit{them}}. \\ \downarrow \\ \textbf{\textit{which}} \\ \textbf{\textit{that}} \end{array}}$	***Which*** or ***that*** can be used as an object in an adjective clause, as in (e) and (f).
(e) The books ***which*** *I bought* were expensive. (f) The books ***that*** *I bought* were expensive. (g) The books **Ø** *I bought* were expensive.	An object pronoun can be omitted from an adjective clause, as in (g). (e), (f), and (g) have the same meaning.

□ **EXERCISE 7. Adjective clauses with WHO, WHO(M), WHICH, and THAT.**
　　　　　　 (Charts 12-3 and 12-4)

Directions: Combine the two sentences into one sentence. Make "b" an adjective clause. Give all the possible forms.

1. a. The pill made me sleepy.　　b. I took it.
　　 → *The pill which I took made me sleepy.*
　　 → *The pill that I took made me sleepy.*
　　 → *The pill Ø I took made me sleepy.*

2. a. The soup was too salty.　　b. I had it for lunch.

3. a. I have a class.　　b. It begins at 8:00 A.M.

4. a. I know a man.　　b. He doesn't have to work for a living.

5. a. The information helped me a lot.　　b. I found it on the Internet.

6. a. The people waved at us.　　b. We saw them on the bridge.

7. a. My daughter asked me a question.　　b. I couldn't answer it.

8. a. The woman predicted my future.
   b. She read my palm.

9. a. Where can I catch the bus?
   b. It goes downtown.

10. a. All of the people can come.
    b. I asked them to my party.

☐ EXERCISE 8. Adjective clauses with WHO and THAT. (Charts 12-3 and 12-4)
Directions: Complete the definitions that begin in Column A with the information given in Column B. Use adjective clauses with **who** or **that** in the definitions.* Consult your dictionary if necessary.

Example: A hammer is a tool . . . .
   → *A hammer is a tool that is used to pound nails.*

Column A

1. A hammer is a tool . . . .
2. A barometer is an instrument . . . .
3. Plastic is a synthetic material . . . .
4. An architect is someone . . . .
5. A puzzle is a problem . . . .
6. A vegetarian is a person . . . .
7. Steam is a gas . . . .
8. A turtle is an animal . . . .
9. A hermit is a person . . . .
10. A pyramid is a structure . . . .

Column B

A. She or he leaves society and lives completely alone.

✓B. It is used to pound nails.

C. It forms when water boils.

D. It is square at the bottom and has four sides that come together in a point at the top.

E. He (or she) designs buildings.

F. It measures air pressure.

G. It can be shaped and hardened to form many useful things.

H. It is difficult to solve.

I. He or she doesn't eat meat.

J. It has a hard shell and can live in water or on land.

---

*NOTE: In usual usage, one pattern is often favored over another.
  (1) As subject pronouns:
   • **who** is more commonly used than **that** (*A doctor is someone who takes care of sick people*);
   • **that** is more commonly used than **which** (*A pencil is an instrument that is used for writing*).
  (2) Object pronouns are usually omitted.

☐ **EXERCISE 9. Adjective clauses. (Charts 12-1 → 12-3)**

Directions: In groups or pairs, provide definitions for the words listed below. Consult your dictionaries if necessary.

Example: A telephone directory is a book . . . .
→ *A telephone directory is a book that lists telephone numbers.*

1. A dictionary is a book . . . .

2. A nurse is someone . . . .

3. Birds are creatures . . . .

4. A key is a piece of metal . . . .

5. A prisoner is a person . . . .

6. A giraffe is an animal . . . .

7. Photographers are people . . . .

8. A hero is a person . . . .

9. An adjective is a word . . . .

10. A friend is a person . . . .

☐ **EXERCISE 10. Object pronouns in adjective clauses. (Charts 12-3 and 12-4)**

Directions: Cross out the incorrect pronouns in the adjective clauses.

1. The books I bought ~~them~~ at the bookstore were expensive.

2. I like the shirt you wore it to class yesterday.

3. Amanda Jones is a person I would like you to meet her.

4. The apartment we wanted to rent it had two bedrooms.

5. My wife and I are really enjoying the TV set that we bought it for ourselves last week.

6. The woman you met her at Aunt Martha's house is a pharmacist.

7. Anna has a cat that it likes to catch birds.

8. The birds that Anna's cat catches them are very frightened.

9. Yesterday, Anna rescued a bird that the cat had brought it into the house. When she set it free, it flew away quickly.

Directions: Write the pronouns that can be used to connect the adjective clauses to the main clause: **who, who(m), which,** or **that.** Also write **Ø** if the pronoun can be omitted.

Example: The manager | who that | fired Tom is a difficult person to work for.

1. The box [   ] I mailed to my sister was heavy.

2. The people [   ] sat in the stadium cheered for the home team.

3. The calendar [   ] hangs in Paul's office has pictures of wildlife.

4. The teenagers counted the money [   ] they earned at the car wash.

5. The people [   ] my brother called didn't answer their phone.

6. The tree branch [   ] was lying in the street was a hazard to motorists.

Directions: <u>Underline</u> the adjective clause. Circle the noun it modifies.

1. I lost the (scarf) <u>I borrowed from my roommate</u>.

2. The food we ate at the sidewalk cafe was delicious.

3. A storekeeper is a person who owns or operates a store.

4. The bus I take to school every morning is usually very crowded.

5. Pizza that is sold by the piece is a popular lunch in many cities and towns throughout the world.

6. Two hundred years ago, people on ships and in coastal towns greatly feared the pirates who sailed the South China Sea and the Gulf of Thailand.

7. The earth receives less than one-billionth of the enormous amount of heat the sun produces. The rest of the sun's energy disappears into outer space.

8. Piranhas are dangerous fish that can tear the flesh off an animal as large as a horse in a few minutes.

9. The heart of education is in a culture's literature. People who read gain not only knowledge but also pleasure. A person who does not read is no better off than a person who cannot read.

10. Cedar waxwings are gray-brown birds that live in most parts of North America. If you see a crested bird that is a little larger than a sparrow and has a band of yellow across the end of its tail, it may be a cedar waxwing.

☐ **EXERCISE 13. Review: adjective clauses. (Charts 12-1 → 12-4)**
Directions: Answer the questions in complete sentences. Use any appropriate pattern of adjective clause. Use ***the*** with the noun that is modified by the adjective clause.

1. • One phone wasn't ringing.
   • The other phone was ringing.
   QUESTION: Which phone did Sam answer?
   → *Sam answered **the** phone that was ringing.*

   QUESTION: Which phone didn't he answer?
   → *He didn't answer **the** phone that wasn't ringing.*

2. • We ate some food from our garden.
   • We ate some food at a restaurant.
   QUESTION: Which food was expensive?
   → ***The*** *food we ate . . . .*

   QUESTION: Which food wasn't expensive?

3. • One student raised her hand in class.
   • Another student sat quietly in his seat.
   QUESTIONS: One of them asked the teacher a question. Which one?
   Which one didn't ask the teacher a question?

4. • One girl won the foot race.
   • The other girl lost the foot race.
   QUESTIONS: Which girl is happy? Which girl isn't happy?

5. • One man was sleeping.
   • Another man was listening to the radio.
   QUESTIONS: One of the men heard the news bulletin about the earthquake in China.
   Which one did? Which one didn't?

6. • One person bought a *(make of car)*.
   • Another person bought a *(make of car)*.
   QUESTION: Which person probably spent more money than the other?

7. • Amanda bought some canned vegetables at a supermarket.
   • Tom picked some fresh vegetables from his grandfather's garden.
   QUESTION: Which vegetables probably tasted fresher than the others?

8. • One young musician practiced hours and hours every day.
   • The other young musician had a regular job and practiced only in the evenings and
     on the weekends.
   QUESTIONS: Which musician showed a great deal of improvement during the course
   of a year? Which one didn't show as much improvement?

9. • One city provides clean water and a modern sewer system for its citizens.
   • Another city uses its rivers and streams as both a source of water and a sewer.
   QUESTIONS: Which city has a high death rate from infectious diseases such as typhoid
   and cholera? Which one doesn't?

12-5 SINGULAR AND PLURAL VERBS IN ADJECTIVE CLAUSES

(a) I know the **man** who **is** sitting over there.	In (a): The verb in the adjective clause *(is)* is singular because **who** refers to a singular noun, *man*.
(b) I know the **people** who **are** sitting over there.	In (b): The verb in the adjective clause *(are)* is plural because **who** refers to a plural noun, *people*.

☐ EXERCISE 14. Subject–verb agreement in adjective clauses. (Chart 12-5)

Directions: Circle the correct word in parentheses. <u>Underline</u> the noun that determines whether the verb should be singular or plural.

1. A saw is a <u>tool</u> that (*(is,)are*) used to cut wood.

2. Hammers are tools that (*is, are*) used to pound nails.

3. I recently met a woman who (*live, lives*) in Montreal.

4. Most of the people who (*live, lives*) in Montreal speak French as their first language.

5. I have a cousin who (*works, work*) as a coal miner.

6. Some coal miners who (*works, work*) underground suffer from lung disease.

7. A professional athlete who (*play, plays*) tennis is called a tennis pro.

8. Professional athletes who (*play, plays*) tennis for a living can make a lot of money.

9. Biographies are books which (*tells, tell*) the stories of people's lives.

10. A book that (*tells, tell*) the story of a person's life is called a biography.

11. I talked to the men who (*was, were*) sitting near me.

12. The woman that (*was, were*) sitting in front of me at the movie was wearing a big hat.

12-6 USING PREPOSITIONS IN ADJECTIVE CLAUSES

			PREP	Obj.	
(a) The man was helpful.		I talked	*to*	*him*.	

Whom, *which*, and *that* can be used as the object of a preposition in an adjective clause.

REMINDER: An object pronoun can be omitted from an adjective clause, as in (d) and (i).

	Obj.		PREP	
(b) The man	*whom*	*I talked to*		was helpful.
(c) The man	*that*	*I talked to*		was helpful.
(d) The man	*Ø*	*I talked to*		was helpful.

	PREP	Obj.		
(e) The man	*to*	*whom*	*I talked*	was helpful.

In very formal English, a preposition comes at the beginning of an adjective clause, as in (e) and (j). The preposition is followed by either *whom* or *which* (not *that* or *who*), and the pronoun CANNOT be omitted.

			PREP	Obj.	
(f) The chair is hard.		I am sitting	*in*	*it*.	

(b), (c), (d), and (e) have the same meaning.

	Obj.		PREP	
(g) The chair	*which*	*I am sitting in*		is hard.
(h) The chair	*that*	*I am sitting in*		is hard.
(i) The chair	*Ø*	*I am sitting in*		is hard.

	PREP	Obj.		
(j) The chair	*in*	*which*	*I am sitting*	is hard.

(g), (h), (i), and (j) have the same meaning.

☐ **EXERCISE 15. Prepositions in adjective clauses. (Chart 12-6)**

Directions: Combine the two sentences in each pair. Use "b" as an adjective clause. Give all the possible forms of the adjective clauses, and <u>underline</u> them.

1. a. The movie was interesting.   b. We went **to** it.
   → *The movie <u>which we went</u> **to** was interesting.*
   → *The movie <u>that we went</u> **to** was interesting.*
   → *The movie <u>**Ø** we went</u> **to** was interesting.*
   → *The movie <u>**to** which we went</u> was interesting.*

2. a. The man is over there.   b. I told you **about** him.

3. a. The woman pays me a fair salary.   b. I work **for** her.

4. a. Alicia likes the family.   b. She is living **with** them.

5. a. The picture is beautiful.   b. Tom is looking **at** it.

6. a. I enjoyed the music.   b. We listened **to** it after dinner.

□ **EXERCISE 16. Prepositions in adjective clauses. (Chart 12-6)**

Directions: Add an appropriate preposition to each sentence.* Draw parentheses around the adjective clause.

1. I spoke _____to_____ a person. The person (I spoke _____to_____) was friendly.

2. We went _____ a movie. The movie we went _____ was very good.

3. We stayed _____ a motel. The motel we stayed _____ was clean and comfortable.

4. We listened _____ a new CD. I enjoyed the new CD we listened _____ .

5. Sally was waiting _____ a person. The person Sally was waiting _____ never came.

6. I talked _____ a man. The man _____ whom I talked was helpful.

7. I never found the book that I was looking _____ .

8. The bank I borrowed money _____ charges high interest on its loans.

9. The news article we talked _____ in class concerned a peace conference.

10. One of the subjects I've been interested _____ for a long time is global economics.

11. The interviewer wanted to know the name of the college I had graduated _____ .

12. Oscar likes the Canadian family _____ whom he is living.

13. The man I was staring _____ started to stare back at me.

14. Organic chemistry is a subject that I'm not familiar _____ .

15. My sister and I have the same ideas about almost everything. She is the one person _____ whom I almost always agree.

16. The person _____ whom you speak at the airline counter will ask to see your passport and ticket.

17. What's the name of the person you introduced me _____ at the restaurant last night? I've already forgotten.

18. My father is someone I've always been able to depend _____ when I need advice or help.

19. Look. The sailor you waved _____ is walking toward us. Now what are you going to say?

20. Your building supervisor is the person _____ whom you should complain if you have any problems with your apartment.

---

*See Appendix 2, p. 463, for a list of preposition combinations.

□ EXERCISE 17. Review: adjective clauses. (Charts 12-1 → 12-6)
Directions: Work in pairs.
Speaker A: Read the cue aloud to your partner.
Speaker B: Combine the sentences, using the second sentence as an adjective clause.
Practice omitting the object pronoun (whom, which, that). Look at your book
only if necessary.
Speaker A: If Speaker B's information is correct, respond with "yes" and repeat the
information.

Example:
SPEAKER A: The taxi was expensive. **I** took it to the airport.
SPEAKER B: The taxi **you** took to the airport was expensive.
SPEAKER A: Yes. The taxi **I** took to the airport was expensive.

1. The plane leaves at 7:08 P.M. I'm taking it to Denver.
2. The university is in New York. I want to go to it.
3. I met the people. You told me about them.
4. The bananas were too ripe. My husband/wife bought them.
5. The shirt/blouse is made of cotton. The teacher is wearing it.
6. The market has fresh vegetables. I usually go to it.

Switch roles.
7. I couldn't understand the woman. I talked to her on the phone.
8. The scrambled eggs were cold. I had them for breakfast at the cafeteria.
9. I had a good time on the trip. I took it to Hawaii.
10. The doctor prescribed some medicine for my sore throat. I went to him yesterday.
11. The cream was spoiled. I put it in my coffee.
12. The fast-forward button on the tape recorder doesn't work. I bought it last month.
13. I'm going to call about the want ad. I saw it in last night's paper.

□ EXERCISE 18. Review: adjective clauses. (Charts 12-1 → 12-6)
Directions: Underline the adjective clauses in the following passages. Circle the nouns that
the adjective clauses modify.

1. Frogs are small, tailless (animals) that live near water.

2. Flowers that bloom year after year are called perennials. Flowers that bloom only one

   season are called annuals.

3. Flamingos are large pink birds that have long legs and curved bills.

4. A fossil is the remains of an animal or plant that lived in the past.

5. A: Who's that boy?

   B: Which boy? Are you talking about the boy who's wearing the striped shirt or the boy who has on the T-shirt?

   A: I'm not talking about either one of them. I'm talking about the boy who just waved at us. Look. Over there. Do you see the kid that has the red baseball cap?

   B: Sure. I know him. That's Al Jordan's kid. His name is Josh or Jake or Jason. Nice kid. Did you wave back?

6. Hiroki is from Japan. When he was sixteen, he spent four months in South America. He stayed with a family who lived near Quito, Ecuador. Their way of life was very different from his. At first, many of the things they did and said seemed strange to Hiroki: their eating customs, political views, ways of expressing emotion, work habits, sense of humor, and more. He felt homesick for people who were like him in their customs and habits.

   As time went on, Hiroki began to appreciate the way of life that his host family followed. Many of the things he did with his host family began to feel natural to him. He developed a strong bond of friendship with them. At the beginning of his stay in Ecuador, he had noticed only the things that were different between his host family and himself. At the end, he appreciated the many things they had in common as human beings despite their differences in cultural background.

7. Many of the problems that exist today have existed since the beginning of recorded history. One of these problems is violent conflict between people who come from different geographical areas or cultural backgrounds. One group may distrust and fear another group of people who are different from themselves in language, customs, politics, religion, and/or appearance. These irrational fears are the source of much of the violence that has occurred throughout the history of the world.

12-7 USING *WHOSE* IN ADJECTIVE CLAUSES

(a) The man called the police. **His car** → **whose car** was stolen.	**Whose*** shows possession. In (a): *His car* can be changed to *whose car* to make an adjective clause. In (b): *whose car was stolen* = an adjective clause.
(b) The man **whose car** *was stolen* called the police.	
(c) I know a girl. **Her brother** → **whose brother** is a movie star.	In (c): *Her brother* can be changed to *whose brother* to make an adjective clause.
(d) I know a girl **whose brother** *is a movie star.*	
(e) The people were friendly. We bought **their house**. → **whose house**	In (e): *Their house* can be changed to *whose house* to make an adjective clause.
(f) The people **whose house** *we bought* were friendly.	

*__Whose__ and __who's__ have the same pronunciation but NOT the same meaning.
Who's = **who is**: Who's (Who is) your teacher?

☐ EXERCISE 19. WHOSE in adjective clauses. (Chart 12-7)
Directions: Combine the two sentences into one sentence. Make "b" an adjective clause. Use **whose**.

SITUATION: You and your friend are at a party. You are telling your friend about the people at the party.

1. a. There is the man.   b. His car was stolen.
    → *There is the man whose car was stolen.*

2. a. There is the woman.   b. Her cat died.

3. a. Over there is the man.   b. His daughter is in my English class.

4. a. Over there is the woman.   b. You met her husband yesterday.

5. a. There is the professor.   b. I'm taking her course.

6. a. That is the man.   b. His daughter is an astronaut.

7. a. That is the girl. b. I borrowed her camera.

8. a. There is the boy. b. His mother is a famous musician.

9. a. They are the people. b. We visited their house last month.

10. a. That is the couple. b. Their apartment was burglarized.

☐ EXERCISE 20. WHOSE in adjective clauses. (Chart 12-7)
Directions: Work in pairs.
Speaker A: Read the cue aloud.
Speaker B: Combine the sentences. Use ***whose***. Look at your book only if necessary.
Speaker A: If Speaker B's information is correct, say "yes" and repeat the sentence.

Example:
SPEAKER A: The people were very kind. **I** stayed at their house.
SPEAKER B: The people whose house **you** stayed at were very kind.
SPEAKER A: Yes, the people whose house **I** stayed at were very kind.

1. The man called the police. His car was stolen.

2. The woman was sad. Her cat died.

3. The man is friendly. His daughter is in my English class.

4. The professor gives hard tests. I'm taking her course.

5. The man is very proud. His daughter is an astronaut.

6. The girl is a good friend of mine. I borrowed her camera.

7. The people were very nice. I visited their house.

Switch roles.
8. I have a friend. Her brother is a police officer.

9. I have a neighbor. His dog barks all day long.

10. I like the people. We went to their house.

11. I thanked the woman. I borrowed her dictionary.

12. The woman shouted "Stop! Thief!" Her purse was stolen.

13. The man is famous. His picture is in the newspaper.

14. I know a girl. Her family never eats dinner together.

☐ EXERCISE 21. Review: adjective clauses. (Chapter 12)
Directions: Which of the following can be used in the blanks: ***who, who(m), which, that, whose,*** and/or ***Ø***?

1. The people _____who / that_____ moved into town are Italian.

2. The lamp _____which / that / Ø_____ I bought downtown is beautiful but quite
   expensive.

3. Everyone _____ came to the audition got a part in the play.

4. Ms. Laura Rice is the teacher _____ class I enjoy most.

5. Flowers _____ grow in tropical climates usually have vibrant colors.

6. The man _____ I found in the doorway had collapsed from exhaustion.

7. I like the people with _____ I work.

8. I have a friend _____ father is a famous artist.

9. The camera _____ I bought has a zoom lens.

10. Students _____ have part-time jobs have to budget their time very carefully.

11. The person to _____ you should send your application is the Director of Admissions.

12. Flying squirrels _____ live in tropical rainforests stay in the trees their entire lives without ever touching the ground.

13. The people _____ window I broke got really angry.

14. Monkeys will eat eggs, grass, fruit, birds, snakes, insects, nuts, flowers, leaves, and frogs. Monkeys will eat almost anything _____ they can find.

15. A: A magazine _____ I read at the doctor's office had an

article _____ you ought to read. It's about the

importance of exercise in dealing with stress.

B: Why do you think I should read an article _____ deals

with exercise and stress?

A: If you stop and think for a minute, you can answer that question yourself. You're

under a lot of stress, and you don't get any exercise.

B: The stress _____ I have at work doesn't bother me. It's

just a normal part of my job. And I don't have time to exercise.

A: Well, you should make time. Anyone _____ job is as

stressful as yours should make physical exercise part of their daily routine.

☐ **EXERCISE 22. Written: adjective clauses. (Chapter 12)**
Directions: Imagine that you are in a room full of people. You know everyone who is there.
I (your reader) know no one. Tell me who these people are. Write your description of
these people. Practice using adjective clauses.

Begin your composition with: *I'm glad you came to the party. Let me tell you about the
people who are here. The woman who . . . .*

☐ **EXERCISE 23. Review: adjective clauses. (Chapter 12)**
Directions: Work in pairs, in groups, or as a class.
Speaker A: Write the main sentence on the board or on a piece of paper for Speaker B to
refer to. Give the cue.
Speaker B: Use Speaker A's information to add an adjective clause to the main sentence.

PART I. MAIN SENTENCE: **The man was nice.**

Example:
SPEAKER A: **I** met him yesterday.
SPEAKER B: The man (whom/that/Ø) **you** met yesterday was nice.

1. He helped me yesterday.
2. I spoke to him on the phone.
3. I called him.
4. He answered the phone.
5. I introduced you to him.
6. I had dinner with him last week.
7. He opened the door for me.
8. I told you about him.

9. (. . .) went to a movie with him last night.
10. He gave me directions to the post office.
11. (. . .) roomed with him.
12. He visited our class yesterday.
13. We visited his house.
14. He helped us at the hardware store.
15. I borrowed his pen.
16. I met him at the party last night.

PART II. MAIN SENTENCE: **Do you know the woman?**

Example:

SPEAKER A: She is standing over there.

SPEAKER B: Do you know the woman who/that is standing over there?

1. (. . .) is talking to her.
2. Her car was stolen.
3. (. . .) is going to marry her.
4. (. . .) is talking about her.
5. She is waving at us.

6. Her apartment was burglarized.
7. She works in that office.
8. She is sitting over there.
9. My brother is engaged to her.
10. Her son was arrested by the police.

PART III. MAIN SENTENCE *(written on the board):* **The movie was good.**

Example:

SPEAKER A: **I** saw it yesterday.

SPEAKER B: The movie which/that **you** saw yesterday was good.

1. I went to it.
2. I watched it on TV last night.
3. (. . .) told me about it.

4. It was playing at *(name of a local theater)*.
5. (. . .) saw it.
6. It starred *(name of an actor/actress)*.

☐ **EXERCISE 24. Review: adjective clauses. (Chapter 12)**

Directions: Use the given information in the list to complete the sentences using adjective clauses. Omit the object pronoun from the adjective clause if possible.

> *Their specialty is heart surgery.*
> ✓*James chose the color of paint for his bedroom walls.*
> *Its mouth was big enough to swallow a whole cow in one gulp.*
> *You drink it.*
> *It erupted in Indonesia recently.*
> *His son was in an accident.*
> *They lived in the jungles of Southeast Asia.*
> *They have been used countless times before in countless ways.*
> *I slept on it in a hotel last night.*

1. The color of paint _____James chose for his bedroom walls_____ was
   an unusual blue.

2. The man _____ called an
   ambulance.

3. My back hurts today. The mattress _____
   was too soft.

4. A volcano _____ killed six
   people and damaged large areas of rice, coconut, and clove crops.

5. Doctors and nurses _____

   are some of the best-trained medical personnel in the world.

6. Early human beings hunted animals for food, including chickens. Originally, chickens

   were wild birds _____ . At

   some point in time, humans learned how to domesticate them and raise them for food.

7. In prehistoric times, there was a dinosaur _____

   _____ .

8. Every glass of water _____ has molecules

   _____ .

☐ **EXERCISE 25. Review: adjective clauses. (Chapter 12)**
Directions: <u>Underline</u> the adjective clauses in the following passage. Circle the noun that
each adjective clause modifies. Work in pairs or groups.
There are ten adjective clauses in the passage (including the one in the first
sentence). Can your team find all of them?

(1) Parents are (people) <u>who provide love, care, and education for children</u>. Parents

may be defined as the principal people who raise a child. These people may or may not

have physically produced the child. Many children are brought up by relatives or other

caring adults when their biological parents, through death, disability, or uncontrollable

circumstances, are not present to care for them. The role of any parents,

biological or not, is to take care of their children's emotional, physical,

and social needs.

(2) Children need love and affection to grow strong emotionally. It

is important for all children to have at least one adult with whom they

can form a loving, trusting relationship. A strong bond with adults is

essential from birth through adolescence. For example, babies who are

not picked up frequently and held lovingly may have slow physical and mental growth even

though they receive adequate food and exercise. Youngsters who are raised in an

institution without bonding with an older person who functions as a parent often have

difficulty forming trusting relationships when they are adults.

(3) In addition to love, children need physical care. Babies are completely dependent upon adults for food, shelter, and safety. Children who are denied such basics in their early lives may suffer chronic health problems and feelings of insecurity throughout their lifetimes. One of the greatest responsibilities that parents have is to provide for the physical well-being of their children.

(4) Children's education is also the responsibility of the parents. Girls and boys must learn to speak, dress themselves, eat properly, and get along with others. They must learn not to touch fire, to look carefully before they cross the street, and not to use violence to solve problems. The lessons that parents teach their children are numerous. As children get older and enter school, teachers join parents in providing the education that young people need in order to become independent, productive members of society.

□ **EXERCISE 26. Adjective clauses. (Chapter 12)**

Directions: <u>Underline</u> the adjective clause and complete each sentence with your own words.

1. One of the things <u>I like best</u>   *is* hot and spicy food.*

2. One of the places I want to visit someday _____

3. One of the people I admire most in the world _____

4. Some of the cities I would like to visit   *are**_____

5. Some of the places I hope to visit someday _____

6. One of the cities I would like to visit while I'm in this country _____

7. One of the programs my roommate likes to watch on TV _____

8. One of the subjects I would like to know more about _____

9. Some of the things I like most in life _____

10. One of the best books I've ever read _____

11. One of the hardest classes I've ever taken _____

12. One of the most fascinating people I've ever met _____

---

*One of the + *plural noun* (+ *adjective clause*) + **singular** *verb*.
Some of the + *plural noun* (+ *adjective clause*) + **plural** *verb*.

☐ **EXERCISE 27. Written: adjective clauses. (Chapter 12)**

Directions: Complete the sentences with your own words.

1. My friend told me about a man who . . . .
2. I have a friend whose . . . .
3. I returned the book that . . . .
4. The person who . . . .
5. The people I . . . .
6. The movie we . . . .
7. The people whose . . . .
8. Do you know the woman that . . . ?
9. The book I . . . .
10. The person to whom . . . .
11. One of the places I . . . .
12. Some of the things I . . . .

☐ **EXERCISE 28. Error analysis: adjective clauses. (Chapter 12)**

Directions: Correct the mistakes.

1. The book that I bought i̶t̶ at the bookstore was very expensive.

2. The woman was nice that I met yesterday.

3. The people which live next to me are friendly.

4. I met a woman who her husband is a famous lawyer.

5. Do you know the people who lives in that house?

6. The professor teaches Chemistry 101 is very good.

7. I wrote a thank-you note to the people who I visited their house on Thanksgiving Day.

8. The people who I met them at the party last night were interesting.

9. I enjoyed the music that we listened to it.

10. The man was very angry who's bicycle was stolen.

11. A clock is an instrument measures time.

12. The apple tree is producing fruit that we planted it last year.

13. Before I came here, I don't have the opportunity to speak to people who their native

    tongue is English.

14. One of the thing I need to get a new alarm clock.

15. The people who was waiting in line for tickets to the game they were happy and

   excited because their team had made it to the championship series.

☐ EXERCISE 29. Adjective clauses. (Chapter 12)
Directions: Discuss one or more of the following topics in groups or as a class. Practice using adjective clauses in your sentences as much as possible (but not every sentence needs to have an adjective clause).

Example:
SPEAKER A: What are the qualities of a friend?
SPEAKER B: A friend is someone you can depend on in times of trouble.
SPEAKER C: A friend is a person who accepts you as you are.
SPEAKER D: Friends don't talk about you behind your back.
SPEAKER E: I agree. A friend is someone you can trust with secrets.
SPEAKER F: Etc.

1. What is your idea of the ideal roommate?
   (Suggested beginning: *An ideal roommate is someone who . . . .*)

2. What kind of people make good leaders?
   (*Good leaders are people who . . . .*)

3. What are the qualities of a good neighbor?
   (*A good neighbor is a person who . . . .*)

4. What kind of people make good parents?
   (*People who . . . .*)

5. What is your idea of the ideal classroom?
   (*Students need a classroom that . . . .*)

6. What are the qualities of a good boss and a bad boss?
   (*A good boss is someone who . . . , but a bad boss . . . .*)

☐ EXERCISE 30. Adjective clauses. (Chapter 12)
Directions: Write a few sentences on one (or more) of the topics in Exercise 29 and/or the following topics. Practice using adjective clauses in some of your sentences.

Additional topics:

1. The qualities of the ideal wife/husband.
2. The qualities of the ideal apartment.
3. The qualities of a good student.
4. The qualities of a good teacher.
5. The qualities of a good novel.

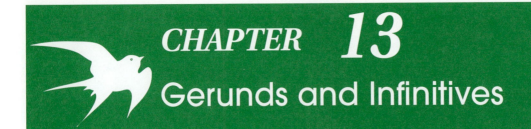

CHAPTER *13*
Gerunds and Infinitives

13-1 VERB + GERUND

verb gerund (a) I ***enjoy*** ***walking*** in the park.	A gerund is the *-ing* form of a verb. It is used as a noun. In (a): *walking* is a gerund. It is used as the object of the verb *enjoy*.

COMMON VERBS FOLLOWED BY GERUNDS
 	
enjoy   (b) I ***enjoy working*** in my garden.
finish   (c) Ann ***finished studying*** at midnight.
stop   (d) It ***stopped raining*** a few minutes ago.
quit   (e) David ***quit smoking***.
mind   (f) Would you ***mind opening*** the window?
postpone   (g) I ***postponed doing*** my homework.
put off   (h) I ***put off doing*** my homework.
keep (on) (i) ***Keep (on) working.*** Don't stop.
consider   (j) I***'m considering going*** to Hawaii.
think about (k) I***'m thinking about going*** to Hawaii.
discuss   (l) They ***discussed getting*** a new car.
talk about (m) They ***talked about getting*** a new car.
	The verbs in the list are followed by gerunds. The list also contains phrasal verbs (e.g., *put off*) that are followed by gerunds.
	
	The verbs in the list are NOT followed by ***to*** + *the simple form of a verb* (an infinitive).
	    INCORRECT: *I enjoy to walk in the park.*
	    INCORRECT: *Bob finished to study.*
	    INCORRECT: *I'm thinking to go to
	                              Hawaii.*
	See Chart 2-5, p. 29, for the spelling of *-ing* verb forms.

(n) I ***considered not going*** to class.	Negative form: ***not*** + *gerund*

□ EXERCISE 1. Verb + gerund. (Chart 13-1)

Directions: Complete the sentences by using gerunds. Add a preposition after the gerund if necessary.

1. It was cold and rainy yesterday, so we postponed ___going to / visiting___ the zoo.

2. The Porters' house is too small. They're considering ___buying/ moving___ ___into /renting___ a bigger house.

3. We discussed _____ Colorado for our vacation.

4. When Martha finished _____ the floor, she dusted the furniture.

5. Sometimes students put off _____ their homework.

6. We had a blizzard yesterday, but it finally stopped _____ around 10:00 P.M.

7. I quit _____ comic books when I was twelve years old.

8. I'm thinking about _____ a biology course next semester.

9. Beth doesn't like her job. She's talking about _____ a different job.

10. I enjoy _____ sports.

11. I'm considering _____ New York City.

12. A: Are you listening to me?
    B: Yes. Keep _____ . I'm listening.

13. A: Do you want to take a break?
    B: No. I'm not tired yet. Let's keep on _____ for another hour or so.

14. A: Would you mind _____ the window?
    B: Not at all. I'd be glad to.

15. A: I'm thinking about not _____ the meeting tomorrow.
    B: Really? Why? I hope you decide to go. We need your input.

Directions: Complete the sentences in the dialogues. Use the expressions in the list or your own words. Be sure to use a gerund in each sentence.

buy a new car	✓ rain
do my homework	read a good book
do things	repeat that
get a Toyota	smoke
go to the zoo on Saturday	tap your fingernails on the table
help him	try

1. A: Would you like to go for a walk?

   B: Has it stopped _____ raining* _____ ?

   A: Yes.

   B: Let's go.

2. A: I've been having a lot of trouble with my old Volkswagen the last couple of months. It's slowly falling apart. I'm thinking about _____ .

   B: Do you think you'll get another Volkswagen?

   A: No. I'm considering _____ .

3. A: What do you usually do in your free time in the evening?

   B: I enjoy _____ .

4. A: Good news! I feel great. I don't cough any more, and I don't run out of breath when I walk up a hill.

   B: Oh?

   A: I quit _____ .

   B: That's wonderful!

5. A: I've been working on this math problem for the last half hour, and I still don't understand it.

   B: Well, don't give up. Keep _____ . If at first you don't succeed, try, try again.

_____

*The object following **stop** is a gerund, NOT an infinitive. *INCORRECT: It stopped to rain.* But in special circumstances, **stop** can be followed by an infinitive of purpose: **in order to** (see Chart 13-9, p. 391). *While I was walking down the hall, I dropped my pen. I stopped to pick it up. = I stopped walking in order to pick it up.*

6. A: Are you a procrastinator?

   B: A what?

   A: A procrastinator. That's someone who always postpones _____

   _____ .

   B: Oh. Well, sometimes I put off _____ .

7. A: What are you doing?

   B: I'm helping Teddy with his homework.

   A: When you finish _____ , could you help me in the

   kitchen?

   B: Sure.

8. A: Could you please stop doing that?

   B: Doing what?

   A: Stop _____ . It's driving me crazy!

9. A: Do you have any plans for this weekend?

   B: Henry and I talked about _____ .

10. A: I didn't understand what you said. Would you mind _____

    _____ ?

    B: Of course not. I said, "Three free trees."

☐ EXERCISE 3. Verb + gerund. (Chart 13-1)

Directions: Complete the sentences in Column A by using a verb from Column B and your own words. Use the verbs in Column B only once.

Example: I often postpone + write

→ *I often postpone writing thank you notes, and then I have to apologize for sending them late.*

Column A	Column B	
1. I often postpone	buy	listen
2. I enjoy	close	love
3. I'm considering	do	make
4. Would you mind	eat	open
5. I finished	exercise	play
6. I'll never stop	finish	take
7. Do you ever think about	give	teach
8. You should keep	go	try
9. Sometimes I put off	help	visit
	learn	watch
	leave	✓write

13-2 *GO + -ING*

(a) ***Did*** you ***go shopping*** yesterday? (b) I ***went swimming*** last week. (c) Bob ***hasn't gone fishing*** in years.	***Go*** is followed by a gerund in certain idiomatic expressions about activities. Notice: There is no ***to*** between ***go*** and the gerund. *INCORRECT: Did you go to shopping?*

COMMON EXPRESSIONS WITH *GO + -ING*

go boating	*go dancing*	*go jogging*	*go (window) shopping*	*go (water) skiing*
go bowling	*go fishing*	*go running*	*go sightseeing*	*go skydiving*
go camping	*go hiking*	*go sailing*	*go (ice) skating*	*go swimming*

☐ **EXERCISE 4. GO + -ING. (Chart 13-2)**

Directions: Answer the questions. Use the expressions with ***go + -ing*** listed in Chart 13-2.

1. Ann often goes to the beach. She spends hours in the water. What does she like to do?
   → *She likes to go swimming.*

2. Nancy and Frank like to spend the whole day on a lake with poles in their hands. What do they like to do?

3. Last summer Adam went to a national park. He slept in a tent and cooked his food over a fire. What did Adam do last summer?

4. Tim likes to go to stores and buy things. What does he like to do?

5. Laura takes good care of her health. She runs a couple of miles every day. What does Laura do every day? (*NOTE: There are two possible responses.*)

6. On weekends in the winter, Fred and Jean sometimes drive to a resort in the mountains. They like to race down the side of a mountain in the snow. What do they like to do?

7. Joe likes to take long walks in the woods. What does Joe like to do?

8. Sara prefers indoor sports. She goes to a place where she rolls a thirteen-pound ball at some wooden pins. What does Sara often do?

9. Liz and Greg know all the latest dances. What do they probably do a lot?

10. The Taylors are going to go to a little lake near their house tomorrow. The lake is completely frozen now that it's winter. The ice is smooth. What are the Taylors going to do tomorrow?

11. Alex and Barbara live near the ocean. When there's a strong wind, they like to spend the whole day in their sailboat. What do they like to do?

12. Tourists often get on buses that take them to see interesting places in an area. What do tourists do on buses?

13. Colette and Ben like to jump out of airplanes. They don't open their parachutes until the last minute. What do they like to do?

14. What do you like to do for exercise and fun?

13-3 VERB + INFINITIVE

(a) Tom **offered to lend** me some money. (b) I've **decided to buy** a new car.	Some verbs are followed by an infinitive: AN INFINITIVE = **to** + *the simple form of a verb.*
(c) I've **decided not to keep** my old car.	Negative form: **not** + *infinitive.*

COMMON VERBS FOLLOWED BY INFINITIVES

want	*hope*	*decide*	*seem*	*learn (how)*
need	*expect*	*promise*	*appear*	*try*
would like	*plan*	*offer*	*pretend*	
would love	*intend*	*agree*		*(can't) afford*
	mean	*refuse*	*forget*	*(can't) wait*

☐ EXERCISE 5. Verb + infinitive. (Chart 13-3)

Directions: Complete the sentences by using infinitives. Add a preposition after the infinitive if necessary.

1. I'm planning ____*to go to / to visit / to fly to*____ Chicago next week.

2. I've decided _____ a new apartment.

3. Jack promised not _____ late for the wedding.

4. I forgot _____ some rice when I went to the grocery store.

5. I would like _____ the Grand Canyon.

6. My husband and I would love _____ Arizona.

7. I need _____ my homework tonight.

8. What time do you expect _____ Chicago?

9. I want _____ a ball game on TV after dinner tonight.

10. You seem _____ in a good mood today.

11. Susie appeared _____ asleep, but she wasn't. She was only pretending.

12. Susie pretended _____ asleep. She pretended not _____
when I spoke to her.

13. The Millers can't afford _____ a house.

14. George is only seven, but he intends _____ a doctor when he grows up.

15. My friend offered _____ me a little money.

16. Tommy doesn't like peas. He refuses _____ them.

17. My wife and I wanted to do different things this weekend. Finally, I agreed
_____ a movie with her Saturday, and she agreed _____
the football game with me on Sunday.

18. I hope _____ all of my courses this term. So far my grades have
been pretty good.

19. I try _____ class on time every day.

20. I can't wait _____ my family again! It's been a long time!

21. I'm sorry. I didn't mean _____ you.

22. I learned (how) _____ when I was around six or
seven.

13-4 VERB + GERUND OR INFINITIVE

(a) It *began* **raining**. (b) It *began* **to rain**.	Some verbs are followed by either a gerund or an infinitive. Usually there is no difference in meaning. (a) and (b) have the same meaning.

COMMON VERBS FOLLOWED BY EITHER A GERUND OR AN INFINITIVE		
begin	*like*★	*hate*
start	*love*★	*can't stand*
continue		

★COMPARE: ***Like*** and ***love*** can be followed by either a gerund or an infinitive:
  I like going/to go to movies. I love playing/to play chess.
Would like and ***would love*** are followed by infinitives:
  I would like **to go** *to a movie tonight. I'd love* **to play** *a game of chess right now.*

□ **EXERCISE 6. Verb + gerund or infinitive. (Charts 13-3 and 13-4)**

Directions: Use the given words to create sentences with gerunds and infinitives.

1. start + snow around midnight
   → *It started snowing around midnight. It started to snow around midnight.*
2. continue + work even though everyone else stopped
3. like + get a lot of e-mails from my friends
4. love + go to baseball games
5. hate + talk to pushy salespeople
6. can't stand + wait in lines for a long time

□ **EXERCISE 7. Verb + gerund or infinitive. (Charts 13-3 and 13-4)**

Directions: Discuss what you like and don't like to do. Use the given ideas to make sentences that begin with words from this list.

I like	*I don't like*	*I don't mind*
I love	*I hate*	
I enjoy	*I can't stand*	

1. cook
   → *I like to cook / I like cooking / I hate to cook / I hate cooking / I don't mind cooking / I don't enjoy cooking, etc.*
2. live in this city
3. wash dishes
4. fly
5. wait in airports
6. read novels in my spare time
7. eat a delicious meal slowly
8. speak in front of a large group
9. play cards for money
10. drive on city streets during rush hour
11. go to parties where I don't know a single person
12. listen to the sounds of the city while I'm trying to get to sleep
13. visit with friends I haven't seen in a long time
14. get in between two friends who are having an argument
15. travel to strange and exotic places

□ **EXERCISE 8. Gerunds vs. infinitives. (Charts 13-1 → 13-4)**

Directions: Complete the sentences with the infinitive or gerund form of the words in parentheses.

1. I need *(study)* _____to study_____ tonight.

2. I enjoy *(cook)* _____cooking_____ fancy meals.

3. Ellen started *(talk)* __to talk / talking__ about her problem.

4. Bud and Sally have decided *(get)* _____ married.

5. We finished *(eat)* _____ around seven.

6. I like *(meet)* _____ new people.

7. My roommate offered *(help)* _____ me with my English.

8. I'd just begun *(watch)* _____ a movie on TV when the phone rang.

9. Please stop *(crack)* _____ your knuckles!

10. Did you remember *(feed)* _____ the cat this morning?

11. I won't be late. I promise *(be)* _____ on time.

12. I'm considering *(move)* _____ to a new apartment.

13. Some children hate *(go)* _____ to school.

14. I forgot *(lock)* _____ the door when I left my apartment this morning.

15. I don't mind *(live)* _____ with four roommates.

16. Shhh. My roommate is trying *(take)* _____ a nap.

17. My boss refused *(give)* _____ me a raise, so I quit.

18. The company will continue *(hire)* _____ new employees as long as new production orders keep *(come)* _____ in.

19. That's not what I meant! I meant *(say)* _____ just the opposite.

20. I want *(go)* _____ *(shop)* _____ this afternoon.

21. Alex seems *(want)* _____ *(go)* _____ *(sail)* _____ this weekend.

22. My wife can't stand *(sleep)* _____ in a room with all of the windows closed.

23. Sam's tomato crop always failed. Finally he quit *(try)* _____ *(grow)* _____ tomatoes in his garden.

24. I enjoy *(be)* _____ a teacher.

Directions: Work in pairs.
Student A: Read the cues. Your book is open.
Student B: Complete the sentences with either ***to go*** or ***going*** + *the name of a place.*
Your book is closed.

Example:
STUDENT A *(book open):* I expect . . . .
STUDENT B *(book closed):* to go (to Mack's Bar and Grill for dinner tonight).
STUDENT A *(book open):* I like . . . .
STUDENT B *(book closed):* to go (to Hawaii). OR going (to Hawaii).

Switch roles.

1. I expect . . . .
2. I like . . . .
3. I would like . . . .
4. I enjoy . . . .
5. I'd love . . . .
6. I promised . . . .
7. I can't stand . . . .
8. I intend . . . .
9. I am thinking about . . . .
10. Are you considering . . . .
11. I've always wanted . . . .
12. I can't afford . . . .

13. I enjoy . . . .
14. I don't need . . . .
15. I'm going to try . . . .
16. I hate . . . .
17. I love . . . .
18. My friend and I discussed . . . .
19. I've decided . . . .
20. Sometimes I put off . . . .
21. Yesterday I forgot . . . .
22. I can't wait . . . .
23. My friend and I agreed . . . .
24. Would you mind . . . .

□ EXERCISE 10. Gerunds vs. infinitives. (Charts 13-1 → 13-4)
Directions: Complete the sentences with a form of the words in parentheses.

1. I want *(stay)* _____to stay_____ home tonight.

2. I want *(relax)* _____ tonight.

3. I want *(stay)* _____ home and *(relax)** _____
   tonight.

4. I want *(stay)* _____ home, *(relax)* _____ , and
   (go) _____ to bed early tonight.

5. I enjoy *(get)* _____ up early in the morning.

6. I enjoy *(watch)* _____ the sunrise.

7. I enjoy *(get)* _____ up early in the morning and *(watch)*
   _____ the sunrise.

---

*When infinitives are connected by ***and***, it is not necessary to repeat ***to***.
   *Example: I need ***to stay*** home ***and*** (to) ***study*** tonight.*

8. I enjoy (get) _____ up early in the morning, (watch) _____ the sunrise, and (listen) _____ to the birds.

9. Mr. and Mrs. Brown are thinking about (sell) _____ their old house and (buy) _____ a new one.

10. Kathy plans (move) _____ to New York City, (find) _____ a job, and (start) _____ a new life.

11. Have you finished (paint) _____ your apartment yet?

12. Steve needs (go) _____ to the shopping mall tomorrow and (buy) _____ winter clothes.

13. Do you enjoy (go) _____ to an expensive restaurant and (have) _____ a gourmet dinner?

14. Most nonsmokers can't stand (be) _____ in a smoke-filled room.

15. Let's postpone (go) _____ abroad until the political situation improves.

16. The children promised (stop) _____ (make) _____ so much noise.

17. Kevin is thinking about (quit) _____ his job and (go) _____ back to school.

18. Linda plans (leave) _____ for Chicago on Tuesday and (return) _____ on Friday.

19. I often put off (wash) _____ the dinner dishes until the next morning.

20. Don't forget (unplug) _____ the coffee pot, (turn off) _____ all the lights, and (lock) _____ the door before you leave for work this morning.

21. Sometimes when I'm listening to someone who is speaking English very fast, I nod my head and pretend (understand) _____ .

22. After Isabel got a speeding ticket and had to pay a big fine, she decided (stop) _____ (drive) _____ over the speed limit on interstate highways.

23. I've been trying (reach) _____ Carol on the phone for the last three days, but she is never at home. I intend (keep) _____ (try) _____ until I finally get her.

☐ **EXERCISE 11. Gerunds vs. infinitives.** (Charts 13-1 → 13-4)

Directions: Create sentences from the given words. Use **I.** Use any tense. Work in pairs, in groups, or as a class.

Example: want and *go*
  → *I want to go (to New York City next week).*

1. *plan* and *go*
2. *consider* and *go*
3. *offer* and *lend*
4. *like* and *visit*
5. *enjoy* and *read*
6. *intend* and *get*
7. *decide* and *get*
8. *seem* and *be*
9. *put off* and *write*
10. *forget* and *go*
11. *can't afford* and *buy*
12. *try* and *learn*
13. *need* and *learn*
14. *would love* and *take*
15. *would like* and *go* and *swim*
16. *promise* and *come*
17. *finish* and *study*
18. *would mind* and *help*
19. *hope* and *go*
20. *think about* and *go*
21. *quit* and *try*
22. *expect* and *stay*
23. *stop* and *eat*
24. *refuse* and *lend*
25. *agree* and *lend*
26. *postpone* and *go*
27. *begin* and *study*
28. *continue* and *walk*
29. *talk about* and *go*
30. *keep* and *try* and *improve*

☐ **EXERCISE 12. Gerunds vs. infinitives.** (Charts 13-1 → 13-4)

Directions: Complete the sentences with the correct form, gerund or infinitive, of the words in parentheses.

A: Have you made any vacation plans?

B: I was hoping *(go)* _____**to go**_____ to an island off the Atlantic coast, but my
       ___1___

   wife wanted *(drive)* _____ down the Pacific coast. We've decided
                                    2

   (compromise) _____ by going to neither coast. We've
                             3

   agreed *(find)* _____ a place where both of us want
                         4

   (go) _____ .
             5

A: So where are you going?

B: Well, we've been considering *(go)* _____ *(fish)* _____ in
                                                    6   7

   Canada. We've also discussed *(take)* _____ a train across central and
                                                       8

   western Canada. We've also been talking about *(rent)* _____ a sailboat
                                                                            9

   and *(go)* _____ *(sail)* _____ in the Gulf of Mexico.
                     10   11

A: Have you ever thought about (stay) _____ home and (relax)
  12

_____ ?
  13

B: That's not a vacation to me. If I stay home during my vacation, I always end up doing

all the chores around the house that I've put off (do) _____ for the past
  14

year. When I go on a holiday, I like (visit) _____ new places and (do)
  15

_____ new things. I enjoy (see) _____ parts of the
  16   17

world I've never seen before.

A: What place would you like (visit) _____ the most?
  18

B: I'd love (go) _____ (camp) _____ in New Zealand. My
  19   20

wife loves (camp) _____ in new places too, but I'm afraid she might
  21

refuse (go) _____ to New Zealand. She doesn't like long plane flights.
  22

A: Why don't you just pick a spot on a map? Then call and make a hotel reservation.

B: Neither of us can stand (spend) _____ two whole weeks at a
  23

luxury hotel. I don't mean (say) _____ anything bad about big hotels,
  24

but both of us seem (like) _____ more adventurous vacations.
  25

A: Well, keep (think) _____ about it. I'm sure you'll figure out a
  26

really great place for your vacation.

B: We'll have to stop (think) _____ about it sometime soon and
  27

make a decision.

A: I can't wait (find) _____ out where you decide (go) _____ .
  28   29

I'll expect (hear) _____ from you when you make a decision. Don't
  30

forget (call) _____ me.
  31

B: Hmmm. Maybe we should go (ski) _____ in Switzerland. Or perhaps
  32

we could go (waterski) _____ on the Nile. Then there's the
  33

possibility of going (hike) _____ in the Andes. Of course, we'd
  34

probably enjoy (swim) _____ off the Great Barrier Reef of
  35

Australia. And we shouldn't postpone *(explore)* _____ the
<u>36</u>

Brazilian rainforest much longer. Someday I'd really like *(climb)* _____
<u>37</u>

to the top of an active volcano and *(look)* _____ inside the crater. Or
<u>38</u>

maybe we could . . . .

13-5 PREPOSITION + GERUND

(a) Kate *insisted **on coming*** with us. (b) We're *excited **about going*** to Tahiti. (c) I *apologized **for being*** late.	A preposition is followed by a gerund, not an infinitive. In (a): The preposition *(on)* is followed by a gerund *(coming)*.

COMMON EXPRESSIONS WITH PREPOSITIONS FOLLOWED BY GERUNDS

*be afraid **of*** (doing something)	*forgive* (someone) ***for***	*plan **on***
*apologize **for***	*be good **at***	*be responsible **for***
*believe **in***	*insist **on***	*stop* (someone) ***from***
*dream **about***	*be interested **in***	*thank* (someone) ***for***
*be excited **about***	*look forward **to***	*be tired **of***
*feel **like***	*be nervous **about***	*worry **about**/be worried **about***

☐ **EXERCISE 13. Preposition + gerund. (Chart 13-5 and Appendix 2)**
  Directions: Complete the sentences with a preposition and the given words.

    1. I'm looking forward   + go to the zoo → *I'm looking forward to going to the zoo.*

    2. Thank you   + open the door

    3. I'm worried   + be late for the concert

    4. Are you interested   + go to the museum with us

    5. I apologized   + be late

    6. Are you afraid   + fly in small planes

    7. Are you nervous   + take your driver's test

8. We're excited	+	go to a soccer game
9. Jack insisted	+	pay the restaurant bill
10. Annie dreams	+	be a horse trainer someday
11. I don't feel	+	eat right now
12. Please forgive me	+	not call you sooner
13. I'm tired	+	live with five roommates
14. I believe	+	be honest at all times
15. Let's plan	+	meet at the restaurant at six
16. Who's responsible	+	clean the classroom
17. The police stopped us	+	enter the building
18. Jake's not very good	+	cut his own hair

□ **EXERCISE 14. Preposition + gerund. (Chart 13-5 and Appendix 2)**

Directions: Work in pairs.

Speaker A: Complete the sentence with a preposition and "doing something."

Speaker B: Ask a question about A's statement. Begin with "What . . ." and end with "doing."

Speaker A: Answer the question in a complete sentence using your own words.

Example: I'm looking forward . . . .

SPEAKER A: I'm looking forward to doing something.

SPEAKER B: What are you looking forward to doing?

SPEAKER A: I'm looking forward to going to a movie tonight.

Switch roles.

1. I'm interested	6. I'm nervous . . . .
2. I'm worried	7. I'm excited . . . .
3. I thanked my friend	8. I feel . . . .
4. I apologized	9. I'm planning . . . .
5. I'm afraid	10. I'm tired . . . .

□ **EXERCISE 15. Preposition + gerund. (Chart 13-5 and Appendix 2)**

Directions: Using the verbs in parentheses, complete the sentences with prepositions and gerunds.

1. I believe ___in___ *(tell)* ___telling___ the truth no matter what.

2. I wish the weather would get better. I'm tired ___of___ *(be)* ___being___ inside all the time.

3. I don't go swimming because I'm afraid _____ *(drown)* _____ .

4. Greg is nervous _____ *(meet)* _____ his girlfriend's parents for the first time.

5. I don't know how to thank you _____ (help) _____ me.

6. Are you interested _____ (go) _____ to a bullfight?

7. I just can't get excited _____ (visit) _____ Disneyland for the third time in two years.

8. Why do you constantly worry _____ (please) _____ your parents?

9. Every summer, I look forward _____ (take) _____ a vacation with my family.

10. Do you feel _____ (tell) _____ me why you're so sad?

11. I apologize _____ (lie) _____ , but I was trying to protect you from the truth. Sometimes the truth hurts.

12. Why do you always insist _____ (pay) _____ for everything when we go out for dinner?

13. I want you to know that I'm sorry. I don't know if you can ever forgive me _____ (cause) _____ you so much trouble.

14. I'm not very good _____ (remember) _____ names.

15. I'm not happy in my work. I often dream _____ (quit) _____ my job.

16. How do you stop someone _____ (do) _____ something you know is wrong?

17. I'm too tired to cook, but I hadn't planned _____ (eat) _____ out tonight.

18. Who's responsible _____ (spill) _____ these coffee beans all over the floor?

19. Anna made a lot of big mistakes at work. That's why she was afraid _____ (lose)* _____ her job.

_____

*Note that lose is spelled with one "o." The word loose, with two "o"s, is an adjective meaning "not tight." (E.g., My shirt is big and loose.) Pronunciation difference: lose = /luwz/; loose = /luws/.

☐ **EXERCISE 16. Preposition + gerund.** (Chart 13-5 and Appendix 2)

Directions: Make up a quiz. Use the given word or phrase + ONE of the suggested verbs in parentheses. Hand your quiz to a classmate to complete. When s/he finishes it, correct the answers.

Example: apologize to (. . .) + (interrupt, be, call)

Quiz item:

You should apologize to Tarik _____ (interrupt)_____ him. OR

I apologized to my friend _____ (be)_____ late. OR

Rosa apologized to me _____ (call)_____ after midnight.

1. thank + (open / help / invite)
2. feel + (go / have / take)
3. worry + (lose / not have / be)
4. insist + (answer / drive / fly)
5. believe + (help / tell / trust)

6. be nervous + (speak / go / get)
7. look forward + (do / stop / skydive)
8. apologize to (. . .) + (sell / give / leave)
9. forgive (. . .) + (lie / take / quit)
10. be excited + (go / hear / move)

13-6 USING *BY* AND *WITH* TO EXPRESS HOW SOMETHING IS DONE

(a) Pat turned off the tape recorder *by pushing* the stop button.	*By* + *a gerund* is used to express how something is done.
(b) Mary goes to work *by bus*. (c) Andrea stirred her coffee *with a spoon*.	*By* or *with* followed by a noun is also used to express how something is done.

BY IS USED FOR MEANS OF TRANSPORTATION AND COMMUNICATION

*by (air)plane**	*by subway***	*by mail*	*by air*
by boat	*by taxi*	*by (tele)phone*	*by land*
by bus	*by train*	*by fax*	*by sea*
by car	*by foot* (OR *on foot*)	*by e-mail*	

OTHERS

by chance	*by mistake*	*by check* (but *in cash*)
by choice	*by hand****	*by credit card*

WITH IS USED FOR INSTRUMENTS OR PARTS OF THE BODY
I cut down the tree *with an ax* (by using an ax).
I swept the floor *with a broom*.
She pointed to a spot on the map *with her finger*.

*airplane = American English; *aeroplane* = British English.

**by subway = American English; *by underground, by tube* = British English.

****The expression **by hand** is usually used to mean that something was made by a person, not by a machine: *This rug was made **by hand**. (A person, not a machine, made this rug.)
COMPARE: *I touched his shoulder **with my hand**.*

Directions: Complete the following by using *by* + a gerund. Use the words in the list or your own words.

eat	smile	wag	wave
drink	stay	wash	✓write
guess	take	watch	

1. Students practice written English ____by writing____ compositions.

2. We clean our clothes _____ them in soap and water.

3. Khalid improved his English _____ a lot of TV.

4. We show other people we are happy _____ .

5. We satisfy our hunger _____ something.

6. We quench our thirst _____ something.

7. I figured out what "quench" means _____ .

8. Alex caught my attention _____ his arms in the air.

9. My dog shows me she is happy _____ her tail.

10. Carmen recovered from her cold _____ in bed and _____ care of herself.

Complete the following with your own words. Use **by** *and gerunds.*

11. You can destroy bacteria in meat _____ it.

12. You can cook an egg _____ it, _____ it, or _____ it.

13. We can improve our English _____ .

14. Each of us, in our own small way, can help conserve the world's natural resources _____ .

15. You can favorably impress a job interviewer _____ .

16. People can improve their health _____ .

17. Parents can help their young children learn to read _____ .

18. We can make the world a better place for future generations _____ _____ .

□ **EXERCISE 18. Using WITH. (Chart 13-6)**

Directions: Complete the sentences using **with** and appropriate words from the list.

✓*a broom*	*a pair of scissors*	*a spoon*
a hammer	*a saw*	*a thermometer*
a needle and thread	*a shovel*	

1. I swept the floor _____ with a broom _____.

2. I sewed a button on my shirt _____.

3. I cut the wood _____.

4. I took my temperature _____.

5. I stirred my coffee _____.

6. I dug a hole in the ground _____.

7. I nailed two pieces of wood together

   _____.

8. I cut the paper _____.

□ **EXERCISE 19. Using BY or WITH. (Chart 13-6)**

Directions: Complete the sentences with **by** or **with**.

1. I opened the door _____ with _____ a key.

2. I went to Cherryville _____ by _____ bus.

3. I dried the dishes _____ a dishtowel.

4. I went from Portland to San Francisco _____ train.

5. Ted drew a straight line _____ a ruler.

6. Is there any way you could touch the ceiling _____ your foot?

7. Some advertisers try to reach target audiences _____ mail.

8. Rebecca tightened the screw in the corner of her eyeglasses _____ her

   fingernail.

9. I called Bill "Paul" _____ mistake.

10. The fastest way to send a copy of a piece of paper halfway around the world is

    _____ fax.

11. The chef sliced the partially frozen meat into thin strips _____ a

    razor-sharp knife.

12. Some people pay their bills _____ computer.

13. Sally protected her eyes from the sun _____ her hand.

14. My grandmother makes tablecloths _____ hand.

13-7 USING GERUNDS AS SUBJECTS; USING *IT* + INFINITIVE

(a) ***Riding*** horses is fun.	(a) and (b) have the same meaning.
(b) ***It*** is fun ***to ride*** horses.	In (a): A gerund *(riding)* is the subject of the sentence.★ Notice: The verb *(is)* is singular because a gerund is singular.
(c) ***Coming*** to class on time is important.	In (b): The word ***it*** is used as the subject of the sentence. The word ***it*** has the same meaning as the infinitive phrase at the end of the sentence: ***it*** means *to ride horses.*
(d) ***It*** is important ***to come*** to class on time.	

★It is also correct (but less common) to use an infinitive as the subject of a sentence: *To ride horses is fun.*

☐ **EXERCISE 20. Gerunds as subjects. (Chart 13-7)**
   Directions: Create sentences with the same meaning by using a gerund as the subject.

   1. It is important to get daily exercise. → *Getting daily exercise is important.*
   2. It isn't hard to make friends.
   3. It is easy to cook rice.
   4. It is relaxing to take a long walk.
   5. Is it difficult to learn a second language?
   6. It is wrong to cheat during a test.
   7. Is it expensive to live in an apartment?
   8. It isn't easy to live in a foreign country.
   9. It takes time to make new friends.

☐ **EXERCISE 21. IT + infinitive. (Chart 13-7)**
   Directions: Create sentences with the same meaning by using ***it*** + an infinitive.

   1. Having good friends is important. → *It's important to have good friends.*
   2. Playing tennis is fun.
   3. Being polite to other people is important.
   4. Learning about other cultures is interesting.
   5. Walking alone at night in that part of the city is dangerous.
   6. Is riding a motorcycle easy?
   7. Having a cold isn't much fun.
   8. Learning a second language takes a long time.
   9. Cooking a soft-boiled egg takes three minutes.

☐ **EXERCISE 22. Gerunds as subjects; IT + infinitive. (Chart 13-7)**
   Directions: Work in pairs.
   Speaker A: Ask the given question. Your book is open.
   Speaker B: Answer the question. Begin with "*It's . . .*" and use an **infinitive**. Your book is closed.
   Speaker A: Respond by saying "*I agree*" followed by a **gerund** subject. (Or, if you wish, say "*I don't agree. I think that . . .*" followed by a gerund subject.)

Example:

SPEAKER A *(book open):* Which is easier: to make money or to spend money?

SPEAKER B *(book closed):* It's easier to spend money than (it is) to make money.

SPEAKER A *(book open):* I agree. Spending money is easier than making money.   OR

I don't agree. I think that making money is easier than spending money.

1. Which is more fun: to study at the library or to go to a movie?
2. Which is more difficult: to write English or to read English?
3. Which is easier: to write English or to speak English?
4. Which is more expensive: to go to a movie or to go to a concert?
5. Which is more interesting: to talk to people or to watch people?

Switch roles.

6. Which is more comfortable: to wear shoes or to go barefoot?
7. Which is more satisfying: to give gifts or to receive them?
8. Which is more dangerous: to ride in a car or to ride in an airplane?
9. Which is more important: to come to class on time or to get an extra hour of sleep in the morning?
10. Which is better: to light one candle or to curse the darkness?

13-8 IT + INFINITIVE: USING *FOR (SOMEONE)*

(a) *You* should study hard. (b) It is important *for you* to study hard. (c) *Mary* should study hard. (d) It is important *for Mary* to study hard. (e) *We* don't have to go to the meeting. (f) It isn't necessary *for us* to go to the meeting. (g) *A dog* can't talk. (h) It is impossible *for a dog* to talk.	(a) and (b) have a similar meaning. Notice the pattern in (b): *it is* + adjective + *for* *(someone)* + infinitive phrase

☐ **EXERCISE 23. Using FOR (SOMEONE). (Chart 13-8)**

Directions: Use the given information to complete each sentence. Use *for (someone)* and an infinitive phrase in each completion.

1. *Students should do their homework.*

   It's important ___for students to do their homework___.

2. *Teachers should speak clearly.*

   It's important _____.

3. *We don't have to hurry.*

   There's plenty of time. It isn't necessary _____.

4. *A fish can't live out of water for more than a few minutes.*

   It's impossible _____ .

5. *Students have to budget their time carefully.*

   It's necessary _____ .

6. *A child usually can't sit still for a long time.*

   It's difficult _____ .

7. *My family always eats turkey on Thanksgiving Day.*

   It's traditional _____ .

8. *People can take trips to the moon.*

   Will it be possible _____

   within the next fifty years?

9. *I usually can't understand Mr. Alvarez.*

   It's hard _____ . He talks too fast.

10. *The guests usually wait until the hostess begins to eat.*

    At a formal dinner party, it's customary _____ .

    After she takes the first bite, the guests also start to eat.

11. *The bride usually feeds the groom the first piece of*
    wedding cake.

    It's traditional _____

    _____ .

12. *I can understand our teacher.*

    It's easy _____ .

☐ **EXERCISE 24. Gerunds as subjects; IT + infinitive. (Charts 13-7 and 13-8)**

Directions: Create sentences by combining ideas from Column A and Column B. Use gerund subjects or *it* + an infinitive.

Example: Riding a bicycle is easy / dangerous / fun / relaxing.   OR
It's easy / dangerous / fun / relaxing to ride a bicycle.

Column A	Column B
1. ride a bicycle	A. against the law
2. read newspapers	B. boring
3. study grammar	C. dangerous
4. play tennis	D. easy
5. steal cars	E. educational
6. listen to a two-hour speech	F. embarrassing
7. predict the exact time of an earthquake	G. exciting
8. forget someone's name	H. frightening
9. walk alone through a dark forest at night	I. fun
10. go fishing with your friends	J. hard
11. know the meaning of every word in a dictionary	K. important
12. be honest with yourself at all times	L. impossible
13. change a flat tire	M. relaxing
14. visit museums	N. a waste of time
15. log on to the Internet	

☐ **EXERCISE 25. IT + FOR (SOMEONE) + infinitive. (Charts 13-7 and 13-8)**

Directions: Create sentences using *it* + *for (someone)* + an infinitive by combining ideas from Columns A, B, and C. Add your own words if you wish.

Example: difficult
  → *It's difficult for me to be on time for class.*
  It's difficult for some people to learn how to swim.
  It's difficult for children to understand adults' behavior.

Column A	Column B	Column C
1. difficult	anyone	spend time with friends
2. easy	children	predict the exact time of an earthquake
3. fun	me	change a flat tire
4. important	most people	be on time for class
5. impossible	some people	understand adults' behavior
6. enjoyable	students	obey their parents
7. interesting		observe animals in their wild habitat
8. possible		visit new places
		learn how to swim
		live on the planet Mars

☐ **EXERCISE 26. IT + FOR (SOMEONE) + infinitive.** (Charts 13-7 and 13-8)

Directions: Complete the sentences with your own words.

1. It's easy for . . . to . . . .

2. It's traditional for . . . to . . . .

3. It's impossible for . . . to . . . .

4. It takes *(a length of time)* for . . . to . . . .

5. It's sensible for . . . to . . . .

6. Is it necessary for . . . to . . . ?

7. It's important for . . . to . . . .

8. It's difficult for . . . to . . . .

☐ **EXERCISE 27. IT + TAKE + infinitive.** (Charts 5-13 and 13-8)

Directions: Use your own words to complete the sentences.

Example: It takes . . . hours to . . . .
→ **It takes** five **hours to** *fly from Los Angeles to Honolulu.*

Example: It takes a lot of work for . . . to . . . .
→ **It takes a lot of work for** *most small businesses* **to** *succeed.*

1. It takes time for . . . to . . . .

2. It takes a lot of money to . . . .

3. It takes . . . minutes to . . . .

4. How long does it take to . . . ?

5. It will take . . . years for . . . to . . . .

6. It takes patience / courage / skill to . . . .

7. It takes hard work for . . . to . . . .

8. It takes stamina and determination to . . . .

13-9 EXPRESSING PURPOSE WITH *IN ORDER TO* AND *FOR*

—*Why did you go to the post office?* (a) I went to the post office *because I wanted to mail a letter.* (b) I went to the post office *in order to mail* a letter. (c) I went to the post office *to mail* a letter.	***In order to*** expresses purpose. It answers the question "Why?" In (c): ***in order*** is frequently omitted. (a), (b), and (c) have the same meaning.

(d) I went to the post office *for some stamps.*
(e) I went to the post office *to buy* some stamps.
  INCORRECT: I went to the post office for to buy some stamps.
  INCORRECT: I went to the post office for buying some stamps.
	For is also used to express purpose, but it is a preposition and is followed by a noun phrase, as in (d).

☐ **EXERCISE 28. Using IN ORDER TO. (Chart 13-9)**

Directions: Add ***in order*** to the sentences whenever possible.

1. I went to the bank to cash a check.
   → *I went to the bank in order to cash a check.*

2. I'd like to see that movie.
   → *(No change. The infinitive does not express purpose.)*

3. Sam went to the hospital to visit a friend.

4. I need to go to the bank today.

5. I need to go to the bank today to deposit my paycheck.

6. On my way home from school, I stopped at the drugstore to buy some shampoo.

7. Carmen looked in her dictionary to find the correct spelling of a word.

8. Masako went to the cafeteria to eat lunch.

9. Jack and Linda have decided to get married.

10. Pedro watches TV to improve his English.

11. I didn't forget to pay my rent.

12. Kim wrote to the university to ask for a catalog.

13. Sally touched my shoulder to get my attention.

14. Donna expects to graduate next spring.

15. Jerry needs to go to the bookstore to buy a spiral notebook.

☐ **EXERCISE 29. Using (IN ORDER) TO. (Chart 13-9)**

Directions: Complete the sentences in Column A by using the ideas in Column B. Connect the ideas with ***(in order) to***.

Example: I called the hotel desk . . .
   → *I called the hotel desk (in order) to ask for an extra pillow.*

Column A	**Column B**
1. I called the hotel desk . . .	A. keep their feet warm and dry
2. I turned on the radio . . .	B. reach the top shelf
3. I looked on the Internet . . .	C. listen to a ball game
4. People wear boots . . .	D. find the population of Malaysia
5. Andy went to Egypt . . .	✓E. ask for an extra pillow
6. Ms. Lane stood on tiptoes . . .	F. chase a stray dog away
7. The dentist moved the light closer to my face . . .	G. help her pay the rent
8. I clapped my hands and yelled . . .	H. get some fresh air and exercise
9. Maria took a walk in the park . . .	I. see the ancient pyramids
10. I offered my cousin some money . . .	J. look into my mouth

□ **EXERCISE 30. Expressing purpose with TO and FOR. (Chart 13-9)**

Directions: Complete the sentences by using *to* or *for*.

1. I went to Chicago _____*for*_____ a visit.

2. I went to Chicago _____*to*_____ visit my aunt and uncle.

3. I take long walks _____ relax.

4. I take long walks _____ relaxation.

5. I'm going to school _____ a good education.

6. I'm going to school _____ get a good education.

7. I'm not going to school just _____ have fun.

8. I'm not going to school just _____ fun.

9. I turned on the radio _____ listen to the news.

10. I listened to the radio _____ news about the earthquake in Peru.

11. I sent a card to Carol _____ wish her a happy birthday.

12. Two police officers came to my apartment _____ ask me about my cousin.

13. Mr. Wong works in his garden _____ the pure pleasure of it.

14. I looked in the encyclopedia _____ information about Ecuador.

15. My three brothers, two sisters, and parents all came to town _____

    attend my graduation.

□ **EXERCISE 31. Expressing purpose with TO and FOR. (Chart 13-9)**

Directions: Answer *why*-questions in your own words. Show purpose by using an infinitive phrase or a *for*-phrase. Work in pairs or as a class.

Example:

SPEAKER A: Yesterday you turned on the TV. Why?

SPEAKER B: Yesterday I turned on the TV (to listen to the news / for the latest news about the earthquake / etc.).

1. You went to the supermarket. Why?

2. You need to go to the bookstore. Why?

3. You went to the post office. Why?

4. You went to the health clinic. Why?

5. You reached into your pocket/purse. Why?

(Switch roles if working in pairs.)

6. You came to this school. Why?

7. You borrowed some money from (. . .). Why?

8. You stopped at the service station. Why?

9. You play (soccer, tennis, etc.). Why?

10. You had to go out last night. Why?

13-10 USING INFINITIVES WITH *TOO* AND *ENOUGH*

***TOO* + ADJECTIVE + (FOR SOMEONE) + INFINITIVE**				
(a)	A piano is	***too*** *heavy*		***to*** *lift.*
(b)	That box is	***too*** *heavy*	***for*** *me*	***to*** *lift.*
(c)	That box is	***too*** *heavy*	***for*** *Bob*	***to*** *lift.*

Infinitives often follow expressions with ***too***. ***Too*** comes in front of an adjective. In the speaker's mind, the use of ***too*** implies a negative result.

COMPARE
The box is too heavy. I can't lift it.
The box is very heavy, but I can lift it.

***ENOUGH* + NOUN + INFINITIVE**			
(d)	I don't have	***enough*** *money*	***to*** *buy* that car.
(e)	Did you have	***enough*** *time*	***to*** *finish* the test?

ADJECTIVE + *ENOUGH* + INFINITIVE			
(f)	Jimmy isn't	*old* ***enough***	***to*** *go* to school.
(g)	Are you	*hungry* ***enough***	***to*** *eat* three sandwiches?

Infinitives often follow expressions with ***enough***.
Enough comes in front of a noun.*
Enough follows an adjective.

****Enough*** can also follow a noun: *I don't have* ***money*** *enough to buy that car.* In everyday English, however, ***enough*** usually comes in front of a noun.

☐ **EXERCISE 32. TOO and ENOUGH + infinitive. (Chart 13-10)**

Directions: Combine the sentences.

PART I. Use ***too***.

1. We can't go swimming today. It's very cold.
   → *It's too cold (for us) to go swimming today.*
2. I couldn't finish my homework last night. I was very sleepy.
3. This jacket is very small. I can't wear it.
4. Mike couldn't go to his aunt's housewarming party. He was very busy.
5. I live far from school. I can't walk there.
6. Some movies are very violent. Children shouldn't watch them.

PART II. Use ***enough***.

7. I can't reach the top shelf. I'm not that tall.
   → *I'm not tall enough to reach the top shelf.*
8. I can't lift a horse. I'm not that strong.
9. It's not warm today. We can't go outside in shorts and sandals.
10. I didn't stay home and miss work. I wasn't really sick, but I didn't feel good all day.

☐ **EXERCISE 33. TOO and ENOUGH + infinitive. (Chart 13-10)**

Directions: Complete the sentences by choosing from the words in *italics*. Use ***too*** or ***enough*** + an infinitive.

1. *strong/lift* I'm not ___strong enough to lift___ a refrigerator.

2. *weak/lift* Most people are ___too weak to lift___ a refrigerator without help.

3. *busy/answer* I was _____ the phone. I let it keep ringing until the caller gave up.

4. *early/get* We got to the concert _____ good seats.

5. *full/hold*   My suitcase is _____

_____ any more clothes.

6. *large/hold*   My suitcase isn't _____

_____ all the

clothes I want to take on my trip.

7. *big/get*   Rex is _____ into

Bobo's doghouse.

8. *big/hold*   Julie's purse is _____ her dog

Pepper.

☐ **EXERCISE 34. TOO and ENOUGH + infinitive. (Chart 13-10)**
Directions: Complete the sentences with **too** and **enough**. Use Ø if nothing is needed.

1. Alan is ____too____ smart ____Ø____ to make that kind of mistake.

2. Alan is ____Ø____ smart ____enough____ to understand how to solve that

problem.

3. My pocket is _____ big _____ to hold my wallet. I always carry

my wallet there.

4. A horse is _____ big _____ for a person to lift.

5. I'm uncomfortable. This room is _____ hot _____. Why don't

you open the window?

6. That watch is _____ expensive _____. I can't afford it.

7. Are you _____ tall _____ to reach that book for me? The green

one on the top shelf. Thanks.

8. Ask John to move that box. He's _____ strong _____ to lift it.

9. I am _____ busy _____ to help you right now.

☐ **EXERCISE 35. TOO and ENOUGH + infinitive. (Chart 13-10)**
   Directions: Complete the following sentences. Use infinitives in the completions.

   1. I'm too short . . . .
   2. I'm not tall enough . . . .
   3. I'm not strong enough . . . .
   4. Last night I was too tired . . . .
   5. Yesterday I was too busy . . . .
   6. A Mercedes-Benz is too expensive . . . .
   7. I don't have enough money . . . .
   8. Yesterday I didn't have enough time . . . .
   9. A teenager is old enough . . . . but too young . . . .
   10. I know enough English . . . . but not enough . . . .

☐ **EXERCISE 36. Review: gerunds vs. infinitives. (Chapter 13)**
   Directions: Complete the sentences with the words in parentheses: gerund or infinitive.

   1. It's difficult for me *(remember)* ____to remember____ phone numbers.

   2. My cat is good at *(catch)* ____catching____ mice.

   3. I bought a newspaper *(look)* _____ at the ads for apartments for rent.

   4. Tourists like *(go)* _____ *(swim)* _____ in the warm
   ocean in Hawaii.

   5. I called my friend *(invite)* _____ her for dinner.

   6. Hillary talked about *(go)* _____ to graduate school.

   7. Sarosh found out what was happening by *(listen)* _____ carefully
   to everything that was said.

   8. Children, stop *(draw)* _____ pictures on the tablecloth!

   9. Professor Amani has a strong accent. It is difficult for his students *(understand)*
   _____ him. He needs *(improve)* _____
   his pronunciation if he wants *(be)* _____ a good lecturer. *(lecture)*
   _____ requires good communication skills.

   10. A: Hi! I'm home!

   B: Welcome back. Did you have a good trip?

   A: Yes, thanks. How's everything? How are my goldfish? I hope you didn't forget

   (feed) _____ them.

   B: Oh, my gosh!

11. Dan's goldfish died when he was away on a trip because his roommate forgot *(feed)*
_____ them. Dan is considering *(get)* _____ a new
roommate.

12. My friend Akihiko has goldfish in a pond in his garden. He enjoys *(feed)*
_____ them one by one with chopsticks.

13. Michelle Yin Yin Ko works sixteen hours a day *(earn)* _____
enough money *(take)* _____ care of her elderly parents and her
three children.

14. It takes care, patience, and a little luck *(take)* _____ a really good
photograph of wildlife.

15. No matter how wonderful a trip is, it's always good *(get)* _____ back
home and *(sleep)* _____ in one's own bed.

16. A: Quit *(stare)* _____ at the phone. Greg isn't going to call.

    B: I keep *(think)* _____ the phone will ring any second.

    A: I don't mean *(be)* _____ unsympathetic, but I think you'd better forget
       about Greg. It's over.

17. It's important to your health for you *(work)* _____ at a job you like. If
you hate *(go)* _____ to your job, you should seriously think about
(look) _____ for a different kind of job. The stress of *(do)*
_____ work you hate day in and day out can damage your health.

18. *(ask)* _____ others about themselves and their lives is one of the
secrets of *(get)* _____ along with other people. If you want
(make) _____ and *(keep)* _____ friends, it is
important *(be)* _____ sincerely interested in other people's lives.

19. I keep *(forget)* _____ *(call)* _____ my friend
Louise. I'd better write myself a note.

20. I like *(travel)* _____ to out-of-the-way places. I don't like *(go)*
_____ to usual tourist places when I'm on holiday.

21. Large bee colonies have 80,000 workers. These worker bees must visit fifty million
flowers *(make)* _____ one kilogram (2.2 pounds) of honey. It's no
wonder that "busy as a bee" is a common expression.

22. Exercise is good for you. Why don't you walk up the stairs instead of *(take)*

    _____ the elevator?

23. Stop *(crack)* _____ those nuts with your teeth! Here. Use a

    nutcracker. Do you want *(be)* _____ toothless by the time you're thirty?

24. Different cultures have different gestures. When North Americans meet someone, they

    usually offer a strong handshake and look the other person straight in the eye. In

    some countries, however, it is impolite *(shake)* _____ hands

    firmly, and *(look)* _____ a person in the eye is equally rude.

25. How close do you stand to another person when you are speaking? North Americans

    prefer *(stand)* _____ just a little less than an arm's length from

    someone. Many people in the Middle East and Latin America like *(move)*

    _____ in closer than that during a conversation.

26. *(smile)* _____ at another person is a universal, cross-cultural

    gesture. Everyone throughout the world understands the meaning of a smile.

□ **EXERCISE 37. Error analysis. (Chapter 13)**
    Directions: Correct the errors.

    1. Do you enjoy ~~to go~~ ^{going} to the zoo?

    2. I went to the store for getting some toothpaste.

    3. Did you go to shopping yesterday?

    4. I usually go to the cafeteria for to get a cup of coffee in the morning.

    5. Bob needed to went downtown yesterday.

    6. I cut the rope by a knife.

    7. I thanked him for drive me to the airport.

    8. Is difficult to learn a second language.

    9. It is important getting an education.

    10. Timmy isn't enough old too get married.

11. Do you want go to swimming tomorrow?

12. I went to the bank for cashing a check.

13. I was to sleepy to finish my homework last night.

14. Is easy this exercise to do.

15. Last night too tired no do my homework.

16. I've never gone to sailing, but I would like to.

17. Reading it is one of my hobby.

18. The man began to built a wall around his garden.

19. I like to travel because you learn too much about other countries and cultures.

20. Instead of settle down in one place, I'd like to travel around the world.

21. My grandmother likes to fishing.

22. Mary would like to has a big family.

☐ EXERCISE 38. Speaking. (Chapter 13)

Directions: Form small groups. Make a list of several topics that can be used for a one-minute impromptu speech. The topics should be gerund phrases. Exchange topics with another group. After your group has its topics, each member in turn should give a one-minute speech to the rest of the group. One group member should keep time. After all the speeches have been given, choose one speech from your group to be presented to the rest of the class. Examples of topics: *eating at fast-food restaurants, traveling to a foreign country, taking care of your health.*

☐ EXERCISE 39. Writing. (Chapter 13)

Directions: What do you do for fun and recreation in your spare time? Write about one or two spare-time activities that you enjoy. What do you do? Where? When? Why? Mention some interesting experiences. Try to get your readers interested in doing the same things in their free time. Do you enjoy exploring caves? Is playing tennis one of your passions? Have you ever gone skydiving? Maybe collecting ceramic horses is one of your hobbies. Have you ever gone waterskiing? Do you enjoy simple pleasures such as walking in a park? Do you go jogging for recreation? Maybe watching sports on television is your way of relaxing. It is important for all of us to have spare-time activities that we enjoy. What are yours?

Directions: Complete the sentences by writing the correct form of the verb in parentheses.

What is your most *(embarrass)* ___**embarrassing**___ experience? Let me tell you

what happened to my Uncle Ernesto when he *(go)* _____ to Norway for a

business meeting last year.

First, I must tell you about my uncle. He *(be)* _____ a businessman from

Buenos Aires, Argentina. He *(manufacture)* _____ a new kind of

computer compass for ships. Computer compasses *(make)* _____ by

many companies in the world, so my uncle *(have)* _____ a lot of

competition for his product. In order to sell his product, he *(need)* _____

(meet) _____ with companies that might want to buy it. He *(travel)*

_____ frequently to other countries.

Last year, he *(go)* _____ to Norway *(meet)* _____ with a

shipping company. It was his first trip to Scandinavia. My Uncle Ernesto *(speak)*

_____ Spanish, of course, and also *(know)* _____ a little

English, but he *(know, not)* _____ any Norwegian. While he

(stay) _____ in Norway, he *(have)* _____ a problem.

Uncle Ernesto *(stay)* _____ at a small hotel in Oslo. One

morning, while he *(get)* _____ ready to take a shower, he *(hear)*

_____ a knock at the door. He *(walk)* _____ to the

door, *(open)* _____ it, and *(find)* _____ no one. He *(take)*

_____ a step out of his room and *(look)* _____ down the

hall. He *(see)* _____ no one. So he *(turn)* _____ *(go)*

_____ back into his room, but the door *(close)* _____! It

(lock) _____, and he *(have, not)* _____

his key. This was a very big problem for my unfortunate uncle because he *(dress, not)*

_____ properly. In fact, he *(wear)* _____

31
32

nothing but a towel. Poor Uncle Ernesto! "What *(I, do)* _____?"

33

he asked himself.

    Instead of *(stand)* _____ in the hallway with only a towel, he

34

(decide) _____ *(get)* _____ help. So he *(start)*

35   36

_____ *(walk)* _____ down the hall toward the

37   38

elevator. He thought about *(knock)* _____ on someone else's door

39

(ask) _____ for help, but decided it was better *(ask)* _____

40   41

the hotel personnel. He hoped the elevator would be empty.

    When he *(reach)* _____ the elevator, he *(push)* _____

42   43

the down button and *(wait)* _____ . When it *(come)* _____ ,

44   45

Uncle Ernesto *(take)* _____ a deep breath and *(get)* _____ in

46   47

even though the elevator wasn't empty. The other people in the elevator *(surprise)*

_____ when they *(see)* _____ a man who *(wrap)*

48   49

_____ in a towel.

50

    Uncle Ernesto *(think)* _____ about *(try)* _____

51   52

(explain) _____ his problem, but unfortunately he *(know, not)*

53

_____ any Norwegian. He said, in English, "Door. Locked. No

54

key." A businessman in the elevator *(nod)* _____ , but he *(smile, not)*

55

_____ . Another man *(look)* _____ at Uncle

56   57

Ernesto and *(smile)* _____ broadly.

58

    After an eternity, the elevator *(reach)* _____ the ground floor.

59

Uncle Ernesto *(walk)* _____ straight to the front desk and *(look)*

60

_____ at the hotel manager helplessly. The hotel manager

61

(have to understand, not) _____
                                                      62

any language *(figure)* _____ out the problem. My uncle
                                    63

(have to say, not) _____ a word. The manager
                                        64

(grab) _____ a key, *(take)* _____ my uncle by the
                    65   66

elbow, and *(lead)* _____ him back to the nearest elevator.
                              67

   My uncle *(embarrass, still)* _____ about
                                                            68

this incident. But he *(laugh)* _____ a lot when he *(tell)* _____
                                        69   70

the story.

☐ **EXERCISE 41. Review of verb forms: writing. (Chapters 1 → 13)**
   Directions: Write a composition about one of the most embarrassing experiences you have
   had in your life.

CHAPTER 14

Noun Clauses

CONTENTS

14-1 NOUN CLAUSES: INTRODUCTION

S V O
(a) I know │ *his address* │.
     (noun phrase)
	Verbs are often followed by objects. The object is usually a noun phrase.★
	In (a): *his address* is a noun phrase;
	         his address is the object of the verb *know*.

S V O
(b) I know │ *where he lives* │.
     (noun clause)
	Some verbs can be followed by noun clauses.★
	In (b): *where he lives* is a noun clause;
	         where he lives is the object of the verb *know*.

O **S V S V** (c) I know *where he lives*.	A noun clause has its own subject and verb. In (c): *he* is the subject of the noun clause; *lives* is the verb of the noun clause.
(d) I know **where my book is**. (noun clause)	A noun clause can begin with a question word. (See Chart 14-2.)
(e) I don't know **if Ed is married**. (noun clause)	A noun clause can begin with **if** or **whether**. (See Chart 14-4, p. 409.)
(f) I know **that the world is round**. (noun clause)	A noun clause can begin with **that**. (See Chart 14-5, p. 414.)

★A **phrase** is a group of related words. It does not contain a subject and a verb.
  A **clause** is a group of related words. It contains a subject and a verb.

14-2 NOUN CLAUSES THAT BEGIN WITH A QUESTION WORD

These question words can be used to introduce a noun clause: *when, where, why, how, who, whom, what, which, whose*.

INFORMATION QUESTION	NOUN CLAUSE	Notice in the examples:
(a) Where *does he live?* (c) When *did they leave?* (e) What *did she say?* (g) Why *is Tom* absent?	(b) I don't know *where **he lives**.* (d) Do you know *when **they left**?** (f) Please tell me *what **she said**.* (h) I wonder *why **Tom is** absent.*	Usual question word order is NOT used in a noun clause. INCORRECT: *I know where does he live.* CORRECT: *I know where he lives.*
(i) ***Who came** to class?* (k) ***What happened?***	(j) I don't know ***who came** to class.* (l) Tell me ***what happened**.*	In (i) and (j): Question word order and noun clause word order are the same when the question word is used as a subject.

*A question mark is used at the end of this noun clause because the main subject and the verb of the sentence *(Do you know)* are in question word order.

     Example: *Do you know when they left?*

Do you know asks a question; *when they left* is a noun clause.

☐ **EXERCISE 1. Information questions and noun clauses. (Charts 5-2 and 14-2)**
    Directions: Are the given words (1) an information question or (2) a noun clause?
- Add "I don't know" and a period to make a sentence with a noun clause. OR
- Add a capital letter and a question mark if the given words are a question.

1. _____I don't know_____ why he left. *(noun clause)*

2. _____ W~~w~~hy did he leave? *(information question)*

3. _____ where she is living

4. _____ where is she living

5. _____ where did Paul go

6. _____ where Paul went

7. _____ what time the movie begins

8. _____ what time does the movie begin

9. _____ how old is Kate

10. _____ why Yoko is angry

11. _____ what happened

12. _____ who came to the party

13. _____ who(m) did you see at the party

14. _____ what did Sue say

15. _____ what Sue is talking about

☐ **EXERCISE 2. Noun clauses that begin with a question word. (Chart 14-2)**

Directions: Complete the dialogues by changing Speaker A's questions to noun clauses.

1. A: Where does Jim go to school?

   B: I don't know ___*where Jim goes*___ to school.

2. A: Where did Natasha go yesterday?

   B: I don't know. Do you know _____ yesterday?

3. A: Why is Maria laughing?

   B: I don't know. Does anybody know _____ ?

4. A: Why is fire hot?

   B: I don't know _____ hot.

5. A: How much does a new Honda cost?

   B: Peter can tell you _____ .

6. A: Why is Mike always late?

   B: Don't ask me. I don't understand _____ late.

7. A: How long do birds live?

   B: I don't know _____ .

8. A: When was the first wheel invented?

   B: I don't know. Do you know

   _____

   _____

   _____ ?

9. A: How many hours does a
      light bulb burn?

   B: I don't know exactly _____

   _____ .

10. A: Where did Emily buy her computer?

    B: I don't know _____ her computer.

11. A: Who lives next door to Kate?

    B: I don't know _____ next door to Kate.

12. A: Who(m) did Julie talk to?

    B: I don't know _____ to.

□ **EXERCISE 3. Information questions and noun clauses. (Charts 5-2 and 14-2)**
  Directions: Ask and answer questions. Only the leader's book is open. Work as a class or in groups.
  Speaker A: Ask a question, using the cue.
  Speaker B: Answer the question, beginning with either *"I don't know . . ."* OR *"I think . . ."* followed by a noun clause.

  Example: Ask (. . .) where (. . .) lives.
  LEADER TO A: Marco, ask Ingrid where Mustafa lives.
    SPEAKER A: Ingrid, where does Mustafa live?
    SPEAKER B: I don't know where Mustafa lives. OR I think that Mustafa lives in Reed Hall.

  1. Ask (. . .) where (. . .) ate breakfast this morning.
  2. Ask (. . .) what (. . .)'s favorite color is.
  3. Ask (. . .) when (. . .) got up this morning.
  4. Ask (. . .) why (. . .) isn't sitting in his/her usual seat today.
  5. Ask (. . .) how (. . .) got to class today.
  6. Ask (. . .) what kind of watch (. . .) has.
  7. Ask (. . .) why (. . .) didn't come to class yesterday.
  8. Ask (. . .) where (. . .) went after class yesterday.

□ **EXERCISE 4. Information questions and noun clauses. (Charts 5-2 and 14-2)**
  Directions: Complete the sentences with the words in parentheses.

  1. A: Where *(Susan, eat)* ___did Susan eat___ lunch yesterday?

     B: I don't know where *(she, eat)* ___she ate___ lunch yesterday.

  2. A: Do you know where *(Jason, work)* _____ ?

     B: Who?

     A: Jason. Where *(he, work)* _____ ?

     B: I don't know.

  3. A: Excuse me.

     B: Yes. How can I help you?

     A: How much *(that camera, cost)* _____ ?

     B: You want to know how much *(this camera, cost)* _____ ,

        is that right?

     A: No, not that one. The one next to it.

  4. A: How far *(you, can run)* _____ without stopping?

     B: I have no idea. I don't know how far *(I, can run)* _____

        without stopping. I've never tried.

5. A: Where *(you, see)* _____ the ad for the computer sale last week?

   B: I don't remember where *(I, see)* _____ it. One of the local papers, I think.

6. A: Ann was out late last night, wasn't she? When *(she, get)* _____ in?

   B: Why do you want to know what time *(she, get)* _____ home?

   A: Just curious.

7. A: What time *(it, is)* _____ ?

   B: I don't know. I'll ask Sara. Sara, do you know what time *(it, is)* _____ ?

   C: Almost four-thirty.

8. A: *(who, invent)* _____ the first refrigerator?

   B: I don't know *(who, invent)* _____ the first refrigerator. Do you?

9. A: Mom, why *(some people, be)* _____ cruel to other people?

   B: Honey, I don't really understand why *(some people, be)* _____ cruel to others. It's difficult to explain.

10. A: I don't care about the future. All I care about is today.

    B: Oh? Well, answer this question for me. Where *(you, spend)* _____ _____ the rest of your life?

    A: What do you mean?

    B: I mean it's important to pay attention to the future. That's where *(you, spend)* _____ the rest of your life.

14-3 NOUN CLAUSES WITH *WHO, WHAT, WHOSE* + *BE*

QUESTION	NOUN CLAUSE	
(a) Who **is** **that boy**? (v s)	(b) Tell me *who* **that boy** **is**. (s v)	A noun or pronoun that follows main verb *be* in a question comes in front of *be* in a noun clause, as in (b) and (d).
(c) Whose pen **is** **this**? (v s)	(d) Tell me *whose pen* **this** **is**. (s v)	
(e) **Who** **is** in the office? (s v)	(f) Tell me **who** **is** in the office. (s v)	A prepositional phrase (e.g., *in the office*) does not come in front of *be* in a noun clause, as in (f) and (h).
(g) **Whose pen** **is** on the desk? (s v)	(h) Tell me **whose pen** **is** on the desk. (s v)	

Directions: <u>Underline</u> and identify the subject and verb of Speaker A's question. Complete Speaker B's noun clause.

1. A: Who <u>is</u> <u>that woman</u>?
        V   S

  B: I don't know ____who that woman is____.

2. A: <u>Who</u> <u>is</u> on the phone?
     S V

  B: I don't know ____who is on the phone____.

3. A: What is a crow?

  B: I don't know _____.

4. A: What is in that bag?

  B: I don't know _____.

5. A: Whose cat is in the driveway?

  B: I don't know _____.

6. A: Whose car is that?

  B: I don't know _____.

7. A: What is a violin?

  B: I don't know _____.

  C: It's a musical instrument that has strings.

8. A: Who is in the doctor's office?

  B: I don't know _____.

9. A: Whose hammer is this?

  B: I don't know _____. Hey, Hank, do you know

  _____?

  C: It's Ralph's.

10. A: Who is Bob's doctor?

  B: I don't know _____

  _____.

11. A: What's at the end of a rainbow?

  B: What did you say, Susie?

  A: I want to know _____

  _____.

□ EXERCISE 6. Noun clauses. (Charts 14-2 and 14-3)

Directions: Work in pairs.

Speaker A: Read the question. Your book is open.

Speaker B: Change the question to a noun clause. Begin your reponse with *"I don't know . . . ."* Your book is closed.

Example: Where does (. . .) live?

SPEAKER A *(book open):* Where does Anita live?

SPEAKER B *(book closed):* I don't know where Anita lives.

Switch roles.

1. Where did (. . .) go yesterday?
2. How old is (. . .)?
3. Where does (. . .) eat lunch?
4. What is (. . .)'s last name?
5. What time does (. . .) usually get up?
6. When did (. . .) get home last night?
7. What time did (. . .) go to bed last night?
8. Who is (. . .)'s best friend?
9. Who did (. . .) call last night?
10. How long has (. . .) been living here?
11. Who wrote *(Tales of the South Pacific)*?
12. What happened in Alaska yesterday?
13. What did (. . .) do yesterday?
14. Who is that girl?
15. Who are those people?
16. What kind of tree is that?
17. Whose (backpack) is that?
18. Whose (gloves) are those?

□ EXERCISE 7. Information questions and noun clauses. (Charts 5-2, 14-2, and 14-3)

Directions: Ask information questions and respond using noun clauses.

Speaker A: Using the given question word, ask any question that you are sure Speaker B cannot answer. (You don't have to know the answer to the question.)

Speaker B: Respond to the question by saying *"I don't know . . . ."* followed by a noun clause. Then you can guess at an answer if you wish.

Example: when

SPEAKER A: When was the first book printed?

SPEAKER B: I don't know when the first book was printed. Probably three or four hundred years ago.

1. where
2. who
3. how far
4. what kind
5. what time
6. whose
7. when
8. why
9. what

14-4 NOUN CLAUSES THAT BEGIN WITH *IF* OR *WHETHER*

YES/NO QUESTION	NOUN CLAUSE	
(a) Is Eric at home? (c) Does the bus stop here? (e) Did Alice go to Chicago?	(b) I don't know *if Eric is at home*. (d) Do you know *if the bus stops here?* (f) I wonder *if Alice went to Chicago*.	When a yes/no question is changed to a noun clause, *if* is usually used to introduce the clause.*
(g) I don't know *if Eric is at home or not*.		When *if* introduces a noun clause, the expression *or not* sometimes comes at the end of the clause, as in (g).
(h) I don't know *whether* Eric is at home (or not).		In (h): *whether* has the same meaning as *if*.

*See Chart 14-11, p. 425, for the use of *if* with *ask* in reported speech.

Directions: Change the yes/no question to a noun clause.

1. YES/NO QUESTION: Is Susan here today?

   NOUN CLAUSE: Can you tell me ___if (whether) Susan is here today___ ?

2. YES/NO QUESTION: Will Mr. Pips be at the meeting?

   NOUN CLAUSE: Do you know _____ ?

3. YES/NO QUESTION: Did Paulo go to work yesterday?

   NOUN CLAUSE: I wonder _____ .

4. YES/NO QUESTION: Is Barcelona a coastal town?

   NOUN CLAUSE: I can't remember _____ .

5. YES/NO QUESTION: Do you still have Yung Soo's address?

   NOUN CLAUSE: I don't know _____ .

□ **EXERCISE 9. Noun clauses that begin with IF or WHETHER. (Chart 14-4)**

Directions: Complete the dialogues by completing the noun clauses. Use *if* to introduce the noun clause.

1. A: Are you tired?

   B: Why do you want to know ___if I am___ tired?

   A: You look tired. I'm worried about you.

2. A: Are you going to be in your office later today?

   B: What? Sorry. I didn't hear you.

   A: I need to know _____ in your office later

   today.

3. A: Do all birds have feathers?

   B: Well, I don't really know for sure _____

   feathers, but I suppose they do.

4. A: Did Rosa take my dictionary off my desk?

   B: Who?

   A: Rosa. I want to know _____ my dictionary off my desk.

5. A: Can Uncle Pete babysit tonight?

   B: Sorry. I wasn't listening. I was thinking about something else.

   A: Have you talked to Uncle Pete? We need to know _____

   _____ tonight.

6. A: Does Al have a flashlight in his car?

   B: I'll ask him. Hey, Al! Al! Fred wants to know _____ a

      flashlight in your car.

   C: Yeah, I do. Why?

7. A: Should I take my umbrella?

   B: How am I supposed to know _____ your

      umbrella? I'm not a weather forecaster.

   A: You're kind of grumpy today, aren't you?

☐ EXERCISE 10. Noun clauses. (Charts 14-2 → 14-4)
   Directions: Change the questions to noun clauses.

1. *Will it rain tomorrow?* I wonder . . . *if it will rain tomorrow.*

2. *What time is it?* I wonder . . . .

3. *What is an amphibian?* Do you know . . . .

4. *Is a frog an amphibian?* Can you tell me . . . .

5. *What's on TV tonight?* I wonder . . . .

6. *What is the speed of sound?* Do you know . . . .

7. *Does sound travel faster than light?* Do you know . . . .

8. *Are dogs colorblind?* Do you know . . . .

9. *Why is the sky blue?* Annie wants to know . . . .

10. *Do insects have ears?* Annie also wants to know . . . .

11. *Have beings from outer space ever visited the earth?*

    I wonder . . . .

12. *How do dolphins communicate with each other?*

    Do scientists know . . . .

13. *Can people communicate with dolphins?*

    I wonder . . . .

□ **EXERCISE 11. Noun clauses. (Charts 14-2 → 14-4)**

Directions: Practice using noun clauses.
Speaker A: Ask the given question. Your book is open.
Speaker B: Restate A's question, beginning with "*You want to know . . . .*" and ask if that is right. Your book is closed.
Speaker A: Tell B if that is right.
Speaker B: Answer the question.

Example: Is (. . .) at the bank?
SPEAKER A *(book open):* Is Gina at the bank?
SPEAKER B *(book closed):* You want to know if Gina is at the bank. Is that right?
SPEAKER A *(book open):* Yes, that's right.
SPEAKER B *(book closed):* I don't know if Gina is at the bank. OR
                            No, Gina isn't at the bank. She's here in class. OR
                            Yes, she is. Gina is at the bank.

Switch roles.

1. Does (. . .) have a bicycle?
2. What time does class end?
3. Can (. . .) sing?
4. What does "delicious" mean?
5. Whose books are those?
6. Is (. . .) married?
7. Where did (. . .) go last night?
8. Does (. . .) have a job?
9. Who is that person?
10. Is there a pay phone in this building?
11. Why is (. . .) absent today?
12. Whose pen is that?
13. How much does a new refrigerator cost?
14. Does (. . .) speak *(name of a language)*?
15. What kind of wristwatch does (. . .) have?
16. Is (. . .) planning to take another English course?
17. Who is the mayor of *(name this city/town)*?
18. Who is in charge of the English classes at this school?

□ **EXERCISE 12. Noun clauses. (Charts 14-2 → 14-4)**

Directions: Answer the questions using the words in **boldface**. Give two or three different answers. Work in groups or as a class.

Example: What do you know?
           where
           → SPEAKER A: I know ***where*** Madagascar is located.
             SPEAKER B: I know ***where*** (. . .)'s dictionary is.
             SPEAKER C: I know ***where*** my parents got married.

QUESTION 1: What do you know?
   a. ***where***
   b. ***what***
   c. ***why***
   d. ***who***
   e. ***whose***

QUESTION 2: What do you NOT know?
   a. ***where***
   b. ***if***
   c. ***why***
   d. ***who***

QUESTION 3: What do you want to know?
    a. *if*
    b. *when*
    c. *what*
    d. *who*

QUESTION 4: What do you wonder?
    a. *why*
    b. *if*
    c. *what*
    d. *who*
    e. *how*
    f. *whether*

☐ EXERCISE 13. Noun clauses. (Charts 14-1 → 14-4)

Directions: What are some of the things you wonder about? Consider the given topics. Create sentences using "*I wonder . . . (**why, when, how, if, whether,** etc.)*." Work in groups or as a class.

Example: fish

    → *I wonder how many fish there are in the world.*
    I wonder how many different kinds of fish there are in the world.
    I wonder how long fish have lived on earth.
    I wonder whether fish can communicate with each other.
    I wonder if fish in fish tanks are happy.
    Etc.

1. birds
2. the earth
3. *(name of a person you know)*
4. events in the future
5. electricity
6. dinosaurs
7. *(topic of your own choosing)*

☐ EXERCISE 14. Noun clauses and questions. (Charts 5-2 and 14-1 → 14-4)

Directions: Create questions and answer them using noun clauses. Work in pairs.
Speaker A: Ask a question. Use the suggestions below. Try to ask a question that Speaker B can't answer.
Speaker B: Answer the question if you can. If you can't, say "*I don't know . . .*" followed by a noun clause. Then you can guess at the answer if you wish.

Example: location of X*

SPEAKER A: Where is Mr. Fong's briefcase right now?
SPEAKER B: Under his desk. OR I don't know where his briefcase is. I suppose he left it at home today.

Switch roles.

1. location of X
2. cost of X
3. owner of X
4. reason for X
5. person who did X
6. country X is from
7. meaning of X
8. time of X
9. amount of X
10. year that X happened
11. type of X
12. distance from X to Y

———————

*"X" simply indicates that the questioner should supply her/his own ideas.

14-5 NOUN CLAUSES THAT BEGIN WITH *THAT*

s **v** **o** (a) I think *that Mr. Jones is a good teacher.* (b) I hope *that you can come to the game.* (c) Mary realizes *that she should study harder.* (d) I dreamed *that I was on the top of a mountain.*	A noun clause can be introduced by the word ***that***. In (a): *that Mr. Jones is a good teacher* is a noun clause. It is the object of the verb *think*. *That*-clauses are frequently used as the objects of verbs that express mental activity. (See the list below.)
(e) *I think **that** Mr. Jones is a good teacher.* (f) *I think Ø Mr. Jones is a good teacher.*	The word ***that*** is often omitted, especially in speaking. (e) and (f) have the same meaning.

COMMON VERBS FOLLOWED BY *THAT*-CLAUSES★

assume that	*feel that*	*learn that*	*read that*
believe that	*hear that*	*notice that*	*say that*
discover that	*hope that*	*predict that*	*suppose that*
dream that	*know that*	*prove that*	*think that*

★The verbs in the above list are those that are emphasized in the exercises. Some other common verbs that can be followed by *that*-clauses are:

agree that	*fear that*	*imagine that*	*realize that*	*reveal that*
conclude that	*figure out that*	*indicate that*	*recall that*	*show that*
decide that	*find out that*	*observe that*	*recognize that*	*suspect that*
demonstrate that	*forget that*	*presume that*	*regret that*	*teach that*
doubt that	*guess that*	*pretend that*	*remember that*	*understand that*

☐ **EXERCISE 15. THAT-clauses. (Chart 14-5)**

Directions: Add the word ***that*** in the appropriate place to mark the beginning of a noun clause.

1. I think ^*that* most people have kind hearts.

2. Last night I dreamed I was at my aunt's house.

3. I believe we need to protect endangered species of animals.

4. I know Matt walks to school every day. I assume he doesn't have a bicycle.

5. Did you notice Ji Ming wasn't in class yesterday? I hope he's okay.

6. I trust Linda. I believe what she said. I believe she told the truth.

7. In yesterday's newspaper, I read half of the people in the world have never used a telephone of any kind in their entire lives.

8. The population of New York City is extraordinarily diverse. Did you know forty percent of the people who live in New York City are foreign born? Many people believe these immigrants are revitalizing the city.

9. A: Do you think a monster really exists in Loch Ness in Scotland?

B: I don't know. Look at this story in the newspaper. It says some investigators say they can prove the Loch Ness Monster exists.

A: You shouldn't always believe what you read in the newspapers.

☐ EXERCISE 16. THAT-clauses. (Chart 14-5)
   Directions: Complete the sentences with your own words. Omit the word **that** if you wish.

1. I believe that . . . .
2. I assume that . . . .
3. Do you realize that . . . ?
4. I can prove that . . . .
5. I predict that . . . .
6. I've heard that . . . .
7. I suppose that . . . .
8. Have you ever noticed that . . . ?
9. Last night I dreamed that . . . .
10. Do you think that . . . ?
11. I've discovered that . . . .
12. Did you know that . . . ?

14-6 OTHER USES OF *THAT*-CLAUSES

(a) **I'm sure that** the bus stops here. (b) **I'm glad that** you're feeling better today. (c) **I'm sorry that** I missed class yesterday. (d) I **was disappointed that** the peace conference failed.	*That*-clauses can follow certain expressions with **be** + *adjective* or **be** + *past participle*. The word **that** can be omitted with no change in meaning: *I'm sure Ø the bus stops here.*

(e) **It is true that** the world is round.
 (f) **It is a fact that** the world is round.
	Two common expressions followed by *that*-clauses are:
	   It is true (that) . . . .
	   It is a fact (that) . . . .

COMMON EXPRESSIONS FOLLOWED BY *THAT*-CLAUSES*

be afraid that	*be disappointed that*	*be sorry that*	*It is true that*
be aware that	*be glad that*	*be sure that*	*It is a fact that*
be certain that	*be happy that*	*be surprised that*	
be convinced that	*be pleased that*	*be worried that*	

*The above list contains expressions emphasized in the exercises. Some other common expressions with **be** that are frequently followed by *that*-clauses are:

be amazed that	*be delighted that*	*be impressed that*	*be sad that*
be angry that	*be fortunate that*	*be lucky that*	*be shocked that*
be ashamed that	*be furious that*	*be positive that*	*be terrified that*
be astounded that	*be horrified that*	*be proud that*	*be thrilled that*

Directions: Add the word ***that*** wherever possible.

1. A: Welcome. We're glad ^that^ you could come.

    B: Thank you. I'm happy to be here.

2. A: Thank you so much for your gift.

    B: I'm so pleased you like it.

3. A: I wonder why Tom was promoted to general manager instead of Ann.

    B: So do I. I'm surprised Ann didn't get the job. I think she is more qualified.

4. A: Are you afraid another nuclear disaster like the one at Chernobyl might occur?

    B: Yes. I'm convinced it can happen again.

5. A: Are you aware you have to pass the English test to get into the university?

    B: Yes, but I'm not worried about it. I'm certain I'll do well on it.

6. A: I'm disappointed my son quit his job. I realize young people must follow their own
       paths, but I'm worried my son's path isn't going to lead him to a rewarding career.

    B: Don't forget he's grown up now and responsible for himself. I think he'll be fine.
       You shouldn't worry about him. He knows what he's doing.

7. It is a fact some ancient Egyptian cats wore earrings.

8. Are you aware dinosaurs lived on earth for one hundred and twenty-five million
    (125,000,000) years? Is it true human beings have lived on earth for only four million
    (4,000,000) years?

9. A: Is it a fact blue whales are the largest creatures on earth?

    B: Yes. In fact, I believe they are the largest creatures that have ever lived on earth.

□ EXERCISE 18. THAT-clauses. (Charts 14-5 and 14-6)

Directions: Read each dialogue. Then use the expressions in parentheses to explain what
the people are talking about.

DIALOGUE 1.   ALICIA: I really like my English teacher.
              BONNIE: Great! That's wonderful. It's important to have a good English
                        teacher.

        (think that, be delighted that)

        → *Alicia thinks that her English teacher is very good.*
         Bonnie is delighted that Alicia likes her English teacher.
         Bonnie thinks that it's important to have a good English teacher.

DIALOGUE 2.   MRS. DAY: How do you feel, honey? You might have the flu.

                  BOBBY: I'm okay, Mom. Honest. I don't have the flu.

(be worried that, be sure that)

DIALOGUE 3.   KIM: Did you really fail your chemistry course? How is that possible?

                 TINA: I didn't study hard enough. I was too busy having fun with my friends. I feel terrible about it.

(be surprised that, be disappointed that)

DIALOGUE 4.   DAVID: Mike! Hello! It's nice to see you.

                 MIKE: It's nice to be here. Thank you for inviting me.

(be glad/happy/pleased that)

DIALOGUE 5.   FRED: Susan has left. Look. Her closet is empty. Her suitcases are gone. She won't be back. I just know it!

                ERICA: She'll be back.

(be afraid that, be upset that, be sure that)

DIALOGUE 6.   JOHN: I heard you were in jail. I couldn't believe it!

                   ED: Neither could I! I was arrested for robbing a house on my block. Can you believe that? It was a case of mistaken identity. I didn't have to stay in jail long.

(be shocked that, be relieved that)

☐ **EXERCISE 19. THAT-clauses. (Charts 14-5 and 14-6)**

Directions: Complete the sentences. Use any appropriate verb form in the *that*-clause. (Notice the various verb forms used in the example.) Omit *that* if you wish.

Example: I'm glad that . . . .

     → *the weather is nice today.*
       Sam is going to finish school.
       I can speak English.

1. I'm pleased that . . . .
2. I'm sure that . . . .
3. I'm surprised that . . . .
4. Are you certain that . . . ?
5. I'm very happy that . . . .
6. I'm sorry that . . . .
7. I'm not sorry that . . . .
8. I'm afraid that . . . .*
9. Are you aware that . . . ?
10. I'm disappointed that . . . .
11. I'm convinced that . . . .
12. Is it true that . . . .
13. It is a fact that . . . .
14. It's not true that . . . .

---

*Sometimes **be afraid** expresses fear:

   I don't want to go near that dog. I'm afraid that it will bite me.

Sometimes **be afraid** expresses polite regret:

   I'm afraid you have the wrong number. = I'm sorry, but I think you have the wrong number.
   I'm afraid I can't come to your party. = I'm sorry, but I can't come to your party.

☐ **EXERCISE 20. THAT-clauses.** (Charts 14-5 and 14-6)

Directions: What are your views on the following topics? Introduce your opinion with an expression from the given list, then state your opinion in a *that*-clause. Discuss your opinions in groups, as a class, or in writing.

Example: guns

→ *I believe that ordinary people shouldn't have guns in their homes.*

I think anyone should be able to have any kind of gun.

I have concluded that countries in which it is easy to get a gun have a higher rate of murder than other countries do.

am certain that	believe that	hope that
am convinced that	can prove that	predict that
am sure that	have concluded that	think that

1. smoking (cigarettes, cigars, pipes)
2. a controversy at your school (perhaps something that has been on the front pages of a student newspaper)
3. a recent political event in the world (something that has been on the front pages of the newspaper)
4. the importance of protecting the environment
5. freedom of the press vs. government-controlled news
6. solutions to world hunger

14-7 SUBSTITUTING *SO* FOR A *THAT*-CLAUSE IN CONVERSATIONAL RESPONSES

(a) A: Is Ana from Peru?
    B: **I think so.** (*so = that Ana is from Peru*)
(b) A: Does Judy live in Dallas?
    B: **I believe so.** (*so = that Judy lives in Dallas*)
(c) A: Did you pass the test?
    B: **I hope so.** (*so = that I passed the test*)
	Think, believe, and ***hope*** are frequently followed by ***so*** in conversational English in response to a yes/no question. They are alternatives to *yes, no,* or *I don't know.*
	So replaces a *that*-clause.
	INCORRECT: I think so that Ana is from Peru.

(d) A: Is Jack married?
    B: **I *don't* think *so.* / I *don't* believe *so.***
	Negative usage of ***think so*** and ***believe so:***
	    do not think so / do not believe so

(e) A: Did you fail the test? B: **I hope *not.***	Negative usage of ***hope*** in conversational responses: *hope not.* In (e): *I hope not = I hope I didn't fail the test.* *INCORRECT: I don't hope so.*

(f) A: Do you want to come with us?
    B: Oh, I don't know. **I guess *so.***
	Other common conversational responses:
	    I guess so. I guess not.
	    I suppose so. I suppose not.

□ EXERCISE 21. Substituting SO for a THAT-clause. (Chart 14-7)

Directions: Restate Speaker B's answers to Speaker A's questions by using a *that*-clause.

1. A: Is Karen going to be home tonight?
   B: I think so. → *I think that Karen is going to be home tonight.*

2. A: Are we going to have a test
   in grammar tomorrow?
   B: I don't believe so.

3. A: Will Margo be at the conference
   in March?
   B: I hope so.

4. A: Can cats swim?
   B: I believe so.

5. A: Do gorillas have tails?
   B: I don't think so.

6. A: Will Janet be at Omar's wedding?
   B: I suppose so.

7. A: Will your flight be canceled because
   of the bad weather in Copenhagen?
   B: I hope not.

□ EXERCISE 22. Substituting SO for a THAT-clause. (Chart 14-7)

Directions: Answer the questions by using **think so** or **believe so** if you are not sure, or **yes** or **no** if you are sure. Work in pairs or as a class.

Example:

SPEAKER A *(book open):*   Does this book have more than 500 pages?
SPEAKER B: *(book closed):* I think / believe so. OR
                 I don't think / don't believe so. OR
                 Yes, it does. / No, it doesn't.

1. Are we going to have a grammar quiz tomorrow?
2. Do spiders have noses?
3. Do spiders have eyes?
4. Is there a fire extinguisher in this building?
5. Is Toronto farther north than New York City?
6. Does the word "patient" have more than one meaning?
7. Don't look at your watch. Is it *(supply a time)* yet?
8. Is next Tuesday the *(supply a date)*?

(Switch roles if working in pairs.)

9. Does the word "dozen" have more than one meaning?
10. Is your left foot bigger than your right foot?
11. Do gorillas eat meat?
12. Is Bangkok farther from the equator than Mexico City?
13. Can I buy a window fan at *(name of a local store)*?
14. Do any English words begin with the letter "x"?
15. Do you know what a noun clause is?
16. Is (. . .) getting married soon?

14-8 QUOTED SPEECH

Sometimes we want to quote a speaker's words—to write a speaker's exact words. Exact quotations are used in many kinds of writing, such as newspaper articles, stories and novels, and academic papers. When we quote a speaker's words, we use quotation marks.

(a) **SPEAKERS' EXACT WORDS** Jane: Cats are fun to watch. Mike: Yes, I agree. They're graceful and playful. Do you own a cat?	(b) **QUOTING THE SPEAKERS' WORDS** Jane said, **"**Cats are fun to watch.**"** Mike said, **"Y**es, I agree. They're graceful and playful. Do you own a cat?**"**

(c) **HOW TO WRITE QUOTATIONS**
1. Add a comma after *said.* * ⟶ Jane said,
2. Add quotation marks. ** ⟶ Jane said, "
3. Capitalize the first word of the quotation. ⟶ Jane said, "Cats
4. Write the quotation. Add a final period. ⟶ Jane said, "Cats are fun to watch.
5. Add quotation marks **after** the period. ⟶ Jane said, "Cats are fun to watch."

(d) Mike said, "Yes, I agree. They're graceful and playful. Do you own a cat?" (e) *INCORRECT: Mike said, "Yes, I agree." "They're graceful and playful." "Do you own a cat?"*	When there are two (or more) sentences in a quotation, put the quotation marks at the beginning and end of the whole quote, as in (d). Do not put quotation marks around each sentence. As with a period, put the quotation marks after a question mark at the end of a quote.
(f) "Cats are fun to watch," Jane said.	In (f): Notice that a comma (not a period) is used at the end of the quoted **sentence** when *Jane said* comes after the quote.
(g) "Do you own a cat?" Mike asked.	In (g): Notice that a question mark (not a comma) is used at the end of the quoted **question**.

*Other common verbs besides *say* that introduce questions: *admit, announce, answer, ask, complain, explain, inquire, report, reply, shout, state, write.*

**Quotation marks are called "inverted commas" in British English.

□ **EXERCISE 23. Quoted speech. (Chart 14-8)**

Directions: Write sentences in which you quote the speaker's exact words. Use ***said*** or ***asked***. Punctuate carefully.

1. ANN: My sister is a student.
   → Ann said, "My sister is a student." OR "My sister is a student," Ann said.

2. ANN: Is your brother a student?

3. RITA: We're hungry.

4. RITA: We're hungry. Are you hungry too?***

***Rita said can come
   (1) at the beginning of the quote: ***Rita said,*** *"I'm tired. I'm going to bed."*
   (2) in the middle of the quote: *"I'm tired,"* ***Rita said.*** *"I'm going to bed."*
   (3) at the end of the quote: *"I'm tired. I'm going to bed,"* ***Rita said.***

5. RITA: We're hungry. Are you hungry too? Let's eat.

6. JOHN F. KENNEDY: Ask not what your country can do for you. Ask what you can do
for your country.

7. THE FOX: I'm going to eat you.*
   THE RABBIT: You have to catch me first!

□ **EXERCISE 24. Quoted speech. (Chart 14-8)**
   Directions: Practice punctuating quoted speech. Notice that a new paragraph signals a change in speakers.

   Both of your parents are deaf, aren't they I asked Roberto.

   Yes, they are he replied

   I'm looking for someone who knows sign language I said. Do you know sign language I asked.

   He said of course I do. I've been using sign language with my parents since I was a baby. It's a beautiful and expressive language. I often prefer it to spoken language.

   A deaf student is going to visit our class next Monday. Could you interpret for her I asked.

   I'd be delighted to he answered. I'm looking forward to meeting her. Can you tell me why she is coming?

   She's interested in seeing what we do in our English classes I said.

   _____

   *In fables, animals are frequently given the ability to speak.

☐ EXERCISE 25. Quoted speech. (Chart 14-8)

Directions: Practice writing quoted speech. Only the teacher's book is open.

1. Write exactly what I say. Identify that I said it. Punctuate carefully.

   a. (Say one short sentence—e.g., *The weather is nice today.*)

   b. (Say two short sentences—e.g., *The weather is nice today. It's warm.*)

   c. (Say two short sentences and one question—e.g., *The weather is nice today. It's warm. Do you like warm weather?*)

2. Write exactly what your classmates say.

   a. (. . .), please say one short sentence.

   b. (. . .), please ask one short question.

   c. (. . .), please say one short sentence and ask one short question.

3. (. . .) and I are going to have a short conversation. Everyone should write exactly what we say.

4. Pair up with another student. Have a brief conversation. Then write your conversation using quoted speech.

☐ EXERCISE 26. Quoted speech. (Chart 14-8)

Directions: Write a composition. Choose one of the following topics.

Topics:
   1. Write a fable from your country in which animals speak. Use quotation marks.
   2. Write a children's story that you learned when you were young. When the characters in your story speak, use quotation marks.
   3. Make up a children's story. When the characters in your story speak, use quotation marks.
   4. Make up any kind of story. When the characters in your story speak, use quotation marks.
   5. Write a joke in which at least two people are talking to each other. Use quotation marks when the people are speaking.
   6. Make up an interview you would like to have with a famous person. Use your imagination. Write the imaginary interview using quotation marks.

14-9 QUOTED SPEECH vs. REPORTED SPEECH

QUOTED SPEECH	**Quoted speech** = giving a speaker's exact words. Quotation marks are used.★
(a) Ann said, "*I'm* hungry."	
(b) Tom said, "*I need* my pen."	
REPORTED SPEECH	**Reported speech** = giving the idea of a speaker's words. Not all of the exact words are used; pronouns and verb forms may change. Quotation marks are NOT used.★
(c) Ann said (that) **she was** hungry.	
(d) Tom said (that) **he needed** his pen.	

★*Quoted speech* is also called "direct speech." *Reported speech* is also called "indirect speech."

Directions: Change the pronouns from the quoted speech to reported speech.

1. Mr. Smith said, "I need help with my luggage."

    → Mr. Smith said that ____he____ needed help with ____his____ luggage.

2. Mrs. Peacock said, "I am going to visit my brother."

    → Mrs. Peacock said that _____ was going to visit _____ brother.

3. Sue and Tom said, "We don't like our new apartment."

    → Sue and Tom said that _____ didn't like _____ new apartment.

4. Joe said to me, "I will call you."

    → Joe said _____ would call _____ .

5. Paul said to me, "I'll meet you at your house after I finish my work at my house."

    → Paul said that _____ would meet _____ at _____

    house after _____ finished _____ work at _____

    house.

14-10 VERB FORMS IN REPORTED SPEECH

(a) QUOTED: Joe said, "I *feel* good." (b) REPORTED: Joe said he *felt* good. (c) QUOTED: Sue said, "I *am* happy." (d) REPORTED: Sue said she *was* happy.	In formal English, if the reporting verb (e.g., *said)* is in the past, the verb in the noun clause is often also in a past form, as in (b) and (d).

—Ann said, "I am hungry."
(e) A: What did Ann just say? I didn't hear her.
  B: She said she *is* hungry.
(f) A: What did Ann say when she got home last night?
  B: She said she *was* hungry.
	In informal English, often the verb in the noun clause is not changed to a past form, especially when words are reported *soon after* they are said, as in (e).
	
	In *later reporting,* however, or in formal English, a past verb is commonly used, as in (f).

(g) Ann *says* (that) she *is* hungry.	If the reporting verb is present tense (e.g., *says),* no change is made in the noun clause verb.

QUOTED SPEECH	REPORTED SPEECH *formal or later reporting*	REPORTED SPEECH *informal or immediate reporting*
He said, "I *work* hard." He said, "I *am working* hard." He said, "I *worked* hard." He said, "I *have worked* hard." He said, "I *am going to work* hard." He said, "I *will work* hard." He said, "I *can work* hard."	He said he *worked* hard. He said he *was working* hard. He said he *had worked* hard. He said he *had worked* hard. He said he *was going to work* hard. He said he *would work* hard. He said he *could work* hard.	He said he *works* hard. He said he *is working* hard. He said he *worked* hard. He said he *has worked* hard. He said he *is going to work* hard. He said he *will work* hard. He said he *can work* hard.

☐ **EXERCISE 28. Reported speech: formal verb forms. (Chart 14-10)**

Directions: Complete the reported speech sentences. Use formal verb forms.

1. Sara said, "I need some help."

   → Sara said (that) she _____*needed*_____ some help.

2. Linda said, "I'm meeting David for dinner."

   → Linda said (that) she _____ David for dinner.

3. Ms. Bell said, "I have studied in Cairo."

   → Ms. Bell said (that) she _____ in Cairo.

4. Bill said, "I forgot to pay my electric bill."

   → Bill said (that) he _____ to pay his electric bill.

5. Barbara said, "I am going to fly to Hawaii for my vacation."

   → Barbara said (that) she _____ to Hawaii for her vacation.

6. I said, "I'll carry the box up the stairs."

   → I said (that) I _____ the box up the stairs.

7. Taufik said to me, "I can teach you to drive."

   → Taufik said (that) he _____ me to drive.

☐ **EXERCISE 29. Quoted vs. reported speech. (Charts 14-9 and 14-10)**

Directions: Change the quoted speech to reported speech. Change the verb in quoted speech to a past form in reported speech if possible.

1. Jim said, "I'm sleepy."
   → *Jim said (that) he was sleepy.*

2. Sally said, "I don't like chocolate."

3. Mary said, "I'm planning to take a trip with my family."

4. Tom said, "I have already eaten lunch."

5. Kate said, "I called my doctor."

6. Mr. Rice said, "I'm going to go to Chicago."

7. Eric said to me, "I will come to your house at ten."

8. Jane said, "I can't afford to buy a new car."

9. Ann says, "I can't afford to buy a new car."

10. Ms. Topp said to me, "I want to see you in my office after your meeting with your supervisor."

14-11 COMMON REPORTING VERBS: *TELL, ASK, ANSWER/REPLY*

(a) Ann **said** that she was hungry. (b) Ann **told me** that she was hungry. (c) Ann **told Tom** that she was hungry. INCORRECT: *Ann told that she was hungry* INCORRECT: *Ann said me that she was hungry.*	A main verb that introduces reported speech is called a "reporting verb." **Say** is the most common reporting verb* and is usually followed immediately by a noun clause, as in (a). **Tell** is also commonly used. Note that **told** is followed by **me** in (b) and by **Tom** in (c). **Tell** needs to be followed immediately by a (pro)noun object and then by a noun clause.
(d) QUOTED: Sue said (to me), "Are you tired?" REPORTED: Sue **asked (me) if** I was tired. (e) Sue **wanted to know if** I was tired. Sue **wondered if** I was tired. Sue **inquired whether or not** I was tired.	**Asked**, not **said**, is used to report questions. Questions are also reported by using **want to know**, **wonder**, and **inquire**.
(f) QUOTED: I said (to Ann), "I am not tired." REPORTED: I **answered/replied** that I wasn't tired.	The verbs **answer** and **reply** are often used to report replies.

*Other common reporting verbs: *Ann **announced**, **commented**, **complained**, **explained**, **remarked**, **stated** that she was hungry.*

☐ **EXERCISE 30. SAY vs. TELL vs. ASK.** (Chart 14-11)

Directions: Complete the sentences with **said**, **told**, or **asked**.

1. Karen ____told____ me that she would be here at one o'clock.

2. Tom ____said____ that he was going to get here around two.

3. Mary ____asked____ me what time I would arrive.

4. Jack _____ that I had a message.

5. Jack _____ me that someone had called me around ten-thirty.

6. I _____ Jack if he knew the caller's name.

7. I had a short conversation with Alice yesterday. I _____ her that I would help her move into her new apartment next week. She _____ that she would welcome the help. She _____ me if I had a truck or knew anyone who had a truck. I _____ her Jason had a truck. She _____ she would call him.

8. My uncle in Chicago called and _____ that he was organizing a surprise party for my aunt's 60th birthday. He _____ me if I could come to Chicago for the party. I _____ him that I would be happy to come. I _____ when it was. He _____ it was the last weekend in August.

□ **EXERCISE 31. SAY vs. TELL vs. ASK.** (Chart 14-11)

Directions: Use *said, told,* and *asked* in reported speech. Work in groups or as a class.
Speaker A: Choose a sentence at random from the list and whisper it to B.
Speaker B: Report what Speaker A said. Use either informal or formal verb forms in the noun clause, as you prefer.*

Example:
SPEAKER A: I need to talk to you after class. *(whispered to B)*
SPEAKER B: Ali told me/said he needed to talk to me after class. *(reported aloud)*

I'll call you tomorrow.	Are you going to be at home tonight?
Can you hear what I'm saying?	Have you ever met *(name of a person)*?
✓I need to talk to you after class.	What are you going to do after class today?
I'm getting hungry.	I'll meet you after class for a cup of coffee.
I walked to school this morning	I'm not going to be in class tomorrow.
Your pronunciation is very good.	Have you seen *(name of a current movie)*?
What kind of food do you like best?	I've already seen *(name of a current movie)*.
Is *(name of a person)* married?	Can you speak *(name of a language)*?
How long have you been married?	Do you know how to cook *(name of a dish)*?
Do you think it's going to rain?	Are you going to take another English class?

□ **EXERCISE 32. Noun clauses and questions.** (Charts 5-2, 14-2 → 14-4, and 14-11)

Directions: Create questions, then report them using noun clauses.
Student A: Write five questions you want to ask Student B about his/her life or opinions. Sign your name. Hand the questions to Student B.
Student B: Report what Student A wants to know. Make your report orally to the class (or to a smaller group) or in writing. Provide the information if you can or want to.

Example:
Student A's list of questions:
1. Where were you born?
2. What is your favorite color?
3. What do you think about the recent election in your country?
4. Who do you admire most in the world?

Student B's report:
1. (Student A) wants to know where I was born. I was born in (Caracas).
2. He/She asked me what my favorite color is/was. Blue, I guess.
3. He/She wants to know what I think about the recent election in my country. I'm very pleased about the election. The new leader will be good for my country.
4. He/She wants to know who I admire most in the world. I'll have to think about that. Probably my parents.

---

*In everyday spoken English, native speakers sometimes change noun clause verbs to past forms, and sometimes they don't. In an informal reporting situation such as in this exercise, either informal/immediate reporting or formal/later reporting tenses are appropriate.

□ **EXERCISE 33. Reported vs. quoted speech. (Charts 14-9 → 14-11)**

Directions: Change the reported speech to quoted speech. Begin a new paragraph each time the speaker changes. Pay special attention to pronouns, verb forms, and word order.

Example: This morning my mother asked me if I had gotten enough sleep last night. I told her that I was fine. I explained that I didn't need a lot of sleep. She told me that I needed to take better care of myself.

WRITTEN: This morning my mother said, "Did you get enough sleep last night?"
"I'm fine," I replied. "I don't need a lot of sleep."
She said, "You need to take better care of yourself."

1. In the middle of class yesterday, my friend tapped me on the shoulder and asked me what time it was. I told her it was two-thirty.

2. I met Mr. Redford at the reception for international students. He asked me where I was from. I told him I was from Argentina.

3. When I was putting on my hat and coat, Robert asked me where I was going. I told him that I had a date with Anna. He wanted to know what we were going to do. I told him that we were going to a movie.

□ **EXERCISE 34. Reported speech. (Charts 14-9 → 14-11)**

Directions: In a written report, change the quoted speech to reported speech. Use formal sequence of tenses.

Example: QUOTED: "What are you doing?" Mr. Singh asked me.
"I'm doing a grammar exercise," I told him.

REPORTED: Mr. Singh asked me what I was doing. I told him (that) I was doing a grammar exercise.

QUOTED CONVERSATION ONE:
"Where's Bill?" Susan asked me.
"He's in the lunch room," I replied.
"When will he be back in his office?" she wanted to know.
I said, "He'll be back around two."

QUOTED CONVERSATION TWO:
"Can you help me clean the hall closet?" Mrs. Ball asked her husband.
"I'm really busy," he told his wife.
"What are you doing?" she wanted to know.
"I'm fixing the zipper on my winter jacket," he replied.
Then she asked him, "Will you have some time to help me after you fix the zipper?"
He said, "I can't because I have to watch a really important ball game on TV."
With a note of exasperation in her voice, Mrs. Ball finally said, "I'll clean the closet myself."

☐ **EXERCISE 35. Reported speech.** (Charts 14-9 → 14-11)

Directions: Complete the written report based on what the people in the picture say. Use the formal sequence of tenses.

AT THE RESTAURANT

One day Susan and Paul were at a restaurant. Susan picked up her menu and looked at it. Paul left his menu on the table. Susan asked Paul _____*what he was going to*

_____*have*_____ . He said _____ anything because

he _____ . He _____ already _____ .

Susan was surprised. She asked him why _____ . He told her

_____ .

☐ **EXERCISE 36. Reported speech.** (Charts 14-9 → 14-11)

Directions: Work in pairs. Each pair should create a short dialogue (five to ten sentences) based on one of the given situations. Each pair will then present their dialogue to the class. After the dialogue, the class will report what was said.

Sample situation: Have a conversation about going to the zoo.
Sample dialogue:
ANN: Would you like to go to the zoo tomorrow?
BOB: I can't. I have to study.
ANN: That's too bad. Are you sure you can't go? It will take only a few hours.
BOB: Well, maybe I can study in the morning and then go to the zoo in the afternoon.
ANN: Great!

Sample report:

  Ann asked Bob if he wanted to go to the zoo tomorrow. Bob said that he couldn't go because he had to study. Ann finally persuaded him to go. She said that it would take only a few hours. Bob decided that he could study in the morning and go to the zoo in the afternoon.

(Notice in the sample report: The writer gives the idea of the speakers' words without necessarily using the speakers' exact words.)

1. Have a conversation in which one of you invites the other to a party.

2. One of you is a teenager, and the other is a parent. The teenager is having problems at school and is seeking advice and encouragement.

3. The two of you are a married couple. One of you is reminding the other about the things s/he should or has to do today.

4. Have a conversation in which one of you persuades the other to begin a health program by taking up a new kind of exercise (jogging, walking, tennis, etc.). Beginning of the dialogue:
   A: I need to get some physical exercise.
   B: Why don't you take up . . . ?
   A: No, I don't want to do that.

5. One of you is fourteen years old, and the other is the parent. The fourteen-year-old wants to stay out late tonight. What will the parent say?

6. One of you is a store detective, and the other is a shoplifter. The store detective has just seen the shoplifter take something.

7. One of you is a stubborn, old-fashioned, uneducated person who thinks the world is flat. The other tries to convince the stubborn one that the world is round.

☐ EXERCISE 37. Error analysis: noun clauses. (Chapter 14)
   Directions: Correct the errors.

1. My friend knows where ~~do~~ I live.

2. I don't know what is your e-mail address?

3. I think so that Mr. Lee is out of town.

4. Can you tell me that where Victor is living now?

5. I asked my uncle what kind of movies does he like.

6. I think, that my English has improved a lot.

7. Is true that people are basically the same everywhere in the world.

8. A man came to my door last week. I don't know who is he.

9. I want to know does Pedro have a laptop computer.

10. They have no children, but their dog understands what do they say.

11. Sam and I talked about his classes. He told that he don't like his algebra class.

12. A woman came into the room and ask me Where is your brother?

13. I felt very relieved when the doctor said, you will be fine. It's nothing serious.

14. I can understand what do I read in the newspaper, but if someone speaks the same

sentences to me, I can't understand what is he saying.

15. My mother asked me that: "When you will be home,,?

☐ **EXERCISE 38. Noun clauses and questions. (Charts 5-2 and 14-1 → 14-4)**
Directions: Do you agree or disagree with the given quote? What do you think about the role of technology in children's education? Discuss in groups or as a class. Write a summary of your views.

"Technology brings into the classroom new capabilities and possibilities in a child's learning environment. However, the most important factor in whether an educational setting is effective for a child is the teacher. The second most critical factor in a child's educational success is the child's home. Technology is far down the list of things that really make a difference, but it can make a difference."

— *John Newsom, Director of Instructional Technology*
Saratoga School District

APPENDIX 1
Phrasal Verbs

CONTENTS

☐ **EXERCISE 1. Preview: phrasal verbs. (Appendix 1)**

Directions: Complete the sentences with the given words. The words may be used more than once.

away	back	off	on	up

1. The children's toys are all over the floor during the day, but before they go to bed, they always **put** their toys _____*away*_____.

2. In the winter, I never go outside without a coat. Before I go out, I always **put** _____ my coat.

3. I took a book from the shelf and then returned it to the exact same place. In other words, when I was finished looking at the book, I **put** it _____ where I found it.

4. Sometimes I postpone doing my homework in the evening and watch TV or talk on the phone instead. I probably should do my homework first, but sometimes I **put** it _____ and do it later.

5. I am not a late sleeper. **I get** _____ early almost every day.

6. I usually take the bus to work. **I get** _____ the bus near my apartment and **get** _____ just a block from my office.

7. We're leaving on May 1. We'll return May 7. As soon as we **get** _____ from our trip on the 7th, we'll call you.

8. When I entered the dark room, **I turned** _____ the lights. When I left, I **turned** them _____ because it's important to save electricity.

A1-1 PHRASAL VERBS: INTRODUCTION

(a) We **put off** our trip. We'll go next month instead of this month. *(put off = postpone)*	In (a): *put off* = a phrasal verb.
(b) Jimmy, **put on** your coat before you go outdoors. *(put on = place clothes on one's body)*	A phrasal verb = a verb and a particle that together have a special meaning. For example, *put off* means "postpone."
(c) Someone left the scissors on the table. They didn't belong there. I **put** them **away**. *(put away = put something in its usual or proper place)*	A particle = a "small word" (e.g., *off, on, away back*) that is used in a phrasal verb.
(d) After I used the dictionary, I **put** it **back** on the shelf. *(put back = return something to its original place)*	Note that the phrasal verbs with *put* in (a), (b), (c), and (d) all have different meanings.

SEPARABLE	Some phrasal verbs are **separable**: a NOUN
(e) We *put* **off** *our* **trip**. = (vb + **particle** + NOUN)	OBJECT can either
(f) We *put our* **trip** **off**. = (vb + NOUN + **particle**)	(1) follow the particle, as in (e), OR (2) come between (separate) the verb and the particle, as in (f).
(g) We *put* **it** **off**. = (vb + PRONOUN + **particle**)	If a phrasal verb is separable, a PRONOUN OBJECT comes between the verb and the particle, as in (g). *INCORRECT: We put off it.*

NONSEPARABLE	If a phrasal verb is **nonseparable**, a NOUN or
(h) I ran **into** *Bob*. = (vb + **particle** + NOUN)	PRONOUN always follows (never precedes) the particle, as in (h) and (i).
(i) I ran **into** *him*. = (vb + **particle** + PRONOUN)	*INCORRECT: I ran Bob into.* *INCORRECT: I ran him into.*

☐ **EXERCISE 2. Phrasal verbs: separable vs. nonseparable. (Charts A1-1 and A1-4)**

Directions: If the phrasal verb is separable, mark SEPARABLE. If it is not separable, mark NONSEPARABLE.

1. CORRECT: I *turned* the light *on*.
    CORRECT: I *turned on* the light.
    turn on =   ☒ SEPARABLE ☐ NONSEPARABLE

2. CORRECT: I *ran into* Mary.
    (INCORRECT: I *ran* Mary *into*.)
    run into =   ☐ SEPARABLE ☒ NONSEPARABLE

3. CORRECT: Joe *looked up* the definition.
    CORRECT: Joe *looked* the definition *up*.
    look up =   ☐ SEPARABLE ☐ NONSEPARABLE

4. CORRECT: I *got off* the bus.
    (INCORRECT: I *got* the bus *off*.)
    get off =   ☐ SEPARABLE ☐ NONSEPARABLE

5. CORRECT: I *took off* my coat.
    CORRECT: I *took* my coat *off*.
    take off =   ☐ SEPARABLE ☐ NONSEPARABLE

6. CORRECT: I *got in* the car and left.
    (INCORRECT: I *got* the car *in* and left.)
    get in =   ☐ SEPARABLE ☐ NONSEPARABLE

7. CORRECT: I *figured out* the answer.
   CORRECT: I *figured* the answer *out*.

   figure out = ☐ SEPARABLE
               ☐ NONSEPARABLE

8. CORRECT: I *turned* the radio *off*.
   CORRECT: I *turned off* the radio.

   turn off = ☐ SEPARABLE
             ☐ NONSEPARABLE

☐ EXERCISE 3. Identifying phrasal verbs. (Chart A1-1)
   Directions: <u>Underline</u> the second part of the phrasal verb in each sentence.

   1. I *figured* the answer <u>out</u>.
   2. The teacher *called* <u>on</u> me in class.
   3. I *made* up a story about my childhood.
   4. I feel okay now. I *got* over my cold last week.
   5. The students *handed* their papers in at the end of the test.
   6. I *woke* my roommate up when I got home.
   7. I *picked* up a book and started to read.
   8. I *turned* the radio on to listen to some music.
   9. When I don't know how to spell a word, I *look* it up in the dictionary.
   10. I opened the telephone directory and *looked* up the number of a plumber.
   11. I *put* my book down and *turned* off the light.

☐ EXERCISE 4. Phrasal verbs: separable vs. nonseparable. (Chart A1-1)
   Directions: Complete the sentences with pronouns and particles. If the phrasal verb is separable, circle SEP. If it is nonseparable, circle NONSEP.

   1. I *got over* my cold. → I got _____over it_____.   SEP   (NONSEP)

   2. I *made up* the story. → I made _____it up_____.   (SEP)   NONSEP

   3. I *put off* my homework. → I put _____.   SEP   NONSEP

   4. I *wrote down* the numbers. → I wrote _____.   SEP   NONSEP

   5. I *ran into* Robert. → I ran _____.   SEP   NONSEP

   6. I *figured* the answer *out*. → I figured _____.   SEP   NONSEP

   7. I *took off* my shoes. → I took _____.   SEP   NONSEP

   8. I *got over* my cold. → I got _____.   SEP   NONSEP

   9. I *turned off* the lights. → I turned _____.   SEP   NONSEP

   10. I *threw away* the newspaper. → I threw _____.   SEP   NONSEP

Group A: Phrasal Verbs (separable)*		
Verb	**Definition**	**Example**
figure out	find the solution to a problem	I *figured out* the answer.
hand in	give homework, papers, etc., to a teacher	We *handed in* our homework.
hand out	give something to this person, then to that person, then to another person, etc.	The teacher *handed out* the test papers.
look up	look for information in a dictionary, a telephone directory, an encyclopedia, etc.	I *looked* a word *up* in the dictionary.
make up	invent (a story)	Children like to *make up* stories.
pick up	lift	Tom *picked up* the baby.
put down	stop holding or carrying	I *put down* the heavy packages.
put off	postpone	We *put off* our trip until next summer.
put on	place clothes on one's body	I *put on* my coat before I left.
take off	remove clothes from one's body	I *took off* my coat when I arrived.
throw away ⎫ **throw out** ⎭	put in the trash, discard	I *threw away* my old notebooks. I *threw out* my old notebooks.
turn off	stop a machine or a light	I *turned off* the lights and went to bed.
turn on	start a machine or a light	I *turned on* the light so I could read.
wake up	stop sleeping	My wife *woke* me *up* at six.
write down	write a note on a piece of paper	I *wrote* his phone number *down*.

*Appendix 1 presents phrasal verbs in small groups to be learned and practiced one group at a time. A complete reference list can be found on pp. 449–452.

☐ EXERCISE 5. Phrasal verbs. (Group A)
 Directions: Complete the sentences with the given particles.

away	*down*	*in*	*off*	*on*	*out*	*up*

1. Before I left home this morning, I put _____**on**_____ my coat.

2. When I got to class this morning, I took my coat _____.

3. The students handed their homework _____.

4. Johnny made _____ a story. He didn't tell the truth.

5. The weather was bad, so we put _____ the picnic until next week.

6. Alice looked a word _____ in her dictionary.

7. Alice wrote the definition _____.

8. My roommate is messy. He never picks _____ his clothes.

9. The teacher handed the test papers _____ at the beginning of the class period.

10. A strange noise woke _____ the children in the middle of the night.

11. When some friends came to visit, Chris stopped watching TV. He turned the television set _____.

12. It was dark when I got home last night, so I turned the lights _____.

13. Peggy finally figured _____ the answer to the arithmetic problem.

14. When I was walking through the airport, my arms got tired. So I put my suitcases _____ for a minute and rested.

15. I threw _____ yesterday's newspaper.

☐ EXERCISE 6. Phrasal verbs. (Group A)
Directions: Complete the sentences with pronouns and particles.

1. A: Did you postpone your trip to Puerto Rico?
   B: Yes, we did. We put _____*it off*_____ until next summer.

2. A: Is Pat's phone number 322-4454 or 322-4455?
   B: I don't remember. You'd better look _____. The telephone directory is in the kitchen.

3. A: Is Mary asleep?
   B: Yes. I'd better wake _____. She has a class at nine.

4. A: Do you want to keep these newspapers?
   B: No. Throw _____.

5. A: I'm hot. This sweater is too heavy.
   B: Why don't you take _____?

6. A: Is that story true?
   B: No. I made _____.

7. A: When does the teacher want our compositions?
   B: We have to hand _____ tomorrow.

8. A: I made an appointment with Dr. Armstrong for three o'clock next Thursday.
   B: You'd better write _____ so you won't forget.

9. A: Do you know the answer to this problem?
   B: No. I can't figure _____.

10. A: Johnny, you're too heavy for me to carry. I have to put _____.
    B: Okay, Mommy.

11. A: Oh, dear. I dropped my pen. Could you pick _____ for me?
    B: Sure.

12. A: How does this tape recorder work?
    B: Push this button to turn _____, and push that button to turn _____.

13. A: I have some papers for the class. Ali, would you please hand _____ for me?
    B: I'd be happy to.

14. A: Timmy, here's your hat. Put _____ before you go out. It's cold outside.
    B: Okay, Dad.

Group B: Phrasal Verbs (nonseparable)		
Verb	**Definition**	**Example**
call on	ask (someone) to speak in class	The teacher *called on* Ali.
come from	originate	Where do these bananas *come from?*
get over	recover from an illness or a shock	Sue *got over* her cold and returned to work.
get off	leave ⎫ a bus/airplane/train/subway	I *got off* the bus at Maple Street.
get on	enter ⎭	I *got on* the bus at Pine Street.
get in	enter ⎫ a car, a taxi	I *got in* the taxi at the airport.
get out of	leave ⎭	I *got out of* the taxi at the hotel.
look into	investigate	Someone needs to *look into* this problem.
run into	meet by chance	I *ran into* Peter at the market.

☐ EXERCISE 7. Phrasal verbs. (Group B)
Directions: Complete the sentences with particles.

1. When I raised my hand in class, the teacher called ____on____ me.

2. While I was walking down the street, I ran _____ an old friend.

3. Fred feels okay today. He got _____ his cold.

4. Last week I flew from Chicago to Miami. I got _____ the plane in Chicago. I got _____ the plane in Miami.

5. Sally took a taxi to the airport. She got _____ the taxi in front of her apartment building. She got _____ the taxi at the airport.

6. I take the bus to school every day. I get _____ the bus at the corner of First Street and Sunset Boulevard. I get _____ the bus just a block away from the classroom building.

7. Mr. Zabidi will look _____ renting a car for his weekend trip.

8. Where do snow leopards come _____?

☐ EXERCISE 8. Review: phrasal verbs. (Groups A and B)
Directions: Complete the sentences with particles and pronouns.

1. I had the flu, but I got ____over it____ a couple of days ago.

2. I was wearing gloves. I took _____ before I shook hands with Mr. Lee.

3. Stacy needed to find the date India became independent. She looked _____ on the computer and wrote _____ in her notebook.

4. I tried to solve the math problem, but I couldn't figure _____.

5. It looked like rain, so I got my raincoat from the closet and put _____ before I left the apartment.

6. A: Have you seen Dan this morning?
   B: Not this morning. I ran _____ at the movie last night.

7. A: Why do you look so worried?

   B: I don't have my homework. My mother threw _____ with the trash this morning. If Ms. Anthony calls _____ in class to answer homework questions, I'll have to tell her what happened.

   A: She'll never believe your story. She'll think you made _____.

8. A: Miss Smith, our supply room is out of pencils again. Why are we always running out of pencils? What is the problem?

   B: I don't know, sir. I'll look _____ right away.

☐ EXERCISE 9. Review: phrasal verbs. (Groups A and B)
Directions: Work in pairs.
Speaker A: Read the cue. Your book is open.
Speaker B: Finish Speaker A's sentence. Your book is closed.

Example:
SPEAKER A *(book open):* Yesterday I cleaned my closet. I found an old pair of shoes that I don't wear anymore. I didn't keep the shoes. I threw . . . .
SPEAKER B *(book closed):* . . . them away/out.

1. The teacher gave us some important information in class yesterday. I didn't want to forget it, so I wrote . . . .
2. When I raised my hand in class, the teacher called . . . .
3. I was carrying a suitcase, but it was too heavy, so I put . . . .
4. I didn't know the meaning of a word, so I looked . . . .
5. I haven't finished my work. I'll do it later. I'm going to put . . . .
6. The lights were off in the dark room, so I turned . . . .
7. (. . .) isn't wearing his/her hat right now. When s/he got to class, s/he took . . . .
8. My pen just fell on the floor. Could you please pick . . . ?

Switch roles.

9. I saw (. . .) at a concert last night. I was surprised when I ran . . . .
10. When you finish using a stove, you should always be careful to turn . . . .
11. When I finished my test, I handed . . . .
12. Is (. . .) sleeping?! Would you please wake . . . ?
13. What's the answer to this problem? Have you figured . . . ?
14. I don't need this piece of paper anymore. I'm going to throw . . . .
15. I had the flu last week, but now I'm okay. I got . . . .
16. I told a story that wasn't true. I made . . . .

Switch roles.

17. Name some means of transportation that you get on.
18. Name some that you get in.
19. Name some that you get off.

Switch roles.

20. Name some that you get out of.

21. Name some things that you turn on.

22. Name some things that you turn off.

	Group C: Phrasal Verbs (separable)	
Verb	**Definition**	**Example**
ask out	ask (someone) to go on a date	Tom *asked* Mary *out.* They went to a movie.
call back	return a telephone call	I'll *call* you *back* tomorrow.
call off	cancel	We *called off* the picnic due to bad weather.
call up	make a telephone call	I *called up* my friend in New York.
give back	return something to someone	I borrowed Al's pen, then I *gave* it *back.*
hang up	hang on a hanger or a hook	I *hung* my coat *up* in the closet.
pay back	return borrowed money to someone	Thanks for the loan. I'll *pay* you *back* soon.
put away	put something in its usual or proper place	I *put* the clean dishes *away.*
put back	return something to its original place	I *put* my papers *back* into my briefcase.
put out	extinguish (stop) a fire, a cigarette	We *put out* the campfire before we left.
shut off	stop a machine or light, turn off	I *shut off* my printer before I left the office.
try on	put on clothing to see if it fits	I *tried on* several pairs of shoes.
turn down	decrease the volume	Sue *turned down* the music. It was too loud.
turn up	increase the volume	Al *turned up* the radio. He likes loud music.

☐ EXERCISE 10. Phrasal verbs. (Group C)

Directions: Complete the sentences with pronouns and particles.

1. A: Could you lend me a couple of bucks?

   B: Sure.

   A: Thanks. I'll pay _____ you back _____ tomorrow.

2. A: The radio is too loud. Could you please turn _____?

   B: Sure.

3. A: I can't hear the TV. Could you please turn _____?

   B: I'd be glad to.

4. A: Have you heard from Jack lately?

   B: No. I think I'll call _____ tonight and see how he is.*

5. A: Someone's at the door. Can I call _____?

   B: Sure.

6. A: Where's my coat?

   B: I hung _____.

_____

*There is no difference in meaning between *I'll call him tonight* and *I'll call him up tonight.*

7. A: Did you leave the water on?

    B: No. I shut _____ when I finished washing my hands.

8. A: May I borrow your calculator? I'll give _____ to you tomorrow.

    B: Sure. Keep it as long as you need it.

9. A: You can't smoke that cigarette in the auditorium. You'd better put

        _____ before we go in.

    B: Okay.

10. A: Do you have any plans for Saturday night?

     B: Yes. I have a date. Jim Olsen asked _____.

11. A: Did you take my eraser off my desk?

     B: Yes, but I put _____ on your desk when I was finished.

     A: Oh? It's not here.

     B: Look under your notebook.

     A: Ah. There it is. Thanks.

12. A: Your toys are all over the floor, kids. Before you go to bed, be sure to

        put _____.

     B: Okay, Daddy.

13. A: Did you go to Kathy's party last night?

     B: She didn't have the party. She called _____.

14. A: This is a nice-looking coat. Why don't you try _____?

     B: How much does it cost?

15. A: That's Annie's toy, Tommy. Give _____ to her.

     B: No!

☐ EXERCISE 11. Review: phrasal verbs. (Groups A, B, and C)

Directions: Complete the sentences with pronouns and particles. Work in pairs, in groups, or as a class.

Example:
SPEAKER A *(book open):* I wanted to be sure to remember (Anna)'s phone number, so I wrote . . . .
SPEAKER B *(book closed):* . . . it down.

1. I can't hear the tape. Could you please turn . . . ?
2. I dropped my book. Could you please pick . . . ?
3. This is a hard problem. I can't figure . . . .
4. I bought these shoes a few days ago. Before I bought them, I tried . . . .
5. Where's your homework? Did you hand . . . ?
6. (. . .) asked (. . .) to go to a movie with him. He asked . . . .
7. We postponed the picnic. We put . . . .
8. I didn't know the meaning of a word, so I looked . . . .

9. We don't need that light. Would you please turn . . . ?

10. My coat was too warm to wear inside, so I took . . . .

(Switch roles if working in pairs.)

11. That music is too loud. Could you please turn . . . ?

12. These papers are for the class. Could you please hand . . . ?

13. (. . .) was going to have a party, but s/he canceled it. S/he called . . . .

14. My coat is in the closet. I hung . . . .

15. The story I told wasn't true. I made . . . .

16. I was cold. So I reached for my sweater and put . . . .

17. (. . .) fell asleep in class, so I woke . . . .

18. I was finished with the tools, so I put . . . .

19. I don't need these papers, so I'm going to throw . . . .

20. Let's listen to the radio. Would you please turn . . . ?

Group D: Phrasal Verbs (separable)		
Verb	**Definition**	**Example**
cross out	draw a line through	I *crossed out* the misspelled word.
fill in	complete by writing in a blank space	We *fill in* blanks in grammar exercises.
fill out	write information on a form	I *filled out* a job application.
fill up	fill completely with gas, water, coffee, etc.	We *filled up* the gas tank.
find out	discover information	I *found out* where he lives.
have on	wear	She *has* a blue blouse *on*.
look over	examine carefully	*Look over* your paper for errors before you hand it in.
point out	call attention to	The teacher *pointed out* a misspelling.
print out	create a paper copy from a computer	I finished the letter and *printed* it *out*.
tear down	destroy a building	They *tore down* the old house and built a new one.
tear out (of)	remove (paper) by tearing	I *tore* a page *out of* a magazine.
tear up	tear into small pieces	I *tore up* the secret note.
turn around } **turn back** } . . .	change to the opposite direction	After a mile, we *turned around/back*.
turn over	turn the top side to the bottom	I *turned* the paper *over* and wrote on the back.

□ EXERCISE 12. Phrasal verbs. (Group D)
   Directions: Complete the phrasal verbs.

1. There was no name on the front of the paper, so I turned it __*over*__ and looked on the back.

2. My wife pointed _____ an interesting article in the newspaper.

3. Before you submit the job application, look it _____ carefully to make sure you've filled it _____ correctly.

4. A: Good news! I've been accepted at the University of Florida.

   B: Great. When did you find _____?

   A: I got a letter in the mail today.

5. A: My roommate moved last week. Before he left, he filled _____ a change-of-address card at the post office, but I'm still getting some of his mail. What should I do?

   B: Cross _____ the old address on a letter and write in his new one. Also write "please forward" on the letter. You don't have to use another stamp.

6. How much does it cost to fill _____ your gas tank?

7. We're doing an exercise. We're filling _____ blanks with prepositions.

8. When I went to Dr. Green's office for the first time, I had to fill _____ a long form about my health history.

9. I made a mistake on the check I was writing, so I tore it _____ and wrote another.

10. An old building was in the way of the new highway through the city, so they tore the old building _____.

11. Sam has his new suit _____ today. He looks very handsome.

12. My employer asked for the latest sales figures, so I went to my computer and quickly printed _____ a new report.

13. I think we're going in the wrong direction. Let's turn _____.

☐ EXERCISE 13. Phrasal verbs. (Group D)

Directions: Work in pairs, in groups, or as a class.

Example:
SPEAKER A *(book open):* When your cup is empty, you fill it . . . .
SPEAKER B *(book closed):* . . . up.

1. I made a mistake, so I crossed it . . . .
2. When you read your composition carefully for mistakes, you look it . . . .
3. When you're done writing something on the computer and you want a hard copy, you print it . . . .
4. You look in reference books when you want to find something . . . .
5. If you want to remove a page from your notebook, you tear it . . . .
6. If you destroy an old building, you tear it . . . .
7. If you tear something into many small pieces, you tear it . . . .

(Switch roles if working in pairs.)

8. If you want to see the back of a piece of paper, you turn it . . . .
9. If you discover you are walking in the wrong direction, you turn . . . .
10. If you put water in a glass to the very top, you fill it . . . .

11. If you give information on an application form, you fill it . . . .

12. When you write words in a blank, you fill the blank . . . .

13. When you're wearing something, we say that you have it . . . .

14. When there's something the teacher wants to make sure we notice, she points it . . . .

Group E: Phrasal Verbs (separable)		
Verb	**Definition**	**Example**
blow out	extinguish (a match, a candle)	He *blew* the candles *out*.
bring back	return	She *brought* my books *back* to me.
bring up	(1) raise (children)	The Lees *brought up* six children.
	(2) mention, start to talk about	He *brought* the news *up* in conversation.
cheer up	make happier	The good news *cheered* me *up*.
clean up	make neat and clean	I *cleaned up* my apartment.
give away	donate, get rid of by giving	I didn't sell my old bike. I *gave* it *away*.
help out	assist (someone)	Could you please *help* me *out?*
lay off	stop employment	The company *laid off* 100 workers.
leave on	(1) not turn off (a light, a machine)	Please *leave* the light *on*.
	(2) not take off (clothing)	I *left* my coat *on* at the movie theater.
take back	return	She *took* a book *back* to the library.
take out	invite out and pay	He *took* Mary *out*. They went to a movie.
talk over	discuss	We *talked* the problem *over*.
think over	consider	I *thought* the problem *over*.
work out	solve	We *worked* the problem *out*.

☐ EXERCISE 14. Phrasal verbs. (Group E)

Directions: Complete the sentences.

1. When I am sad, my friends can always cheer me ___up___ .

2. These are bad economic times. Businesses are laying _____ hundreds of workers.

3. After I lit the candles, I blew _____ the match.

4. Jack and Ann are having some problems in their marriage, but they are trying hard to
   work them _____ .

5. When they have a problem, they always try to talk it _____ to make sure they are
   communicating with each other.

6. A: I'm leaving. Should I turn the TV off?

   B: No. Please leave it _____ .

7. Saturday night I took my parents _____ to a fancy restaurant.

8. After dinner, Michael helped me clean _____ the kitchen.

9. I was brought _____ in the South.

10. You're welcome to borrow my tools, but when you finish, please be sure to bring them
    _____ .

11. Don't forget to take the video _____ to the store today.

12. I didn't take off my hat when I came inside. I left it _____.

13. I hate to bring this problem _____, but we need to talk about it.

14. A: Are you going to accept the job offer?

    B: I don't know. I'm still thinking it _____.

15. I can't sell this old sofa. I guess I'll give it _____. Someone will be able to use it.

16. My parents usually help me _____ with a little money when I'm having trouble paying my bills.

☐ EXERCISE 15. Phrasal verbs. (Group E)
Directions: Work in pairs, in groups, or as a class.

Example:
SPEAKER A *(book open):* If I am sad, you will try to cheer me . . . .
SPEAKER B *(book closed):* . . . up.

1. You need to return that book to the library. You need to take it . . . .

2. I lost my job. The company I'm working for laid me . . . .

3. If you don't need the light from a candle anymore, you blow it . . . .

4. If we need to discuss something, we need to talk it . . . .

5. You walked into a cold building. Instead of taking your coat off, you left it . . . .

6. If you give your old clothes to charity, you give them . . . .

7. When we have a problem to solve, we need to work it . . . .

8. If I lend you something, I want you to return it to me. I want you to bring it . . . .

(Switch roles if working in pairs.)

9. Parents feed, educate, and love their children. They bring their children . . . .

10. When I finish using my computer, I don't turn it off each time. Instead, I often leave it . . . .

11. Someone offered you a job. Before you give an answer, you need some time to think it . . . .

12. When you take guests to a restaurant and pay the bill, you take them . . . .

13. If you introduce a topic into a conversation, you bring it . . . .

14. If you make a mess, you need to clean it . . . .

15. You rented a video. When you were finished with it, you took it . . . .

16. When friends need our assistance, we offer to help them . . . .

A1-2 PHRASAL VERBS: INTRANSITIVE

(a) The machine *broke down.* (b) Please *come in.* (c) I *fell down.*	Some phrasal verbs are intransitive; i.e., they are not followed by an object.

Group F: Phrasal Verbs (intransitive)		
Verb	**Definition**	**Example**
break down	stop functioning properly	My car *broke down* on the highway.
break out	happen suddenly	War *broke out* between the two countries.
break up	separate, end a relationship	Ann and Tom *broke up*.
come in	enter a room or building	May I *come in*?
dress up	put on nice clothes	People usually *dress up* for weddings.
eat out	eat outside of one's home	Would you like to *eat out* tonight?
fall down	fall to the ground	I *fell down* and hurt myself.
get up	get out of bed in the morning	What time did you *get up* this morning?
give up	quit doing something or quit trying	I can't do it. I *give up*.
go on	continue	Let's not stop. Let's *go on*.
go out	not stay home	Jane *went out* with her friends last night.
grow up	become an adult	Jack *grew up* in Sweden.
hang up	end a telephone conversation	When we finished talking, I *hung up*.
move in (to)	start living in a new home	Some people *moved in* next door to me.
move out (of)	stop living at a place	My roommate is *moving out*.
show up	come, appear	Jack *showed up* late for the meeting.
sit back	put one's back against a chair back	*Sit back* and relax. I'll get you a drink.
sit down	go from standing to sitting	Please *sit down*.
speak up	speak louder	I can't hear you. You'll have to *speak up*.
stand up	go from sitting to standing	I *stood up* and walked to the door.
start over	begin again	I lost count, so I *started over*.
stay up	not go to bed	I *stayed up* late last night.
take off	ascend in an airplane	The plane *took off* 30 minutes late.

☐ EXERCISE 16. Phrasal verbs. (Group F)

Directions: Complete the sentences.

1. A: Are you comfortable?

   B: Yes. This is a very comfortable chair.

   A: Good. Now just sit __back__ and take it easy. There's nothing to worry about.

2. A: I'm exhausted. I can't go _____. I have to stop and rest.

   B: Let's sit in the shade of that tree. I'll get you some water.

3. A: I don't feel like cooking tonight. Let's eat _____.

   B: Okay. Where do you want to go?

4. A: Are you going to get dressed _____ for the symphony tonight?

   B: Yes. I think so. You?

5. A: What time do you usually get _____ in the morning?

   B: Around seven.

6. A: Knock, knock. Hello? Is anyone here? Professor Cook?

   B: Ah, Miss Sweeney. Hello. Come _____, come _____. Here, have a seat. Please sit _____.

7. A: I couldn't print out my composition.

   B: Why not?

   A: My printer broke _____.

8. A: Are you going to bed soon?

   B: No. I think I'll stay _____ for a while and read.

9. A: When I saw a pregnant woman on the crowded bus, I stood _____ and gave her my seat.

   B: Good for you. That's very considerate.

10. A: I don't feel like staying home. Let's go _____ this evening. I'm bored.

    B: How about going to a movie?

    A: Great! Let's go!

11. A: A riot broke _____ after the soccer finals.

    B: I find it hard to believe that people riot over a sports event.

12. A: Are you all right? What happened?

    B: I tripped on the rug and fell _____.

    A: Let me help you up.

13. A: Shall we begin the meeting without Ms. Lane?

    B: Yes. She'll probably show _____ soon, but we can begin without her.

14. A: When are Bill and Gloria getting married?

    B: They're not. They broke _____.

15. A: Don't forget that Grandma is a little hard of hearing.

    B: I won't. I'll be sure to speak _____ when I'm talking to her.

16. There's an empty apartment next to mine. My neighbors moved _____. Why don't you move _____? It'd be fun to live next door to each other.

17. A: It's been fun talking to you, but I need to hang _____ now.

    B: Okay. Let's talk again tomorrow.

18. I can't solve this math problem. I give _____.

19. Dan had trouble figuring out what to say in his letter to his girlfriend. He had to start _____ three times.

20. My flight was supposed to leave at 6:30, but the plane didn't take _____ until nearly 8:00.

☐ EXERCISE 17. Phrasal verbs. (Group F)

Directions: Work in pairs, in groups, or as a class.

Example:
SPEAKER A *(book open)*:   Don't stop. I'm enjoying your story. Please go . . . .
SPEAKER B *(book closed)*: . . . on.

1. If I'm sitting and then get to my feet, I stand . . . .

2. If you don't feel like staying at home, you go . . . .

3. When you put on nice clothes for a special affair, you dress . . . .

4. If you're not tired at night, instead of going to bed you stay . . . .

5. When you play soccer, sometimes you fall . . . .

6. When a fax machine stops working, you say that it broke . . . .

7. You walk to a chair, and then you sit . . . .

Switch roles.

8. If you relax into the chair, you sit . . . .

9. If two people end a relationship, they break . . . .

10. After you stop sleeping in the morning, you get . . . .

11. If you continue to do something and don't stop, you go . . . .

12. If a war begins, you say that it broke . . . .

13. If I invite you to enter my house, I say, "Please come . . . ."

14. If you eat at a restaurant instead of at home, you eat . . . .

15. If you ask someone to speak more loudly, you ask them to speak . . . .

16. When someone arrives for a meeting, you say that he or she shows . . . .

17. When you decide a problem is impossible to solve, you give . . . .

18. An airplane increases its speed on the runway, and then it takes . . . .

A1-3 THREE-WORD PHRASAL VERBS

	Some two-word verbs (e.g., *drop in*) can become three-word verbs (e.g., *drop in on*).
(a) Last night some friends *dropped in*.	In (a): *drop in* is not followed by an object. It is an intransitive phrasal verb (i.e., it is not followed by an object).
(b) Let's *drop in on* Alice this afternoon.	In (b): *drop in on* is a three-word phrasal verb. Three-word phrasal verbs are transitive (they are followed by objects).
(c) We *dropped in on* **her** last week.	In (c): Three-word phrasal verbs are nonseparable (the noun or pronoun follows the phrasal verb).

Group G: Phrasal Verbs (three-word)		
Verb	**Definition**	**Example**
drop in (on)	visit without calling first or without an invitation	We *dropped in on* my aunt.
drop out (of)	stop attending (school)	Beth *dropped out of* graduate school.
fool around (with)	have fun while wasting time	My son likes to *fool around with* his friends on the weekends.
get along (with)	have a good relationship with	I *get along* well *with* my roommate.
get back (from)	return from (a trip)	When did you *get back from* Hawaii?
get through (with)	finish	I *got through with* my work before noon.
grow up (in)	become an adult	Hamid *grew up in* Sweden.
look out (for)	be careful	*Look out for* that car!
run out (of)	finish the supply of (something)	We *ran out of* gas.
sign up (for)	put one's own name on a list	Did you *sign up for* the school trip?
watch out (for)	be careful	*Watch out for* that car!

☐ EXERCISE 18. Phrasal verbs. (Group G)
Directions: Complete the phrasal verbs.

1. Look __out__ ! There's a car coming!

2. Look __out__ __for__ that car!

3. Where did you grow _____?

4. I grew _____ _____ Springfield.

5. I couldn't finish the examination. I ran _____ _____ time.

6. A: What did you do yesterday?

   B: Nothing much. I just fooled _____ .

7. A: Hi, Chris! What's up? I haven't seen you in a long time. Where have you been?

   B: I went to California last week to visit my brother.

   A: Oh? When did you get _____ _____ California?

   B: Just yesterday.

8. A: Where's Jack? He hasn't been in class for at least two weeks.

   B: He dropped _____ _____ school.

9. A: Watch _____ _____ that truck!

   B: What truck?

10. A: What time do you expect to get _____ _____ your homework?

    B: In about an hour, as soon as I finish reading this chapter.

11. A: I haven't seen the Grants for a long time. Let's drop _____ _____ them this evening.

    B: We'd better call first. They may not like unexpected company.

12. A: I want to change my room in the dorm.

    B: Why?

    A: I don't get _____ _____ my roommate.

13. A: I signed _____ _____ Mrs. Grant's art class.

    B: You're lucky. I tried to sign _____ too, but it was full.

Group H: Phrasal Verbs (three-word)		
Verb	**Definition**	**Example**
come along (with)	accompany	Do you want to *come along with* us?
come over (to)	visit the speaker's place	Some friends are *coming over* tonight.
cut out (of)	remove with scissors or knife	I *cut* an article *out of* today's paper.
find out (about)	discover information about	When did you *find out about* the problem?
get together (with)	join, meet	Let's *get together* after work today.
go back (to)	return to a place	I *went back to* work after my illness.
go over (to)	(1) approach (2) visit another's home	I *went over to* the window. Let's *go over to* Jim's tonight.
hang around (with) **hang out (with)** }	spend undirected, idle time	John likes to *hang around* the coffee shop. Kids like to *hang out with* each other.
keep away (from)	not give to	*Keep* matches *away from* children.
set out (for)	begin a trip	We *set out for* our destination at dawn.
sit around (with)	sit and do nothing	You can't just *sit around*. Do something.

☐ EXERCISE 19. Phrasal verbs. (Group H)

    Directions: Complete the sentences.

1. A: Are you busy tonight?

    B: No.

    A: Would you like to come ___*along*___ ___*with*___ us to the movie?

2. A: I need to talk to you. When can we get _____?

    B: How about tomorrow morning?

3. My teenage daughter is lazy. All she wants to do is hang _____ _____ her friends.

4. I saw a young child who was all alone. He was crying. I went _____ _____ him and asked if I could help.

5. How did you find _____ _____ the change in the schedule?

6. It's a long trip. We'd better set _____ early.

7. Keep that cat _____ _____ me! I'm allergic.

8. Do you want to come _____ tonight? We could watch a movie or something.

9. There was a funny cartoon in the newspaper. I cut it _____ for my aunt.

10. A: I was born in Viet Nam, but I haven't been there for many years.

    B: Do you expect to go _____ _____ Viet Nam again someday?

    A: Yes.

11. A: What did you do at your aunt's?

    B: Not much. We just sat _____ and talked about the relatives who weren't there.

A1-4 PHRASAL VERBS: A REFERENCE LIST*

A **ask out** . . . . *ask (someone) to go on a date*

B **blow out** . . . . *extinguish (a match, a candle)*

    break down . . . . *stop functioning properly*

    break out . . . . *happen suddenly*

    break up . . . . *separate, end a relationship*

    bring back . . . . *return*

    bring up . . . . *(1) raise (children)*

                                                          (2) mention, start to talk about

C **call back** . . . . *return a telephone call*

    call off . . . . *cancel*

    call on . . . . *ask (someone) to speak in class*

    call up . . . . *make a telephone call*

    cheer up . . . . *make happier*

    clean up . . . . *make neat and clean*

    come along (**with**) . . . . *accompany*

    come from . . . . *originate*

    come in . . . . *enter a room or building*

    come over (**to**) . . . . *visit the speaker's place*

    cross out . . . . *draw a line through*

    cut out (**of**) . . . . *remove with scissors or knife*

D **dress up** . . . . *put on nice clothes*

    drop in (**on**) . . . . *visit without calling first or without an invitation*

    drop out (**of**) . . . . *stop attending (school)*

E **eat out** . . . . *eat outside of one's home*

F **fall down** . . . . *fall to the ground*

    figure out . . . . *find the solution to a problem*

*For more information about phrasal verbs and their meanings, see dictionaries written especially for second language learners, such as the *Longman Advanced American Dictionary,* the *Longman Dictionary of Contemporary English,* the *Collins* COBUILD *English Learner's Dictionary,* or the *Oxford Advanced Learner's Dictionary.*

	fill in	*complete by writing in a blank space*
	fill out	*write information on a form*
	fill up	*fill completely with gas, water, coffee, etc.*
	find out (about)	*discover information*
	fool around (with)	*have fun while wasting time*
G	**get along (with)**	*have a good relationship with*
	get back (from)	*return from (a trip)*
	get in	*enter a car, a taxi*
	get off	*leave a bus/an airplane/a train/a subway*
	get on	*enter a bus/an airplane/a train/a subway*
	get out of	*leave a car, a taxi*
	get over	*recover from an illness or a shock*
	get together (with)	*join, meet*
	get through (with)	*finish*
	get up	*get out of bed in the morning*
	give away	*donate, get rid of by giving*
	give back	*return (something) to (someone)*
	give up	*quit doing (something) or quit trying*
	go on	*continue*
	go back (to)	*return to a place*
	go out	*not stay home*
	go over (to)	(1) *approach*
		(2) *visit another's home*
	grow up (in)	*become an adult*
H	**hand in**	*give homework, test papers, etc., to a teacher*
	hand out	*give (something) to this person, then to that person, then to another person, etc.*
	hang around/out (with)	*spend undirected time*
	hang up	(1) *hang on a hanger or a hook*
		(2) *end a telephone conversation*
	have on	*wear*
	help out	*assist (someone)*
K	**keep away (from)**	*not give to*
	keep on	*continue*
L	**lay off**	*stop employment*
	leave on	(1) *not turn off (a light, a machine)*
		(2) *not take off (clothing)*
	look into	*investigate*

	look over	*examine carefully*
	look out (**for**)	*be careful*
	look up	*look for information in a dictionary, a telephone directory,n an encyclopedia, etc.*
M	**make up**	*invent (a story)*
	move in (**to**)	*start living in a new home*
	move out (**of**)	*stop living at a place*
P	**pay back**	*return borrowed money to (someone)*
	pick up	*lift*
	point out	*call attention to*
	print out	*create a paper copy from a computer*
	put away	*put (something) in its usual or proper place*
	put back	*return (something) to its original place*
	put down	*stop holding or carrying*
	put off	*postpone*
	put on	*put clothes on one's body*
	put out	*extinguish (stop) a fire, a cigarette*
R	**run into**	*meet by chance*
	run out (**of**)	*finish the supply of (something)*
S	**set out** (**for**)	*begin a trip*
	shut off	*stop a machine or a light, turn off*
	sign up (**for**)	*put one's name on a list*
	show up	*come, appear*
	sit around (**with**)	*sit and do nothing*
	sit back	*put one's back against a chair back*
	sit down	*go from standing to sitting*
	speak up	*speak louder*
	stand up	*go from sitting to standing*
	start over	*begin again*
	stay up	*not go to bed*
T	**take back**	*return*
	take off	*(1) remove clothes from one's body*
		(2) ascend in an airplane
	take out	*invite out and pay*
	talk over	*discuss*
	tear down	*destroy a building*
	tear out (**of**)	*remove (paper) by tearing*

tear up	*tear into small pieces*
think over	*consider*
throw away/out	*put in the trash, discard*
try on	*put on clothing to see if it fits*
turn around ⎱	
turn back ⎰	*change to the opposite direction*
turn down	*decrease the volume*
turn off	*stop a machine or a light*
turn on	*start a machine or a light*
turn over	*turn the top side to the bottom*
turn up	*increase the volume*

W   **wake up** . . . . *stop sleeping*

watch out (**for**)	*be careful*
work out	*solve*
write down	*write a note on a piece of paper*

APPENDIX 2
Preposition Combinations

CONTENTS

A2-1   PREPOSITION COMBINATIONS: INTRODUCTION

(a) Ali is **absent** **from** class today.
             adj   + prep
 	
(b) This book **belongs** **to** me.
             verb + prep
	At, from, of, on, and *to* are examples of prepositions.*
	
	Prepositions are often combined with adjectives, as in (a), and verbs, as in (b).

*See Chart A2-2, p. 463, for a list of prepositions.

☐ **EXERCISE 1. Preview: preposition combinations. (Chart A2-2)**

Directions: These sentences contain a sampling of the preposition combinations in this Appendix. Complete the sentences with prepositions. How many do you already know? Which ones do you still need to learn?

1. Tom is devoted _____to_____ his family.

2. I'm afraid I don't agree _____ you.

3. I wasn't aware _____ the problem.

4. I'm excited _____ the concert.

5. Are you satisfied _____ your progress?

6. She warned us _____ the coming storm.

7. What's the matter _____ him?

8. It doesn't matter _____ me.

9. I got rid _____ my old bicycle.

10. I don't approve _____ smoking in public.

11. The solution is clear _____ me.

12. Who is responsible _____ this?

13. The hotel provides guests _____ towels.

14. Protect your eyes _____ the sun.

15. He filled my cup _____ hot tea.

Directions: The prepositions in the column on the left are the correct completions for the blanks. To test yourself and practice the preposition combinations, follow these steps:

(1) **Cover** the ANSWERS column with a piece of paper.

(2) Complete the SENTENCES.

(3) Then remove the paper and check your answers.

(4) Then **cover** both the ANSWERS and the SENTENCES to complete your own REFERENCE LIST.

(5) Again check your answers.

Preposition Combinations: Group A		
Answers	**Sentences**	**Reference List**
from	He was absent ___from___ work.	**be absent** ___from___ s.t.**
of	I'm afraid ___of___ rats.	**be afraid** ___of___ s.t./s.o.**
about	I'm angry ___about___ it.	**be angry** _____ s.t.
at / with	I'm angry _____ you.	**be angry** _____ s.o.
about	I'm curious _____ many things.	**be curious** _____ s.t./s.o.
to	This is equal _____ that.	**be equal** _____ s.t./s.o.
with	I'm familiar _____ that book.	**be familiar** _____ s.t./s.o.
of	The room is full _____ people.	**be full** _____ (people/things)
for	I'm happy _____ you.	**be happy** _____ s.o.
about	I'm happy _____ your good luck	**be happy** _____ s.t.
to	He's kind _____ people and animals.	**be kind** _____ s.o.
to	She's always nice _____ me.	**be nice** _____ s.o.
to	Are you polite _____ strangers?	**be polite** _____ s.o.
for	I'm ready _____ my trip.	**be ready** _____ s.t.
for	She's thirsty _____ knowledge.	**be thirsty** _____ s.t.

**s.t. = "something"   s.o. = "someone"

☐ **EXERCISE 2. Preposition combinations. (Group A)**

Directions: Complete the sentences with prepositions.

1. Mr. Porter is nice ___to___ everyone.

2. Kathy was absent _____ class yesterday.

3. Are you ready _____ the test?

4. I'm angry _____ Greg.

5. Are you afraid _____ dogs?

6. Sometimes people aren't kind _____ animals.

7. One inch is equal _____ 2.54 centimeters.

8. I'm thirsty _____ a big glass of water.

9. Joe has good manners. He's always polite _____ everyone.

---

*Appendix 2 presents preposition combinations in small groups to be learned and practiced one group at a time.

10. I'm not familiar _____ that book. Who wrote it?

11. Children ask "Why?" a lot. They are curious _____ everything.

12. Anna got a good job that pays well. I'm very happy _____ her.

13. Anna is very happy _____ getting a new job.

14. Jack's thermos bottle is full _____ coffee.

☐ EXERCISE 3. Review: preposition combinations. (Group A)

Directions: Make up a review quiz for a classmate. On a separate piece of paper, write sentences with the preposition combinations in Group A, but omit the preposition. Leave a blank for a classmate to write in the correct preposition. When your classmate has finished the quiz you wrote, correct his or her answers.

Example: 1. Are you afraid _____ loud noises?

2. It's important to be nice _____ other people.

3. (Etc.)

☐ SELF-STUDY PRACTICE. Group B.

Directions: The prepositions in the column on the left are the correct completions for the blanks. Follow the same steps you used for Group A on page 454.

Preposition Combinations: Group B		
Answers	**Sentences**	**Reference List**
for	I admire you _____ **for** _____ your honesty.	**admire** s.o. _____ **for** _____ s.t.
for	He applied _____ a job.	**apply** _____ s.t.
with	I argued _____ my husband.	**argue** _____ s.o.
about / over	We argued _____ money.	**argue** _____ s.t.
in	My parents believe _____ me.	**believe** _____ s.o./s.t.
from	I borrowed a book _____ Oscar.	**borrow** s.t. _____ s.o.
with	I discussed the problem _____ Jane.	**discuss** s.t. _____ s.o.
with	Please help me _____ this.	**help** s.o. _____ s.t.
to	I introduced Sam _____ Helen.	**introduce** s.o. _____ s.o./s.t.
at	I laughed _____ the joke.	**laugh** _____ s.t./s.o.
for	I'm leaving _____ Rome next week.	**leave** _____ (a place)
at	Don't stare _____ me.	**stare** _____ s.o./s.t.

☐ EXERCISE 4. Preposition combinations. (Group B)

Directions: Complete the sentences with prepositions.

1. I borrowed this dictionary _____ Pedro.

2. Could you please help me _____ these heavy suitcases?

3. Sue, I'd like to introduce you _____ Ed Jones.

4. You shouldn't stare _____ other people. It's not polite.

5. Do you believe _____ ghosts?

6. Are you laughing _____ my mistake?

7. I admire my father _____ his honesty and intelligence.

8. I argued _____ Anna _____ politics.

9. I discussed my educational plans _____ my parents.

10. I applied _____ admission to the University of Massachusetts.

11. We're leaving _____ Cairo next week.

12. Mrs. Wertz smiled _____ her grandchildren.

☐ SELF-STUDY PRACTICE. Group C.
Directions: The prepositions in the column on the left are the correct completions for the blanks. Follow the same steps you used for Group A on page 454.

Preposition Combinations: Group C		
Answers	**Sentences**	**Reference List**
of	I'm aware _____ the problem.	**be aware** _____ s.t./s.o.
for	Smoking is bad _____ you.	**be bad** _____ s.o./s.t.
to	The solution is clear _____ me.	**be clear** _____ s.o
about	Alex is crazy _____ football.	**be crazy** _____ s.t.
from	Jane is very different _____ me.	**be different** _____ s.o./s.t.
for	Venice is famous _____ its canals.	**be famous** _____ s.t.
to / with	She's friendly _____ everyone.	**be friendly** _____ s.o.
for	Fresh fruit is good _____ you.	**be good** _____ s.o.
for	I'm hungry _____ some chocolate.	**be hungry** _____ s.t.
in	I'm interested _____ art.	**be interested** _____ s.t.
about	I'm nervous _____ my test scores.	**be nervous** _____ s.t.
with	I'm patient _____ children.	**be patient** _____ s.o.
of	My parents are proud _____ me.	**be proud** _____ s.o./s.t.
for	Who's responsible _____ this?	**be responsible** _____ s.t./s.o.
about	I'm sad _____ losing my job.	**be sad** _____ s.t.
to	A canoe is similar _____ a kayak.	**be similar** _____ s.o./s.t.
of / about	I'm sure _____ the facts.	**be sure** _____ s.t.

☐ EXERCISE 5. Preposition combinations. (Group C)
Directions: Complete the sentences with prepositions.

1. I don't understand that sentence. It isn't clear _____ me.

2. Mark Twain is famous _____ his novels about life on the Mississippi River.

3. I'm hungry _____ some chocolate ice cream.

4. Our daughter graduated from the university. We're very proud _____ her.

5. A lot of sugar isn't good _____ you. It is bad _____ your teeth.

6. Who was responsible _____ the accident?

7. My coat is similar _____ yours, but different _____ Ben's.

8. Some people aren't friendly _____ strangers.

9. My daughter is crazy _____ horses. She is very interested _____ them.

10. Sara knows what she's talking about. She's sure _____ her facts.

11. Are you aware _____ the number of children who die each day throughout the world? According to one report, 40,000 children die each day, mostly due to malnutrition and lack of minimal medical care.

☐ SELF-STUDY PRACTICE. Group D.

Directions: The prepositions in the column on the left are the correct completions for the blanks. Follow the same steps you used for Group A on page 454.

Preposition Combinations: Group D		
Answers	**Sentences**	**Reference List**
with	I agree _____ you.	**agree** _____ s.o.
about	I agree with you _____ that.	**agree with** s.o. _____ s.t.
in	We arrived _____ Toronto at six.	**arrive** _____ (*a city/country*)
at	We arrived _____ the hotel.	**arrive** _____ (*a building/room*)
about	We all complain _____ the weather.	**complain** _____ s.t./s.o.
about	Sally complained to me _____ my dog.	**complain to** s.o. _____ s.t.
of	A book consists _____ printed pages.	**consist** _____ s.t.
with	I disagree _____ you.	**disagree** _____ s.o.
about	I disagree with you _____ that.	**disagree with** s.o. _____ s.t.
from	She graduated _____ Reed College.	**graduate** _____ (*a place*)
to	Ted invited me _____ a picnic.	**invite** s.o. _____ s.t.
to	We listened _____ some music.	**listen** _____ s.t./s.o.
for	Jack paid _____ my dinner.	**pay** _____ s.t.
to	I talked _____ Anna.	**talk** _____ s.o.
about	We talked _____ her problem.	**talk** _____ s.t.
on	A salesman waited _____ a customer.	**wait** _____ s.o.
for	We waited _____ the bus.	**wait** _____ s.t.

☐ EXERCISE 6. Preposition combinations. (Group D)

Directions: Complete the sentences with prepositions.

1. Tom paid _____ his airplane ticket in cash.

2. Joan graduated _____ high school two years ago.

3. I waited _____ the bus.

4. Jim is a waiter. He waits _____ customers at a restaurant.

5. I have a different opinion. I don't agree _____ you.

6. I arrived _____ this city last month.

7. I arrived _____ the airport around eight.

8. I listened _____ the news on TV last night.

9. This exercise consists _____ verbs that are followed by certain prepositions.

10. Jack invited me _____ his party.

11. I complained _____ the landlord _____ the leaky faucet in the kitchen.

12. Annie disagreed _____ her father about the amount of her weekly allowance.

13. Did you talk _____ Professor Adams _____ your grades?

□ **EXERCISE 7. Review: preposition combinations. (Groups A and B)**
   Directions: Complete the sentences with prepositions.

1. Dan is always nice _____ everyone.

2. A: How long do you need to keep the Spanish book you borrowed _____ me?

   B: I'd like to keep it until I'm ready _____ the exam next week.

3. A: Why weren't you more polite _____ Alan's friend?

   B: Because he kept staring _____ me all evening. He made me nervous.

4. A: We're going to beat you in the soccer game on Saturday.

   B: No way. Two of your players are equal _____ only one of ours.

   A: Oh yeah? We'll see.

5. Stop pouring! My cup is already full _____ coffee.

6. May I please borrow some money _____ you? I'm thirsty _____ an ice cream soda, and we're walking right by the ice cream shop.

7. A: Do you believe _____ astrology?

   B: I'm really not familiar _____ it.

8. A: Mike, I really admire you _____ your ability to remember names.
   Will you help me _____ the introductions?

   B: Sure. Ellen, let me introduce you _____ Pat, Andy, Debbie, Olga, Ramon, and Kate.

□ **EXERCISE 8. Review: preposition combinations. (Groups A, B, C, and D)**
   Directions: Complete the sentences with prepositions.

1. Everyone is talking _____ the explosion in the high school chemistry lab.

2. Carlos was absent _____ class six times last term.

3. Fruit consists mostly _____ water.

4. Our children are very polite _____ adults, but they argue _____ their playmates all the time.

5. Three centimeters is equal _____ approximately one and a half inches.

6. I'm not ready _____ my trip. I haven't packed yet.

7. I borrowed some clothes _____ my best friend.

8. Are you familiar _____ ancient Greek history?

9. I discussed my problem _____ my uncle.

10. Someday astronauts will travel _____ another solar system.

11. Jennifer arrived _____ this city last Tuesday.

12. Jack's plane arrived _____ the airport in Mexico City two hours ago.

13. I admire you _____ your ability to laugh _____ yourself when you make a silly mistake.

14. A: Why are you staring _____ the wall?

    B: I'm not. I'm thinking.

15. A: Are you two arguing _____ each other _____ your in-laws again?

    B: Do you know what his father did?

    C: Oh yeah? Listen _____ what her sister said.

    A: Shhh. I don't want to hear any of this. Stop complaining _____ me _____ your relatives. I don't agree _____ either of you.

☐ **SELF-STUDY PRACTICE. Group E.**

Directions: The prepositions in the column on the left are the correct completions for the blanks. Follow the same steps you used for Group A on page 454.

	Preposition Combinations: Group E	
Answers	**Sentences**	**Reference List**
about	She asked me _____ my trip.	**ask** s.o. _____ s.t. (inquire)
for	She asked me _____ my advice.	**ask** s.o. _____ s.t. (request)
to	This book belongs _____ me.	**belong** _____ s.o.
about / of	I dreamed _____ my girlfriend.	**dream** _____ s.o./s.t.
about	Do you know anything _____ jazz?	**know** _____ s.t.
at	I'm looking _____ this page.	**look** _____ s.t./s.o.
for	I'm looking _____ my lost keys.	**look** _____ s.t./s.o. (search)
like	Anna looks _____ her sister.	**look** _____ s.o. (resemble)
to	I'm looking forward _____ vacation.	**look forward** _____ s.t.
to	Your opinion doesn't matter _____ me.	**matter** _____ s.o.
with	Something is the matter _____ the cat.	**be the matter** _____ s.t./s.o.
for	I'm searching _____ my lost keys.	**search** _____ s.t./s.o.
from	She separated the boys _____ the girls.	**separate** *(this)* _____ *(that)*
about / of	I warned them _____ the danger.	**warn** s.o. _____ s.t.

Directions: Complete the sentences with prepositions.

1. What's the matter _____ you? What's wrong?

2. We can go out for dinner, or we can eat at home. It doesn't matter _____ me.

3. To make this recipe, you have to separate the egg whites _____ the yolks.

4. I don't know anything _____ astrology.

5. I'm looking forward _____ my vacation next month.

6. Dennis dreamed _____ his girlfriend last night.

7. Right now I'm doing an exercise. I'm looking _____ my book.

8. Jim can't find his book. He's looking _____ it.

9. Jim is searching _____ his book.

10. I asked the waitress _____ another cup of coffee.

11. I asked Rebecca _____ her trip to Japan.

12. Does this pen belong _____ you?

13. The city was warned _____ the hurricane in advance.

□ SELF-STUDY PRACTICE. Group F.
Directions: The prepositions in the column on the left are the correct completions for the blanks. Follow the same steps you used for Group A on page 454.

	Preposition Combinations: Group F	
Answers	**Sentences**	**Reference List**
to	I apologized _____ my friend.	**apologize** _____ s.o.
for	I apologized _____ my behavior.	**apologize** _____ s.t.
of	I don't approve _____ Al's behavior.	**approve** _____ s.t.
to / with	I compared this book _____ that book.	**compare** *(this)* _____ *(that)*★
on	I depend _____ my family.	**depend** _____ s.o./s.t.
of / from	He died _____ heart disease.	**die** _____ s.t.
from	The teacher excused me _____ class.	**excuse** s.o. _____ s.t.
for	I excused him _____ his mistake.	**excuse** s.o. _____ s.t. (forgive)
for	I forgave him _____ his mistake.	**forgive** s.o. _____ s.t.
of	I got rid _____ my old clothes.	**get rid** _____ s.t./s.o.
to	What happened _____ your car?	**happen** _____ s.t./s.o.
on	I insist _____ the truth.	**insist** _____ s.t.
from	I protected my eyes _____ the sun.	**protect** s.t./s.o. _____ s.t./s.o.
on	I am relying _____ you to help me.	**rely** _____ s.o./s.t.
of	Mr. Lee took care _____ the problem.	**take care** _____ s.t./s.o.
for	Thank you _____ your help.	**thank** s.o. _____ s.t.

★Also possible: *I compared this **and** that.* (***And*** is not a preposition. A parallel structure with ***and*** may follow ***compare***.)

Directions: Complete the sentences with prepositions.

1. I apologized _____ Ann _____ stepping on her toe.

2. I thanked Sam _____ helping me fix my car.

3. My grandfather doesn't approve _____ gambling.

4. Please forgive me _____ forgetting your birthday.

5. My friend insisted _____ taking me to the airport.

6. Please excuse me _____ being late.

7. Children depend _____ their parents for love and support.

8. In my composition, I compared this city _____ my hometown.

9. Umbrellas protect people _____ rain.

10. We're relying _____ Jason to help us move into our new apartment.

11. We had mice in the house, so we set some traps to get rid _____ them.

12. What happened _____ your finger? Did you cut it?

13. My boss excused me _____ the meeting when I became ill.

14. What did old Mr. Hill die _____?

□ SELF-STUDY PRACTICE. Group G.
Directions: The prepositions in the column on the left are the correct completions for the blanks. Follow the same steps you used for Group A on page 454.

Answers	Sentences	Reference List
to	I'm accustomed _____ hot weather.	**be accustomed** _____ s.t.
to	I added a name _____ my address book.	**add** *(this)* _____ *(that)*
on	I'm concentrating _____ this exercise.	**concentrate** _____ s.t.
into	I divided the cookie _____ two pieces.	**divide** *(this)* _____ *(that)*
from	They escaped _____ prison.	**escape** _____ *(a place)*
about	I heard _____ the prison escape.	**hear** _____ s.t./s.o.
from	I heard about it _____ my cousin.	**hear about** s.t. _____ s.o.
from	The escapees hid _____ the police.	**hide** (s.t.) _____ s.o.
for	We're hoping _____ good weather.	**hope** _____ s.t.
by	I multiplied 8 _____ 2.	**multiply** *(this)* _____ *(that)*
to / with	I spoke _____ the teacher.	**speak to/with** _____ s.o.
about	We spoke to Dr. Carter _____ my problem.	**speak** _____ s.t.
about	I told the teacher _____ my problem.	**tell** s.o. _____ s.t.
from	I subtracted 7 _____ 16.	**subtract** *(this)* _____ *(that)*
about	I wonder _____ lots of curious things.	**wonder** _____ s.t.

Preposition Combinations: Group G

Directions: Complete the sentences with prepositions.

1. Shhh. I'm trying to concentrate _____ this math problem.

2. How did the bank robbers escape _____ jail?

3. Did you tell your parents _____ the dent in their new car?

4. We're hoping _____ good weather tomorrow so we can go sailing.

5. Did you hear _____ the earthquake in Turkey?

6. I heard _____ my sister last week. She wrote me a letter.

7. I spoke _____ Dr. Rice _____ my problem.

8. I'm not accustomed _____ cold weather.

9. When you divide 2 _____ 6, the answer is 3.

10. When you subtract 1 _____ 6, the answer is 5.

11. When you multiply 6 _____ 3, the answer is 18.*

12. When you add 6 _____ 4, the answer is 10.**

13. George wondered _____ his team's chances of winning the tennis tournament.

14. Sally hid her journal _____ her younger sister.

☐ EXERCISE 12. Review: preposition combinations. (Groups E, F, and G)
Directions: Complete the sentences with prepositions.

1. He insisted _____ knowing the truth.

2. I was wondering _____ that!

3. What's the matter _____ you today?

4. He hid the money _____ his wife.

5. We separated the ducks _____ the chickens.

6. I apologized _____ my boss _____ my mistake.

7. We got rid _____ the cockroaches in our apartment.

8. Who does this book belong _____?

9. The prisoners escaped _____ their guards.

10. What happened _____ you?

11. I'm sorry. Please forgive me _____ my error.

12. What did Mr. Grant die _____?

13. Parents protect their children _____ harm.

14. Shh. I'm trying to concentrate _____ my work.

_____

*Also possible: *multiply 6 **times** 3*
Also possible: *add 6 **and 4; add 6 **plus** 4*

15. I rely _____ my friends for their help.

16. I don't approve _____ his lifestyle.

17. The official warned us _____ the danger of traveling there.

18. Fresh vegetables are good _____ you.

19. We're looking forward _____ your visit.

20. Does it matter _____ you what time I call this evening?

A2-2 PREPOSITION COMBINATIONS: A REFERENCE LIST

A

be absent from
be accustomed to
   add *(this)* to *(that)*
be acquainted with
   admire *(someone)* for *(something)*
be afraid of
   agree with *(someone)* about *(something)*
be angry at / with *(someone)* about / over *(something)*
   apologize to *(someone)* for *(something)*
   apply for *(something)*
   approve of
   argue with *(someone)* about / over *(something)*
     arrive at *(a building / a room)*
     arrive in *(a city / a country)*
   ask *(someone)* about *(something)*
   ask *(someone)* for *(something)*
be aware of

B

be bad for
   believe in
   belong to
be bored with / by
   borrow *(something)* from *(someone)*

C

be clear to
   combine with
   compare *(this)* to / with *(that)*
   complain to *(someone)* about *(something)*
be composed of
   concentrate on
   consist of
be crazy about
be crowded with
be curious about

D

   depend on *(someone)* for *(something)*
be dependent on *(someone)* for *(something)*

be devoted to
   die of / from
be different from
   disagree with *(someone)* about *(something)*
be disappointed in
   discuss *(something)* with *(someone)*
   divide *(this)* into *(that)*
be divorced from
be done with
   dream about / of
   dream of

E

be engaged to
be equal to
   escape from *(a place)*
be excited about
   excuse *(someone)* for *(something)*
   excuse from
be exhausted from

F

be familiar with
be famous for
   feel about
   feel like
   fill *(something)* with
be finished with
   forgive *(someone)* for *(something)*
be friendly to / with
be frightened of / by
be full of

G

   get rid of
be gone from
be good for
   graduate from

H

   happen to
be happy about *(something)*

be happy for *(someone)*
hear about / of *(something)* from *(someone)*
help *(someone)* with *(something)*
hide *(something)* from *(someone)*
hope for
be hungry for

I

insist on
be interested in
introduce *(someone)* to *(someone)*
invite *(someone)* to *(something)*
be involved in

K
be kind to
know about

L

laugh at
leave for *(a place)*
listen to
look at
look for
look forward to
look like

M
be made of
be married to
matter to
be the matter with
multiply *(this)* by *(that)*

N
be nervous about
be nice to

O
be opposed to

P

pay for
be patient with
be pleased with / about
play with
point at
be polite to
prefer *(this)* to *(that)*
be prepared for

protect *(this)* from *(that)*
provide *(someone)* with
be proud of

Q
be qualified for

R

read about
be ready for
be related to
rely on
be responsible for

S
be sad about
be satisfied with
be scared of / by
search for
separate *(this)* from *(that)*
be similar to
speak to / with *(someone)* about *(something)*
stare at
subtract *(this)* from *(that)*
be sure of / about

T

take care of
talk about *(something)*
talk to / with *(someone)* about *(something)*
tell *(someone)* about *(something)*
be terrified of / by
thank *(someone)* for *(something)*
think about / of
be thirsty for
be tired from
be tired of
translate from *(one language)* to *(another)*

U
be used to

W

wait for
wait on
warn about / of
wonder about
be worried about

Index

A/an, 312–313, 326–327 *(Look on pages 312 through 313 and on* *pages 326 through 327.)*	The numbers following the words listed in the index refer to page numbers in the text.
Consonants, 13*fn.* *(Look at the footnote on page 13.)*	The letters *fn.* mean "footnote." Footnotes are at the bottom of a page or the bottom of a chart.

NOTES

NOTES

NOTES

NOTES

NOTES

<u>NOTES</u>

NOTES